The Pursuit of Power

William H. McNeill

The
Pursuit of Power

Technology, Armed Force, and Society
since A.D. 1000

The University of Chicago Press

William H. McNeill
*is the Robert A. Milliken Distinguished
Service Professor of History at the University of Chicago.*
His many books include Venice: The Hinge of Europe, 1081–1797;
The Metamorphosis of Greece since World War II; *and*
The Rise of the West: A History of the Human Community,
which received the National Book Award.

The University of Chicago Press, Chicago 60637
Basil Blackwell Publisher Limited

©1982 by William H. McNeill
All rights reserved. Published 1982
Printed in the United States of America
90 89 88 87 86 85 84 83 82   5 4 3 2 1

Library of Congress Cataloging in Publication Data

McNeill, William Hardy, 1917–
The pursuit of power.

Includes index.
1. Military art and science—History.
2. Military history, Medieval.   3. Military
history, Modern.   4. World politics.   I. Title.
U37.M38   355'.02'09   81-24095
ISBN 0–226–56157–7   AACR2

Contents

Preface

The *Pursuit of Power* is meant to be a twin to my earlier book, *Plagues and Peoples*. The latter sought to discern major landmarks in the interaction of human populations and microparasites, paying special attention to the relatively abrupt niche changes that organisms undergo from time to time when some new mutation or penetration of a new geographical environment allows them to escape briefly from older ecological limits. This book undertakes a similar inquiry into changes in patterns of macroparasitism among human kind. Disease germs are the most important microparasites humans have to deal with. Our only significant macroparasites are other men who, by specializing in violence, are able to secure a living without themselves producing the food and other commodities they consume. Hence a study of macroparasitism among human populations turns into a study of the organization of armed force with special attention to changes in the kinds of equipment warriors used. Alterations in armaments resemble genetic mutations of microorganisms in the sense that they may, from time to time, open new geographic zones for exploitation, or break down older limits upon the exercise of force within the host society itself.

Nevertheless, I have refrained from using the language of epidemiology and ecology in describing changes in the way armed force has been organized among human beings, partly because it involves a metaphorical extension of the strict meaning of the term "macroparasitism," and partly because symbiotic relationships between efficient armed forces and the society supporting them commonly exceeded the parasitic drain on local resources required for their maintenance. Microparasitic symbiosis is also important in disease ecology. Indeed I argue in *Plagues and Peoples* that civilized, that

vii

is, disease-experienced, populations had a lethal advantage over isolated communities whenever some new contact exposed the inexperienced population to unfamiliar infections. A well-equipped and organized armed force, making contact with a society not equally well organized for war, acts in much the same way as the germs of a disease-experienced society do. The weaker community, in such an encounter, may suffer heavy loss of life in combat. More often it suffers its principal losses from exposure to economic and epidemiological invasions that are made possible by the military superiority of the stronger people. But whatever the exact combination of factors, a society unable to protect itself by force from foreign molestation loses its autonomy and may lose its corporate identity as well.

A profound ambivalence inheres in warfare and organized human violence. On the one hand, sociality achieves its highest expression in acts of heroism, self-sacrifice, and prowess. The bonds of solidarity among warriors are fierce and strong. Indeed, human propensities find fullest expression in having an enemy to hate, fear, and destroy and fellow-fighters with whom to share the risks and triumphs of violent action. Our remote hunting ancestors banded together to lead such a life, though their foes were animals more often than other men. But old psychic aptitudes remain near the surface of our consciousness still, and fit men for war in far-reaching ways.

On the other hand, organized and deliberate destruction of life and property is profoundly repugnant to contemporary consciousness, especially in view of the quantum jump in human capacity to kill impersonally and at a distance that has occurred since 1945. The technology of modern war, indeed, excludes almost all the elements of muscular heroism and simple brute ferocity that once found expression in hand-to-hand combat. The industrialization of war, scarcely more than a century old, has erased the old realities of soldiering without altering ancient, inherited psychic aptitudes for the collective exercise of force. This constitutes a dangerous instability. How armed forces, weapons technology, and human society at large can continue to coexist is, indeed, a capital question of our age.

Examining the pursuit of power in former times, and analyzing changes in older balances between technology, armed force, and society will not solve contemporary dilemmas. It may, nonetheless, provide perspective and, as is the wont of historical awareness, make simple solutions and radical despair both seem less compelling. Muddling through in the face of imminent disaster was the fate of all past generations. Perhaps we will do the same, and others after us. Moreover, since we must still make decisions every day, it probably helps to know a little more about how we got into our present awesome dilemma.

The Pursuit of Power attests to a modest faith in the utility of such knowledge, which may, conceivably, provide a ground for wiser action. Even if that turns out to be false, there remains the pale, cerebral, but nonetheless real delight of knowing something about how things were different once and then swiftly got to be the way they are.

This book, almost two decades in the making, was stimulated, initially, by a reviewer of *The Rise of the West* who remarked that I had unaccountably lost track of the interaction between military technology and political patterns when dealing with modern times after highlighting this relationship in earlier ages. *The Pursuit of Power* is thus a belated footnote to *The Rise of the West*.

Across the years, my thinking about technology, armed force, and society profited enormously from the patience of successive generations of students at the University of Chicago who let me test my ideas in class, and responded with a tonic mix of interest, enthusiasm, skepticism, and incomprehension. I also owe a great deal to Ph.D. dissertations written at the University of Chicago by Barton C. Hacker, Walter McDougall, Stephen Roberts, Howard Rosen, and Jon Sumida, each of whom taught me things I would not otherwise know and, by looking over what I wrote here, helped me avoid mistakes.

The manuscript has also been read, in whole or in part, by colleagues at Chicago, John Boyer, Ping-ti Ho, Halil Inalcik, and Emmet Larkin. In addition, Michael Howard and Hartmut Poggo von Strandmann of Oxford, Paul Kennedy of East Anglia, John Guilmartin of the United States Air Force, and Dennis Showalter of Colorado College have generously given me the benefit of their expertise. I owe a further special debt to three graduate students of Chinese history, Hugh Scogin and James Lee of Chicago and Steven Sagi of Hawaii, each of whom took an interest in my researches for chapter 2 and helped to pilot me through the intricacies of Chinese historiography. Robin Yates of Cambridge also generously gave time to improving that chapter.

Finally, the nurturing matrix of the University of Chicago was supplemented both by the University of Hawaii, which invited me to discourse on the subject matter of this book by appointing me Burns Visiting Professor in the winter of 1979, and by Oxford University and Balliol College, which afforded me the same hospitality during my tenure of the Eastman Professorship in 1980–81.

With this encouragement and stimulus, the book has now come to its final shape. Needless to say, remaining defects and infelicities are my very own. They would be far more numerous without the scrutiny of my wife Elizabeth and daughter Ruth, who resolutely attempted, here as elsewhere, to make me write better by insisting that I say what I really mean and mean what I actually say.

28 November 1981

1

Arms and Society in Antiquity

I n a limited sense, the industrialization of war is almost as old as civilization, for the introduction of bronze metallurgy made specially skilled artisans indispensable for the manufacture of weapons and armor. Moreover, bronze was rare and expensive. Only a few privileged fighting men could possess a full panoply. It followed that warrior specialists emerged alongside metallurgical specialists, one class enjoying near monopoly of the other's product, at least to begin with.

But the phrase "industrialization of war" does not really fit the ancient river valley civilizations, whether of Mesopotamia, Egypt, India, or China. In the first place, priests and temples competed with warriors and army commanders as consumers of bronze and other artisan products; and the earliest rulers probably based their power more on their religious than on their military roles. In the second place, in society at large the great majority of the population remained in the fields, toiling to produce food for their own support. Surpluses were small; and the number of rulers—whether priestly or military or both—and of artisans remained proportionately modest. Moreover, within that small number, the industrial element was inconspicuous. Arms and armor, once molded into shape, lasted indefinitely, and even if blunted or dented in battle could be restored to usefulness with a little sharpening or hammering. Armorers therefore remained relatively few, even in proportion to warriors.

Since tin and copper ores did not usually occur in the same places, and since tin was relatively scarce and often had to be sought at great distances, the really critical limit upon ancient metallurgy and warmaking capacity was more often the availability of suitable metal ingots or ores than manufacturing skill. Traders and transport personnel, in other words, mattered more than artisans. Public policy had to take into account relations with potential metal suppliers who lived beyond the range of direct administrative control. Safeguarding trade routes from rivals and marauders was also important and sometimes difficult. On the other hand, availability of skilled metal workers could usually be taken for granted once the appropriate artisan tradition had become established in the community.

Wars were normally fought with existing stocks of arms and armor, modified only by gains or losses through capture in the course of operations. What an army needed along the way was food and forage. Hence the availability of food constituted the principal limit upon military action and the size of armies. Occasionally and by exception, an outbreak of epidemic disease intervened to alter military balances abruptly—miraculously, indeed, as the biblical account of the Assyrian failure before Jerusalem in 701 B.C. attests.[1]

Guarding against disease and other evidences of divine displeasure was the province of priests with their knowledge of religious rituals and prayers. Doing something to increase local supplies of food and forage for the support of an itinerant army was the province of rulers and administrators. It was always easiest to rely on direct exercise of force, i.e., to plunder local food producers by seizing their stocks of grain or animals in order to consume them on the spot or at very short remove. Such an army had to overwhelm opposition quickly and then move on, for it rapidly exhausted local supplies, leaving devastation in its rear. Peasants deprived of their stocks were likely to starve and were sure to have the greatest difficulty in finding seed for their fields in the following year. Several years, even decades, had to pass before the ravages of such a campaign could be remedied.

The career of Sargon of Akkad, who plundered all the lands of Mesopotamia around his capital city of Kish about 2250 B.C., illustrates the potentialities and limits of this sort of organized robbery. As one of his inscriptions declares:

> Sargon, king of Kish, thirty-four campaigns won, the walls he destroyed as far as the shore of the sea.... To Sargon, the king, the hand of Enlil [chief of the gods] a rival did not permit. Fifty-four thousand men daily in his presence eat food.[2]

1. 2 Kings 19:20–36.
2. G. A. Barton, ed. and trans., *Royal Inscriptions of Sumer and Akkad* (New Haven, 1929), pp. 109–11.

A perpetual following of 54,000 men no doubt gave the great conqueror an assured superiority over any local rival; hence his thirty-four victorious campaigns. But to keep such a force in being also required annual campaigning, devastating one fertile landscape after another in order to keep the soldiers in victuals. Costs to the population at large were obviously very great. Indeed Sargon's armies can well be compared to the ravages of an epidemic disease that kills off a significant proportion of the host population yet by its very passage confers an immunity lasting for several years. Sargon's armies did the same, since the diminished productivity of the land that resulted from such plundering made it impractical for an army of similar size to pass that way again[3] until such time as population and the area under cultivation had been restored.

But just as an epidemic disease will become endemic whenever interaction between the infectious organism and the host population becomes sufficiently massive and intimate, so also in war. Hence if we shift attention from the time of Sargon to the time of the Achaemenid Empire (539–332 B.C.), we see that war had become less destructive to a great king's subjects during that long interval of time. When Xerxes determined on his famous invasion of Greece (480–479 B.C.), for example, he issued commands from his palace at Persepolis, instructing his agents to gather food supplies from territories under their control, and deliver them to stations along the intended route of march. As a result, Xerxes was able to march into Greece with an army a little larger than Sargon's without devastating the landscapes through which he passed. To be sure, he could not maintain such a force for more than a few weeks in a land as poor in local food supplies as Greece. So, when a handful of Greek cities in the extreme south refused to submit, the Great King had to withdraw a substantial part of his invading force, because there was no way he could feed the entire army in the field over the winter.[4]

As far as we can tell, the passage of Xerxes' army did not interrupt

3. In the words of a contemporary:
    Against Kasalla [a neighboring region] he marched, and
        he turned Kasalla into mounds and heaps of ruins;
    he destroyed (the land and left not) enough for a bird
        to rest thereon.
L. W. King, ed. and trans., *Chronicles concerning Early Babylonian Kings* (London, 1907), pp. 5–6.
    4. Herodotus is of course the basic source for the Persian campaign, but his figures for the size of Xerxes' forces are hopelessly exaggerated. My understanding of the logistics of Xerxes' campaign derives primarily from G. B. Grundy, *The Great Persian War* (London, 1901) and Charles Hignett, *Xerxes' Invasion of Greece* (Oxford, 1963).

the flow of tax and rent payments in the regions through which it marched. Quite the contrary: it was the regular flow of such income, concentrated into storage magazines along the army's route of march, that immunized the local populations against destructive exposure to plunder. The mutual benefit of such a system of regulated exactions as compared to Sargon's system of predation is obvious. The king and his army secured a surer supply of food and could march farther and arrive at the scene of battle in better condition than if they had stopped to plunder along the way. The peasant populations, likewise, by handing over a more or less fixed portion of their harvest to tax and rent collectors, escaped sporadic destitution and risk of starvation. However difficult it may have been to make such payments—and the condition of the peasantry in ancient empires can be assumed to have approached the minimum required for biological survival—the superior predictability and regularity of taxes and rents made Xerxes' imperial system preferable to Sargon's unrestrained pillage, even though pillage could occur only at intervals of several years, whereas taxes and rents were exacted annually. Hence, even though levying taxes and rents pitted the interests of rulers and landlords against those of the peasant producers, both parties had a real interest in substituting such regulated exactions for plundering.

The development of tax and rent systems in other ancient empires is less vividly attested in surviving documents than is the case in the Middle East. Nevertheless, it is clear that similar imperial, bureaucratic systems arose in ancient China, in India, and presently also in the Mediterranean world with the rise of Rome. Amerindian civilizations, too, though at a remove in time, developed comparable administrative systems for transferring agricultural surplus into the hands of the agents of a distant ruler, who used the food and other goods that thus came under his control for warfare or for worship, as he and his close advisers determined.

It is worth pointing out that warfare was not always preeminent. Rulers sometimes preferred to organize elaborate religious ceremonies and grandiose construction enterprises instead of devoting their resources to the maintenance of armies. In ancient Egypt, where geographic conditions made the task of border defense relatively simple, pharoahs of the Fifth Dynasty mobilized the manpower of the country to build pyramids—one per reign—whose remarkable size attests the vast number of workers they were able to summon to the task. Even in war-torn Mesopotamia, temple-building competed with military operations as a consumer of tax income. And in other ages and places, division of resources between warfare and welfare[5] varied indefinitely in antiquity as in more recent times.

Yet it seems correct to say that, regardless of the ends to which resources were put, large-scale public action in antiquity was always achieved by means of command. The ruler or his agent and subordinate issued an order and others obeyed. Human beings are probably fundamentally attuned to this mode of public management by childhood experience, since parents routinely issue commands and instructions which children are expected (and often compelled) to obey. Parents know more and are physically stronger than children; ancient kings also knew more because of superior access to information relayed up and down the administrative hierarchy; and with the help of professionalized soldiery they were also stronger than their subjects. Sometimes they were also living gods, with access to still another form of power.

The awkward element in the entire structure was long-distance trade and the people who conducted it. Yet some imports from afar were essential. For example, the tin needed to make bronze was usually unobtainable close by. Commands were incapable of compelling populations to dig the ore, smelt it into ingots, and then carry it across the sea and land to the place where kings and high priests wanted it. Other scarce products were similarly recalcitrant to the straightforward methods of command mobilization. Rulers and men of power had to learn to deal with possessors of such commodities more or less as equals, substituting the manners and methods of diplomacy for those of command.

The transition was, no doubt, slow and difficult. In very early times, kings organized military expeditions to secure needed commodities from afar. This, for example, is how Gilgamesh, king of Uruk (ca. 3000 B.C.?) prepared for a trip to get timber from distant cedar forests:

"But I will put my hand to it
And will cut down the cedar.
An everlasting name I will establish for myself!
Orders, my friend, to the armorers I will give;
Weapons they shall cast in our presence."
Orders to the armorers they gave.

5. Propitiation of the gods through more splendid ceremonies, and assurance of immortality through more massive tombs, counted as welfare as much as canal and dike construction to extend the area of irrigated land. Such enterprises were all calculated to increase the harvest.

The craftsmen sat down and held a conference.
Great weapons they cast.
Axes of three talents each they cast.
Great swords they cast . . .[6]

But raiding in search of scarce commodities was a high-risk enterprise.
Gilgamesh, the tale informs us, lost his friend and companion, Enkidu,
after their return from the cedar forest—a kind of poetic justice for
Enkidu's refusal to make a deal, as the following passage indicates:

So Huwawa [lord of the cedar forest] gave up.
Then Huwawa said to Gilgamesh:
"Let me go Gilgamesh; thou shalt be my master,
And I will be thy servant. And the trees
That I have grown on my mountains,
I will cut down, and build thee houses."
But Enkidu said to Gilgamesh:
"Do not hearken to the word which Huwawa has spoken;
Huwawa must not remain alive."[7]

Whereupon, the two heroes killed Huwawa, and returned triumphantly to Uruk, presumably bringing the cedar logs with them.

The decision to kill Huwawa reflected a highly unstable constellation of power. Gilgamesh could not long remain in the cedar forest: only momentarily could he bring superior force to bear, and that with difficulty. As soon as the expeditionary force withdrew, Huwawa's power to defy the wishes of strangers would have been restored had Enkidu and Gilgamesh not killed him. Obviously, an adequate timber supply for Uruk was hard to assure by such methods, regardless of whether Gilgamesh accepted or refused Huwawa's proffered submission.

A more reliable way to get scarce resources from regions too far away to be folded into the ordinary command structure was to offer some tangible commodity in exchange, i.e., to substitute trading for raiding. What civilized societies could offer, characteristically, were products of specialized artisan skills, developed initially for the delectation of gods and rulers.

Such luxury objects, of course, were rare; only a few could ever

---

6. A. Heidel, ed. and trans., *The Gilgamesh Epic and Old Testament Parallels* (Chicago, 1946), tablet III, col. iv, lines 156–67. The Gilgamesh epic is known through fragments of several different versions, all much later than the historic date of Gilgamesh. Still the texts undoubtedly embody archaic elements, reflecting conditions in Sumer near the beginning of civilized development.

7. Ibid., tablet V, col. iv, lines 20–28.

possess them. For many centuries, therefore, trade was largely confined to exchanges of scarce commodities between rulers and administrators of civilized lands and local potentates of distant parts. Civilized rulers and officials were the only people who had access to luxury products made on command by specially skilled artisans. Moreover, civilized rulers and officials were only interested in offering such goods to those distant power-wielders who could organize the necessary labor for digging ore, cutting timber or performing whatever other tasks were necessary to prepare and then start the commodity in question on its way to civilized consumers. Such trade, therefore, tended to replicate civilized command structures in surrounding human communities (sometimes in miniature to begin with) in much the same way that DNA and RNA replicate their complex molecular structures in favorable environments.

Bargaining over terms of trade could and did respond partly to market forces of supply and demand and partly to considerations of power, prestige, and ritual. Dependence on distant suppliers who were not firmly subject to imperial words of command constituted a limit upon the management of ancient empires. But it was rarely encountered, since most of the commodities really important for maintenance of armies and administrative bureaucracies—the twin pillars of Xerxes' and every other great king's power—were available from within the boundaries of the state, and could be effectively mobilized by command. Of these, food was by far the most important. Everything else was dwarfed by the simple fact that men (and transport animals) could not remain active for more than a few days without eating.

The contrast between trade relations with outsiders and administration within the bounds of the state was not as great as the above remarks might suggest. Local governors and other administrators who served the king as his agents in the localities had to be rewarded for their services by an appropriate mix of perquisites, praise, and punishment. Command mobilization worked only when men obeyed; and obedience had often to be purchased at a price which differed only in degree from the price paid to more distant and more fully independent local potentates.

Early civilizations existed by virtue of transfer of food from its producers to rulers and men of power who supported themselves, along with a following of military and artisan specialists, on the food so secured. Sometimes, too, the labor power of the food-producing majority was conscripted for some sort of public works: digging a canal, fortifying a city, or erecting a temple. This basic transfer of resources from the many to a few was supplemented by a circulation of luxury goods among members of the ruling elites—partly gift-giving from the great to followers and subordinates, partly tribute from subordinates to the great. Trade across political frontiers was really a variation within this larger pattern of exchanges among men of power. It differed from such exchanges in being more easily interrupted, and less strongly colored by patterns of deference and condescension of the kind that prevailed within the ruling elites of civilized states.[8]

Another feature of ancient empires deserves emphasis, to wit, the fact that there was an optimal size for such polities. The smooth functioning of a tax-collecting administration required the king to reside for at least part of each year in a capital city. Information needed for meting out reward and punishment to key servants of the crown could best be concentrated in a single locality. Such matters had to be attended to promptly, or else the administrative machine would quickly run down and cease to be capable of concentrating resources at anything like maximal capacity. It was equally vital to maintain a bodyguard around the person of the ruler, sufficient to overawe or defeat any likely rival who might meditate revolt. This, too, was best achieved by residing much of the time in some central location where natural routes of transport, especially waterways, made it feasible to gather necessary stores of food year in and year out from the surrounding countryside.

But if a capital city was essential, and if residence by the ruler for part or all of the year in the capital was likewise essential, then a limit was automatically imposed on the extension of imperial frontiers. To exert sovereign power effectively, a ruler had to be able to bring superior force to bear if forcibly challenged either by revolt from within or by attack from without. But if the ruler and his bodyguard had to reside at least part of the year in a capital city, then a march of more than about ninety days from the capital became risky. When he invaded Greece, Xerxes trespassed far beyond the

8. In the Far East, however, in the first century B.C. the Chinese empire established a pattern of "tribute trade" with neighboring rulers. Ritual deference was central in this relationship; indeed the Chinese authorities paid dearly in tangible commodities for the ceremonial acknowledgment of their superiority. Yet in another sense the Hsiung-nu and other border folk, in submitting differentially to the Chinese court rituals, opened themselves to Sinification, paying thereby a high, if intangible, price. Cf. the interesting analysis of this relationship in Yü Ying-shih, *Trade and Expansion in Han China: A Study in the Structure of Sino-Barbarian Economic Relations* (Berkeley and Los Angeles, 1967).

ninety-day radius of action from his capital in Iran.[9] As a result, his campaigning season was cut too short to win decisive victory. By invading Greece the Persians had in fact exceeded the practical limit of imperial expansion. Other empires in other parts of the earth conformed to similar limits, except when no formidable enemy existed beyond the imperial frontiers. In such cases comparatively modest garrisons and peripherally mounted expeditionary forces (like the one Xerxes took with him to Greece) might suffice to enforce and extend sovereignty. This seems to have been the case, for example, in southern China during most phases of Chinese expansion beyond the Yangtse. When, however, the Chinese encountered effective local resistance, their armies met the same fate as Xerxes' did in Greece. Vietnam owes its historical independence to this fact.

Transport and provisioning were, therefore, the principal limits ancient rulers and armies confronted. The supply of metal and weaponry, though important, was seldom a critical variable; and the industrial aspect of warfare remained correspondingly trivial. Nevertheless, one can detect in the historic record a series of important changes in weapons-systems resulting from sporadic technical discoveries and inventions that sufficed to change preexisting conditions of warfare and army organization. Far-reaching social and political upheavals accompanied such changes, as one would expect; and the clutter of ancient dynastic and imperial history achieves a modicum of intelligibility when the rise and fall of empires is viewed within the framework of systematic changes in the military basis of political power.[10]

The first such horizon point has already been mentioned: the introduction of bronze weapons and armor at or near the very beginning of civilized history, starting in Mesopotamia about 3500 B.C. Before imperial command structures of the sort that Xerxes had at his disposal became firmly rooted in ancient Mesopotamia, the next important weapons-system change occurred. This was the result of radical improvements in the design of war chariots. Mobility and firepower were raised to a new level with the invention, soon after 1800 B.C., of light

---

9. Conclusive proof of Xerxes' time of march is unattainable, but cf. the careful discussion of what a century or more of scholarship has been able to surmise in Hignett, *Xerxes' Invasion of Greece,* app. 14, "The Chronology of the Invasion," pp. 448–57. Herodotus tells us that Xerxes' army took three months to go from the Hellespont to Athens (8.51.1).

10. The points raised in the balance of this chapter are more extensively discussed in William H. McNeill, *The Rise of the West: A History of the Human Community* (Chicago, 1963).

but sturdy two-wheeled vehicles that could dash about the field of battle behind a team of galloping horses without upsetting or breaking down. The critical improvement that made chariots supreme instruments of war was the invention of the spoked wheel with a friction-reducing hub-and-axle design. Manufacturing hubbed wheels from wood, making them accurately circular and dynamically balanced so that rapid motion while carrying several hundredweight would not rack them to pieces was no easy task and required specialized wheelwrights' skills. The compound bow—short but strong—was a scarcely less important part of the charioteers' equipment, and its construction also required a high level of craftsmanship.[11]

When chariot design was perfected, a skilled archer standing beside the driver could shower arrows on opposing infantry forces while enjoying comparative impunity, owing to the rapidity of the chariot's motion. On open ground, fast-moving chariots could easily bypass infantry, or cut them off from their supply base. Nothing could stop them—at least in the early years when chariots were new—although rough ground or steep slopes always offered a secure refuge from chariot-warriors. But since all major centers of civilized life were located on flat ground at the time the chariot style of warfare was introduced, this limitation was not critically important. What was critical was access to horseflesh, along with the skills of wheelwrights and bowmakers. Bronze metallurgy also remained important, for charioteers carried swords and spears and protected themselves with metallic armor, as civilized warriors had long been accustomed to doing.

The population best able to take advantage of the possibilities of chariot warfare were steppe dwellers, whose way of life assured an easy access to horses. Accordingly, waves of barbarian conquerors equipped with chariots overran all the civilized lands of the Middle East between 1800 and 1500 B.C. The newcomers established a series

11. Whether compound bows, which get extra power by facing wood with expansible sinew on one side and by compressible horn on the other, were new with the charioteers or had been known earlier is a disputed point. Yigael Yadin, *The Art of Warfare in Biblical Lands in the Light of Archaeological Study*, 2 vols. (New York, 1963), 1:57, says that these bows were invented by the Akkadians of Sargon's era. The basis for this view is a stele representing Naram Sin, Sargon's grandson and successor, with a bow whose shape resembles that of later compound bows. But how to interpret the curve of a bow recorded in stone is obviously indecisive. On the compound bow and its capacities see W. F. Paterson, "The Archers of Islam," *Journal of the Economic and Social History of the Orient* 9 (1966):69–87; Ralph W. F. Payne-Gallwey, *The Crossbow, Medieval and Modern, Military and Sporting: Its Construction, History, and Management* (London, 1903), appendix.

of "feudal" states, in which a small elite of chariot warriors exercised decisive military force and shared the practical exercise of sovereignty with overlords whose commands were effective only when a majority of the chariot-owning class concurred. As victorious bands of charioteers spread out over conquered Middle Eastern lands, they gathered into their own hands most of the available agricultural surplus, either as plunder (in their initial onset) or as rents (when exactions became somewhat more regular). The effect was to weaken central authority, although in the Middle Eastern lands, where bureaucratic traditions of imperial government had already begun to develop, it did not take long for revived central authorities to make the new military technology their own. After 1520 B.C., for example, the New Kingdom of Egypt used gold from Nubia to hire charioteers, thus securing a standing, professional force that proved superior to all rivals for several generations.

In China and India the arrival of chariotry signalled more drastic change. In India, charioteers disrupted the older Indus civilization about 1500 B.C., and a "dark age" lasting several centuries intervened before a new pattern of civilized life began to emerge. In China, an opposite transformation occurred, for a new chariot-using dynasty, the Shang, presided over the development of a more sharply differentiated society than had previously existed in the valley of the Yellow River. The enhanced levels of luxury and income commanded by the noble class of Shang charioteers allowed several characteristic skills of subsequent Chinese civilization to define themselves more clearly than before.

In Europe, chariots seem to have mattered less. To be sure, the shift from Minoan to Mycenaean hegemony in the Aegean region was accompanied or swiftly followed by the arrival of chariots in Greece. Within a few centuries chariots also appeared in distant Scandinavia and remote Britain. But if what Homer tells us about Mycenaean battle tactics is correct, the European warriors failed to use the chariot's combination of mobility and firepower to good effect. Instead, Homer's heroes dismounted from their chariots to fight on foot with spears and other close-combat weapons, using their chariots for show and as mere conveniences in coming and going from the field of battle.[12]

12. See, for example, book 16, lines 426 ff. However absurd, Homer's report may be accurate. The tactics he describes may have been a function of numbers and terrain. To succeed, a chariot charge required a critical mass—enough arrows and charging chariots to break opposing infantry and persuade foot soldiers to flee. But in a land like Greece,

Chariots were expensive, both because of the workmanship that went into their construction and because of the costliness of feeding horses on grain in landscapes where year-round grass was not to be found. Societies dominated by chariot-warriors were therefore narrowly aristocratic. A very small warrior class was in a position to control the lion's share of whatever agricultural surplus could be wrested from the peasant producers. Artisans and traders, bards and even priests danced attendance on the ruling military élites. When such élites were ethnically alien to the majority—as was often the case—a pervasive lack of sympathy between ruler and ruled resulted.

Social balances swung the other way very sharply when the next major change of weapons-systems brought a radical democratization of war to the ancient world. The discovery of how to make serviceable tools and weapons of iron occurred somewhere in eastern Asia Minor about 1400 B.C., but the new skill did not spread widely from its point of origin until after about 1200 B.C. When it did, metal became enormously cheaper, for deposits of iron were widespread in the earth's crust and the charcoal required for smelting was not difficult to make. For the first time it became feasible for common people to own and use metal, at least in small amounts. In particular, iron plowshares improved cultivation and allowed the expansion of tillage onto heavier clay soils. Wealth increased as a result, slowly but surely. Ordinary cultivators began to benefit for the first time from something they could not make themselves. Peasants in other words began to profit tangibly from the differentiation of skills that was the hallmark of civilization. As this occurred, civilized social structures became far more secure than previously. Overthrow of a ruling élite did not any longer invite a nearly total collapse of social differentiation, as had sometimes happened previously, e.g., in the Indus valley.

As far as warfare was concerned, the cheapness of iron meant that a relatively large proportion of the male population could acquire metal arms and armor. Ordinary farmers and herdsmen thereby achieved a new formidability in battle, and the narrowly aristocratic structure of society characteristic of the chariot age altered abruptly. A more democratic era dawned as iron-welding invaders overthrew ruling élites that had based their power on a monopoly of chariotry.

---

where hills abound and fodder for horses is short, chariots had to remain few—too few, perhaps to achieve decisive effect in battle. Yet, like Cadillacs of the recent past, the prestige of the chariot after its victories in the Middle East was such that every local European chieftain was eager to have one, whether or not he could use it effectively in war.

Hillsmen and other barbarians living on the fringes of civilized society profited most directly from the new cheapness of metal. In such communities, moral solidarity between leaders and followers was firm and easy, since a traditional and rudely egalitarian style of life united the entire population. Charioteers could not afford to arm the superior numbers of their subjects to match the newly formidable metal-clad barbarians: that would merely assure local rebellion against their power. Hence the chariot aristocracies, lacking firm support from below, were overthrown by barbarian tribesmen whose shields and helmets of iron protected them from charioteers' arrows well enough to make the formerly invincible chariot tactics ineffective in battle.

In the Middle East, the diffusion of iron-working skills therefore precipitated a new round of invasions and migrations between 1200 and 1000 B.C. New peoples—Hebrews, Persians, Dorians, and many others—entered the historical record, inaugurating a barbarous and much more egalitarian age. As the author of Judges says, at the close of a bloody tale of violence and mayhem:

> In those days there was no king in Israel; everyone used to do as he pleased.[13]

Yet egalitarianism and disorderly local violence proved evanescent. Soon the superior value of professionalized troops became apparent. Traditions of centralized government, surviving in Egypt and Babylonia from before the chariot invasions, were available to ambitious state builders, like Saul and David and their various rivals. After 1000 B.C., therefore, bureaucratic monarchies again began to dominate the Middle East, each supported by a standing body of troops, supplemented by militia levies in time of need. Since income to support the military professionals came from taxation, the way was open for the development of the kind of command structure that sustained Xerxes' vast empire.

Assyrian kings were the most successful practitioners of the art of bureaucratic management of armed force in the early Iron Age. They developed an army in which ascribed rank defined who should command and who obey. Standard equipment, standard units, a ladder of promotion open to talent: these familiar bureaucratic principles of army management all appear to have been either introduced or made standard by Assyrian rulers. A parallel civil bureaucracy proved itself capable of assembling food stocks for a proposed campaign, of build-

13. Judges 21:25 (Theophile J. Meek, trans.).

ing roads to facilitate military movement across long distances, and of mobilizing labor for the erection of fortifications.

Precedents going all the way back to the third millennium B.C. can be found for many of the administrative patterns that the Assyrians made normal; but historians' appraisal of the Assyrian achievement has commonly been colored by the fact that we inherit from the Bible a hostile portrait of the fierce conquerors who destroyed the kingdom of Israel in 722 B.C. and came within a hairsbreadth of doing the same to the kingdom of Judah in 701 B.C. Yet it seems no exaggeration to say that the fundamental administrative devices for the exercise of imperial power which remained standard in most of the civilized world until the nineteenth century A.D. first achieved unambiguous definition under the Assyrians between 935 and 612 B.C. The conquering kings also put considerable ingenuity into the development of new military equipment and formations. They invented a complex array of devices for beseiging fortified cities, for example, and carried a siege train with them on campaign as a matter of course. Altogether, a radical rationality seems to have pervaded Assyrian military administration, making their armies the most formidable and best disciplined that the world had yet seen.

Ironically, readiness to experiment with new military modes may have accelerated Assyria's downfall. Cavalrymen, mounted directly on the backs of their horses, were a new element in the military coalition that sacked the capital of Nineveh in 612 B.C. and thereby destroyed the Assyrian empire forever. No one knows for sure when the practice of riding on horseback first became normal, nor where. But early representations of horseback-riding show Assyrian soldiers astride.[14] It seems likely therefore, that in their restless search for more effective ways of managing armed force, Assyrians discovered how to ride and retain control of a horse while using both hands to shoot with a bow. At first they did so by pairing riders so that one man held the reins for both mounts while the second drew the bow. This arrangement replicated the long-standing cooperation between driver and

14. Men occasionally rode horseback as early as the fourteenth century B.C. This is proved by an Egyptian statuette of the Amarna age, now in the Metropolitan Museum of New York. See photograph in Yadin, *Art of Warfare in Biblical Lands,* 1:218; another equestrian figure, from the British Museum, of the same age is reproduced, ibid., p. 220. The difficulty of remaining firmly on a horse's back without saddle or stirrups was, however, very great; and especially so if a man tried to use his hands to pull a bow at the same time—or wield some other kind of weapon. For centuries horseback riding therefore remained unimportant in military engagements, though perhaps specially trained messengers used their horses' fleetness to deliver information to army commanders. So, at least, Yadin interprets another, later, representation of a cavalryman in an Egyptian bas-relief recording the Battle of Kadesh (1298 B.C.).

bowman that had made chariot fighting possible. Such paired cavalry-men were, in fact, charioteers sans chariot. After learning to ride their team directly, charioteers could simply unhitch the chariot, which had become an unnecessary encumbrance.[15] Subsequently, man and horse became so attuned to one another that solitary riders dared to drop the reins and use both hands to bend their bows.

Most historians assume that steppe nomads, who benefited spectac-ularly from the cavalry revolution, were the pioneers of this new means of exploiting the speed and endurance of horseflesh. That may be true, but there is no evidence for such a view. The fact that nomads in the later ages became past masters at riding and shooting does not prove that they invented the technique; it only shows that they were in a position to take fuller advantage of the new style of warfare than other peoples. The initial use of paired cavalrymen in the Assyrian army surely makes it look as though they had been the principal pioneers of this new way to exploit the fleetness of horseflesh in war.

· Even after steppe nomads took to horseback in sufficient numbers to organize massive raids on civilized lands, several centuries passed before the techniques of cavalry warfare spread throughout the length and breadth of the Eurasian grasslands. The horizon point for cavalry raiding from the steppe was about 690 B.C. when a people known to the Greeks as Cimmerians overran most of Asia Minor. This, in-cidentally, was nearly two centuries after Assyrians had begun to use cavalry on a significant scale in war. The Cimmerians inhabited the grassy plains of the Ukraine, and returned thither after devastating the kingdom of Phrygia. Subsequently a new people, the Scythians, mi-grated west from the Altai region of central Asia and overran the Cim-merians. The newcomers sent a swarm of horsemen to raid the Middle East for a second time in 612 B.C. and shared in the plunder of Nineveh.

These two great raids announced the onset in the Middle East of a new era in military matters that lasted, in essentials, until the four-teenth century A.D. In the Far East, records of cavalry harassment from Mongolia and adjacent regions do not become unambiguous until the fourth century B.C., although some scholars think that the collapse of the western Chou Dynasty in 771 B.C. may have been a result of a Scythian cavalry raid from the Altai region.[16]

The enduring consequences of the cavalry revolution in Eurasia

15. For photographs of a bas-relief portraying Assyrian paired cavalrymen see Yadin, 2:385.
16. Karl Jettmar, "The Altai before the Turks," Museum of Far East Antiquities, Stockholm, *Bulletin* 23 (1951):154–57.

were far-reaching. Steppe populations, once they had mastered the arts of horsemanship and acquired the skills to make bows, arrows, and all necessary accoutrements from materials available to them locally, had a cheaper and more mobile armed force at their command than civilized peoples could easily put into the field. Steppe warriors could therefore raid civilized lands lying to the south of them almost with impunity, unless rulers were able to replicate barbarian levels of mobility and morale within their own armed establishments.

Setting a thief to catch a thief was one obvious tactic. This was, in fact, what Xerxes and his Achaemenid predecessors resorted to for the protection of their exposed frontier upon the steppe. Most Chinese rulers did the same. By paying tribesmen to defend the border against would-be raiders, an impervious membrane could be stretched along the frontier. But this sort of arrangement was always liable to break down. Border guards were continually tempted to join forces with those outer barbarians whom they were paid to oppose, since in the short run plunder was likely to bring richer returns than they could ever hope to achieve by renegotiating rates of pay with governmental authorities.

Within this general framework, endlessly variable military, diplomatic, and economic relationships between steppe tribesmen and civilized rulers and bureaucrats ensued across the next two thousand years. Protection payments alternated with raids; occasionally destructive plundering impoverished all concerned. The rise and fall of steppe war confederations around individual captains, who were often charismatic leaders like the greatest of them, Genghis Khan (1162–1227), introduced another variable. But despite endless perturbations of the political and military relationships between grassland and plowland, peoples of the steppe enjoyed a consistent advantage because of their superior mobility and the cheapness of their military equipment. This produced a pattern of recurrent nomad conquests of civilized lands.

Whenever local defenses weakened, for whatever reason, nomad raiding could be expected to snowball year by year, as news of successful plundering expeditions spread across the steppe. If local defenses crumbled completely, raiders were tempted to remain permanently in occupation of the lands that had been unable to protect themselves. Thereupon, of course, raiders became rulers and soon recognized the advantage to themselves of substituting taxation for plunder and of protecting their taxpaying subjects from rival predators. Under these conditions, locally effective defense might be expected to arise, at least for a while, until the new rulers lost their tribal cohesion and surrendered their warlike habits for the comforts of urban living—in which case, renewal of the cycle of raid and conquest was likely to take place.

A second pattern also asserted its power over steppe populations. Both temperature and precipitation diminished from west to east across the steppe. In Mongolia climatic conditions of the grasslands became harsh for humans and animals alike. Eastward in Manchuria, increasing rainfall brought richer pastures and temperatures became a little milder. The result of this geographical layout was that tribesmen, given a choice, preferred to leave Mongolia, pushing towards better pasture by moving either east or west. The Scythians, presumably, were responding to the superior attractions of the western steppelands when they moved from the Altai to the Ukraine in the eighth century B.C. Others followed them in succeeding centuries, bringing first speakers of Indo-European tongues, then Turks, and finally Mongols into eastern Europe, each people obeying the dictates of the geographic gradient of the Eurasian steppe.

Thus two currents of population displacement resulted from the cavalry revolution. Sporadically, steppe tribesmen succeeded in conquering one or another of the civilized lands that abutted on the grasslands—China, the Middle East, or Europe as the case might be. This movement from pasture land to cultivated land coexisted with an east-west current of migration within the steppelands proper. In the one case, nomads had to surrender their established way of life by becoming landlords and rulers of civilized countrysides. In the other, the familiar nomad patterns could persist under somewhat eased conditions. Efforts by civilized rulers and armies to hold back the nomad pressure were only sporadically successful. Even the Great Wall of China was ineffective in stopping raids and conquest.

Geographical and sociopolitical conditions maintained a fluctuating equilibrium between grassland and farmland. Insufficient rainfall made farming in much of the steppe impractical. To be sure, in the better-watered regions, like the Ukraine, grain farming was very rewarding, since wheat, too, is a kind of grass. In that region, accordingly, and in similar regions in Manchuria, in Asia Minor, and in Syria, nomad occupation of natural grassland competed with grain farming as alternative ways of exploiting the soil. Nomad warriors who decided to remain as permanent occupants of these marginal farmlands often drove plowing peasants entirely from the scene; yet the greater food-producing capacity of a landscape that was farmed meant that time and again, in periods of peace and population growth, fields would creep out into the grasslands, until some new military-political upheaval brought new raiding, new destruction, and a local return to pastoralism.

Recurrent ebb and flow of the boundaries between plowing peasants and herding pastoralists accordingly took place within rather broad regions of the Middle East and eastern Europe for more than two thousand years, between 900 B.C. and A.D. 1350. On the whole, the military advantage that cavalry tactics conferred upon nomads during this long period meant that pastoral land use tended to expand, while agricultural exploitation of the soil always halted considerably short of its climatic limits.

In the Far East, the monsoon pattern of rainfall created a sharper transition between farmland and grassland. Moreover, the relatively high returns that intensive Chinese methods of cultivation got from the loess soil of the semiarid northern provinces was so much superior to anything which pasturage could bring in from the same landscape that the reestablishment of cultivation in that frontier zone of China seems to have occurred relatively rapidly each time nomad raiding disrupted agricultural occupation of the loess soils.[17]

Geographical and socioeconomic factors were assisted in defining the oscillating equilibrium between nomad tribesmen and settled agriculturalists by a further change in weapons-systems, not so far-reaching as those previously referred to but important enough to transform patterns of social structure in much of western Asia and most of Europe. Between the sixth and first centuries B.C., Iranian landowners and warriors developed a large, powerful breed of horse capable of carrying an armored man[18] on its back. Such horses were often protected by some sort of metaled garment to ward off arrows. So burdened, they could not keep up with the steppe ponies' unimpeded canter. Still, a force of armored cavalrymen at least partially arrow-proof, and itself capable of offensive action with either bow or lance, constituted a far more effective form of local self-defense against steppe raiders than civilized lands had previously been able to

17. Nevertheless, peasants were uprooted from most of the loess soils of north China at least twice. Mongol raids of the thirteenth and fourteenth centuries and nomad attacks in the centuries after the collapse of the Han Dynasty in the third century A.D. were severe enough and prolonged enough to destroy agricultural settlement in wide districts of north China—or so imperfect population statistics suggest. Cf. Ping-ti Ho, *Studies in the Population of China, 1368–1953* (Cambridge, Mass., 1959), and Hans Bielenstein, "The Census of China during the Period 2–742 A.D.," Museum of Far Eastern Antiquities, Stockholm, *Bulletin* 19 (1947):125–63.

18. Assyrian bas-reliefs show cavalrymen with metaled corselets. As in so many other military matters, the Assyrians seem to have pioneered armored cavalry too.

provide. The great horses had to be fed of course, and natural pasture was scarce in most cultivated landscapes. But by consuming planted fodder crops—alfalfa above all—the great horses no longer competed with humans by eating grain.[19] The cultivation of alfalfa therefore cheapened the cost of keeping big horses enormously, and made it feasible for Iranians to maintain a numerous and formidable armored cavalry on cultivated ground. Such warriors were capable of guarding local peasants from most nomad raiding parties, and had a clear self-interest in doing so, since their own livelihood depended directly on the work of the peasants they protected.

Heavy armored cavalry, Iranian style, was therefore definitely worth the cost to populations exposed to steppe raids. But where city walls protected the politically active portion of the population, the military supremacy that such a system of local self-defense conferred upon the possessors of great horses was sometimes unacceptable. Hence the new techniques spread only slowly to the Mediterranean coastlands. Roman armies experimented with the new style of armored cavalry, beginning in the time of Hadrian (r. 177–38),[20] but "cataphracts" (as these fighting men were called in Greek) remained very few to begin with. Moreover, in Roman and early Byzantine times they were paid in cash rather than allowed, as in Iran, to draw their incomes directly from the villagers whom they protected and among whom they lived.[21] A thoroughgoing feudal reorganization of Byzantine society did not occur until after A.D. 900, lagging far behind Latin Europe, which had taken that path within a century of the time that Charles Martel introduced the new style of cavalry to the Far West in A.D. 732.

To be sure, the Franks used the great horse in a new way. Instead of carrying bows, the knights of Latin Christendom preferred close-in combat with lance, mace, and sword. This departure from eastern

19. A field planted to alfalfa in effect cost next to nothing, for grain fields had to be fallowed every other year to keep down weeds. By planting alfalfa in the ground instead of leaving the soil fallow, a useful crop could be garnered while bacterial action on the roots of the alfalfa actually enriched the soil with nitrogen and so made subsequent grain harvests richer than would otherwise have been the case. Even the amount of work required to plant and harvest a field of alfalfa was not notably greater than the mid-season plowing necessary for a field left fallow; for it was only thus that the natural seeding of weeds could be interrupted and the soil readied for grain. Alfalfa kept back unwanted weeds almost as well as mid-season plowing simply by shading the soil with its leaves.

20. John W. Eadie, "The Development of Roman Mailed Cavalry," *Journal of Roman Studies* 57 (1967):161–73.

21. This Byzantine policy resembled the way the New Kingdom of Egypt reconciled the superior technology of chariot warfare with Old Kingdom traditions of bureaucratic centralism.

styles of warfare matched Homer's heroes' disdain for archery. It differed from the apparent irrationality of Homeric misuse of chariots, inasmuch as knightly tactics were in fact exceedingly effective. The reason was that a knight's charge, delivered at full gallop, concentrated an enormous momentum at the lance tip. Only an army similarly equipped could hope to counter such concentrated force. To keep a firm seat at the moment of impact required the rider to brace his feet against a pair of heavy stirrups. Stirrups, apparently, were invented only about the turn of the fifth-sixth centuries A.D., and spread so rapidly across Eurasia that it is impossible now to tell where that apparently simple device was first introduced. The invention made the charge of western knights enormously formidable on the battlefield and also increased the effectiveness of steppe cavalry, since an archer could aim more accurately with stirrups to stabilize his seat atop a galloping horse.[22]

The rise of heavy armored cavalry in western Asia and in western Europe constituted a reprise of the impact of chariotry on social and political structures some eighteen hundred years earlier. Whenever superior force came to rest in the hands of a few elaborately equipped and trained individuals, it became difficult for central authorities to prevent such persons from intercepting most of the agricultural surplus and consuming it locally. "Feudalism" was the result, even though in both Iran and the Mediterranean lands, old imperial forms and pretensions lingered on to provide models and precedents for reconstruction of more effective authority when the balance of power in matters military again shifted in favor of centralized forms of administration.[23]

The Far East developed differently. In spite of Emperor Wu-ti's expedition of 101 B.C. which introduced the great horses of Iran into China, these animals never became very important in the Far East. Crossbows, capable of knocking an armored man from his horse at a distance of 100 yards or more, were readily available in China. This went far to cancel the effectiveness of the new heavy armored cavalry. Moreover, Chinese rulers preferred to use the resources which taxation concentrated in their hands to maintain a suitable balance between payments to professionalized border guards on the one hand, and diplomatic gift-payments to potentates across the frontier on the other. Matching balances within Chinese society between taxpayers and tax consumers, as defined by the Han emperors (202B.C.–A.D.

22. On stirrups and knights see Lynn White, Jr., *Medieval Technology and Social Change* (Oxford, 1962); John Beeler, *Warfare in Feudal Europe, 730–1200* (Ithaca, N.Y., 1971), pp. 9–30.

23. Shadowy survival of older command structures had also occurred in the chariot age and facilitated the rebuilding of Iron Age monarchies.

220), were long retained and readily restored, even after sporadic breakdowns due to bureaucratic corruption or unusually severe barbarian attacks.

Within any of the paradigms defined by a dominant weapons-system, ups and downs of discipline and training constituted important local variables; and the occasional appearance of great captains added another dramatic dimension to the political-military scene. Alexander the Great of Macedon (r. 336–323 B.C.) was such a figure, and without him it is hard to believe that the Hellenic cultural imprint would have traveled as far eastward into Asia as it did in the wake of his armies.

Mohammed's career and that of the community of the faithful that formed around him were still more remarkable. Moslem victories rested entirely on a new social discipline and religious faith that united all the tribes of Arabia into a single armed polity without affecting the design of weaponry in the slightest. Yet the Moslems created a new, relatively centralized empire in the Middle East and North Africa, and shored up urban, mercantile, and bureaucratic elements in society throughout a broad territory—all the way from Iraq to Spain—at a time when the balance of military forces in adjacent lands favored feudal devolution.

More unmistakably than any other major event in world history, the rise of Islam and the establishment of the early caliphate proves that ideas, too, matter in human affairs and can sometimes enter decisively into the balance of forces so as to define long-lasting and fundamental human patterns. In a given time and place, where alternate social structures are in competition, conscious choice and emotional conviction can make the difference in determining which pattern will prevail. The rise and propagation of Islam did so in the Middle East, giving decisive impetus to the urban and bureaucratic as against the feudal principle of military and social organization.

The power of Islam was never more tellingly demonstrated than in Iran, where the conversion of rural cavalrymen to the new faith involved their abandonment of the military style of life that had for centuries provided an effective guard against steppe raiding. The result was that Iran became permeable once more to infiltration from the steppe, as the appearance of Turkish raiders and rulers from the tenth century onwards amply demonstrated.

Prior to A.D. 1000, the preponderance of command systems for mobilizing human and material resources for large-scale enterprises was never in doubt. Wars were fought and taxes were collected by command. Public works were built by command. Settlement of border regions was carried through by command.[24] When rulers found that they needed something which could not be obtained by issuing a command, they had to bargain for it, of course; and much internal administration, even in the most efficiently bureaucratized states, depended on bargaining (whether tacit or explicit) between central authorities and local governors, landowners, chieftains, priesthoods, and other potentates.

Power relationships across political frontiers partook of the same character, with the difference that intermediaries who moved back and forth across lines of jurisdiction were in a position to emancipate themselves from subordination to any of the public command systems in whose interstices they conducted their affairs. Instead of seeking rank, dignity, and the income appropriate to a niche in existing hierarchies of command, such persons could seek simply to maximize their material profit from exchanges at either end of, or along, their route of travel.[25]

But such behavior had limits. Anyone who accumulated large amounts of wealth while remaining independent of military-political command structures faced the problem of safeguarding what he had gained. Unless a merchant could count on the protection of some formidable man of power, there was nothing to restrain local potentates from seizing his property any time his goods came within reach. To gain effective protection was likely to be costly—so costly as to inhibit large-scale accumulation of private capital.

Moreover, in most civilized societies, the prestige and deference paid to men of power, i.e., to bureaucrats and landowners, was matched by a general distrust of and disdain for merchants and men of the marketplace. Anyone who succeeded in profiting from trade, therefore, was likely to see the advantage of acquiring land, or in some other way of gaining access to a place in some local command hierarchy.

Accordingly, trade and market-regulated behavior though present from very early times,[26] remained marginal and subordinate in civilized societies before A.D. 1000. Most persons lived out their lives without responding to market incentives in any way. Customary

24. James Lee, pending Ph.D. diss., University of Chicago.
25. Cf. the perceptive remarks of Denis Twitchett, "Merchant Trade and Government in Late T'ang," *Asia Major* 14 (1968): 63–95, on the role of merchants in China.
26. A rich find of cuneiform tablets from about 1800 B.C. in Anatolia shows merchant colonies from a mother city, Assur, flourishing as part of a trade net that extended from the Persian Gulf northward through Mesopotamia. These ancient Assyrian traders shipped tin eastward and carried textiles manufactured in central Mesopotamia west-

routine dominated everyone's behavior. Large-scale changes in human conduct, when they occurred, were more likely to be in response to commands coming from some social superior than to any change in supply and demand, buying and selling.

Much more important than any human action in most people's lives were natural disasters like crop failure and epidemic outbreaks of disease. Even the sporadic ravages of armed raiders—coming from nowhere and disappearing into the distance when their work was done—partook of the character of natural disaster from the point of view of the plowing peasants who were their principal victims. Scope for deliberate conscious action remained very small. Human beings were part of an ecological equilibrium whose impact on their survival was not cushioned by anything like our modern skills, organization, and capital. Custom and immemorial routine provided precise guidelines in most life circumstances. Change, whether conscious and in accord with someone's intent or generated in moments of desperation when old patterns of life had broken down, remained sporadic and exceptional.

Getting enough to eat was the central task of life and presented a perpetual problem for most persons. Everything else took second place. The industrial basis of large-scale enterprises though real enough—public works required tools as much as armies required weapons—was a trivial element in the sense that access to tools and weapons was seldom felt to be a real limit upon what human beings could or did undertake.

The commercialization, followed in due season by the industrialization, of war began to get under way, in a more meaningful sense, only after A.D. 1000. The transformation was slow at first; it attained runaway velocity only in very recent centuries. The following chapters will attempt to survey the major benchmarks in that momentous change.

---

ward. They appear to have behaved as private capitalists, quite in the spirit of medieval merchants two thousand years later. Family firms exchanged letters: hence the archive. Profits were high—up to 100 percent in a single year, if all went well. Cf. M. T. Larsen, *The Old Assyrian City-State and Its Colonies,* Studies in Assyriology, vol. 4 (Copenhagen, 1976). Clearly rulers and men of power along the way permitted their donkey caravans to get through, perhaps because of the strategic value of the tin. But the archive is silent about such arrangements. For traders and their role in ancient Mesopotamia generally, see also A. Leo Oppenheim, "A New Look at the Structure of Mesopotamian Society," *Journal of the Economic and Social History of the Orient* 10 (1967): 1–16.

2

The Era of Chinese Predominance, 1000-1500

Remarkable changes came to Chinese industry and armaments after about A.D. 1000, anticipating European achievements by several hundred years. Yet new patterns of production, even when they had attained massive scale, eventually broke up as remarkably as they had arisen. Government policy altered, and the social context that first fostered change subsequently resisted or at least failed to encourage, further innovation. China therefore lost its leading place in industry, power politics, and war. Previously marginal, half-barbarous lands—Japan to the east and Europe far to the west—supplanted the Mongol rulers of China as the most formidable wielders of weapons in the world.

Yet before China's preeminence over other civilizations faded, a new and powerful wind of change began to blow across the southern seas that connected the Far East with India and the Middle East. I refer to an intensified flow of goods and movement of persons responding mainly to market opportunities. In seeking riches or a mere livelihood, a growing swarm of merchants and peddlers introduced into human affairs far more pervasive changeability than earlier centuries had ever known.

China's remarkable growth in wealth and technology was based upon a massive commercialization of Chinese society itself. It therefore seems plausible to suggest that the upsurge of market-related behavior that ranged from the sea of Japan and the south China seas to the Indian Ocean and all the waters that bathe the coasts of Europe took decisive impetus from what happened in China. In this fashion, one hundred million people,[1] increasingly caught up within a com-

1. This is the population total suggested by Ping-ti Ho, "An Estimate of the Total

mercial network, buying and selling to supplement every day's livelihood, made a significant difference to the way other human beings
made their livings throughout a large part of the civilized world. Indeed, it is the hypothesis of this book that China's rapid evolution
towards market-regulated behavior in the centuries on either side of
the year 1000 tipped a critical balance in world history. I believe that
China's example set humankind off on a thousand-year exploration of
what could be accomplished by relying on prices and personal or
small-group (the partnership or company) perception of private advantage as a way of orchestrating behavior on a mass scale.

Obedience to commands did not of course disappear. Interaction
between command behavior and market behavior lost none of its
complex ambivalence. But political authorities found it less and less
possible to escape the trammels of finance, and finance depended
more and more on the flow of goods to markets which rulers could no
longer dominate. They, too, like humbler members of society, were
more and more trapped in a cobweb of cash and credit, for spending
money proved a more effective way of mobilizing resources and manpower for war and for other public enterprises than any alternative.
New forms of management and new modes of political conduct had to
be invented to reconcile the initial antipathy between military power
and money power; and the society most successful in achieving this act
of legerdemain—western Europe—in due season came to dominate
the world.

Europe's rise will be the theme of the next chapters. This one seeks
to examine the springs and limits of China's transformation, and its
initial impact on the rest of the world.

Market and Command in Medieval China

In trying to understand what put China in the lead, and how its
technological headstart on the rest of the civilized world crumbled
away, one soon runs into difficulty. Historians of China have yet to
work through the voluminous records from the T'ang (618–907),
Sung (960–1279), Yüan (1260–1368), and Ming (1368–1644) dynasties with the appropriate questions in mind. A generation or more will
be required before they can attain a clear vision of the regional variations and social and economic transformations of China that underlay
the rise and decay of a high technology iron and coal industry and of a

---

Population in Sung-Chin China," *Etudes Song I: Histoire et institutions,* ser. 1 (Paris,
1970), p. 52.

naval hegemony that extended briefly throughout the Indian Ocean. In the meanwhile, active hypothesis is all that can be hoped for.[2]

All the same, scholars working in the field have assembled some startling data about Chinese accomplishments. Robert Hartwell, for example, in three remarkable articles,[3] has traced the history of iron-working in north China in the eleventh century. The technical basis of the large-scale development that then occurred was already old in China. Blast furnaces, using an ingenious bellows that produced a continuous flow of air, had been known for up to one thousand years[4] before the ironmasters of north China began to fuel such furnaces with coke during the first decades of the eleventh century, thereby solving a persistent fuel problem in the tree-short landscape of the Yellow River valley. Coke, too, had been used for cooking and domestic heating for at least two hundred years before being put to use in ferrous metallurgy.[5]

Yet even if the separate techniques were old, the combination was new; and once coke came to be used for smelting, the scale of iron and steel production seems to have surged upward in quite extraordinary fashion, as the following figures for iron production in China show:[6]

2. Stefan Balazs was the great pioneer with his "Beiträge zur Wirtschaftsgeschichte der T'ang Zeit," *Mitteilungen des Seminars für orientalische Sprachen zu Berlin* 34 (1931): 21–25; 35 (1932): 27–73, and his later essays gathered in two overlapping collections, Etienne Balazs, *Chinese Civilization and Bureaucracy* (New Haven, 1964) and *La bureaucratie céleste: Recherches sur l'économie et la société de la Chine traditionelle* (Paris, 1968). Yoshinobu Shiba, *Commerce and Society in Sung China* (Ann Arbor, Mich., 1970) offers a sample of recent Japanese scholarship, which also influences the essays collected in John W. Haeger, ed., *Crisis and Prosperity in Sung China* (Tucson, Ariz., 1975), and a bold effort at synthesis by Mark Elvin, *The Pattern of the Chinese Past* (Stanford, Calif., 1973). For an interesting attempt to put China's economic history into the context of contemporary theory of economic "development" see Anthony M. Tang, "China's Agricultural Legacy," *Economic Development and Cultural Change* 28 (1979): 1–22.

3. Robert Hartwell, "Markets, Technology and the Structure of Enterprise in the Development of the Eleventh-Century Chinese Iron and Steel Industry," *Journal of Economic History* 26 (1966): 29–58; "A Cycle of Economic Change in Imperial China: Coal and Iron in Northeast China, 750–1350," *Journal of Economic and Social History of the Orient (JESHO)*, 10 (1967): 103–59; "Financial Expertise, Examinations and the Formulation of Economic Policy in Northern Sung China," *Journal of Asian Studies* 30 (1971): 281–314.

4. Joseph Needham, *The Development of Iron and Steel Technology in China* (London, 1958), p. 18.

5. The use of coal as fuel in ironworking also was of long standing; but the method used to prevent the iron from becoming useless by contamination with sulphur from the coal was to encase the ore to be smelted in cylindrical clay containers. This meant small-scale production and high fuel consumption. Cf. ibid., p. 13, and pl. 11, showing modern craftsmen using such hand-sized crucibles.

6. Hartwell, "Markets, Technology and the Structure of Enterprise," p. 34. As Hartwell points out, these statistics parallel British output in the early phases of the industrial revolution. As late as 1788, when Britain too had begun to shift to coke fuel for

Year	Tons
806	13,500
998	32,500
1064	90,400
1078	125,000

Such statistics are of course derived from official tax records, and may therefore systematically underestimate production, since small-scale "backyard" smelting must sometimes have escaped official notice. On the other hand, growth may be partly a statistical artifact, if for some reason or other official concern with iron and steel production became more energetic in the eleventh century.[7] Yet even if this apparent growth is partly a matter of more thorough reporting, Hartwell has shown that within a relatively small region of north China, on or adjacent to bituminous coal fields (suitable for coking) in northern Honan and southern Hopei, production went from nothing to 35,000 tons per annum by 1018. Large-scale enterprises arose in these locations, employing hundreds of full-time industrial laborers, whereas iron smelting in other parts of China seems usually to have remained a part-time occupation for peasants who worked as ironmakers in the agricultural off season.

The new scale of enterprise could flourish only when there was a ready market for large amounts of iron and steel. That in turn depended on transportation, and on price relationships that made it attractive for families (perhaps, as Hartwell suggests, originally land-owners) to build and manage the new metallurgical establishments. For about a century, these conditions did coexist. Canals connected the capital of the northern Sung dynasty, K'ai-feng, with the new iron and steel producing centers in Honan and Hopei; and the capital constituted a vast market for metal. Iron was used for coinage,[8] for weapons, in construction, and for tools. Government officials supervised minting and weapons manufacture closely and in 1083 saw fit also to monopolize the sale of agricultural implements made of iron.

Chinese history offered ample precedent for this decision. Ever since Han times (202 B.C.–A.D. 220) iron had rivaled salt as a commodity attracting official attention. By monopolizing the distribution of these two materials, and selling them at arbitrarily heightened

---

ferrous metallurgy, total iron output in England and Wales was only 76,000 tons, just 60 percent of China's total seven hundred years earlier!

7. Chinese population estimates encounter this same difficulty, as had long been recognized.

8. Only in Szechuan; elsewhere coinage was copper.

prices, state revenue could readily be enlarged. The decision of 1083 thus represented a reversion to old, well-established patterns of taxation,[9] though one may readily believe that resulting high prices may have inhibited the expansion of private, civilian uses for iron and steel, and thereby helped to check any further growth of production.

Hartwell has not tried to estimate the end uses to which Chinese iron and steel were put in the eleventh century. Only scattered data survive. A single order for 19,000 tons of iron to make currency pieces, and a mention of two government arsenals in which 32,000 suits of armor were produced each year, give a glimpse of the scale of government operations in K'ai-feng in the late eleventh century when iron from the new foundries was pouring into the capital at an ever increasing rate. But such information does not permit any estimate of how much went into armaments as against coinage, construction, and the decorative arts.[10] How much iron and steel escaped governmental manufactories and entered the private sector also remains unknowable, though Hartwell believes some did.

Even if the decision in 1083 to monopolize the sale of agricultural implements made of iron resulted in restricted production, it is worth pointing out that official management of the economy in medieval China had attained a good deal of self-consciousness and sophistication. The theory was concisely expressed by Po Chü-i (ca. 801) as follows:

> Grain and cloth are produced by the agricultural class, natural resources are transformed by the artisan class, wealth and goods are circulated by the merchant class, and money is managed by the ruler. The ruler manages one of these four in order to regulate the other three.[11]

Currency management took on modern characteristics. Paper money had been introduced in parts of China as early as 1024; later, by 1107, the practice was extended to the capital region itself.[12] A

9. Cf. Esson M. Gale, *Discourse on Salt and Iron* (Leiden, 1931).

10. Iron and steel were used in bridges, pagodas, and statues. Cf. Needham, *Iron and Steel Technology*, pp. 19–22; Hartwell, "A Cycle of Economic Change," pp. 123–45; Hartwell, "Markets, Technology and the Structure of Enterprise, pp. 37–39.

11. Hartwell, "Financial Expertise," p. 304.

12. Yang Lien-sheng, *Money and Credit in China: A Short History* (Cambridge, Mass., 1952), p. 53. Robert Hartwell, "The Evolution of the Early Northern Sung Monetary System, A.D. 960–1025," *Journal of the American Oriental Society* 87 (1967): 280–89. Paper money was, initially, backed by silver. "If there was the slightest impediment in the flow of paper money, the authorities would unload silver and accept paper money as payment for it. If any loss of popular confidence was feared, then not a cash's worth of

shift from taxes in kind to taxes in money gained rapid headway. According to one calculation, annual tax receipts in cash rose from sixteen million strings of cash early in the Sung dynasty (i.e., soon after A.D. 960) to about sixty million per annum in the decade 1068–78.[13] By that time more than half of the entire governmental income probably took the form of cash payments.[14]

Obviously, such changes registered far-reaching alteration in society and the economy, at least in the most developed parts of China. What seems to have happened was that with the improvement of transport, through canal building and removal of natural obstacles to navigation in streams and rivers, local differences in landscape and resources allowed even the very humble to specialize their production. Agricultural yields rose markedly as diverse crops suited to differing soils and climates began to supplement one another. Improved seed and systematic application of fertilizers also worked wonders. Innumerable peasants began to supplement what they produced for their own support by buying and selling in local markets. On top of this, part-time artisanal activity eked out agricultural income for millions. Proliferating market exchanges—local, regional, and trans-regional—allowed spectacular increases in total productivity, as all the advantages of specialization that Adam Smith later analyzed so persuasively came into operation.[15]

A rising level of population meant that poverty did not disappear. On the contrary, while some became rich by skillful manipulation of the market, others became paupers. Their plight became painfully conspicuous in the imperial capital and other cities. Impoverished rural folk swarmed into towns hoping for gainful employment, and begged or starved when it was not to be had. Efforts to organize public relief, beginning in 1103, were only sporadically effective, as a memorial of 1125 makes clear:

> In winter the collapsing people are not being cared for. The
> beggars are falling down and sleeping in the streets beneath the

the accumulated reserves of gold and silver in the province concerned would be moved elsewhere." Elvin, *Pattern of the Chinese Past,* p. 160, translating Li Chien-nung, *Sung-Yüan-Ming ching-chi-shih-kao* (Peking, 1957), p. 95. A cash was a small coin, punctured in the center and used for larger transactions attached to strings of standard length.

13. Edmund H. Worthy, "Regional Control in the Southern Sung Salt Administration," in Haeger, *Crisis and Prosperity,* p. 112.

14. Yang, *Money and Credit,* p. 18.

15. Yoshinobu Shiba, "Commercialization of Farm Products in the Sung Period," *Acta Asiatica* 19 (1970): 77–96; Peter J. Golas, "Rural China in the Song," *Journal of Asian Studies* 39 (1980): 295–99.

imperial carriage. Everyone sees them and the people pity them and lament.[16]

Under the remorseless pressure of circumstance, therefore, even the humblest members of Chinese society were compelled to enter the market whenever they could, seeking always to increase their overall material well-being. As a writer of the early fourteenth century put it:

> These days, wherever there is a settlement of ten households, there is always a market for rice and salt. . . . At the appropriate season, people exchange what they have for what they have not, raising or lowering the prices in accordance with their estimate of the eagerness or diffidence shown by others, so as to obtain the last small measure of profit. This is of course the usual way of the world. Although Ting-ch'iao is no great city, its river will still accommodate boats and its land routes carts. Thus it, too, serves as a town for peasants who trade and artisans who engage in commerce.[17]

Or again:

> All the men of An-chi county can graft mulberry trees. Some of them take their living solely by sericulture. For subsistence it is necessary that a family of ten persons rear ten frames of silkworms. . . . Supplying one's food and clothing by these means insures a high degree of stability. One month's toil is better than a whole year's exertion at farming.[18]

On top of such local exchanges, an urban hierarchy arose, starting with rural towns, then provincial cities, and rising to a few truly metropolitan centers located along the Grand Canal that connected the Yangtse valley with that of the Yellow River. At the apex, and dominating the whole exchange system, was K'ai-feng, the capital of

16. Quoted in Hugh Scogin, "Poor Relief in Northern Sung China," *Oriens extremus* 25 (1978): 41.

17. Ting-ch'iao was located in the lower Yangtse region. This passage comes from a local gazetteer, written between 1330 and 1332, quoted from Yoshinobu Shiba, "Urbanization and the Development of Markets on the Lower Yangtse Valley," in Haeger, *Crisis and Prosperity*, p. 28. Shiba's essay admirably connects the commercialization of specific localities with landscape variations (hill vs. flood plain), transport networks, and population growth. Obviously, not all of China was as highly developed as the region of the lower Yangtse valley. But it was what happened in that region and in the lower reaches of the Yellow River plain that set the pace for the new social and economic developments of the eleventh to the fifteenth centuries.

18. Ibid., p. 36, translating Ch'en Fu, *Treatise on Agriculture*, first printed in 1154.

the northern Sung.[19] After 1126 the city of Hang-chou, at the other end of the Grand Canal, where the southern Sung dynasty established its headquarters, played a similarly dominating role.

Against this background of commercial expansion and agricultural specialization, the growth of the iron and steel production of the eleventh century seems less amazing. It was, indeed, only part of a general upsurge of wealth and productivity resulting from specialization of skills and fuller utilization of natural resources that intensifying market exchanges permitted and encouraged. Yet the vigorous pursuit of private advantage in the marketplace, especially when it allowed upstart individuals to accumulate conspicuous amounts of wealth, ran counter to older Chinese values. Moreover, these traditional values were firmly and effectually institutionalized in the government. Officials, recruited by examination based on the Confucian classics, habitually looked askance at the more flamboyant expressions of the commercial spirit. Thus, for example, a high official named Hsia Sung (d. 1051) wrote:

> ... since the unification of the empire, control over the merchants has not yet been well established. They enjoy a luxurious way of life, living on dainty foods and delicious rice and meat, owning handsome houses and many carts, adorning their wives and children with pearls and jades, and dressing their slaves in white silk. In the morning they think about how to make a fortune, and in the evening they devise means of fleecing the poor. ... In the assignment of corvee duties they are treated much better by the government than average rural households, and in the taxation of commercial duties they are less rigidly controlled than commoners. Since this relaxed control over merchants is regarded by the people as a common rule, they despise agricultural pursuits and place high value on an idle living by trade.[20]

Since official doctrine held that the emperor "should consider the Empire as if it formed a single household,"[21] the right of imperial officials to intervene and alter existing patterns of production and exchange was never in doubt. The only issue was whether a given policy was practically enforceable and whether it would serve the

19. Cf. Etienne Balazs, "Une Carte des centres commerciaux de la Chine à la fin du XIe siècle," *Annales: Economies sociétés, civilisations* 12 (1957): 587–93.
20. Shiba, "Urbanization," p. 43.
21. A phrase attributed to anonymous Confucian literati in a remarkable debate on state economic policy that occurred in 81 B.C. Cf. Gale, *Discourse on Salt and Iron,* p. 74.

general interest. Confiscatory taxation of ill-gotten gains always smacked of justice and retribution. The all too obvious suffering of the poor reinforced the case against the rich merchants and ruthless engrossers of the market. Yet Sung officials recognized that indiscriminate resort to such a policy might cost the state dearly by diminishing tax revenue in future years. Officials therefore struggled to reconcile justice with fiscal expediency, and long-range with short-range advantage. For a while, in the eleventh century, their policies allowed rapid technological development and expansion of iron and steel production in geographically favored regions accessible to the capital. Hartwell has explored the truly spectacular result for us.

But large-scale commercial and industrial enterprises were vulnerable to decay for the same reasons that had caused them to burgeon. Interruption of communications with the capital or collapse of official demand for iron and steel products would be sure to disrupt the industry. Changes of tax rates or of prices paid by the government could choke off production—perhaps more slowly, but no less surely.

Assuredly, conditions did alter so that the growth of iron and steel production in the K'ai-feng economic region decayed in the twelfth century, but statistics disappear after 1078 because of gaps in surviving records. Forty-eight years later, in 1126, regular administration was disrupted when tribesmen from Manchuria, known as Jürchen, conquered K'ai-feng and set up a new regime in north China (the Ch'in dynasty). The defeated Sung withdrew to the south, making the Huai River the northern frontier of their shrunken domain. A century afterward Genghis Khan's armies defeated the Jürchen (by 1226), and the victor assigned the area in which the ironworks lay to one of the Mongol princes as an appanage. Later when Genghis' grandson, the founder of the Yüan dynasty, Kublai Khan, ascended the throne (1260) and undertook the conquest of southern China, direct imperial administration was again imposed on the iron-producing region of Hopei and Honan. Accordingly, it once more becomes possible to estimate output for the 1260s. By that time, iron production of this region had shrunk from a recorded peak of 35,000 tons per annum in 1078 to about 8,000 tons annually, and was exclusively consigned, as one might expect, to equip the Mongol armies with armor and weapons.[22]

The Yüan dynasty's military demand for iron and steel did not, in and of itself, suffice to restore production to anything like the former level. One reason was the disruption of canal transportation in north

22. Hartwell, "A Cycle of Economic Change," p. 147.

China. This, in turn, was part of an enormous disaster that occurred in 1194, when the Yellow River broke through its restraining dikes and, after flooding vast areas of the most fertile land in north China, eventually found a new path to the sea. The work necessary to restore the canal system was never undertaken. Hence iron production in Honan and Hopei remained at relatively modest levels thereafter. By 1736 the once busy blast furnaces, coke ovens, and steel manufactories were abandoned entirely, even though plenty of coking coal remained at hand and beds of iron ore were not far distant. Production was not resumed until the twentieth century.

Clearly, information is too fragmentary to permit anyone to figure out exactly what happened, either in the period of expansion and technical breakthrough or in the period of constriction and decay. But it is clear that governmental policy was always critically important. The distrust and suspicion with which officials habitually viewed successful entrepreneurs meant that any undertaking risked being taken over as a state monopoly. Alternatively, it could be subjected to taxes and officially imposed prices which made the maintenance of existing levels of operation impossible. This is what seems to have happened to the technologically innovative ironworks in the north which, if they had continued to expand, would have been capable of supplying China with cheaper and far more abundant iron and steel than any other people of the world had hitherto enjoyed.

The abortion of coke-fired ferrous technology was the more remarkable considering that the army maintained by the northern Sung dynasty grew to be over a million men, and its appetite for iron and steel was enormous. Nevertheless, military demand was blunted by the fact that it could become effective only with the consent of governmental officials; and the civil officials who disdained captains of industry actively distrusted and feared captains of men, since organized military force constituted a well-recognized potential challenge to their control of Chinese society.

After the first years of reunification (in the 960s), which involved offensive campaigning, Sung military policy became strictly defensive. The main problem, as always, was how to keep the nomads across the northwestern frontier from raiding settled Chinese landscapes. Nomad cavalry could outstrip Chinese footsoldiers; but footsoldiers, armed with crossbows and stationed in fortified garrison posts thickly scattered throughout the frontier zone, could hold off cavalry attacks quite effectually. If a raiding party chose to bypass such defended places in order to penetrate deeper into China, the Sung government's response was to rely initially on a "scorched earth" policy that aimed at bringing everything of value within city walls.[23] If raiders lingered, the central imperial field army, normally stationed in the environs of the capital, could be sent to harass and drive back the intruders. The field army was partly a cavalry force; its role was as much to countervail and overawe potentially rebellious border units as to protect the interior from barbarian raiding.[24]

This strategy became inadequate only if raiding parties snowballed into really large invading armies and acquired the organization and weaponry needed to attack city walls with success. This is what happened in 1127 when the Jürchen conquered K'ai-feng. To guard against such disaster, Sung policy relied on diplomacy, buying immunity from raids with "gifts" to powerful barbarian neighbors. From a nomad chieftain's point of view, luxury goods received as gifts in connection with diplomatic intercourse (in exchange, to be sure, for horses or other gifts from him to make the transaction symmetrical) often seemed better than the randomly assorted objects that could be secured by plunder.

From the viewpoint of Chinese officialdom, a passive defense policy had the advantage of making it easier to assure civilian dominance within China. An army that was assigned to garrison duty and seldom took the field for active campaigning could be kept in leading-strings by carefully regulating its flow of supplies. Civilian officials, charged with the duty of providing food and weapons to local military commanders, could in any dispute expect to balance one military leader off against another. This made it relatively easy to nip rebelliousness in the bud, should any military captain find himself tempted to bring armed force to bear on decision-making at imperial headquarters.[25] If

23. Cf. Herbert Franke, "Siege and Defense of Towns in Medieval China," in Frank A. Kierman, Jr., and John K. Fairbank, eds., *Chinese Ways in Warfare* (Cambridge, Mass., 1974), pp. 151–201.

24. Laurence J. C. Ma, *Commercial Development and Urban Change in Sung China (960–1279)* (Ann Arbor, Mich., 1971), p. 100. An encyclopedia of the Sung period summed up the military policy of the founder of the dynasty as follows: "He comprehended the value of strengthening the root and weakening the branches." Wang Ying-lin, *Yü Hai,* cited in Lo Ch'iu-ch'ing, "Pei-sung ping-chih yen-chiu" (The military service of the northern Sung Dynasty), *Hsin-ya Hsueh-pao* (New Asia Journal), 3 (1957): 180, translated by Hugh Scogin.

25. The risk of military rebellion by border troops had been vividly demonstrated under the T'ang when a barbarian general rebelled in 755 and nearly toppled that dynasty from the throne. The rebellion did paralyze the central civilian administration, making the next two hundred years of Chinese history a period of thinly veiled local warlordism. It was in reaction to this experience that Sung military policy was devised soon after the country was (mostly) reunited under an unusually successful warlord,

the cost was loss of field mobility and vulnerability to large-scale, well-organized nomad attack, the Sung authorities were willing to pay the price. Only so could civilian authority be assured within China; only so could the mandarins be sure of dominating all sides of Chinese life.

Two aspects of this situation seem worth comment. First, from the point of view of the ruling elite, the policy towards Chinese army commanders was not fundamentally different from their policy towards barbarian chieftains outside the imperial boundaries. Divide and rule, while pacifying undependable elements by assigning goods, titles, and ritual roles to military leaders, was the recipe the Sung officials followed, whether within or beyond China's frontiers. Policy called for giving as little in the way of goods and prestige as was safe. The temptation for officials on the spot was always to divert wealth for personal and family uses, even if it meant risk of armed reaction, whether from within or from without imperial borders.

Military men and barbarian chieftains confronted precisely parallel temptations. Raiding or rebellion might bring immediate access to booty and plunder more valuable than anything they could ever wring out of the reluctant Chinese officials. On the other hand, such gains were risky and could not continue indefinitely. Everyone concerned had therefore always to weigh long-term benefit against short-term gain. Since judgments in fact fluctuated, this meant that even the most cunningly contrived defense system was potentially unstable. Very sudden changes in the balance of military force along the frontier were always possible, if border guards ceased to resist the barbarian enemies, or if those enemies were able to unite into really formidable armies and acquire the means of besieging and breaking into walled cities and defended strongpoints. The sudden victories won by the Jürchen after 1122, culminating in the capture of K'ai-feng just four years later, illustrate this inherent instability.[26]

In the second place, Sung official policy towards armed men and organized violence was not fundamentally different from govern-

---

Chao K'uang-yin, the founder of the dynasty. He, in effect, set out to throw down the ladder by which he had ascended to the throne by establishing administrative patterns that would put every conceivable obstacle in the way of armed rebellion by military commanders. On the T'ang revolt cf. Edwin G. Pulleybank, *The Background of the Rebellion of An Lu-shan* (London, 1955); on Sung military policy see Jacques Gernet, *Le monde chinois* (Paris, 1972), pp. 272–75; Edward A. Kracke, Jr., *Civil Service in Early Sung China, 960–1067* (Cambridge, Mass., 1953), pp. 9–11; Karl Wittfogel and Feng Chia-sheng, *History of Chinese Society, Liao, 907–1125* (Philadelphia, 1949), pp. 534–37.

26. For details of the Jürchen conquest, see Jing-shen Tao, *The Jürchen in Twelfth Century China: A Study of Sinicization* (Seattle and London, 1976), pp. 14–24.

mental policy towards merchants and others who enriched themselves by skillful or lucky manipulation of the growing market system of China. Like organized resort to armed force, private riches acquired by personal shrewdness in buying and selling violated the Confucian sense of propriety. Such persons could be tolerated, even encouraged, when their activity served official ends. But to allow merchants or manufacturers to acquire too much power, or accumulate too much capital, was as unwise as to allow a military commander or a barbarian chieftain to control too many armed men. Wise policy aimed at breaking up undue concentrations of wealth just as an intelligent diplomacy and a well-designed military administration aimed at preventing undue concentrations of military power under any one command. Divide and rule applied in economics as much as in war. Officials who acted on that principle could count on widespread popular sympathy, since plundering armies and ruthless capitalists seemed almost equally detestable to the common people.

The technology of Chinese armament also lent itself to the maintenance of bureaucratic supremacy. Since Han times, and perhaps before, crossbows had been the principal missile weapon of Chinese armies.[27] The crossbow had two salient characteristics. First, a crossbow was about as easy to use as a modern handgun. No special strength was needed to cock it. A longbow required years of practice to develop sufficient strength in thumb and fingers to draw the bow to its full arc, whereas once a crossbow had been cocked, all the archer had to do was to place the arrow in firing position, and sight along the stock until a suitable target came into view. A few hours of target

27. No satisfactory account of the development of the crossbow in China seems to exist. A Chinese text, *Spring and Autumn Annals of Wu and Yüeh,* attributes the invention of the crossbow to a man named Ch'in, from whom the invention passed to three local magnates and from them to Ling, ruler of the state of Ch'u in south central China from 541 to 529 B.C. Archaeological evidence tends to support this dating, for several tombs of the fifth and fourth centuries B.C. contained crossbows. The first notable improvement in crossbow design came in the eleventh century, when Li Ting invented the foot stirrup (about 1068), allowing use of the back and leg muscles for cocking the bow. Correspondingly stronger bows could then be brought into use. I owe these bits of information to personal communications from Steven F. Sagi of the University of Hawaii and Robin Yates of Cambridge University. Published materials seem hopelessly inadequate. Cf. C. M. Wilbur, "History of the Crossbow," *Smithsonian Institution Annual Report, 1936* (Washington, D.C., 1937), pp. 427–38; Michael Loewe, *Everyday Life in Early Imperial China* (London, 1968), pp. 82–86; Noel Barnard and Sato Tamotsu, *Metallurgical Remains of Ancient China* (Tokyo, 1975), pp. 116–17. For European crossbows the admirable work by Ralph W. F. Payne-Gallwey, *The Crossbow, Medieval and Modern, Military and Sporting: Its Construction, History and Management* (London, 1903), offers clear and abundant information, and includes a little on modern Chinese crossbows as well.

Chinese Crossbow Manufacture

This woodcut from a seventeenth-century encyclopedia shows how the arc was strengthened by lamination. In the figure below, the crossbow is shown with a magazine holding ten arrows. Cocking the bow released an arrow from the magazine, which then fell into shooting position. Details of the cocking and trigger mechanism do not show clearly, though these were the parts requiring most exact skill in manufacture.

Reproduced from Sung Ying-Hsing, *T'ien-Kung K'ai-Wu,* translated by E-tu Zen Sun and Shiou-Chuan Sun (University Park, Pa.: Pennsylvania State University Press, 1966), p. 266.

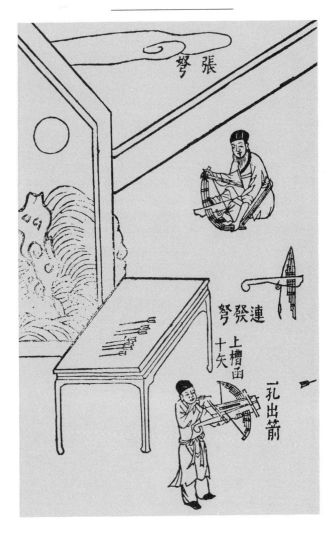

practice allowed an ordinary man to use a crossbow quite effectively. Yet Chinese crossbows of the thirteenth century were lethal up to four hundred yards.[28]

Second, the simple skill required for using a crossbow was counterbalanced by the high skill needed for its manufacture. An army of crossbowmen had to rely on expert artisans to produce precisely shaped trigger mechanisms and other necessary parts. Moreover, to supply such craftsmen with everything required to manufacture crossbows in large numbers was not easy. A powerful crossbow was compounded of laminated wood, bone, horn, and sinew, all cunningly fitted together to assure maximal springiness when bent out of its unstressed shape. The art of making such compound bows, however, was highly developed throughout the Eurasian steppelands. What distinguished crossbows was their trigger mechanism, which had to be made strong enough to withstand heavy stress when the bow was cocked and awaiting discharge. Only skilled artisans with access to appropriate supplies of metal could make a reliable trigger.[29]

A market economy, ranging across diverse landscapes, was better able to assure a suitable flow of the requisite materials into artisan workshops than any but the most efficient command economy. The same consideration applied to the varied machines for projecting stones, arrows, and incendiary materials with which Chinese armies of the eleventh century were also equipped.[30] Explosive mixtures, in-

28. Corinna Hana, *Berichte über die Verteidigung der Stadt Te-an während der Periode K'ai-hsi, 1205–1209* (Wiesbaden, 1970). As we shall see in chapter 3, powerful crossbows checked the expansion of knighthood in the thirteenth century when these weapons became common in Mediterranean Europe. In China, crossbows may have helped to discourage reliance on the Iranian style of heavily armored cavalry, for if a crossbowman could knock even an armored cavalryman off his horse, it made no sense to invest in the heavy horse and the expensive armor that put Iranian barons and European knights at the apex of their respective societies. Heavily armored cavalry, after some three centuries of importance in China, disappeared in the seventh century. It is, however, not certain that Chinese crossbows were powerful enough to penetrate armor before the invention of the foot stirrup in the eleventh century. Cf. Joseph Needham, *The Grand Titration: Science and Society in East and West* (London, 1969), pp. 168–70.

29. For a literary account of bowmaking and prints showing crossbow artisans at work, see Sung Ying-Hsing, *T'ien-Kung K'ai-Wu,* translated as *Chinese Technology in the 17th Century,* by E-tu Zen Sun and S. C. Sun (Univeristy Park, Pa., 1966), pp. 261–67. Weaker bows could be made of simpler material; indeed it was even possible to shape a workable trigger entirely out of wood; but such weapons lacked the power needed to penetrate armor. For an account of nineteenth-century Chinese crossbows made of wood and designed to fire a magazine of arrows at a very rapid rate, see Payne-Gallwey, *The Crossbow,* pp. 237–42. These weak but ingenious weapons (actually used against British troops in the 1860s) relied on poisoned arrows to make their wounds dangerous.

30. Sergej Aleksandrović Skoljar, "L'artillerie de jet à l'époque Song," in Françoise

cluding gunpowder, joined this array of complicated weaponry about the year 1000. Explosives were valued initially as incendiaries, but the Chinese began to exploit the propulsive power of gunpowder after about 1290, when the first true guns seem to have been invented.[31]

Chinese technical innovation, indeed, appears to have concentrated specially on weaponry in the Sung period. Technological advances among the barbarians perhaps impelled the Chinese to try to keep ahead. At any rate, before their conquest of north China in 1126, the Jürchen and other barbarian neighbors of China gained increasing access to products of Chinese artisanal skills. Improved armor and a greater supply of metal for weapons was the major symptom of this change. Clearly the Sung rulers faced a narrowing technical gap between themselves and their principal rivals—a gap that practically disappeared after the conquest of north China by the barbarians. Faced with this sort of threat, Sung authorities began systematically to reward military inventors, as the following passage illustrates:

> In the third year of the K'ai Pao period of the reign of Sung T'ai-Tse [i.e., A.D. 969] the general Feng Chi-Sheng, together with some other officers, suggested a new model of fire arrow. The Emperor had it tested, and (as the test proved successful) presents of gowns and silk were bestowed upon the inventors.[32]

With such patronage in high places, obstacles to innovation were minimized.

The city-based, defensive character of Sung strategy also encouraged technical experiment. It made sense to expend ingenuity and resources preparing complicated and powerful machines of war to defend city walls and other fixed positions, whereas such machinery initially was far too cumbersome for use by armies designed to take the field and move rapidly across open country. Only later, when catapults and gunpowder weapons had become really powerful, did the Mon-

Aubin, ed., *Etudes Song,* ser. 1 (Paris, 1978), pp. 119–42; Joseph Needham, "China's Trebuchets, Manned and Counter-weighted," in Bert S. Hall and Delno C. West, eds., *On Pre-modern Technology and Science: A Volume of Studies in Honor of Lynn White, Jr.* (Malibu, Calif., 1976), pp. 107–38.

31. Joseph Needham, "The Guns of Khaifengfu," *Times Literary Supplement,* 11 January 1980; Herbert Franke, "Siege and Defense of Towns in Medieval China," in Kierman and Fairbank, *Chinese Ways in Warfare,* pp. 161–79; L. Carrington Goodrich and Feng Chia-sheng, "The Early Development of Firearms in China," *Isis* 36 (1946): 114–23; Wang Ling, "On the Invention and Use of Gunpowder in China," *Isis* 37 (1947): 160–78.

32. Quoted from Wang Ling, "Gunpowder," p. 165. According to Wang Ling, the fire arrows in question may have been tipped with gunpowder that exploded on impact.

gols demonstrate that these devices could be used to break down city gates and walls as well as to defend them.[33]

Successful administration of an army that grew to count more than a million men in its ranks, and that relied on complex weaponry to fend off more mobile attackers, obviously depended on the prior articulation of Sung China's economy through market relationships, transport improvements, and technically competent administration. New patterns of recruitment into officialdom through examinations helped to assure a relatively proficient civilian management;[34] but despite all the mandarins' skills and wiles, the tasks of supplying the army may have strained the precarious balance between military and civilian command elements in Chinese society on the one hand and the newly ebullient market behavior of private persons on the other. The famous reform minister, Wang An-Shih (d. 1086) could write: "The educated men of the land regard the carrying of arms as a disgrace"; yet in the 1060s an official calculation revealed that 80 percent of the government's income, fifty-eight million strings of cash, was necessary to support the million and more despised soldiers who garrisoned China.[35] Concerned officials, seeking to economize on military expenditure, were in a position to throttle the ferrous metallurgy of Honan and Hopei simply by setting prices at uneconomic levels; but no one now knows whether this is actually what happened or whether something else disrupted the industry.

However costly their policies may have been in the long run, westerners in the twentieth century can surely sympathize with the problem Confucian officials faced in trying to balance one disturbing element—professionalized violence—against another equally disturbing element—professionalized pursuit of profit. Neither conformed to traditional propriety. Indeed, merchants and military men frequently flaunted their moral deficiencies with brazen unconcern for others. Uninhibited linkage between military and commercial enterprise, such as was to take place in fourteenth- to nineteenth-century Europe, would have seemed truly disastrous to Chinese officials. As long as men educated in the traditions of Confucian statecraft retained political authority, such a dangerous confluence would not be permitted. Instead, systematic restraints upon industrial expansion, commercial

---

33. For a detailed account of how machines and men were mobilized to defend a provincial city against the Jürchen see Hana, *Berichte über die Verteidigung der Stadt Te-an.*

34. Kracke, *Civil Service in Early Sung China.*

35. The quotation and figures for the army's cost come from Hsiao Ch'i Ch'ing, *The Military Establishment of the Yüan Dynasty* (Cambridge, Mass., 1978), pp. 6–7.

expansion, and military expansion were built into the Chinese system of political administration.

The career of a twelfth-century ironmaster named Wang Ko offers an instructive example *in parvo* of how the system worked, though obviously he represents an extreme case. Starting from nothing, Wang Ko became a rather considerable ironmaster in south-central China, with something like five hundred men in his employ. His furnaces used charcoal, not coke; indeed, his initial start came from getting possession of a tree-covered mountainside where charcoal could be produced. For reasons not clearly stated in the surviving record, Wang Ko quarreled with local officials in 1181. When they sent a detachment of soldiers to enforce their will, he mobilized his workmen to beat them off, and then followed up with an attack on the town where the officials resided. But his workmen deserted him; he had to flee, and was later caught and executed.[36] Such a career shows how economic entrepreneurship and irregular exercise of armed force could merge into one another; and how entrenched officialdom enforced its will against both forms of impropriety.

Yet going over to a cash basis for government finance in the eleventh century risked infection of officialdom itself by the commercial mentality. This became most clearly apparent in south China. South of the Yangtse, a mountainous topography hindered transport by canals and riverways. Merchants had therefore to take to the open sea, and once sea trade among Chinese coastal provinces became well established, it was easy to extend trade relations to more distant parts. Indeed, commerce with populations that were not subject to imperial administration could be made to contribute handsomely to governmental income through excise taxes. Officials managing such taxes sometimes sought to promote overseas trade in a spirit reminiscent of mercantilist Europe, and might even invest government funds in ventures that promised to increase income and bring back rare and valued goods. In words attributed to the emperor himself:"The profits from maritime commerce are very great. If properly managed they can be millions. Is it not better than taxing the people?"[37] The emperor knew whereof he spoke, for by 1137 something like a fifth of his government's income came from excise taxes on maritime trade.[38]

36. Wolfram Eberhard, "Wang Ko: An Early Industrialist," *Oriens* 10 (1957): 248–52, tells this tale.

37. Ma, *Commerical Development and Urban Change in Sung China,* p. 34. The phrases come from an imperial decree issued in 1137.

38. Ibid., p. 38. Cf. Lo Jung-pang, "Maritime Commerce and Its Relation to the Sung Navy." *JESHO* 12 (1969): 61–68.

This partial coalescence between mercantile and official outlooks reached its apogee under the Mongols (the Yüan dynasty, 1227–1368), who did not share the Confucian disdain for shrewd traders. Marco Polo's reception at Kublai's court illustrates this fact. He was, indeed, only one of many foreign merchants whom Kublai appointed as tax collectors and to other key administrative posts in his empire.[39] Under the Ming (1368–1644) reaction against the alliance between mercantile and military enterprise set in, though not at once, for some of its most spectacular results came early in the fifteenth century, when Chinese fleets explored the Indian Ocean for political-commercial purposes.

The imperial venture into the Indian Ocean built upon a naval tradition that took shape with the establishment of the southern Sung dynasty. When K'ai-feng fell to the Jürchen in 1126, a scion of the ruling house fled to the south and proved able to defend the remnant of the empire at the river barriers that still protected him from the barbarians of the north. He did so by creating a navy. Instead of relying on infantry forces stationed in fortified strongholds along a land frontier, as the northern Sung had done, after 1126 the southern Sung government came to rely on specially designed warships to guard against the Jürchen horsemen.

Initially the Sung navy was used primarily on inland waterways. New types of vessels, including armored ships driven by treadmills and paddle wheels, were invented for river and canal fighting. Crossbowmen and pikemen provided the main offensive and defensive element, but large projectile-throwing machines of the kind that had long been used in land sieges and for the defense of fortified places were also mounted on the bigger vessels. It was, in general, an adaptation of methods of land warfare to shipboard, each ship playing the role of mobile strongpoint. Equipping such a navy, numbering hundreds of ships and manned by as many as 52,000 men,[40] required an even more complex assemblage of raw materials and manufactured parts than the land army of the northern Sung had required. All the

39. Herbert Franz Schurmann, *Economic Structure of the Yüan Dynasty* (Cambridge, Mass., 1967), pp. 3–4. Herbert Franke, "Ahmed: Ein Beitrag zur Wirtschaftsgeschichte Chinas unter Qubilai," *Oriens* 1 (1948): 222–36, describes the rise and fall of the most spectacularly successful of these outsiders. He was a Moslem born in Transcaucasia who became chief administrator of the salt and other monopolies. Yet the greater scope the Mongols accorded to merchants went along with such an energetic mobilization of shipping for state purposes that Chinese seaborne trade suffered serious setback, according to Lo Jung-pang, "Maritime Commerce," pp. 57–100.

40. Joseph Needham, *Science and Civilization in China* (Cambridge, 1971), 4, pt. 3:476.

materials required for shipbuilding—timbers, rope, sails, fittings—were added to the relatively complex requirements land forces had already imposed on the Chinese economy. An urban base and a market-articulated supply system were even more essential than before; but the passive defense policy pursued by the northern Sung was modified by the fact that the new warships were quite mobile and could be concentrated against an attacker far more readily than infantry forces could ever be.

When, in due course, the armies of Genghis Khan overran the Jürchen domains in north China and then, after a pause of half a century, attacked the south as well, they had first to overcome the navy that had long been the principal bulwark of the Sung regime. This required Kublai Khan to build a navy of his own. With its help he besieged Hsiang-yang, one of the main Sung strongholds on the Yangtse River, for five years before being able to break through. Thereafter, most of the Sung navy went over to the victors, making the final stages of the conquest comparatively easy.[41]

After his victory, Kublai continued to build up his naval strength but changed its character, since the subsequent naval enterprises he undertook were ventures overseas. Accordingly, ships designed to navigate the open oceans became the backbone of the Chinese fleet.[42] Yet despite a truly imperial scale of construction—it is recorded that a total of 4,400 ships attempted the invasion of Japan in 1281—Kublai's naval expeditions met with no enduring success. Japanese warriors, in combination with an opportune typhoon, destroyed the invading force of 1281; and a later venture against Java (1292), though it met with initial victories, also failed to establish enduring control over that distant island.

What might have been more significant for the long run (but turned out not to be) was the use of seagoing ships to supplement grain deliveries from south to north along the inland waterways. By the early part of the fourteenth century, as much grain was carried in seagoing vessels as moved on the canals. Improvement of navigation techniques shortened the trip from the Yangtse mouth to Tientsin to

41. For details of the naval war see Jose Din Ta-san and F. Olesa Muñido, *El poder naval chino desde sus orígenes hasta la caída de la Dinastia Ming* (Barcelona, 1965), pp. 96–98.

42. Needham, *Science and Civilization in China* 3, pt. 3, sec. 29, "Nautical Technology," pp. 379–699, constitutes a thorough and persuasive study of Chinese shipbuilding and naval history. My remarks on naval development derive mainly from this work, supplemented by Din Ta-san and Olesa Muñido, *El poder naval chino,* and by three articles by Lo Jung-pang, "China as a Sea Power," *Far Eastern Quarterly* 14 (1955): 489–503; "The Decline of the Early Ming Navy," *Oriens extremus* 5 (1958): 149–68; and "Maritime Commerce and Its Relation to the Sung Navy," *JESHO* 12 (1969): 57–107.

ten days—far faster than cargo could travel through the Grand Canal. But local rebellion and disorders in the south soon began to interfere with massive long-distance shipment of grain and other commodities, and piracy at sea became a problem as well. Hence even before the final collapse of the Mongol rule in China (1368), shipments by sea had diminished to trivial proportions. Indeed, the entire tax system that concentrated extra grain in the north for use of the government broke down. Local warlords arose, one of whom succeeded in ousting his rivals and reuniting all of China under a new native dynasty, the Ming (1368–1644).

To begin with, the new dynasty combined the military policy of the southern Sung with that of the northern Sung. That is to say, the first Ming emperors set out to maintain a vast infantry army to guard the frontier against the nomads as well as a formidable navy to police internal waterways and the high seas. In 1420, the Ming navy comprised no fewer than 3,800 ships, of which 1,350 were combat vessels, including 400 especially large floating fortresses, and 250 "treasure" ships designed for long-distance cruising.[43]

The famous admiral Cheng Ho commanded the "treasure" ships in his cruises to the Indian Ocean (1405–33). His largest vessels probably displaced about 1,500 tons compared to the 300 tons of Vasco da Gama's flagship that reached the Indian Ocean from Portugal at the end of that same century. Everything about these expeditions eclipsed the scale of later Portuguese endeavors. More ships, more guns, more manpower, more cargo capacity, were combined with seamanship and seaworthiness equivalent to anything Europeans of Columbus' and Magellan's day had at their command. Everywhere he went—from Borneo and Malaysia to Ceylon and beyond to the shores of the Red Sea and the coast of Africa—Cheng Ho asserted Chinese suzereignty and sealed the relationship with tribute/trade exchanges. In the rare cases when his powerful armada met resistance, he used force, seizing a recalcitrant ruler from Ceylon, for example, in 1411, and carrying him back for disciplining at the Chinese imperial court.[44]

Supplementing such official exchanges, privately managed overseas trade burgeoned in China from about the thirteenth century. Mer-

43. Needham, *Science and Civilization in China* 4, pt. 3:484.

44. It is possible that Cheng Ho's first voyage was undertaken to secure China's sea approaches at a time of an anticipated overland attack by Tamurlane, who died in 1405 while preparing a massive assault on China. For this suggestion see Lo Jung-pang, "Policy Formulation and Decision Making on Issues Reflecting Peace and War," in Charles O. Hucker, ed., *Chinese Government in Ming Times: Seven Studies* (New York, 1969), p. 54.

chants and capitalists built and operated large ships. Standard patterns for management of crew and cargo, for sharing risks and gains, and for settling disputes arising from transactions at a distance came to be well defined.[45] Lands close to China's coast—Manchuria, Korea, Japan— were common destinations; but Chinese shipping had begun to enter the Indian Ocean several decades before Cheng Ho's imperial squadrons first went there. The scale of Chinese trade in south Asia and east Africa seems to have spurted upwards from the middle of the twelfth century. The best index of this is offered by sherds of Chinese porcelain found along the African coast. They can be dated quite accurately, and show that trade started as early as the eighth century (presumably carried in Moslem ships); but quantities increased sharply after 1050, when Chinese vessels regularly began to enter the Indian Ocean by rounding the Malay peninsula instead of sending goods across the Kra Isthmus by land portage, which had been the usual practice in earlier centuries.[46]

Just as the rapid growth of coke-fueled blast furnaces in the eleventh century leads someone attuned to European history to suppose that an industrial revolution of general significance ought to have followed, so the overseas empire China had created by the early fifteenth century impels a westerner to think of what might have been if the Chinese had chosen to push their explorations still further. A Chinese Columbus might well have discovered the west coast of America half a century before the real Columbus blundered into Hispaniola in his vain search for Cathay. Assuredly, Chinese ships were seaworthy enough to sail across the Pacific and back. Indeed, if the like of Cheng Ho's expeditions had been renewed, Chinese navigators might well have rounded Africa and discovered Europe before Prince Henry the Navigator died (1460).

But the officials of the imperial court chose otherwise. After 1433 they launched no more expeditions to the Indian Ocean, and in 1436 issued a decree forbidding the construction of new seagoing ships. Naval personnel were ordered to man the boats that plied the inland

45. For details of how Chinese overseas shipping and trade were financed, and how ships were commanded, controlled, and crewed, see Shiba, *Commerce and Society in Sung China*, pp. 15–40. For a survey of what Chinese merchants knew about the world beyond the oceans, see Chau Ju-kua, *On the Chinese and Arab Trade in the 12th and 13th Centuries,* trans. Friedrich Hirth and W. W. Rockhill (St. Petersburg and Tokyo, 1914).
46. August Toussaint, *History of the Indian Ocean* (Chicago, 1966), pp. 74–86; Paul Wheatley, *The Golden Khersonese: Studies in the Historical Geography of the Malay Peninsula before 1500 A.D.* (Kuala Lumpur, 1961), pp. 292–320; K. Mori, "The Beginning of Overseas Advance of Japanese Merchant Ships," *Acta Asiatica* 23 (1972): 1–24.

waters of the Grand Canal, and the seagoing warships were allowed to
rot away without being replaced. Shipbuilding skills soon decayed,
and by the mid-sixteenth century the Chinese navy was unable to fend
off the pirates who became a growing nuisance along the China
coast.[47]

This withdrawal was partly a result of bureaucratic infighting among
rival cliques of courtiers. Cheng Ho was a Moslem by birth, probably
of Mongol descent.[48] This gave a foreign flavor to his overseas ad-
ventures; and Chinese Confucian officials grew to distrust things
foreign. He was also a eunuch, and eunuchs, too, came under attack in
the Ming court when one of them recklessly led an expedition against
the Mongols in 1449 and succeeded only in allowing the barbarians to
capture the emperor in person.[49] But this episode pointed to a more
fundamental reason for official abandonment of overseas ventures. A
formidable and feared enemy existed across the land frontier,
whereas, until the rise of "Japanese" piracy in the late fifteenth century, there was no rival on the seas whom the Chinese had to fear.

The issue, accordingly, became a choice between an offensive as
against a defensive military policy. In 1407 the Ming navy led an
expedition to Annam (modern Vietnam), but between 1420 and 1428
Chinese forces there met a series of reverses. A decision to withdraw
was finally made in 1428. Against this background the memorial to the
emperor, written in 1426 when the struggle in Annam was at a critical
stage, sounds strangely familiar to American ears:

> Arms are the instruments of evil which the sage does not use
> unless he must. The noble rulers and wise ministers of old did not
> dissipate the strength of the people by deeds of arms. This was a
> far-sighted policy. . . . Your minister hopes that your majesty . . .
> would not indulge in military pursuits nor glorify the sending
> of expeditions to distant countries. Abandon the barren lands
> abroad and give the people of China a respite so that they could de-
> vote themselves to husbandry and the schools. Thus there would
> be no wars and suffering on the frontier and no murmuring in the
> villages, the commanders would not seek fame and the soldiers

47. Lo Jung-pang, "The Decline of the Early Ming Navy," pp. 149–68; Kuei-sheng
Chang, "The Maritime Scene in China at the Dawn of the Great European Discoveries,"
Journal of the American Oriental Society 94 (1974): 347–59.

48. Cf. John V. G. Mills, ed. and trans., Ma Huan, *Ying-yai Sheng-ian: Overall
Survey of the Ocean's Shores* [1433] (Cambridge, 1970), Introduction.

49. For a detailed account of this ill-fated military enterprise see Fredrick W. Mote,
"The Tu-mu Incident of 1449," in Kierman and Fairbank, *Chinese Ways in Warfare,* pp.
243–72.

would not sacrifice their lives abroad, the people from afar would voluntarily submit and distant lands would come into our fold, and our dynasty would last for 10,000 generations.[50]

Given the choice between defense of a threatened frontier close to the new capital at Peking and costly offensive operations overseas, it is not hard to understand why the Ming authorities opted for retrenchment.

A further consideration which may have played a part was this: in 1417, construction of deep-water locks was completed throughout the length of the Grand Canal connecting the Yangtse with the Yellow River valleys. Such locks were newly invented, and their construction meant that vessels could use the canal twelve months in the year without having to worry about high and low water. Always before, for about six months of the year, the canal had been unavailable to large boats, and sometimes traffic halted completely until the rains raised the water level. Building new locks assured year-round grain deliveries to the north via inland water routes. Reliance on ocean shipping to supplement traffic in the Grand Canal became unnecessary, and there was no longer any need to police the high seas to assure sufficient food for the capital. Officials, therefore, saw no compelling reason to authorize the heavy expenditures needed to keep the navy in a state of readiness. Accordingly they let it quietly disintegrate.

What about private entrepreneurs' interest in ocean voyaging? Clearly, the livelihood of several thousand persons depended on the overseas trading that had flourished so markedly in the coastal cities of south China. These traders and sailors did not tamely submit when the government prohibited foreign trade in 1371, with periodic reaffirmations across the ensuing two centuries.[51] Overseas voyages continued, though on a reduced scale, since the costs of doing business outside the law were significantly higher than before. Bribing officials to overlook illegal transactions usually cost more than the 10–20 percent levies in kind assessed on foreign goods under the Sung in the time when Chinese overseas trade had swelled so rapidly.[52] The pos-

50. A memorial written by Fan Chi and quoted by Lo Jung-pang, "The Decline of the Early Ming Navy," p. 167. For details of this decision to withdraw see Lo Jung-pang, "Policy Formulation and Decision Making," in Hucker, *Chinese Government in Ming Times*, pp. 56–60.

51. Prohibition of overseas trade was renewed in 1390, 1394, 1397, 1433, 1449, and 1452 according to Matsui Masato, "The Wo-K'uo Disturbances of the 1550's," *East Asian Occasional Papers* 1 (Asian Studies Program, University of Hawaii, Honolulu, 1969), pp. 97–107.

52. Jitsuzo Kuwabara, "P'u Shou-keng: A Man of the Western Regions," *Memoirs of the Research Department of the Toyo Bunko* 7 (1935): 66.

sibility of accumulating large private capital from the profits of seafaring became correspondingly slim, inasmuch as any official had ample reason to confiscate a merchant's illegally gotten gains whenever they came to his attention.

For about two centuries, from 1371 to 1567, when the Ming government again authorized Chinese ships to sail to foreign lands under suitable regulation and with official permission, Chinese seamen and merchants had therefore to go outside the law to continue their way of life. Enough of them did so to constitute a nuisance to the Ming government. The officials called them "Japanese" pirates, thereby excusing themselves for not being able or willing to suppress them effectively. A few Japanese did join the pirates' ranks, but most of the seamen operating illegally off the Chinese coast in the fifteenth and sixteenth centuries were ethnic Chinese. Like Wang Ko the ironmaster and his work force, these Chinese pirate-traders lacked enough popular support ever to challenge the organized might of the Ming government seriously. After 1567, when a more or less satisfactory modus vivendi between officialdom and overseas entrepreneurs was achieved, piracy subsided and the crisis passed. But two centuries of illegal operation obviously hindered the development of Chinese overseas trade prior to that date and made it much easier for European merchants to gain a foothold in the Far East.[53]

Both in iron smelting and shipping, therefore, Chinese achievements which anticipated later European technical triumphs were absorbed into the ongoing reality of Chinese life without making much difference in the long run. Chinese merchants and manufacturers themselves subscribed to the value system that limited their roles in society to comparatively modest proportions. They proved this by investing in land and in education for their sons, who thus joined the dominant landowning class and could compete for a place in the ranks of officialdom.[54]

As a result, the traditional ordering of Chinese society was never really challenged. The governmental command structure, balanced (sometimes perhaps precariously) atop a pullulating market economy, never lost ultimate control. Ironmasters and shipbuilders, along with

53. On the "Japanese" pirates see Kwan-wai So, *Japanese Piracy in Ming China during the 16th Century* (Lansing, Mich., 1975); Louis Dermigny, *La Chine et l'occident: la commerce à Canton au XVIIIe siècle* (Paris, 1964), 1:95–99.

54. For examples, admittedly from a later age, see Ping-ti Ho, "Salt Merchants of Yang-chou," *Harvard Journal of Asiatic Studies* 17 (1954): 130–68.

everybody else in Chinese society, were never autonomous. When officials allowed it, technical advances and increase in the scale of activity could occur in dazzlingly rapid fashion. But, correspondingly, when official policy changed, reallocation of resources in accordance with changed priorities took place with the same rapidity that had allowed the upthrust of iron and steel production in the eleventh century and of shipbuilding in the twelfth to the fifteenth centuries.

The advantages of an economy sustained by complex market exchanges yet responding to politically inspired commands were well illustrated by these episodes. Chinese resources could be channeled toward the accomplishment of some public purpose—whether building a fleet, improving the Grand Canal, defending the frontier against the nomads, or building a new capital—on a grand, truly imperial scale. The vigorous market exchange system operating underneath the official command structure enhanced the flexibility of the economy. It also increased wealth and greatly expanded the resources of the country at large. But it did not displace officialdom from its controlling position. On the contrary, new wealth and improved communications enhanced the practical power Chinese officials had at their disposal. The fact that China remained united politically from Sung to modern times with only relatively brief periods of disruption between regimes is evidence of the increased power government personnel wielded. Discrepancies between the ideals of the marketplace and those of government were real enough; but as long as officials could bring overriding police power to bear whenever they were locally or privately defied, the command element in the mix remained securely dominant. Market behavior and private pursuit of wealth could only function within limits defined by the political authorities.

For this reason the autocatalytic character that European commercial and industrial expansion exhibited between the eleventh and the nineteenth centuries never got started in China. Capitalists in China were never free for long to reinvest their profits at will. Anyone who accumulated a fortune attracted official attention. Officials might seek to share privately in an individual's good fortune by accepting bribes; they might instead adjust taxes and prices so as to allow the state to tap the new wealth; or they might prefer preemption, and simply turn the business in question into a state monopoly. In particular instances various combinations of these policies were always negotiable. But in every encounter the private entrepreneur was at a disadvantage, while officials had the whip hand. This was so, fundamentally, because most

Chinese felt that any unusual accumulation of private wealth from trade or manufacture was profoundly immoral, since it could only arise when an entrepreneur systematically cheated others by buying cheap and selling dear. Official ideology and popular psychology thus coincided to reinforce the advantage officials had in any and every encounter with merely private men of wealth.

Market Mobilization beyond China's Borders

Though the capitalist spirit was thus kept firmly under control, the rise of a massive market economy in China during the eleventh century may have sufficed to change the world balance between command and market behavior in a critically significant way. China swiftly became by far the richest, most skilled, and most populous country on earth. Moreover, the growth of the Chinese economy and society was felt beyond China's borders; and as Chinese technical secrets spread abroad, new possibilities opened in other parts of the Old World, most conspicuously in western Europe.

Even before gunpowder, the compass, and printing began to revolutionize civilized societies beyond China's borders, there was a preliminary phase when intensified long-distance commerce raised the significance of market relationships to new heights, preparing the way for a longer, more sustained economic take-off than any that occurred within Chinese borders.

Unfortunately, little is known about the growth of trade in the southern seas. Arab seafarers and before them Greco-Roman and Indonesian seamen had traversed the Indian Ocean and adjacent waters for many centuries before the Chinese appeared there. Sumerians in all probability had communicated with peoples of the Indus valley by sea at the very beginning of civilized history, and various Indian peoples also sailed to and fro across the tropical waters where summer and winter monsoons, blowing alternately in opposite directions for about half the year, made navigation relatively safe and easy, even for small and lightly built vessels.

What seems certain is that the scale of trade through the southern seas grew persistently and systematically from 1000 onwards, despite innumerable temporary setbacks and local disasters. Behavior attuned to the maintenance of such trade became more and more firmly embedded in everyday routines of human life. The production of spices, such as pepper, cloves, cinnamon, and the rest, which played so conspicuous a role in Europe's medieval trade, began to dominate the lives of many thousands of people in southeast Asia and adjacent islands. All who cultivated and prepared these commodities for shipment, along with sailors, merchants and everyone connected with the collection, assortment, and transport of spices came to depend for their everyday livelihood on precarious linkages with consumers thousands of miles away. The same was true for the producers of hundreds of other commodities entering long-distance trade nets, from rarities like rhinoceros horn to items of mass production and consumption like cotton and sugar.[55]

Such specialization and interdependence duplicated what had happened earlier in China, with the difference that trade in the south China Sea and Indian Ocean crossed political boundaries. As a result, merchants faced greater uncertainty on the one hand and enjoyed greater freedom on the other. Malaya and other key places along the trade routes—Ceylon and southern India, together with ports on the African coast and in southern Arabia as well—were governed by rulers whose income came to depend in very large part upon dues levied on shipping. But once a ship put out to sea, local rulers lost control, whereas ship captains were free within fairly wide limits to seek out the cheapest place to come ashore and do business. If a ruler became too greedy, resentful captains could find another port of call. Under these circumstances, patterns of trade could alter rapidly in response to changes in political regimes, and new entrepôts could rise to importance very quickly.

This happened at Malacca, for example. That emporium, built in a dismal swamp, almost inaccessible by land, had no importance before the turn of the fourteenth-fifteenth centuries. It started as a piratical headquarters, where goods seized at sea could be re-sorted and dispatched to advantageous destinations. Then, in the first years of the fifteenth century it became a port of more general resort for peaceable shipping, and within a few decades dominated the trade of the region round about—becoming the principal entrepôt for the spices produced in the "Spice Islands" lying further east. Malacca rose, of course, at the expense of other, alternate ports. Safe harborage and moderate dues attracted trade; so did compulsion exercised by armed vessels policing the Malaccan straits between Sumatra and the mainland. Force therefore mattered in Malacca's rise, along with the protection from piracy such force could bring. Naval force had to be sustained by taxation levied on goods passing through the port. A delicate

55. Archibald Lewis, "Maritime Skills in the Indian Ocean, 1368–1500," *JESHO* 16 (1973): 254–58, compiled a long list of goods traded.

balance between the two governed the scale of trade and the number of ships that showed up to pay dues.[56]

Though details are beyond recovery, it is reasonable to think that a process of trial and error gradually defined the acceptable limits of taxation a local ruler could exact from passing merchants and traders. If he lowered the costs of protection and harborage he could hope to attract new business; if he took too much, he would see traffic diminish sharply.[57] A ruler who took too little (if there ever was one) might not be able to maintain effective armed control of his territory or of adjacent seas. One who took too much might suffer the same fate, if ships and merchants succeeded in eluding his grasp to the detriment of his income. In other words, a kind of market asserted itself among the political rulers of the shores of the Indian Ocean, setting what can be called protection rent at a level that permitted the continuance and (after 1000 or so) the systematic expansion of trade.[58]

This system may well have been very old. Presumably, ancient Mesopotamian kings and captains began to define protection rents in the earliest phases of organized long-distance trade. Assuredly, the Moslems, when they conquered the Middle East (634–51) brought with them from the trading cities of the Arabian peninsula a well-articulated idea of how trade should be conducted. The Koran afforded appropriate sanction,[59] and Mohammed's early career as a merchant offered a morally unimpeachable model. The impulse towards broadened market behavior that came from China's commercialization was therefore a reinforcement rather than a novelty.

56. On Malacca see Wheatley, *The Golden Khersonese,* pp. 306–20.

57. Sung records nicely illustrate how the system worked. In 1144 officials raised import duties to 40 percent of declared value, only to see trade languish and receipts diminish, with the result that in 1164 the old rate of 10 percent was restored. Lo Jung-pang, "Maritime Commerce," p. 69.

58. My conception of how merchants and rulers interacted along Asia's southern shores is largely shaped by Niels Steensgaard, *The Asian Trade Revolution of the Seventeenth Century: The East India Companies and the Decline of the Caravan Trade* (Chicago, 1974), pp. 22–111. Steensgaard describes a situation existing about 1600, and he is concerned primarily with caravan trade; but the strategy of trade and taxation probably did not much alter from early times until after 1600, and rulers' relations with merchants who traveled overland were not notably different from those who came in ships. The concept of "protection rent" was invented by Frederick Lane, "Economic Consequences of Organized Violence," *Journal of Economic History* 18 (1958): 401–17, and his investigations of medieval Italian enterprise in the Mediterranean also provided me with a model for what I believe happened along the shores of the Indian Ocean. Lewis, "Maritime Skills in the Indian Ocean," pp. 238–64, offers a very suggestive survey of the subject, though he does not raise the question of relations between rulers and merchants directly.

59. Sura IV, 29: "O Believers, consume not your goods between you in vanity, except there be trading by your agreeing together." Arthur J. Arberry, trans., *The Koran Interpreted* (London, 1955).

Indeed, the transformation of Chinese economy and society in Sung times may best be conceived of as an extension to China of mercantile principles that had been long familiar in the Middle East. Buddhist monks and central Asian caravan traders were the first intermediaries.[60] Their linkages with nomads of the open steppe created another strategically important, trade-prone community, whose impact upon China and other civilized populations of the Old World was assured by the military effectiveness the nomad way of life conferred upon steppe dwellers.

What was new in the eleventh century, therefore, was not the principle of market articulation of human effort across long distances, but the scale on which this kind of behavior began to affect human lives. China's belated arrival at a market articulation of its economy acted like a great bellows, fanning smoldering coals into flame. New wealth arising among a hundred million Chinese began to flow out across the seas (and significantly along caravan routes as well) and added new vigor and scope to market-related activity.[61] Scores, hundreds, and perhaps thousands of vessels began to sail from port to port within the Sea of Japan and the South China Sea, the Indonesian Archipelago and the Indian Ocean. Most voyages were probably relatively short, and goods were reassorted at many different entrepôts along the way from original producer to ultimate consumer. Business organizations remained simple, often familial, partnerships. Hence an increasing flow of commodities meant a great number of persons moving to and fro on shipboard or sitting in bazaars, chaffering over prices.

As is well known, a similar upsurge of commercial activity took place in the eleventh century in the Mediterranean, where the principal carriers were Italian merchants sailing from Venice, Genoa, and other ports. They in turn brought most of peninsular Europe into a more and more closely articulated trade net in the course of the next three hundred years. It was a notable achievement, but only a small part of the larger phenomenon, which, I believe, raised market-regulated behavior to a scale and significance for civilized peoples that had never been attained before. Rulers of old-fashioned command societies simply were unable to dominate behavior as thoroughly as in earlier times. Peddlers and merchants made themselves useful to rulers and subjects alike and could now safeguard themselves against

---

60. This is the central thesis of Stefan Balazs, "Beiträge zur Wirtschaftsgeschichte der T'ang Zeit" (n. 2 above), and of Jacques Gernet, *Les aspects économiques du Bouddhisme dans la société chinoise du Ve au Xe siècle* (Saigon, 1956).

61. My late colleague, Marshall G. S. Hodgson, *The Venture of Islam* (Chicago, 1974), 2:403–4, made the same suggestion several years ago, with the same lack of evidence to back up the hypothesis.

confiscatory taxation and robbery by finding refuge in one or another port of call along the caravan routes and seaways, where local rulers had learned not to overtax the trade upon which their income and power had come to depend.

Thus, after about 1100, what had previously been a smoldering fire, bursting out only sporadically into intenser flame, began to escape from official control and gradually turned into a general conflagration. Eventually, in the nineteenth century, market behavior flamed so high that it melted down the inimical command structure of the Chinese empire itself, although it took nine centuries before this catastrophe to Confucian China became possible.

In its initial stages this commercial transformation seemed of little importance to chroniclers and men of letters generally. Hence historians can only reconstruct what occurred by using scattered sources, painstakingly piecing together a general picture of what happened from merest fragments. This has been done for medieval Europe—mainly during the past thirty to forty years—but not elsewhere. As a result, historians know a good deal about how western Europeans developed trade relations among themselves and with Moslems of the eastern Mediterranean shoreline. It was precisely in the eleventh century, when China's conversion to cash exchanges went into high gear, that European seamen and traders made the Mediterranean a miniature replica of what was probably happening simultaneously in the southern oceans.[62] A systematic shift from piracy to trade occurred at almost the same time along the Atlantic face of Europe, where Vikings had previously raided Christian Europe.[63] These separate sea networks were then combined into one single interacting whole after 1291, when a Genoese sea captain seized control of the straits of Gibraltar from a Moslem ruler who had previously interdicted through passage for Christian vessels.[64]

Thus, if one takes a synoptic view of the rise of commerce in the Old World, the multiple linkages within China between north and south that arose through improvements of inland waterways were matched, though on a somewhat smaller scale, by a similar development in the Far West some centuries later. European rivers, and the open seas connecting them, provided a network of natural waterways

---

62. Cf. William H. McNeill, *Venice: The Hinge of Europe, 1081–1797* (Chicago, 1974), pp. 1–39.

63. Cf. Archibald R. Lewis, *The Northern Seas: Shipping and Commerce in Northern Europe, A.D. 300–1100* (Princeton, 1958).

64. Robert Lopez, *Genova Marinara nel Duecento: Benedetto Zaccaria, ammiraglio e mercanti* (Messina-Milan, 1933).

that needed rather less artificial improvement than was the case in China. By the later fourteenth century, wool, metal, and other raw materials from the north and west came to be exchanged for wine, salt, spices, and fine manufactures from the south; and an ever more elaborate grain trade supplemented by expanding fisheries everywhere sustained urban populations. The intra-European market, in turn, hitched up with Moslem-managed trade networks of the Middle East and North Africa, and with the commerce of the southern oceans. The same Italian cities that organized Europe's interregional exchanges were the main trade partners with Moslem and Jewish merchants of the eastern Mediterranean. These Levantines, in turn, were connected with deeper Asia and Africa by commercial links that tied all the diverse peoples of the ecumene more and more closely together between the eleventh and the fifteenth centuries.

A more or less homogeneous organizational pattern and level of technique apparently established itself as a lubricant for trade throughout the southern seas, all the way from the south China coast to the Mediterranean. Regular use of a decimal system of numerical notation and of the abacus was one conspicuous and important accompaniment of this growth of trade. The value of such systems for facilitating calculations of all sorts is difficult to exaggerate and can be compared only to the cheapening of literacy that the invention of alphabetic writing had allowed some twenty-three hundred years earlier.

In addition to this fundamental simplification of numerical calculation, the long-distance trade of the southern seas depended on a cluster of institutional conventions. Rules for partnerships, means for adjudicating disputed contracts, and bills of exchange that allowed settlement of debts across long distances with a minimal transport of hard currency probably had an ecumenical scope. The same applies to rules for managing ships—how to divide profit among those aboard, organize responsibility, insure against loss, and the like. Moslem and Christian practices in these matters were nearly identical; what little is known of how the Chinese managed long-distance sea trade seems to match up quite exactly.[65]

65. For the Mediterranean, Robert S. Lopez and Irving W. Raymond, *Medieval Trade in the Mediterranean World* (New York and London, 1955), is a useful starting place. For the Indian Ocean, Michel Mollat, ed., *Sociétés et compagnies de commerce en orient et dans l'océan indien: Actes du huitième colloque internationale d'histoire maritime, Beyrouth, 1966* (Paris, 1970) is the best available summary of what little is known. For China, Shiba, *Commerce and Society in Sung China,* pp. 15–40. For interesting sidelights on the India trade, and its congruence with Mediterranean patterns, see S. D. Goitein, *Studies in Islamic History and Institutions* (Leiden, 1968), pp. 329–50.

Nor were the seas the only important medium of long-distance travel. From about the beginning of the Christian era, caravans had begun to link China with the Middle East and with India. Animal packtrains moving from oasis to oasis through the desert or semi-desert country of central Asia resembled ships moving from port to port. The conditions of successful operation were similar. Protection rent had to be adjusted by a process of trial and error until an optimal level at which local rulers and long-distance traders could support one another most efficiently was discovered.

Such arrangements were perpetually liable to disruption. Plunder and outright confiscation always tempted local power wielders, and alternate routes were less easy to find overland than when crossing open water. Nevertheless, caravan connections between China and western Asia were never broken off for very long after the first such ventures achieved success. In the course of the next ten centuries, the customs and attitudes that allowed the caravan trade to thrive filtered northward into the steppe and forest zones of Eurasia. Gradually a north-south exchange of slaves and furs for the goods of civilization supplemented the east-west flow of goods that initially sustained the caravans.

To be sure, evidence is scanty and indirect. The main register of northward penetration of trade patterns is the spread of civilized religions among the oasis and steppe peoples of Asia—Buddhism, Nestorian Christianity, Manicheanism, Judaism, and, most successful of them all, Islam. Tribute missions dating back to Han times, when nomad rulers visited the Chinese capital and received "gifts" from the emperor and gave "gifts" in return, also attest to penetration of the steppe by a ritualized and heavily politicized form of trade. But for the most part we do not know very much about how nomads and traders entered into symbiotic relationships with one another.[66]

Yet pastoral nomads found the advantages of trade with civilized populations very compelling. Apart from the symbolic value of luxury goods and the practical usefulness of metal for tools and weapons, both of which assumed great importance in nomad society by or before the tenth century, a nomad population could greatly expand its food supply by modifying a diet prodigally rich in protein through trading off some of their animals and animal products for cereals. The upper classes of civilized societies—and especially those in China where animal husbandry was poorly developed—were willing to pay

66. Luc Kwanten, *Imperial Nomads: A History of Central Asia, 500–1500* (Philadelphia, 1979), conveniently summarizes the current state of knowledge.

handsomely for animals and animal products because the work force under their control could not raise equivalent livestock nearly as cheaply as the nomads did.

China's trade with the nomads achieved quite elaborate organization under the Han,[67] but it is impossible to follow the ups and downs or regional patterns of ebb and flow, which must have been extreme. Probably trade relations between steppe and cultivated land tended to become more important during the first millenium of the Christian era. The prominent place merchants held in Mongol society in the time of their greatness is proof that trading and traders were securely at home among the heirs of Genghis Khan.

The Mongol conquest of China in the thirteenth century opened up new possibilities for nomad tribesmen. Under Kublai and his successor, for example, the garrison of Karakorum received more than half a million bushels of grain each year from China, delivered by wagons that took four months to make the round trip.[68] Such deliveries supplemented the meat and milk products available locally to allow more people to survive on the steppe than could otherwise have done so. But dependence on grain supplies from afar also meant risk of real disaster should deliveries be cut off. As long as Mongols ruled China, grain deliveries were assured; but when the Ming dynasty came to power (1368), Chinese authorities were tempted to embargo grain export as a way of bringing pressure on their steppe neighbors. They actually did so in 1449. The Mongol response was to go to war, with the result that they captured the person of the emperor.[69] Anything less would have meant starvation for at least part of the population of the steppe.

It is worth pointing out that nomads (as well as transhumant pastoralists in Mediterranean Europe) shared this kind of vulnerability with city folk. Urban populations, too, suffered catastrophe with any prolonged interruption of food supply. Cities, especially big cities, survived only on the strength of a smoothly functioning transport system capable of bringing food from afar. Nomads and transhumant pastoralists were particularly well fitted to undertake the overland transport tasks involved in feeding inland cities, since they possessed

67. Cf. Yü Ying-shih, *Trade and Expansion in Han China: A Study in the Structure of Sino-Barbarian Economic Relations* (Berkeley and Los Angeles, 1967), p. 209 and passim.

68. According to Hsiao Ch'i Ch'ing, *The Military Establishment of the Yüan Dynasty,* pp. 59–60, between 200,000 and 300,000 shih of grain were delivered annually to Karakorum. A shih weighed 157.89 pounds, or roughly three bushels of millet, two and three-fourths bushels of wheat.

69. Jacques Gernet, *Le Monde chinois* (Paris, 1972), p. 351.

suitable pack animals in large numbers. In fact, it seems plausible to say that a social alliance between urban populations and animal husbandmen became the backbone of Islamic society. This alliance expanded from its birthplace in Arabia across most of the Middle East, as city folk were persuaded or compelled to cooperate with nomads to exploit the grain-growing majority. As for the peasantries, they were all but helpless, being rooted to the soil by their routines of life and unable to achieve the mobility (or market participation) that urban and pastoral life both came to depend upon.[70]

Anticipating what occurred on the seas in the eleventh century, linkages between steppe populations and civilized lands seem to have crossed a critical threshold in the tenth century. Beginning about 960, Turkish tribesmen infiltrated the central regions of the Islamic world in such numbers as to be able to seize power in Iran and Mesopotamia. Another Turkish people, the Pechenegs, flooded into the Ukraine in the 970s, cutting the Russians off from Byzantium. Simultaneously, along the northwest Chinese border a series of newly formidable states came into existence, beginning with the Kitan empire (907–1125).

These political events reflect the fact that in both China and the Middle East (though not perhaps among the Pechenegs) nomad military organization and effectiveness transcended earlier tribal limits in the tenth century. This was partly a matter of improved equipment. Metaled corselets and helmets, for example, became commonplace when trade with civilized societies gave nomads, like the Kitan, access to such goods in quantity. The Kitan also learned to use siege machines—catapults and the like—thus overcoming the earlier impotence of raiding horsemen when confronted by fortifications. But new equipment was less important than new patterns of social and military organization. In the course of the tenth century, civilized models of command and military discipline took root among steppe peoples, supplanting or at least modifying old tribal structures. The Kitan, for example, organized their army according to a decimal system, with commanders for tens, hundreds, and so on, just as the ancient Assyrians had done. The Turks who took power in Iran and Mesopotamia were even more radically detribalized, having become

---

70. On the alliance between pastoralists and city people in Islam see Xavier de Planhol, *Les fondements géographiques de l'histoire de l'Islam* (Paris, 1968), pp. 21–35. On the phenomenon in Christian Balkan society, see William H. McNeill, *The Metamorphosis of Greece since World War II* (Chicago, 1978), pp. 43–50.

slave soldiers in the service of civilized rulers before seizing power in their own right.[71]

The enhancement of nomad military power through interpenetration with civilized societies climaxed in the thirteenth century. Genghis Khan (r. 1206–27) united almost all the steppe peoples into one single command structure. His army was also arranged on a decimal system, led at each level (10s, 100s, 1,000s) by persons who had earned the right to command by success in the field. As this formidable and expansible army (defeated steppe enemies were simply folded into the structure, starting at the bottom as common soldiers) penetrated civilized ground in north China and central Asia, the Mongol commanders took over any and every new form of weaponry they encountered. Thus they brought Chinese explosives into Hungary in the campaign of 1241, and used Moslem siege engines in China— more powerful than any the Chinese had yet seen—in the campaigns of 1268–73 against the southern Sung. Similarly, as we have already noticed, Kublai Khan first annexed and then transformed the southern Sung navy into an oceanic fleet in order to launch attacks on Japan and other lands overseas.

Yet the enormous successes that came to Mongol arms in the thirteenth century carried their own unique nemesis. As had happened before to other steppe conquerors, after two or three generations the comforts and delectations of civilization undermined the hardihood and military cohesion of Mongol garrisons. This was normal and to be expected, and led to the eviction of the Mongol soldiery from all of China in 1371. In western Asia and Russia, Mongols were not driven out but instead dissolved into the numerically superior Turkish-speaking warrior population of the western steppe after the end of the thirteenth century, when subordination to the Great Khan in Peking ceased to have even ritual significance.

But on top of this normal pattern whereby steppe conquerors were partly absorbed and partly repulsed by civilized communities, two accidental by-products of the Mongol empire of Asia radically weakened steppe peoples vis-à-vis their civilized neighbors. One was the demographic disaster to Eurasian nomads that resulted from the arrival of the plague, known in European history as the Black Death

71. For the Kitan as representative of a new "generation" of nomad society see Gernet, *Le monde chinois,* p. 308; for Middle Eastern slave soldiers see Patricia Crone, *Slaves on Horses: The Evolution of the Islamic Polity* (New York, 1980); Daniel Pipes, *Slave Soldiers and Islam: The Genesis of a Military System* (New Haven, 1981).

(1346). The plague bacillus probably became epidemic among burrowing rodent populations of the steppe for the first time in the fourteenth century. The infection was presumably introduced into the new
environment by Mongol horsemen who brought it back from their
campaigns in Yunnan and Burma, where endemic plague already
existed among local populations of burrowing rodents. Once the
bacillus established itself on the steppe, nomad populations found
themselves systematically exposed to lethal infection of a kind that
had never been known there before. Radical depopulation and even
the complete abandonment of some of the best pasture land of Eurasia
was the result.

By degrees, folkways effectively insulating steppe dwellers from the
new infection may have arisen. This certainly occurred in the Manchurian portion of the steppe, for such practices were in force there in the
1920s, when the most recent serious outbreak of plague among
human populations took place in that part of the world. But this sort
of readjustment took time. For two centuries or more after 1346,
steppe populations appear to have been much reduced in number by
their exposure to a new and very lethal disease that Mongol expansion
across hitherto insuperable distances had brought in its train.[72]

The resulting interruption of demographic movement out of the
steppe towards cultivated lands disrupted what had long been one of
the fundamental currents of human migration in the Old World. By
the time the steppe peoples began demographic recovery, a new factor, also traceable back to the Mongol breakthrough of older geographic barriers, came into play: the use of firearms that could counter
nomad archers on the battlefield. Effective small-arms were not generally available to civilized armies until after about 1550; but as they
spread, nomad superiority in battle suffered its final erosion. Instead
of being able to encroach on agricultural ground, as nomads had been
able to do since about 800 B.C., peasants began to invade the cultivable portions of the Eurasian grasslands, making fields where pasture
had previously prevailed. The eastward expansion of Russia and the
westward expansion of China under the Manchus between 1644 and
1911 registered this reversal of human settlement patterns politically.
It is ironic to think that the diffusion of gunpowder weaponry, which
led to the final eclipse of steppe military power in the mid-eighteenth

---

72. Arguments and evidence for this reconstruction of events are presented in William
H. McNeill, *Plagues and Peoples* (New York, 1976), pp. 149–65, 190–96.

century, was a by-product of the Mongols' military success, and of the radical rationality they exhibited in their management of weapons design, logistics, and command. Yet so it was.

In the Middle East and India, Turkish soldiery harnessed in tandem to Arab, Iranian, and Indian urban populations came to power between the tenth and sixteenth centuries. Warriors of nomad background assimilated Islamic urban culture and then combined with urban traders and associated artisans to exploit the peasant grain producers of the countryside with a ruthlessness that may have had the effect of limiting economic development in the mid-regions of Eurasia.[73] Whether for this or other reasons, economic devolution seems to have taken place in the Arab heartland of Islam. Merchants in Iraq and adjacent regions achieved a higher level of wealth and social prestige in the tenth and eleventh centuries than ever before; but after 1200 their prominence and probably their wealth too diminished.[74] The irrigation system of Iraq decayed, and the fundamental productivity of the landscape shrank back accordingly. Perhaps the change in climate that made the thirteenth century an especially good time in northwestern Europe, with warm, dry summers and correspondingly good grain harvests meant drought and agricultural setback in the Middle East. If so, even in proximity to cities, grazing areas must have expanded at the expense of grainfields, a development which in turn would tend to refresh and reinforce the nomadic element in the Islamic body politic.[75]

At any rate, the Moslem world failed to take full advantage of the new technical possibilities opened up by the diffusion of Chinese skills in the wake of the Mongol unification of Eurasia. To be sure, the Ottoman Turks used improvements in cannon design to capture Constantinople in 1453; but the craftsmen who cast the cannon for Mohammed the Conqueror were Hungarian. Even as early as the mid-fifteenth century it appears to be true that gun founders of Latin Christendom had achieved a technical lead over cannon makers in other parts of the civilized world, including China.

73. John E. Woods, *The Aqquyunlu: Clan, Confederation, and Empire: A Study in 15th/9th Century Turko-Iranian Politics* (Minneapolis, 1976), offers a sample of how urban and tribal elements interacted and (usually) allied with one another to form one of the many unstable states into which the realm of Islam divided after A.D. 1000.

74. Cf. S. D. Goitein, "The Rise of the Near Eastern Bourgeoisie in Early Islamic Times," *Journal of World History* 3 (1957): 583–604.

75. I am not aware of any scholarly discussion of climate change in the Middle East in these centuries. For Europe see Emmanuel LeRoy Ladurie, *Histoire du climat depuis l'an mil* (Paris, 1967).

How Latin Christians achieved this proficiency, and the recklessness with which they proceeded in the following centuries to commercialize war more effectively and enthusiastically than any other population on earth, is the theme of the next chapter.

3

The Business of War in Europe, 1000-1600

In the year 1000 the part of Europe known as Latin Christendom was overwhelmingly rural. Nearly everyone lived in villages where social roles were defined by a delicate interaction between tradition and the personal qualities of the individuals filling each role. In an emergency, every able-bodied person was expected to help with local defense—whether by carrying valuables to some fortified spot for safekeeping or by some more aggressive action against threatening outsiders. To be sure, with the spread of knighthood from its place of origin between the Rhine and the Seine rivers, a more effective defense against attack put most of the responsibility for meeting and repelling would-be plunderers on the shoulders of a small class of men who rode expensive war-horses and were trained in the use of arms from childhood. Knights' weapons and armor were, of course, a product of specialized craftsmen, though very little is known about the manufacture and distribution of the arms and armor upon which the knights of Latin Christendom relied.[1] Ordinary villagers supported the new military experts with contributions in kind. The quantity and character of such payments quickly achieved a customary definition, stabilizing social relations around the fundamental distinction between knights and commoners.

Priests and monks and bards fitted into this simple social hierarchy with no difficulty, but the handful of merchants and itinerant peddlers who also made a living in that rural society represented a potentially disruptive element. Market behavior was deeply alien to the social outlook of village life. Merchants or peddlers, coming as strangers into an unsympathetic environment, had to attend to their own defense.

1. Cf. J. F. Fino, "Notes sur la production de fer et la fabrication des armes en France au moyen âge," *Gladius* 3 (1964): 47–66.

This introduced a second relatively well-armed element into society. It was connected with the knightly establishment of the countryside only by a series of unstable negotiated truces.

Another way of describing this situation is to say that for several centuries on either side of the year 1000 the weakness of large territorial polities in Latin Christendom required merchants to renegotiate protection rents at frequent intervals. Moving amidst a warlike, violence-prone society,[2] European merchants had a choice between attracting and arming enough followers to defend themselves, or, alternatively, offering a portion of their goods to local potentates as a price for safe passage. In other civilized societies (with the possible exception of Japan), merchants were less ready to use arms on their own behalf and more inclined to cater to preexisting rent and tax-based authorities and depend upon their protection.

The merger of the military with the commercial spirit, characteristic of European merchants, had its roots in the barbarian past. Viking raiders and traders were directly ancestral to eleventh-century merchants of the northern seas. A successful pirate always had to reassort his booty by buying and selling somewhere. In the Mediterranean, the ambiguity between trade and raid was at least as old as the Mycenaeans. To be sure, trading had supplanted raiding when the Romans successfully monopolized organized violence in the first century B.C., but the old ambiguities revived in the fifth century A.D. when the Vandals took to the sea. Thereafter, from the seventh century until the nineteenth, cultural antipathy between Christian and Moslem justified and sustained a perpetual razzia upon the seas that bounded Europe to the south.

The knightly Latin Christian society that defined itself in the century or so before the year 1000 proved capable of far-ranging conquest and colonization. The Norman invasion of England in 1066 is the most familiar example of this capacity; but a geographically more

---

2. The rise of knighthood did not produce a submissive, nonviolent peasantry in Europe. Habits of bloodshed were deep-seated, perennially fed by the fact that Europeans raised both pigs and cattle in considerable numbers but had to slaughter all but a small breeding stock each autumn for lack of sufficient winter fodder. Other agricultural regimes, e.g., among the rice-growing farmers of China and India, did not involve annual slaughter of large animals. By contrast, Europeans living north of the Alps learned to take such bloodshed as a normal part of the routine of the year. This may have had a good deal to do with their remarkable readiness to shed human blood and think nothing of it. Cf. the *Saga of Olav Trygveson* for the primal ferocity of northern Europe. Also Georges Duby, *The Early Growth of the European Economy: Warriors and Peasants from the Seventh to the Twelfth Century* (London, 1973), pp. 96, 117, 163, 253, and passim.

extensive expansion occurred east of the Elbe where, by the mid-thirteenth century, German knights and settlers extended their sway across the north European plain as far as Prussia. Further east and north along the Baltic coast German knights imposed their rule on native peasantries all the way to the Gulf of Finland in the same century. On other frontiers Latin Christians also exhibited remarkable aggressiveness: in Spain and southern Italy at the expense of Moslems and Byzantines and, most spectacularly of all, in the distant Levant, where the First Crusade (1096–99) carried an army of knights all the way to Jerusalem.

By 1300, however, this sort of expansion had reached its limits. Climatic obstacles set bounds to the indefinite extension of the fields, cultivated by the moldboard plow, that provided the basic foodstuffs supporting western European society. When seed-harvest ratios sank too low, as happened in arid parts of Spain or in the cold chill of northern and eastern Europe, the heavy plow and the draft animals required to drive it through the soil had to give way to cheaper agricultural techniques. Along the same borderlands the relatively dense settlement that the moldboard plow could sustain yielded to more thinly populated landscapes in which pastoralism, hunting, gathering, and fishing played a more important part than they did in the heartland of Latin Christendom. Wherever knightly conquests outran the moldboard plow, social patterns differed from those of the west European heartlands. The resulting political regimes were often unstable and short-lived, as in the Levant where the crusading states disappeared after 1291, or in the Balkans, where Latin dominion, dating from the Fourth Crusade (1204), was largely supplanted by local dynasts as early as 1261. In Spain and Ireland, on the contrary, and along the east coast of the Baltic, conquest societies became enduring marginalia to the main body of Latin Christendom. Similarly, in Poland, Bohemia, and Hungary, kingdoms that consolidated around the effort needed to repel German knights took a form divergent from, yet closely related to, the knight and peasant pattern of western Europe.[3]

Pioneering the Business of War in Northern Italy

The military expansion of Latin Christendom in the eleventh century was accompanied by an expansion of the scope for market behavior.

3. Light cavalry and small scratch plows were cheaper than their west European equivalents and fitted an environment in which seed-harvest ratios were lower than in the more fertile west. The firmness of connection between lord and peasant was less in

As in China in the same age, places where transport and communications were unusually easy led the way. In Mediterranean lands, Europe's commercial development was also affected by the fact that skills were readily imported from adjacent, more developed societies (i.e., from Byzantium and from Moslem countries). To begin with, this configuration gave primacy to Italy. A secondary commercial center arose in the Low Countries where the navigable Rhine, Meuse, and Scheldt rivers converge. Overland portage routes linked these two main nodes of commercial and artisan activity; and exchanges between the two regions were consummated at a series of fairs held in Champagne. Little by little more time and effort went into production for market sale, sometimes at a distance. Specialization led to increased wealth, and altered social balances in favor of merchant-capitalists. In the most active economic centers, the preeminence of knights and of social leadership based on rural relationships came into question before the end of the twelfth century.

These social and economic changes were reinforced by a parallel weakening of knightly supremacy in war. In the eleventh century a few hundred Norman knights had been able to conquer and rule south Italy and Sicily; a few thousand sufficed to seize and hold Jerusalem at the very end of the century. Yet, in the twelfth century, an army of German knights met unexpected defeat in northern Italy at Legnano (1176) when they vainly charged pikemen who had been put in the field by the leagued cities of northern Italy. The military might of the Lombard League, attested by that victory, was essentially defensive, like the town walls which had begun to sprout wherever traders and artisans had become numerous enough to require and pay for this kind of protection.

The result was a standoff, in Italy at least, between older and newer forms of warfare and social leadership. Armed townsmen sought to control the surrounding countryside. How else assure safe passage for their goods and the punctual delivery of food within city walls? Sometimes an accommodation between rural landholders and the ruling elements of nearby towns proved possible; sometimes noble land- holders moved into town to mingle with and rival the urban upper class of merchant-capitalists. On top of this, from the eleventh century onward, the rival claims of emperor and pope divided Italy. Both aspired to exercise a general hegemony over the existing medley of

---

the east, and ties to a particular set of fields was weaker for nobles and peasants alike because scratch plow cultivation made it comparatively easy to start afresh on new land prepared for cultivation by the age-old technique of slash and burn.

local rulers and jurisdictions, but only sporadically were they able to enforce overriding authority.

The military balance of power within Italy was as uncertain as the political. Traders, artisans, and their hangers-on in the larger towns were able to defend themselves from knightly attack as long as they sustained the discipline required to man city walls or array a formation of pikemen in the field. But this was hard to do in a world where primary social bonds were rapidly giving way to market behavior affecting and affected by persons and events hundreds of miles away. Consequent civic strife weakened urban defenses. Party conflict was fed by the larger political controversies of the peninsula and often was also envenomed by collision of interests between rich and poor, employer and employee. Under these circumstances, the practice of hiring strangers to fight on behalf of the citizens became increasingly important. But this meant that the ambiguous relationship between employer and employee, which already distracted the internal life of the wealthier Italian cities, extended to military matters as well.

Clearly, as trade and artisan specialization began to affect more and more people, primary relations within the local communities of Europe ceased to be effective regulators of everyday conduct. This opened up vast new problems of social and military management. A few cities in northern Italy pioneered effective response, for it was within their walls that impersonal market relationships first began to dominate the behavior of scores of thousands of persons.

A new factor came to the fore between the eleventh and thirteenth centuries when cities like Barcelona and Genoa expanded the scale of crossbow manufacture to such a point as to make that weapon critically important in battle. Crossbows were initially valued primarily for defending ships, since a handful of crossbowmen, stationed in a crow's nest atop the mainmast, could make successful boarding even of a lightly crewed merchant vessel exceedingly difficult. But by the closing decades of the thirteenth century, crossbowmen became skilled and numerous enough to make a difference in land warfare as well. The ever-victorious career of the Catalan Company between 1282 and 1311 demonstrated crossbowmen's newfound offensive capability, even when pitted against the most formidable horsemen of the age. For the Catalans first destroyed a (mostly French) army of knights in Sicily in 1282, and then went on in ensuing decades to defeat Turkish light cavalry with equal decisiveness on several Balkan and Anatolian battlefields. As in China, the manufacture of large numbers of powerful crossbows required metal-working specialists, but the crossbow's

simplicity in use made it a great equalizer in the field. Armored cavalrymen need not always prevail when any able bodied commoner could
pull the trigger and unleash a crossbow bolt capable of knocking a
knight from his horse at a distance of a hundred yards or more. No
wonder the weapon was banned at the Second Lateran Council (1139)
as being too lethal for Christians to use against one another!

Crossbows and pikes had to be supplemented by cavalry for flank
protection and the pursuit of a vanquished foe. This obviously made
war far more complicated than it had been when a headlong charge by
a group of knights dominated the battlefields of Europe. Simple personal prowess, replicated within knightly families across the generations, was no longer enough to win battles or maintain social dominion. Instead, an art of war was needed. Someone had to be able to
coordinate pikes, crossbows, and cavalry. Infantrymen needed training to assure steadiness in the ranks, for, were their formation to break
apart, individual pikemen would find themselves at the mercy of
charging knights; and the time required to cock a crossbow meant that
archers, too, became vulnerable each time they discharged their
weapons, unless some field fortification or an unbroken array of
friendly pikes could protect them until they were ready to shoot again.

Not surprisingly, Italian citizens were not able to achieve the elaborate coordination needed for such an art of war all at once. Cities in
other parts of Europe lagged still farther behind, relying mainly on
passive defense behind city walls. Nevertheless, the military balance
within Europe altered fundamentally with the transformation that
townsmen and their trading brought to rural society between 1000
and 1300. On balance, the complexity of the new art of war reinforced
localism. If prosperous cities found it difficult to exploit the new
techniques, it was doubly difficult for older territorial units—principalities, kingdoms, and, largest of all, the Holy Roman Empire, to
manage the new military resources effectively. Hence the changing
forms of economic and military power that arose in Latin Europe
during the eleventh and twelfth centuries led to the collapse of the
imperial fabric in the thirteenth. This was followed a generation later
by the failure of the papacy to erect a universal monarchy on the ruins
of the Holy Roman Empire (clear by 1305).

Both empire and papacy were heritages from the Roman past.
Memories of that past and its glories died hard, at least among political
theorists, who reluctantly reconciled themselves to the political
pluralism of rival sovereign states only in the seventeenth century.
Had Popes Innocent III (1198–1216) and Boniface VIII (1294–1303)

been able to make good their vision of a Christendom obedient to papal governance, subjecting local fighting men as well as peasants and townsmen to clerical control, western Europe would have come to resemble China, where the Son of Heaven exercised jurisdiction over peasants, townsmen, landowners, and soldiers through a corps of officials imbued with Confucian principles.

Of course Christianity was not the same as Confucianism, yet in interesting ways thirteenth-century administration of the Roman church paralleled Chinese bureaucratic procedures. At least a rudimentary education was required to qualify bishops and other high-ranking clergymen for office. Appointments were subject to papal review, at least in principle. Office was not hereditary, and a career open to talent often attracted gifted and ambitious men into clerical ranks. In all these respects Christian prelates of the thirteenth century resembled Confucian officials of Sung China.

Moreover, Christian doctrine was quite as hostile to the ethos of the marketplace as was Confucianism. The condemnation of usury was more explicit and emphatic in Christian theology than anything to be found in Confucian texts; and distrust between Christian clerics and Christian men-at-arms resembled the gulf separating Chinese mandarins from the soldiery of the Celestial Empire, though it was not nearly so wide. Had papal monarchy proved feasible, western Europe's history would not have duplicated China's bureaucratic experience, but divergences would surely have been far fewer than they actually were. In fact, however, the papal bid for effective sovereignty throughout Latin Christendom failed as miserably as the German emperors' efforts had previously done. Christendom remained divided into locally divergent political structures, perpetually at odds with one another and infinitely confused by overlapping territorial and jurisdictional claims.

This political situation permitted a remarkable merger of market and military behavior to take root and flourish in the most active economic centers of western Europe. Commercialization of organized violence came vigorously to the fore in the fourteenth century when mercenary armies became standard in Italy. Thereafter, market forces and attitudes began to affect military action as seldom before.[4] The art

4. The closest parallel from the European past takes us back to classical times when Greek mercenaries responded to a Mediterranean-wide market, both within Greece and beyond its borders. See. H. W. Parkes, *Greek Mercenary Soldiers from the Earliest Times to the Battle of Ipsus* (Oxford, 1933) for interesting details about the first stages of this development. The rise of Rome, however, meant monopolization of the Mediterranean market for military service after 30 B.C. Victory for the old-fashioned command

of war began to evolve among Europeans with a rapidity that soon
raised it to unexampled heights. The history of the globe between
1500 and 1900 testified to Europe's uniqueness in these matters, and
the arms race that continues to strain world balances in our own time
descends directly from the intense interaction in matters military that
European states and private entrepreneurs inaugurated during the
fourteenth century. What happened, and how it happened, therefore,
deserve careful analysis.

First the general background. In many parts of Europe, hard times
set in slightly before the end of the thirteenth century. Population
pressed hard against available resources in Italy and the Low Countries. Wood supplies began to run short. Climate became distinctly
colder, provoking widespread famines. Harsh divergence of interest
between rich and poor, employer and employed, troubled European
society. Urban uprisings and peasants' revolts registered some of these
difficulties, but all were eclipsed by the demographic disaster that set
in after 1346 when the Black Death first began to ravage western
Europe. Within a generation, a quarter to a third of the entire population of Europe died of bubonic infection. Recovery to pre-plague
levels did not occur until after 1480.

With such a record it is obvious that the fourteenth century was not
a very comfortable time for most Europeans. Yet there were counter
trends that in the long run proved more significant than the century's
long catalog of disasters. A fundamental advance in naval architecture
took place between 1280 and 1330,[5] as a result of which larger, stout-
er, and more maneuverable ships could for the first time sail the seas
safely in winter as well as in summer. All-weather ships were soon able
to spin a more coherent commercial web around Europe's coastline
than had previously been possible. The price of wool in Southampton,
of cloth in Bruges, of alum in Chios, of slaves in Caffa, of spices in
Venice, and of metal in Augsburg all began to interact in a Europe-

principle of mobilizing resources for war ensued, and became applicable to peaceable as
well as to military affairs after depopulation set in during the third century A.D. It was
no accident that the major period of weapons development in the ancient Mediterranean world occurred in the centuries when competing rulers applied commercial principles to the tasks of military mobilization. On the remarkable development of artillery
in the Hellenistic age, see E. W. Marsden, *Greek and Roman Artillery: Historical Development* (Oxford, 1969); Barton C. Hacker, "Greek Catapults and Catapult Technology:
Science, Technology, and War in the Ancient World," *Technology and Culture* 9 (1968):
34–50; W. W. Tarn, *Hellenistic Military and Naval Development* (Cambridge, 1930).

5. Cf. William H. McNeill, *Venice: The Hinge of Europe* (Chicago, 1974), pp. 48–51.
The new ships relied mainly on crossbows for defense—probably a critical factor in
increasing the prevalence and importance of that weapon in Mediterranean warfare
from the eleventh century onwards.

wide market. Bills of exchange facilitated payment across long distances. Credit became a lubricant of commerce and also of specialized, large-scale artisan production. A more complexly differentiated, potentially richer, yet correspondingly vulnerable economy began to control more human effort than in earlier centuries. Cities of north Italy and a secondary cluster of towns in the Low Countries remained the organizing centers of the whole system of exchanges.

Geographically, waters which had previously been effectively separated from each other became for the first time parts of a single sea room. The Black Sea to the east and the North Sea to the west fell within the extended scope of Italian-based shipping. Previously, the risks of seafaring in winter and on stormy seas had combined with political barriers at the Straits of Gibraltar and at the Dardanelles and Bosphorus to isolate these bodies of water from each other. Similarly, German shipping based in the Hansa ports linked the Baltic with the North Sea coast, where exchanges with the Italian-dominated seaways of the south occurred. The Baltic lands, indeed, entered upon a frontier boom in the fourteenth century at a time when other parts of Europe were troubled first by overpopulation and then by plague and social strife. Salt imported from the south enabled Baltic populations to preserve herring and cabbage through the winter. This assured a vastly improved diet, and an improved diet soon made manpower available for cutting timber and raising grain for export to the food-and-fuel-deficient Low Countries and adjacent regions.

Another economically important advance took place in the field of hard rock mining. In the eleventh century, German miners of the Harz mountains began to develop techniques for penetrating solid rock to considerable depths. Fracturing the rock and removing it was only part of the problem. Ventilation and drainage were no less necessary, not to mention the skills required for finding ore, and refining it when found. As these techniques developed, each reinforcing and expanding the scope of the others, mining spread to new regions, moving from the Harz mountains eastward to the Erzgebirge in Bohemia during the thirteenth century and then to Transylvania and Bosnia in the course of the fourteenth and fifteenth centuries. Silver was the principal metal the German miners sought; but copper, tin, coal, and iron could also be mined more cheaply and in greater abundance by using techniques initially developed by silver miners.[6]

6. No satisfactory account of the techniques of European mining before the sixteenth century seems to exist. Maurice Lombard, *Les métaux dans l'ancien monde du Ve au XIe siècle* (Paris, 1974) breaks off just when European mining surged ahead. T. A. Richard,

Overall, therefore, the picture of European economic development in the fourteenth century is not completely black. However acute local hardships and the plague disaster may have been, the market for goods of common consumption—grain, wool, herring, salt, metal, timber, and the like—became far more pervasive. This affected an expanding proportion of the work force and enriched the continent as a whole. Yet the new wealth remained precarious. Price fluctuations and changes in supply and demand brought severe suffering to thousands of individuals from time to time, because their livelihood had come to depend on what happened in distant markets over which they could have no personal control.

The primary managers of the commercial economy of Europe were Italians, operating from such towns as Venice, Genoa, Florence, Siena, and Milan. They bought and sold wholesale, brought new techniques to backwoods regions (e.g., organizing or reorganizing salt mines in Poland and tin mines in Cornwall), and, above all, extended credit to (or withheld it from) lords, clerics, and commoners.

Clerical, royal, and princely administration, as well as long-distance trade, mining, shipping, and other large-scale forms of economic activity, all became dependent on loans from Italian bankers. The relationship was not an easy one. The prohibition of usury in canon law created an aura of impropriety around credit operations. Reckless and impecunious monarchs could invoke the wickedness of usury to justify repudiation of their debts. Such an act could have widely ramifying consequences. The bankruptcy of the English King Edward III in 1339, for example, triggered a general financial crisis in Italy and provoked the first clearly recognizable business cycle in European history.

Taking a personal part in the defense of their hometowns could scarcely seem worthwhile to international merchants and bankers who found it easier and more comfortable to hire someone else to man the walls or ride into battle. A hired professional was also likely to be a better and more formidable soldier than a desk-bound banker or

---

Man and Metals (New York, 1932), 2:507–69, has scattered data; Charles Singer, ed., *A History of Technology* (Oxford, 1956), 2:11–24, marks no advance; John Temple, *Mining: An International History* (London, 1972) is equally uninformative. The difficulty presumably lies in the fact that mining skills developed on an artisan basis and were not recorded in writing until 1555 when George Bauer's masterwork was published as Agricola, *De re metallica,* complete with instructive illustrations of technical procedures. Richard, Singer, and Temple depend entirely on what Agricola has to say for technical matters. Painstaking archaeology will be required before modern scholars can discover when and where technical advances took place before *De re metallica* suddenly opens up a view of what European miners of the sixteenth century had accomplished.

harassed businessman. Efficiency and personal inclination thus tended to coincide. As a result the town militia that in the twelfth and thirteenth centuries defended Italian cities against all comers began to give way to hired bands of professional fighting men.

This change was not simply a matter of convenience for the rich: the poor, too, found military duty increasingly burdensome. Campaigns became lengthier and well-nigh perennial. Having reduced their surrounding countrysides to subjection during the eleventh and twelfth centuries, adjacent cities began to enter upon border quarrels and trade wars against one another. A civic militia could not permanently garrison border strongpoints located as much as fifty miles from the city itself, since militiamen could not afford to stay away from home for indefinite periods of time.

Conversely, as professional bodies of troops came into being, their superior skill made militia men unlikely to prevail in battle, especially when success depended on the difficult coordination of infantry and cavalry movements. A further factor debilitating Italian civic militias was the growing alienation between upper and lower classes within the cities themselves, which made it difficult for rich and poor to cooperate wholeheartedly, whether in military or civil affairs. By about 1350, therefore, Italian civic militias had become archaic holdovers from a simpler past, seldom called into action and of dubious military value. Instead, organized violence came to be exercised mainly by professional troops, commanded by captains who negotiated contracts with appropriate city officials for specified services and time periods.[7]

Initially, the decay of primary group solidarity within the leading cities of Italy and of the town militias which were its military expression invited chaos. Armed adventurers, often originating from north of the Alps, coalesced under informally elected leaders and proceeded to live by blackmailing local authorities, or, when suitably large payments were not forthcoming, by plundering the countryside. Such "free companies" of soldiers became more formidable as the fourteenth century advanced. In 1354, the largest of these bands, numbering as many as 10,000 armed men, accompanied by about twice as many camp followers, wended its way across the most fertile parts of central Italy, making a living by sale and resale of whatever plunder

7. On the shift from town militia to professional soldiery see Michael E. Mallett, *Mercenaries and Their Masters: Warfare in Renaissance Italy* (London, 1974), pp. 1–51; D. P. Waley, "The Army of the Florentine Republic from the 12th to the 14th Centuries," in Nicholai Rubenstein, ed., *Florentine Studies* (London, 1968), pp. 70–108; Charles C. Bayley, *War and Society in Renaissance Florence: The "De Militia" of Leonardo Bruni* (Toronto, 1961).

the soldiers did not consume directly on the spot. Such a traveling company was, in effect, a migratory city, for cities, too, lived by extracting resources from the countryside through a combination of force or threat of force (rents and taxes) on the one hand and more or less free contractual exchanges (artisan goods for food and raw materials) on the other.

The spectacle of a wealthy countryside ravaged by wandering bands of plundering armed men was as old as organized warfare itself. What was new in this situation was the fact that enough money circulated in the richer Italian towns to make it possible for citizens to tax themselves and use the proceeds to buy the services of armed strangers. Then, simply by spending their pay, the hired soldiers put tax monies back in circulation. Thereby, they intensified the market exchanges that allowed such towns to commercialize armed violence in the first place. The emergent system thus tended to become self-sustaining. The only problem was to invent mutually acceptable contractual forms and practical means for enforcing contract terms.

From a taxpayer's point of view, the desirability of substituting the certainty of taxes for the uncertainty of plunder depended on what one had to lose and how frequently plundering bands were likely to appear. In the course of the fourteenth century, enough citizens concluded that taxes were preferable to being plundered to make the commercialization of organized violence feasible in the richer and better-governed cities of northern Italy. Professionalized fighting men had precisely parallel motives for preferring a fixed rate of pay to the risks of living wholly on plunder. Moreover, as military contracts (Italian *condotta,* hence *condottiere,* contractor) developed, rules were introduced specifying the circumstances under which plundering was permissible. Thus, in becoming salaried, soldiering did not entirely lose its speculative economic dimension.

The merging of military enterprise into the market system of Italy passed through two distinguishable stages. By the 1380s self-constituted "free companies" had disappeared. Instead it became usual for cities to enter into contracts with captains who promised to hire and command a body of troops in exchange for agreed payments of money. In this way, a city could choose just what kind of a force it wished to have for a particular campaigning season; and by careful inspection of the force in question, magistrates, representing the taxpayers, could hope to pay for what they got, and no more. Contracts were drawn up initially for a single campaign and for even shorter periods of time. Troops were hired for a specific action: an assault on some neighboring border fortress or the like. The relationship was conceived simply as an emergency service.

A short-term contractual relationship, however, carried relatively high costs. Each time an agreed period of service expired, the soldiers faced a critical transition. If new employment could not be found, they had a choice between plundering for a living or shifting to some more peaceable occupation. Whether to disperse or remain leagued together as a single body of men was a related and no less critical decision. Obviously, to remain successful a captain had to find new contracts. Frequent shifts of employers and a careful husbanding of the *condottiere*'s salable resources—horses, men, arms, and armor—was a necessary implication of short-term contracts.

Friction and distrust between employer and employed was built into such a relationship, for both parties constantly had to look ahead to a time when their contractual relationship would come to an end. The free market in organized violence meant that today's employee might become tomorrow's enemy. Consciousness of this possibility meant that solidarity of sentiment between mercenary troops and the authorities who paid them was not, initially, very great.

But this fragility was uncomfortable to both sides, and by degrees, as the perennial succession of military emergencies became apparent to city magistrates and taxpayers, the advantages of making longer-term contracts became obvious. By the early decades of the fifteenth century, accordingly, long-term associations between a particular captain and a given city became normal. Lifetime service to a single employer became usual, though such ties were only the result of repeated renewals of contracts, each of which might run for two to five years.

Regular employment of the same captain went hand in hand with stabilization and standardization of the personnel under his command. Long-term professional soldiers were arranged into units of fifty or a hundred "lances." A "lance" originally meant an armored knight and the following he brought with him into the field. But commercialization soon required standardization of personnel and equipment, making each lance into a combat team of three to six men, armed differently but mutually supportive in battle and linked by close personal relations. Regular muster and review then allowed magistrates to verify the physical reality of what they were paying for. Reciprocally, terms of service achieved contractual definition. In this way a regular standing army of known size and capability emerged in the better-governed cities of Italy during the first half of the fifteenth century.

Venice, when it launched its first campaigns aimed at conquest on *terra firma* (1405) took the lead in regularizing military *condotta* along these lines. Venetian precocity arose in part from the fact that similar practices had long prevailed in the fleet. Since before the First Crusade, salaried rower-soldiers, formed into standard ships' companies, had been employed season after season to make Venetian power effective overseas. Management of semi-permanent land forces required only modest readjustment of such practices.[8] Florence, on the other hand, lagged far behind in its adaptation to the new conditions of war, partly, at least, because humanistically educated magistrates like Machiavelli were dazzled by Roman republican institutions. Accordingly, they deplored the collapse of the town militia, and feared military coups d'état and the costs of professionalism so much that they sacrificed military efficiency in favor of economy and faithfulness to old traditions of citizen self-defense.

The Florentine fear of coups d'état was well grounded. Many ambitious *condottieri* did indeed seize power from civic officers by illegal use of force. The greatest city to experience this fate was Milan, which became a military despotism after 1450, when Francesco Sforza took power and began to use the resources of the city to support his military following on a permanent basis. Venice managed to escape any such fate, partly by careful supervision of potential usurpers, partly by dividing contracts among several different, mutually jealous captains, and partly by bestowing civic honors and gifts upon loyal and successful *condottieri* and arranging suitable marriages for them with members of the Venetian aristocracy.

Whether by usurpation or assimilation, therefore, outstanding *condottieri* quickly worked their way into the ruling classes of the Italian cities. As that occurred, the first phase of institutional adjustment between the old political order and newfangled forms of military enterprise can be said to have been achieved. The cash nexus came to be reinforced by a variety of sentimental ties connecting professional wielders of armed force to the newly consolidated states that divided sovereignty over the Italian landscape. A captain and his men might still shift employers, however, if some unusual advantage beckoned, or if his or the company's pride were injured by some apparent preference for a rival.

8. And had been initiated by hiring Balkan Christians, the so-called "stradioti," shortly before the venture onto the Italian mainland began. Cf. Freddy Thieret, *La Roumanie vénetienne au moyen âge* (Paris, 1959), p. 402.

The existence of such rivalries and the difficulty of adjusting them smoothly was, indeed, the principal weakness of the Venetian and Milanese military systems. No single captain could be appointed commander-in-chief of all Venetian armed forces without creating such jealousy among the subordinate commanders as to invite irrational displays of prowess or explicit disobedience on the field of battle. Only by assigning rival captains to separate "fronts" could friction be avoided; but this, of course, reduced the flexibility and military value of the armed establishment as a whole. Sforza, too, had similar problems in adjusting relationships among his subordinate commanders after his takeover of Milan in 1450.

The way around this sort of inefficiency was for civil administrators to enter into contractual relationships with smaller and smaller units, down to the single "lance." This practice became increasingly common in both Venice and Milan by the 1480s. Civil officials thereby acquired a far greater control over the state's armed forces, since they now could appoint whomever they wished to command an appropriate number of assembled "lances." The effect was to promote the emergence of a corps of officers whose careers depended more on ties with civic officials who had the power of appointment and less on ties with the particular soldiers who from time to time might come under a given officer's command. Such a pattern of subordination assured effective political control of organized force. Coups d'état ceased to be a serious threat.

A remarkably flexible and efficient system of warfare, relating means to ends according to financial as well as diplomatic calculations, thus came into being in the Po valley by the end of the fifteenth century. Its establishment constituted a second stage in the institutional adjustment to the commercialization of warfare by Italian cities.

Obviously, since states were relatively few and individual "lances" were numerous, terms of trade tilted strongly in favor of the employer and against the employee. The entire evolution, indeed, may be viewed as a development from a nearly free market (when blackmail and plundering defined protection costs by means of innumerable local "market" transactions) towards oligopoly (when a few great captains and city administrators made and broke contracts), followed by quasi-monopoly within each of the larger and better-administered states into which Italy divided. From a different point of view, one may say that an almost unadulterated cash nexus gave way by degrees to more complex linkages among armed men and with their employers. These linkages combined esprit de corps with bureaucratic subordination, loyalty to a commander, and (in Venice at least) also to the state.

However complex and variable from case to case, the overall result was to stabilize relationships between the civil and military elements in Italian society. This in turn allowed the leading Italian city-states to function as great powers in the politics of the age. In 1508, for example, the Venetians staved off attack by the so-called League of Cambrai, in which Pope Julius II, Emperor Maximilian, the king of France, and the king of Spain combined against them. Only in collision with the Turks did Venetian military might prove insufficient.

Later, when Italian cities became pawns and prizes in the wars between France and Spain, observers like Machiavelli (d. 1527) came to disdain the virtuosity with which Venice and Milan had adapted their administrative practices to the dictates of an age in which human relations in general and military relations in particular could no longer be managed on a face-to-face basis in accordance with custom and status, but responded instead to impersonal and imperfectly understood market relations. Until very recently, Machiavelli's attack on mercenary soldiering seemed persuasive to nineteenth- and twentieth-century historians whose own experience of war emphasized the value of citizen-soldiers and patriotism. But in an age when military professionalism promises to make citizen-soldiers obsolete once again, scholars have begun to recognize the way in which the best-governed Italian cities anticipated, in the fifteenth century, military arrangements that became standard north of the Alps some two centuries later.[9]

The fact remains that by collecting tax monies to pay soldiers who proceeded to spend their wages and thereby helped to refresh the tax base, Italian city administrations showed how a commercially articulated society could defend itself effectively. By inventing administrative methods for controlling soldiers and tying their self-interest more and more closely to continued service with the same employer, these cities altered the incidence of instability inherent in market relationships.

9. These remarks on Italian military organization depend primarily on Mallett's magnificent book *Mercenaries and Their Masters,* and his chapter "Venice and Its Condottieri, 1404–54" in John R. Hale, ed., *Renaissance Venice* (London, 1973), pp. 131–45. Cf. also John R. Hale, "Renaissance Armies and Political Control: The Venetian Proveditorial System, 1509–1529," *Journal of Italian History* 2 (1979): 11–31, and Piero Pieri, *Il Rinascimento e la crisi militare italiana* (Turin, 1952), which offers abundant information but generally endorses the traditionally negative appraisal of mercenary soldiering.

Put differently, efficient tax collection, debt-funding, and skilled, professional military management kept peace at home, and exported the uncertainties of organized violence to the realm of foreign affairs, diplomacy, and war. States that lagged in developing an efficient internal administration of armed force, like Florence and Genoa, continued to experience sporadic outbreaks of civil violence. Venice, the most successful innovator in the management of armed force, entirely escaped domestic upheavals, though it barely survived external attacks provoked by the Republic's long series of diplomatic and military successes on Italian soil.

The Gunpowder Revolution
and the Rise of Atlantic Europe

The Italian state system as a whole (together with the economic relationships that concentrated financial resources so remarkably in a few Italian cities) was vulnerable to two different, yet interconnected, processes of change. First the most obvious: political rivalries and diplomatic alliances among competing states could not be confined to the Italian peninsula itself. When newly consolidated monarchies, commanding comparatively vast territories, chose to intervene in Italian affairs, the sovereignty of mere city-states, however skillfully managed, could not permanently be maintained. This was signaled towards the close of the fifteenth century, when first the Ottoman Empire (1480) and then France (1494) dispatched powerful expeditionary forces to Italian soil. Though both soon withdrew, divided Italy's inability to check massive outside intervention became clear to all concerned. In the next century the peninsula accordingly became a theater of war where foreign powers competed for control of Italians' superior wealth and skill.

The second source of instability was technological. Commercialization of military service depended upon, and simultaneously helped to sustain, the commercialization of weapons' manufacture and supply. After all, a soldier without appropriate arms was of little value, whereas an armed man might sell his services at a price related to the kind of arms he possessed and the skill with which he could use them. Easy and open access to arms was therefore a sine qua non of mercenary war.

Ordinary long-distance trade also depended upon free access to weapons, for an unarmed ship or caravan could not expect to arrive safely at its destination. Indeed, successful trade across political frontiers required the same delicate combination of diplomatic negotiation, military readiness, and financial acumen that was needed for successful management of close-in defense of the city and its dependent territory. Perhaps the relationship should be put the other way: skills and aptitudes developed for the successful pursuit of long-distance trade, upon which the wealth and power of the great cities of Italy had come to depend, provided the model and context within which Italians invented a new and distinctively European pattern of diplomacy and war.

The system maintained strong incentives for continued improvements of weapons design. When many different purchasers entered the market, and many different artisan shops produced arms and armor for the public, any change in design that cheapened the product or improved its performance could be counted on to attract prompt attention and propagate itself rapidly. Accordingly an arms race, of the kind that has often manifested itself among European peoples subsequently, broke out in the fourteenth century. It centered mainly in Italy. The effect at first was to confirm and strengthen the formidability of Italian armed forces; before long, however, new weaponry began to favor larger states and more powerful monarchs.

As long as the race lay between ever more efficient crossbows and more and more elaborate plate armor, Italian workshops and artisan designers kept the lead. This was the agenda of the fourteenth century, beginning with the introduction of a simple "stirrup" (1301) (known in China since the eleventh century) that allowed archers to cock their crossbows faster, and going on to the design of increasingly powerful bows, substituting steel for wood in the arc of the bow after about 1350, and then employing a windlass to pull back the string (1370).[10] Thereafter, crossbow design stood still. Inventiveness concentrated instead on gunpowder weapons. But before that time, each improvement in the power of crossbows was matched by improvements in the design of armor. Milan was a major locus for the manufacture of armor, but the production of crossbows does not seem to have had any comparable center, unless it was Genoa. That city became famous among northern rulers as the place from which to recruit crossbowmen; and perhaps the Genoese enjoyed a certain primacy in crossbow manufacture. But hard data seem lacking.

The next episode in the technological race between offensive and

10. Ralph W. F. Payne-Gallwey, *The Crossbow, Medieval and Modern, Military and Sporting: Its Construction, History and Management* (London, 1903), pp. 62–91 and passim.

defensive weapons involved the use of guns. The idea that the explosive power of gunpowder, if suitably confined, might be made to shoot a projectile with previously unattainable force seems to have dawned almost simultaneously upon European and Chinese artificers. At any rate, the earliest drawings that clearly attest the existence of guns date from 1326 in Europe and from 1332 in China. Both drawings portray a vase-shaped vessel, armed with an oversized arrow that projects from its mouth. This certainly suggests a single origin for the invention, wherever it was actually made.[11]

But even if the idea of guns as well as of gunpowder reached Europe from China, the fact remains that Europeans very swiftly outstripped the Chinese and every other people in gun design, and continued to enjoy a clear superiority in this art until World War II. But Italians do not ever appear to have attained the primacy as gunfounders that they had enjoyed in crossbow manufacture and armor making, perhaps because European guns quickly became giant tubes, weighing more than a ton. This put Italians at a disadvantage, since they had to import metal from the north, and overland portage was expensive. Except in the case of untransportable objects, like the guns that battered down Constantinople's walls in 1453, it was easier to refine the ore and to produce finished metal goods close beside the mining sites. Italian metal workers therefore could not easily compete with gunfounders nearer the source of supply. Consequently as soon as guns became critical weapons in war, Italian technical primacy in the armaments industry decayed.

Before considering the early development of gunpowder weapons, it seems best to glance briefly at what had been happening north of the Alps, where the feudal system, according to which a knight owed his lord military service in return for a grant of income-producing land, was much more firmly established than it had ever been in Italy. When the Hundred Years War (1337–1453) began, the French king still relied primarily on the infeudated chivalry of his kingdom to meet and repel the English invaders,[12] though by the time of the Battle of

11. Cf. L. Carrington Goodrich, "Early Cannon in China," *Isis* 55 (1964): 193–95; L. Carrington Goodrich and Feng Chia-sheng, "The Early Development of Firearms in China," *Isis* 36 (1946): 114–23; and Joseph Needham, "The Guns of Khaifengfu," *Times Literary Supplement,* 11 January 1980. On early guns in Europe innumerable books exist, of which O. F. G. Hogg, *Artillery, Its Origin, Heyday, and Decline* (London, 1970) is a worthy recent example.

12. Feudal service had already been partially monetized by the fact that after a stated period of time (usually forty days) the lord was expected or required to pay his knights a daily allowance to permit them to remain under arms. Since the English remained in France winter and summer, their arrival put an intolerable strain on traditional patterns

Crécy (1346) he had taken the precaution of supplementing the knightly array with crossbowmen hired in Genoa, hoping thereby to counterbalance the mercenary longbowmen in the English army.

From the beginning, English armies in France were promised pay, but seldom received it in the field. Instead, they lived off the country by seizing food and forage for immediate consumption, hoping all the while for some windfall—a hoard of silver or a great man's ransom—that would bring them at least temporary riches. Circulation of goods through buying and selling had not developed to a sufficient level in most of France for anything like the regulated fiscality of Italian mercenary service to stabilize itself. Nevertheless, the transfers of tangible wealth that resulted from the passage of plundering armies—melting down church treasure, for example—must have stimulated market exchange. The hordes of sutlers and camp followers who attended English and French armies in the field regularly bought and sold; and so of course did the soldiers when they failed to get exactly what they wanted by stealing and plundering. As earlier in Italy, an army in the field with its continual appetite for supplies acted like a migratory city. In the short run the effect on the French countryside was often disastrous; in the long run armies and their plundering expanded the role of buying and selling in everyday life.[13]

As a result, by the time the French monarchy began to recover from the squalid demoralization induced by the initial English victories and widespread disaffection among the nobility, an expanded tax base allowed the king to collect enough hard cash to support an increasingly formidable armed force. This was the army which expelled the

---

of short-term feudal service among the French. Among the English, earlier wars of conquest in Wales and Scotland had already triggered the development of a semiprofessional royal army of mercenaries. On recruitment into English expeditionary forces, see Kenneth Fowler, ed., *The Hundred Years War* (London, 1971), pp. 78–85; H. J. Hewitt, *The Organization of War under Edward III, 1338–62* (Manchester, 1966), pp. 28–49.

13. Cf. the masterful work by Phillipe Contamine, *Guerre, état et société à la fin du moyen âge: Etudes sur les armées des rois de France, 1337–1494* (Paris, 1972). On English armies: Hewitt, *Organization of War under Edward III, 1338–62;* K. B. McFarlane, "War, Economy and Social Change: England and the Hundred Years War," *Past and Present* 22 (1962): 3–17; Edward Miller, "War, Taxation and the English Economy in the Late Thirteenth and Early Fourteenth Centuries," in J. M. Winter, ed., *War and Economic Development* (Cambridge, 1975), pp. 11–31; and the essays in Fowler, *The Hundred Years War* (n.12 above) are pertinent. For the economic consequences of plunder, cf. Fritz Redlich, *De Praeda Militare: Looting and Booty, 1500–1800* (Wiesbaden, 1956), and especially his major work *The German Military Enterpriser and His Work Force,* 2 vols. (Wiesbaden, 1964), 1:118 and passim. Redlich's data come from a later time, but the fact that he was trained as an economist and brought an economist's vocabulary to bear on the phenomena of plunder and mercenary soldiering gives his work a unique value.

English from France by 1453 after a series of successful campaigns. The same force allowed Louis XI (1461–83) to take possession of a large part of the inheritance of Charles the Bold of Burgundy after that ruler met his death in a battle against the Swiss (1477). The kingdom of France thus emerged on the map of Europe between 1450 and 1478, centralized as never before and capable of maintaining a standing professional army of about 25,000 men year in and year out, with an extreme upper limit of 80,000 available for mobilization in time of crisis.[14]

Mere numbers, however, do not tell the tale. The French army that drove the English out of Normandy and Guienne, 1450–53, did so by bringing heavy artillery pieces to bear on castle walls, one after another, whereupon previously formidable defenses came tumbling down in a matter of hours, if the garrison did not prefer to surrender. A century of rapid development of cannon design lay behind this dramatic demonstration of the power gunpowder weapons had attained.

From the very beginning, the explosive suddenness with which a gun discharged somehow fascinated European rulers and artisans. The effort they put into building early guns far exceeded their effectiveness, since, for more than a century after 1326, catapults continued to surpass anything a gun could do, except when it came to making noise. Yet this did not check experimentation.[15]

The first important change in gun design was to substitute a spherical shot (usually made from stone) for the arrowlike projectiles of the earliest guns. This went along with a shift from the early vase shape to a tubular design for the gun itself, allowing expanding gases from the

14. These figures come from Contamine, *Guerre, état et société*, pp. 317–18. In 1478 France's 4,142 "lances" outnumbered Milan's more than 4 to 1. This offers a rough measure of the way in which the French monarchy had outstripped the Italian city-state scale of war by the close of the fifteenth century. Ibid., p. 200.

15. Cf. Thomas Esper, "The Replacement of the Longbow by Firearms in the English Army," *Technology and Culture* 6 (1965): 382–93. Sexual symbolism presumably attached itself to guns from the beginning, and perhaps goes far to explain European artisans' and rulers' irrational investment in early firearms. I owe this idea to Barton C. Hacker, who explored parallel psychological drives behind the development of tanks in the interwar decades in "The Military and the Machine: An Analysis of the Controversy over Mechanization in the British Army, 1919–1939" (Ph.D. diss., University of Chicago, 1968). Yet even if this sort of psychological resonance explains otherwise unintelligible behavior, it does not explain why Europeans were especially susceptible. The character of western Europe's political institutions and the militaristic habits of urban dwellers who manufactured (and paid for) the new guns seem necessary factors in converting psychological drives from mere fantasy into hard metal. Cf. J. R. Hale, "Gunpowder and the Renaissance: An Essay in the History of Ideas," in Charles H. Carter, ed., *From Renaissance to Counter-Reformation: Essays in Honor of Garret Mattingly* (London, 1966), pp. 133–34.

Artillery Development in Europe, 1326–1500

These four drawings show how European craftsmen and rulers collaborated to develop a formidable artillery out of the ineffective toy depicted in 1326 (a). The two giant stone-throwing bombards, one of wrought iron (b) and one cast in bronze (c), were superseded in the second half of the fifteenth century by mobile siege artillery (d) that used denser iron cannonballs and accelerated them more rapidly by burning "corned" powder. The result was a weapon that could demolish any existing

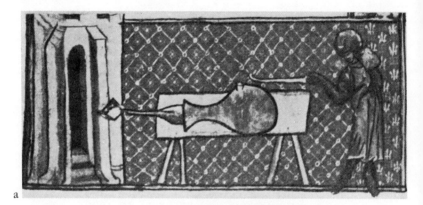

a

b

fortification in no more than a few hours.

a, Berhard Rathgen, *Das Geschütz im Mittelalter* (Berlin: VDI, 1928), Tafel 4, Abbildung 12. Miniature from the manuscript of Walter de Milimete, at Oxford, A.D. 1326.

b, Ibid., Tafel 7, Abbildung 22. Stone throwing bombard, Vienna, made about A.D. 1425.

c, A. Essenwein, *Quellen zur Geschichte der Feuerwaffen* (Leipzig: F. A. Brockhaus, 1877), vol. 2, pl. A. XXI–XXII. Brunswick bombard, cast in 1411 and recorded in a copperplate drawing in 1728.

d, Ibid., pl. A.LXXII–LXXIII. Gun cast for Emperor Maximilian between 1500 and 1510, reproduced from Codex icon. 222, Münich Königlichen Hof- und Staatsbibliothek.

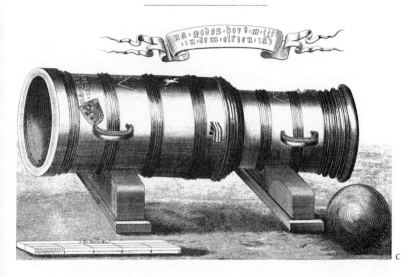

c

d

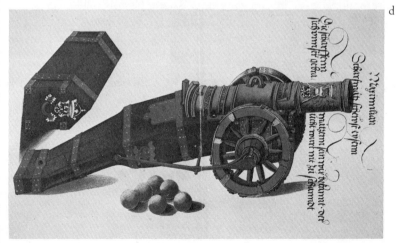

explosion to accelerate the projectile while it traveled the length of the barrel. Such a design produced far higher velocities than had been attainable before.

Higher velocities, in turn, induced gunmakers to try for bigger and bigger calibers on the theory that a larger projectile would exercise decisive shattering force on enemy fortifications. Bigger guns carrying heavier projectiles and larger charges of powder had to be made stronger. The earliest giant guns were fabricated by welding bars of wrought iron together; but such "bombards" were liable to burst. A more satisfactory solution was to employ metal-casting techniques which European bell makers had already developed to a high degree of perfection. Guns cast as a single piece of bronze or brass proved far more reliable than any built-up design, all of which were, accordingly, abandoned.

By 1450, therefore, supplies of copper and tin to make bronze and of copper and zinc to make brass became critically important for Europe's rulers. When the new guns spread to Asia, a second bronze age set in. It lasted for about a century until technicians imported into England from the Continent discovered in 1543 how to cast satisfactory iron cannon. They thereby cheapened big guns to about a twelfth of their former cost, just as the iron-age blacksmiths had cheapened swords and helmets in the twelfth century B.C.[16]

Strictly speaking, therefore, the second bronze age lasted less than a century (1453–1543). But English ironmasters could not supply every ruler of Europe; and even after the Swedes and Dutch developed an international trade in iron guns in the 1620s, bronze and brass cannon continued to be preferred. Thus, for example, it was only in the 1660s, when Colbert set out to build a navy and needed thousands of guns for his ships and shore installations, that the French went over to

16. Theodore A. Wertime, *The Coming of the Age of Steel* (Leiden, 1961), pp. 67–69; H. R. Schubert, *History of the British Iron and Steel Industry from c. 450 B.C. to A.D. 1775* (London, 1957), pp. 164 ff. On the Continent, cast iron cannon actually dated back to the mid-fifteenth century but were often defective, so the cheapness of the metal was counteracted by the frequency of failure. England retained an effective monopoly of serviceable cast iron cannon for half a century, largely because minute chemical trace elements in the ore used by the Sussex ironmasters made the metal less likely to develop flaws as it cooled.

Military demand for cannon slacked off after 1604 when England made peace with Spain (and the Dutch soon followed suit). Growing fuel shortages deepened the economic depression that then set in in Sussex; and two decades later Sweden began casting iron guns of high quality, thanks to the import of Walloon techniques of blast furnace construction and metal casting. Thereafter the Swedes dominated the international market in iron cannon until late in the eighteenth century. Cf. Eli Heckscher, "Un grand chapître de l'histoire de fer: le monopole suèdois," *Annales d'histoire économique et sociale* 4 (1932): 127–39.

iron guns.[17] Prior to that time, access to copper and tin was of vital strategic importance to the rulers of the world.

Economic patterns registered this fact. The importance of central European copper and silver mines increased sharply, for example. The burst of prosperity in south Germany, Bohemia, and adjacent regions in the late fifteenth century reflected a mining boom in those parts of Europe; so did the financial empire raised by the Fuggers and other south German bankers, who briefly rivaled older Italian centers for managing large-scale interregional economic enterprises.[18] A similar period of economic effervescence in the West Country of England was related to intensified exploitation of the Cornish tin mines. Likewise, Japanese copper and Malayan tin became critically important when the sovereign value of bronze artillery became apparent to the rulers of India and the Far East in the sixteenth and seventeenth centuries.

The substitution of iron for bronze and brass cannon eventually undercut central Europe's mining prosperity. Cheap silver from the New World began to compete with the products of European mines at almost exactly the same time that copper mining was affected by the appearance of cheaper gunmetal. But the setback in central Europe was offset by gains elsewhere. England in the sixteenth and Sweden in the seventeenth century profited most directly from the new importance of iron in cannon making. The political and military history of Europe turned to some degree on these facts.

Long before the second bronze age came to a close, gun design underwent a second major advance. The bombards of the mid-fifteenth century were so big (often thirty inches or more in diameter and twelve to fifteen feet long) that they could be moved only with the greatest difficulty. The cannon that breached Constantinople's walls in 1453, for example, were cast on the spot, since it was easier to bring the raw materials to the scene of action and build the necessary furnaces and molds outside the walls than it would have been to move the finished guns. However powerful their discharge, the immobility of such giant weapons was a serious handicap and an obvious challenge to gunfounders.

Between 1465 and 1477 an arms race between France and Burgundy[19] provided artisans and rulers with means and motive to invent a practical solution to the problem. The gunfounders of the Low Countries and France discovered that much smaller weapons could do

17. Maurice Daumas, ed., *Histoire générale des techniques* (Paris, 1965), 2:493.

18. Cf. Léon Louis Schick, *Un grand homme d'affaires au début du XVIe siècle: Jacob Fugger* (Paris, 1957), pp. 8–27.

19. A convenient shorthand to refer to the territories gathered together by dukes of Burgundy between 1363 and 1477. The Low Countries constituted the richest part of

the same damage as bombards of three times the size if the gun tubes were made strong enough to fire denser iron cannonballs instead of stones. Iron cannonballs were also cheaper to make and could often be reused, whereas giant stone projectiles shattered on impact and were difficult and expensive to shape by hand and transport to the scene of action.

A second technical improvement came in at the same time: the practice of forming gunpowder into small grains or "corns." This allowed a more rapid ignition, since the exposed surfaces of the separate corns could all burn at once. The explosion became correspondingly more powerful, for rapidly generated gases had less time to leak out around the cannonball while it accelerated along the barrel.[20] This put additional strain on the gunmetal of course, but the bronze founders of the Low Countries discovered how to thicken the critical area around the chamber, where the explosion occurred, and tapered the thickness of the barrel towards the cannon mouth in proportion to the drop-off of pressure behind the projectile.

With suitable mounting and strong enough horses, powerful siege guns of about eight feet in length, designed to fire an iron ball of between twenty-five and fifty pounds, could travel cross-country with relative ease. This required specially designed gun carriages, with stout axles and wheels and long "trails" extending behind the gun. By mounting the gun on trunnions near its center of gravity, it became possible to elevate the tube to any desired angle without dismounting it from the carriage on which it traveled. Recoil could be absorbed by allowing the gun and its carriage to jerk backwards a few feet. To fire again, it might be necessary to wheel the carriage forward to the initial firing position, but this could be done by using simple levers and without hitching the horses. When it was time to move on, a few minutes sufficed to lift the trails from the ground, put a limber underneath, and set off. Rapid transition from traveling position to firing position and vice versa was matched by the fact that these guns could go wherever a heavy wagon and team could pass. In essence, the siege gun design developed in France and Burgundy between 1465 and 1477 lasted until the 1840s, with only marginal improvement.[21]

their domains, which, however, extended irregularly southward to the Swiss border. For half a century before the death of Charles the Bold in 1477 the dukes of Burgundy seemed about to reconstitute the kingdom of Lotharingia which had been interposed between France and Germany by the division of the Carolingian empire in 843.

20. Daumas, *Histoire générale des techniques,* 2:487.

21. Carlo M. Cipolla, *Guns, Sails and Empires: Technological Innovation and the Early Phases of European Expansion, 1400–1700* (New York, 1965), pp. 1–73, is by far the

Guns of this radically new design accompanied the French army that invaded Italy in 1494 to make good Charles VIII's claim to the throne of Naples. The Italians were overawed by the efficiency of the new weapons. First Florence and then the pope yielded after only token resistance; and on the single occasion when a fortress on the border of the kingdom of Naples did try to resist the invaders, the French gunners required only eight hours to reduce its walls to rubble. Yet not long before, this same fortress had made itself famous by withstanding a siege of seven years.[22]

The clumsy bombards of 1453 had already altered the balance between besieger and besieged, but the resulting disturbance to established power relationships was enormously magnified by the French and Burgundian invention of mobile siege guns between 1465 and 1477. Wherever the new artillery appeared, existing fortifications became useless. The power of any ruler who was able to afford the high cost of the new weapons was therefore enhanced at the expense of neighbors and subjects who were unable to avail themselves of the new technology of war.

In Europe, the major effect of the new weaponry was to dwarf the Italian city-states and to reduce other small sovereignties to triviality. The French and Burgundians did not long retain a monopoly, of course; nearby territorial monarchs quickly acquired siege guns of the new design, including the Hapsburg emperors and the Ottoman sultans.[23] A mighty struggle among the newly consolidated powers of Europe ensued, lasting through most of the sixteenth century and reducing the Italian city-states to the condition of pawns to be fought over.

Yet the ingenuity that made Italian skills the cynosure of all who encountered them was not baffled for long by the heightened power of siege guns. As a matter of fact, even before encountering the formidable new French guns in 1494, Italian military engineers had been

---

most incisive account of early development of artillery in Europe that I have seen. In the nineteenth century, detailed and more or less antiquarian writing on artillery achieved striking refinement with such works as A. Essenwein, *Quellen zur Geschichte der Feuerwaffen*, 2 vols. (Leipzig, 1877; republished in facsimile, Graz, 1969). On the Burgundian development of artillery, cf. C. Brusten, *L'armée bourguignonne de 1455 à 1468* (Brussels, 1954); Claude Gaier, *L'industrie et le commerce des armes dans l'anciennes principautés belges du XIIIe à la fin du XVe siècle* (Paris, 1973).

22. Christopher Duffy, *Siege Warfare: The Fortress in the Early Modern World, 1494–1660* (London, 1979), pp. 8–9.

23. The Hapsburgs shared the Burgundian inheritance with the French in 1477 and thus fell heir directly to the gunfounding capabilities of the Low Countries. For the Ottomans cf. John F. Guilmartin, Jr., *Gunpowder and Galleys: Changing Technology and Mediterranean Warfare at Sea in the 16th century* (Cambridge, 1974), pp. 255–56.

experimenting for half a century in desultory fashion with ways to make old fortifications better able to withstand gunfire. After that date the problem assumed an entirely new urgency for every existing political authority in Italy. The country's best brains were devoted to seeking a solution, including those of Leonardo da Vinci and Michelangelo.[24]

Partly by accident, or perhaps one should say through hasty improvisation, the Italians quickly discovered that loosely compacted earth could absorb cannon shot harmlessly. The Pisans, besieged by the Florentines in 1500, made this discovery when they built an emergency wall of earth inside their endangered ring wall. As a result, when cannon fire brought the stones of their permanent fortification tumbling down, a new obstacle confronted the besiegers which they were unable to cross. To make a rampart of earth, one had to dig: and by shaping the resulting hole in the ground so as to give it a vertical forward face, the ditch thus formed became a sort of negative, or inverted, wall, presenting an attacker with a very difficult obstacle, and one that was entirely proof against destruction by cannon.[25]

This fundamental idea, later embodied in more permanent forms, with masonry facings to the ditch, went far to solve the problem of how to protect against gunfire. Bastions and outworks, armed with guns and defended by ditches, were soon added. When properly located, such outworks could bring a withering crossfire against anyone trying to cross the ditch and assault the wall. Outworks' artillery also had a second role to play, for by directing counter battery fire against the besiegers' guns, the accuracy and force of the attack could be sharply reduced.[26]

By the 1520s, fortifications on the new Italian model were again quite capable of resisting even the best-equipped attackers. But their cost was enormous. Only the wealthiest states and cities could afford the scores of cannon and the enormous labor of construction required by the *trace italienne,* as this type of fortification came to be called beyond the Alps.

---

24. Albrecht Dürer, a pupil of Italians in many things, came back from his Italian travels with an interest in the problem, and has the distinction of having published the first book on fortification ever printed, *Etliche Underricht zur Befestigung der Stett Schloss und Flecken* (Nuremberg, 1527). This volume is more remarkable for the grandiose works Dürer recommends as protections against cannon than for the practicality of his designs. Cf. Duffy, *Siege Warfare,* pp. 4–7.

25. Duffy, *Siege Warfare,* p. 15.

26. John R. Hale, "The Development of the Bastion, 1440–1534," in John R. Hale, ed., *Europe in the Late Middle Ages* (Evanston, Ill., 1965), pp. 466–94.

Nevertheless, by checking the sovereignty of siege cannon so quickly, the *trace italienne* played a critical role in European history. By the 1530s, as cannon-proof fortifications began to spread from Italy to other parts of Europe, high technology once again favored local defenses, at least in those regions where governments could afford the cost of the new fortifications and the large number of cannon they required. This put a very effective obstacle in the way of the political consolidation of Europe into a single imperial unity at almost the same time that such a possibility became conceivable, thanks to the extraordinary collection of territories that the Hapsburg heir, Charles V of Ghent, acquired between 1516 and 1521. As Holy Roman Emperor of the German nation, Charles laid claim to a vague primacy over all of Christendom; and as ruler of Spain, the Low Countries, and of broad regions in Germany, he seemed to have the resources to give new substance to the ancient imperial dignity.

His first enterprise, after putting down rebellion in Spain, was to drive the French out of Italy. By 1525 he had succeeded; and in the following decades his troops (mainly Spanish) made good their control over both Naples and Milan. He thereby reduced the other Italian states to uneasy dependence, sporadically punctuated by futile efforts to throw off what was often felt to be a Spanish yoke. Success in Italy, however, provoked cooperation between French and Ottoman rivals to the Hapsburg power in the larger theater of the Mediterranean, while, in the north, German princes resisted consolidation of Charles's imperial authority by resorting to military action whenever they judged it necessary.

Obviously, fortifications capable of resisting superior field forces for long periods of time could play a critical role in checking empire-building. Construction of such fortresses therefore went on apace, first mainly in Italy, later in more peripheral parts of Europe. As a result, after 1525, large-scale battles, which had been characteristic of the first two and a half decades of the Italian wars, ceased. Sieges set in instead. Imperial consolidation halted halfway, with Spanish garrisons in Naples and Milan supporting an unstable Hapsburg hegemony in Italy. By the 1560s, a similar barrier halted Ottoman expansion, as the new style of fortress arose in such places as Malta (besieged vainly by the Turks in 1565) and along the Hungarian frontier.

In their first decades, before the Italian landscape became thickly dotted with cannon-proof fortifications, the Italian wars (1499–1559) had served as a forcing house for the development of effective infantry firearms, and for the invention of tactics and field fortifications to

How Europeans Checked the Gunpowder Revolution

These drawings by a French architect of the nineteenth century, E. Viollet-le-Duc, show how an emergency response to walls crumbling under gunfire was developed into a new style of fortification that made sieges once again long and difficult to conduct. The drawing upper left shows a shallow ditch and emergency wall, with gun ports, erected behind a newly made breach, thus confronting the attackers with a further formidable obstacle to their capture of the city. Below is a cross-section of the fully

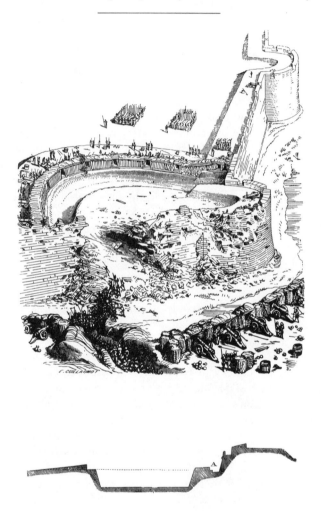

developed trace italienne, *showing the way in which ditch and walls were combined to protect a city from gunfire. Note that the shallow angle of the glacis on the left of the ditch made it impossible to strike the wall with direct fire unless cannon could be mounted on the very lip of the ditch, as in the drawing on the right. Yet that shows how even after the wall had been breached and the moat filled with debris, a suitably designed bastion could still make an assault very costly to the attackers.*

E. Viollet-le-Duc, *Dictionnaire raisonné de l'architecture française du IXe au XVIe siècle* (Paris, 1858), vol. 1:420 (fig. 57), 452 (fig. 75), and 441 (fig. 72).

utilize the firepower that muskets and arquebuses began to exhibit in battle. The French failure in Italy, in fact, can be attributed largely to an excessive reliance on Swiss pikemen, heavy cavalry, and their famous siege guns. The Spanish were readier than the French to experiment with musketry as a supplement to pike formations and proved especially adept at making use of field fortification to protect infantry from cavalry attack.

As a result, the so-called Spanish *tercios* emerged from the Italian wars as the most formidable field force in Europe. A *tercio* comprised a mass of pikemen who protected a fringe of musketeers posted around the central square of pikes. This formation proved capable of withstanding cavalry attack in the open field and could charge an enemy with lowered pikes just as effectively as the Swiss, who had invented this tactic. Only occasionally did artillery play much of a role in battles; it was too difficult to get heavy guns to the battlefield in time.

The tactics of the Spanish *tercios* gave a decisive battlefield role to infantry, not only in defense but in attack as well. Until the sixteenth century the prestige of knighthood in battle had lingered stubbornly, especially in France and Germany, where knighthood was deeply rooted in the social structure of the countryside. But after 1525 or so, the idea that a gentleman could fight on foot with almost as much dignity as if he were mounted became irresistible in practice, even among the French and Germans. Cavalry, after all, had almost no role in siege warfare, which became the principal growing point in the art of war for the ensuing half-century.

Despite all the skill brought to bear on the art of combining different arms and formations in battle to achieve success, Spanish victories in the field always fell short of assuring a general supremacy for the Hapsburg cause. As long as the defeated party had a multitude of prepared fortifications to fall back upon, where the shattered remnants of a field force could take refuge and expect to resist for many months, even a series of victories did not suffice to establish hegemony.

Hence, the superiority of Spanish soldiers in battle, although it did allow Charles V to drive the French from Italy, did not allow him to overthrow the independent power of the French monarchy. Nor was he able to suppress the autonomy of German princes or the diverse local immunities of his Netherlandish subjects, even when they began to espouse various forms of Protestant heresy. As a result, perpetual competition among European states continued to provoke sporadic arms races, when from time to time a new technology seemed capable of conferring significant advantage in war upon its possessor.

In other parts of the earth, however, the Italian riposte to cannon fire was not forthcoming. Instead, the edge that mobile siege cannon gave to their possessors allowed a series of relatively vast gunpowder empires to come into existence across much of Asia and all of eastern Europe. The Portuguese and Spanish overseas empires of the sixteenth century belong to this class, for they were defended (and in the Portuguese case created) by ship-borne artillery, which differed from that of land-based powers mainly in being more mobile. Ming China (1368–1644) depended less upon cannon that did such upstart empires as the Mughal in India (founded 1526), the Muscovite in Russia (founded 1480), and the Ottoman (after 1453) in eastern Europe and the Levant. The Safavid empire in Iran depended less on gunpowder weaponry than did its neighbors, though under Shah Abbas (1587–1629) the centralizing effect of the new technology of war manifested itself there too. Similarly, in Japan the establishment of a single central authority after 1590 was facilitated by the way small arms and even a small number of cannon made older forms of fighting and fortification at least partially obsolete.

The extent of the Mughal, Muscovite, and Ottoman empires was defined in practice by the mobility of their respective imperial gun parks. In Russia, the Muscovites prevailed wherever navigable rivers made it possible to bring heavy guns to bear against existing fortifications. In the interior of India, where water transportation was unavailable, imperial consolidation remained precarious, since it required

---

A European Army of the Sixteenth Century in Marching Order

This bird's-eye view (following page) shows how the European art of war combined different arms and formations in the sixteenth century. Cavalry, light and heavy artillery, pikemen, and arquebus-carrying infantry are accompanied by supply wagons that could double as emergency field fortification around the encamped army's perimeter. Flags projecting above the array of pikes signified subordinate units of command, which allowed maneuver on the battlefield. This is an idealized portrait; in practice guns could seldom keep up with marching troops, and ground was almost never flat enough to permit an army to move forward in such a broad-front formation.

Leonhardt Fronsperger, *Von Wagenburgs und die Feldlager* (Frankfurt am Main, 1573; facsimile reproduction, Stuttgart, Verlag Wilh. C. Rübsamen, 1968).

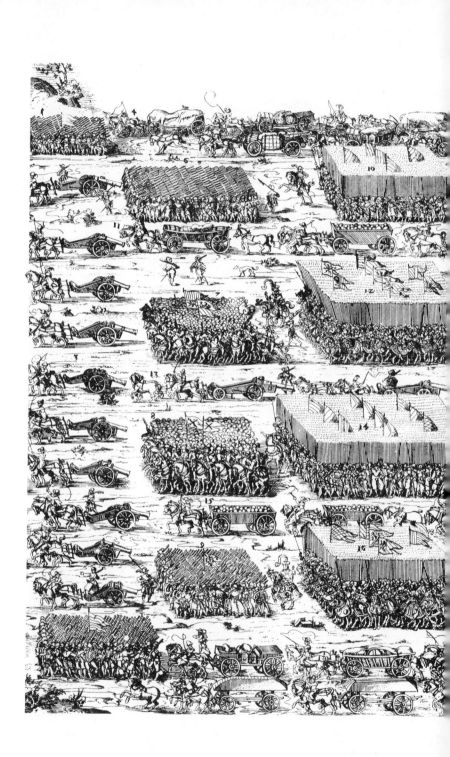

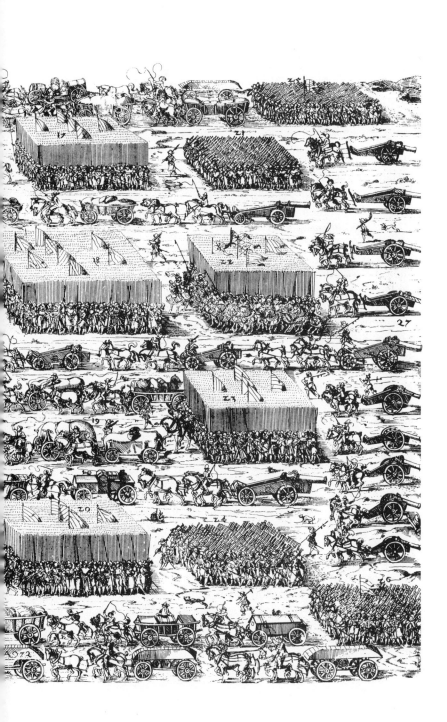

great effort to cast guns on the spot, as Babur (1526–30) did, or else to haul them overland, as his grandson Akbar (1566–1605) did. But in each of these states, even in those immediately abutting upon western Europe, once a decisive advantage accrued to central authorities through the use and monopolization of heavy guns, further spontaneous improvements in gunpowder weapons ceased. Rulers had come into possession of what obviously seemed to be an ultimate weapon, however difficult it might sometimes be for heavy artillery to be brought to bear in a given locality. There was little incentive to experiment with new devices. On the contrary, anything that might tend to make existing artillery pieces obsolete must have seemed wantonly wasteful and potentially dangerous to those in power.

In western Europe, on the contrary, improvements in weapons design continued to be eagerly sought after. Whenever anything new really worked, it spread from court to court, shop to shop, and camp to camp with quite extraordinary rapidity. Not surprisingly, therefore, the equipment and training of European armed forces soon began to outstrip those of other parts of the civilized world. Western Europe's emerging battlefield superiority became apparent to the Ottoman Turks in the war of 1593–1606, when, for the first time, Turkish cavalry met disciplined infantry gunfire.[27] The Russians discovered a similar gap between themselves and their neighbors to the west in the course of the Livonian war (1557–82).[28] Asian states only discovered the discrepancy later. By that time the gap between their own military skill and that of the Europeans had become much greater than was the case at the turn of the seventeenth century—often too great to be bridged successfully without first submitting to foreign invasion and conquest. Europe's extraordinary global imperialism of the eighteenth and nineteenth centuries became possible as a result.

In this connection it is worth pointing out that in most of Asia the second bronze age, like the first, gave military power to a small body of foreigners who ruled over subject populations by virtue of their control over a sovereign weapon of war—chariots supported by fortified encampments in the first case, cannon backed up by cavalry in the second. It is true that Ming China and Tokugawa Japan departed from this pattern; but when China came under Manchu rule (1644–1912), it too came to be governed by a small ruling stratum of foreign

27. Halil Inalcik, "The Socio-Political Effects of the Diffusion of Firearms in the Middle East," in V. J. Parry and M. E. Yapp, eds., *War, Technology and Society in the Middle East* (London, 1975), pp. 199–200.

28. Richard Hellie, *Enserfment and Military Change in Muscovy* (Chicago, 1971), pp. 152–68.

conquerors. Only Japan remained ethnically homogeneous. Hence it is not surprising that the Japanese could call on a sense of national emergency to justify drastic political, technological, and social reforms in the nineteenth century, whereas a pervasive distrust between rulers and ruled hampered other Asian regimes in their efforts to react effectively to the threat of European power.

That threat was not recognized in the fifteenth and sixteenth centuries by the more powerful Asian rulers, since, when Europeans first appeared off their coasts, they conformed to already familiar roles as traders and missionaries. Asian governments had long had to cope with the unruliness of merchants and ships' crews from foreign parts. Even if European ships were more formidable than those which had preceded them in Asian waters, their number was at first so small that established ways of dealing with seafaring strangers seemed to suffice.

To be sure, small trading states were immediately threatened by the naval superiority the newcomers enjoyed. Some of these endangered states appealed for help to the mightiest Moslem ruler of the age: the Ottoman sultan. Turkish authorities responded by building a fleet in the Red Sea to protect the Moslem holy places in the first instance, and secondly to operate in the Indian Ocean, as opportunity might dictate. The Turks also sent artillery experts to distant Sumatra, where they reinforced the resistance capabilities of local Moslem governments. But the Ottoman effort in the Indian Ocean met with only local and limited success because the Mediterranean style of naval warfare, of which they were masters, was becoming obsolescent thanks to the rapid development of cannon.

This calls for a little explanation. Mediterranean naval fighting, from antiquity, turned upon ramming and boarding. This required light, fast, maneuverable war galleys with large crews for rowing and for hand-to-hand combat at sea. Such a force also constituted an army on land whenever the ships were beached and their crews went ashore to besiege a fortress, raid the countryside, or merely to seek fresh water and a good night's sleep. Then, in the thirteenth century, the invention of all-weather sailing vessels injected a new element into Mediterranean fighting. The new ships, using crossbows in hitherto unprecedented numbers, relied on missiles to keep their foes at a distance. Merchant vessels needed nothing more.

Matters changed far more radically with the development of efficient cannon in the last decades of the fifteenth century. European seamen quickly grasped the idea that the guns which were dramatically revolutionizing land warfare could do the same at sea. Stoutly built all-weather sailing ships of the sort already in use in Atlantic waters could readily be converted into floating gun platforms—comparable in their concentrated firepower to the bastions with which military engineers were simultaneously beginning to protect city walls. Such floating bastions, being readily maneuverable, made missiles decisive offensively as well as defensively. The impact of a cannonade on lightly constructed ships was as catastrophic as the initial impact of the same guns on castle walls; and its effect lasted much longer, since no technical riposte to the supremacy of heavy-gunned ships at sea was discovered until twentieth-century airplanes and submarines came along.

A far-ranging change in naval relationships resulted. Mediterranean galleys, built for speed, were pitifully vulnerable to cannon if they allowed themselves to come within range. So were the merchant ships of the Indian Ocean, whose light construction suited the monsoon winds but made it impossible for local seamen to meet the Europeans on anything like even terms by fitting guns to their own vessels. The recoil of a heavy gun was, after all, almost as destructive to lightly built craft as the impact at the other end of the cannonball's trajectory.

Cannon, in the forms developed by French and Burgundian gunfounders between 1465 and 1477, were admirably suited for use aboard a stoutly built ship. The only modification required was to design a different kind of gun carriage, capable of absorbing recoil by rolling backwards across the deck, and thus, conveniently, bringing the cannon mouth inboard to allow reloading. Return to firing position required the crew to pull the gun forward with special tackle, since firing inboard risked igniting the ship. But the new guns were so heavy that they had to be carried near the waterline to avoid dangerous topheaviness. This meant they had somehow to fire through the sides of the hull itself. Cutting gunports just above the waterline, and equipping them with stout, waterproof covers that could be secured when no fighting was expected made a formidable broadside compatible with general seaworthiness. As early as 1514 a warship built for King Henry VIII of England pioneered this design. Some seventy years later, Sir John Hawkins lowered the "castles" fore and aft to improve the sailing qualities of Queen Elizabeth's warships. With these changes, the adaptation of oceangoing vessels to the artillery revolution of the fifteenth century was effectively achieved. Thereafter, European ships could count on crushing superiority in armed encounters with vessels of different design on every ocean of the earth.

Heavy guns, routinely carried by ordinary merchant ships, allowed the amazingly rapid expansion of European dominion over American (beginning 1492) and Asian (beginning 1497) waters. The easy Portuguese success off the port of Diu in India against a far more numerous Moslem fleet (1509) demonstrated decisively the superiority that their long-range (up to 200 yards) weapons gave to European seamen against enemies whose idea of a sea battle was to close, board, and fight it out with hand weapons. As long as cannon-carrying ships could keep their distance, the old-fashioned boarding tactics were utterly unable to cope with flying cannonballs, however inaccurate long-range bombardment may sometimes have been.

In the Mediterranean, the eclipse of ramming and boarding tactics lagged considerably behind the rise of the new Atlantic style of naval warfare. Until 1581, when a truce between the Ottoman Empire and Spain ended more than a century of recurrent fleet actions, galleys remained the mainstay of Mediterranean navies.[29] The fact that Spain was accustomed to launching its main naval effort against the Turks inhibited the Spaniards from accepting the logic of gunned warships as wholeheartedly as English and Dutch interlopers upon Spanish and Portuguese colonial empires were to do. When Charles V's son, King Philip II of Spain (r. 1556–98), at length lost patience and decided to invade England, the fleet he assembled for the purpose (1588) was better prepared for close-in fighting than for cannonading at a distance, even though the galleons that constituted the backbone of the Spanish fleet were stoutly built vessels, intended for Atlantic crossings, and carried an appropriate number of guns. But they were clumsy to maneuver and could not successfully return the fire of the nimbler English ships. The English, however, were unable to sink the Spanish galleons by gunfire alone. Hence, the major disaster to the Armada was due to storms encountered on the return trip around Scotland.

Nevertheless, the defeat of the Spanish Armada deserves its traditional fame, for King Philip's failure demonstrated the inadequacy of the Mediterranean style of naval warfare in oceanic waters. Neither the Spanish nor the Ottoman governments, wedded as they were to Mediterranean naval techniques and conceptions, could effectively compete on the high seas with the new, Atlantic-based sea power of Holland, England, and, ere long, of France as well. The consequent transfer of supremacy at sea to northwestern Europe had much to do with the general decline of the Mediterranean lands that became

29. Cf. John F. Guilmartin, Jr., *Gunpowder and Galleys,* for a very penetrating discussion of the rationality behind the conservatism of Mediterranean sea tactics.

manifest in the first decades of the seventeenth century. In effect, the roar of Dutch and English naval guns closed off the last avenue of escape from the economic and ecological impasse confronting Mediterranean populations, so skillfully explored for us by Fernand Braudel.[30]

The Market Asserts Control

An important feature of European sea power in the sixteenth century was its quasi-private character. In England, for instance, the Royal Navy was only beginning to differentiate itself from the merchant marine; indeed, most of the ships that exchanged shots with the Spaniards in 1588 were merchantmen whose ordinary pursuits smacked almost as much of raid as of trade. The same was true of the Armada itself, which numbered forty armed merchantmen and only twenty-eight specialized warships.[31]

Dutch, English, and French merchantmen had the advantages and disadvantages of an interloper when they ventured into the exclusive preserves claimed by the Spanish and Portuguese governments. They could try legal trade in any port of Europe, or go outside the law by raiding the Spanish Main, dabbling in the slave trade, or smuggling on some other coast, depending on what seemed most advantageous to the captain and owners. Year after year suitably armed vessels could expect to pay their way by returning to their home port with a mix of booty and trade goods, varying with the opportunities the ship encountered in the course of its voyage.

It was a dangerous business, no doubt, in which command of superior force at the moment of contact often made the difference between success and failure. Robbers always risked being robbed by someone stronger; and ready resort to armed force involved danger to life and limb analogous to what soldiers faced on land. The investors back home, who made each voyage possible by buying shares with which the costs of fitting out the ship and hiring the crew were met, also faced high risks, since many ships never returned and others came back with little to show for the effort expended. But against such failures must be set the occasional spectacular windfall, like the fortune paid out by Sir Francis Drake after his first voyage around the world (1577–80).[32]

30. Fernand Braudel, *The Mediterranean and the Mediterranean World in the Age of Phillip II,* 2 vols. (New York, 1972, 1973).

31. Garret Mattingly, *The Defeat of the Spanish Armada* (London, 1959), pp. 215–16.

32. Investors received a dividend of 4,700 percent, according to ibid., p. 87.

Even parsimonious governments like those of Manuel of Portugal (1495–1521) and Elizabeth of England (1558–1603), found reason to encourage this kind of voyaging. Both of these monarchs personally invested in overseas ventures, thereby lending the weight of royal authority to such enterprises, yet without committing the government to meeting their costs. The Portuguese king was the more ambitious, seeking to monopolize for his personal account all of the profits of the spice trade. But to do so he had to enter into partnership with Genoese bankers, who were the only people able to supply the necessary amount of ready cash for equipping the king's ships. Interest on his debts on the one hand, and peculation by his agents on the other, cut into Manuel's profit very heavily. Consequently, the Portuguese king found it hard to cash in personally, although others around him were notably successful in doing so.

Elizabeth of England was more modest. She never aspired to monopolize the overseas enterprise of her kingdom and chose which voyages to invest in from a mix of pecuniary and political considerations. She was shrewd on both counts, and profited handsomely from her investments.[33]

The Dutch case was different, inasmuch as public authority in Holland and Zeeland after about 1570 came to be wielded by merchant oligarchs among whom private and public business calculations were more intimately mingled and less tinged by considerations of prestige and prowess than was the case in countries where a royal court existed. The Spanish regime stood at an opposite extreme, for in King Philip's realms state enterprise played an ever larger role in mercantile as well as in military undertakings. This was because English, Dutch, and French privateers captured so much Spanish and Portuguese shipping between 1568 and 1603 that they almost drove Iberian private merchantmen from the seas. State-owned galleons only partially filled the gap.[34] Yet the Spanish state was only able to outfit its ships and soldiers by virtue of loans made by bankers and private speculators, many of them foreigners.

Thus, despite differences of degree, in every instance European ventures on the oceans were sustained by a combination of public, quasi-public, and relentlessly private enterprise. The resulting mix

33. An Admiralty Court judge in 1590 wrote: "Her Majesty hath gotten and saved by these reprisals since they began [five years previously in 1585] above 200,000 pounds." Kenneth R. Andrews, *Elizabethan Privateering, 1585–1603* (Cambridge, 1964), p. 22. Since Elizabeth's annual income amounted to about £300,000, this was no trivial increment.

34. Other factors, especially tax rates and timber costs, also worked against private Iberian maritime enterprise. Cf. Andrews, *Elizabethan Privateering.*

responded sensitively to new economic opportunities. Each voyage was a new proposition, requiring new decisions by everyone concerned. Investors who subscribed to successive voyages had frequent opportunities to shy away from unprofitable undertakings and could redeploy their resources anytime they saw a better chance to reap a profit.

As long as European overseas enterprises were managed in this fashion, armed force on the seas was made to pay for itself by a relatively close conformity to the dictates of the capital market. Effort and energy expended by individual captains and their crews acted like the molecules of an expanding gas, probing everywhere the limits of profitable transactions. And whenever a captain returned with unusually handsome profits, other ships soon followed.

For this reason, the Portuguese intrusion into the Indian Ocean in 1497 was not an evanescent epiphenomenon of world history, as the much larger Chinese naval expeditions to the same waters earlier in the century had turned out to be. Instead, an unceasing succession of European ships visited Asian shores, seizing whatever opportunities for trade and plunder came their way.

As European ships gradually became more numerous, their capacity to affect Asian economic and political life increased until, eventually, even the greatest land empires of Asia were unable to resist European power. This extraordinary shift took three centuries to reach its climax, by which time the Europeans' mix of market and military enterprise had undergone considerable modification. But until the nineteenth century, sea trade and privateering remained intimately connected; and even after the development of regular navies in the second half of the seventeenth century, prize money awarded for the capture of enemy vessels remained an important part of the income naval officers and crews could look forward to.

On land, the mingling of mercenary and military motives never worked as smoothly as on the sea. Noblemen, disdainful of pecuniary calculations in principle if not always in practice, played the leading role in European armies. Their ideals of prowess and personal honor were fundamentally incompatible with the financial, logistical, and routine administrative aspects of military management. On the sea, prowess was firmly subordinated to finance because before a ship sailed it had to be fitted out with a rather complicated assortment of supplies which could only be gathered together by payments of money. On land, the expenses armies incurred were no less real, but supply was not crisply divided into the costs of equipping separate units for distinct enterprises. As a result, financial limits were diffuse and acted only clumsily to limit the size of armies and military expenditure in general.

Part of the difficulty was that the men who made decisions about raising armies and planning campaigns were utterly out of sympathy with pecuniary calculation. War was an affair of honor, prestige, heroic self-assertion. To regulate it according to the grubby selfishness of bankers and moneylenders seemed fundamentally wrong to the majority of rulers and their ministers. On the other hand, the persons who lent money to sovereigns had little to say in military administration. How the king chose to use the money he borrowed was not supposed to concern the lender. Hence no one routinely calculated the balance between costs of military enterprises and likely returns, whereas for shipping ventures overseas the investors in each voyage measured their costs against prospective returns as shrewdly as they knew how.

By giving away valuable rights—most commonly the right to collect future taxes—rulers could borrow enough money to equip a larger army than their tax revenues could support on a continuing basis. In the absence of adequate tax support, such forces had to supplement pay by resorting to plunder, i.e., by living directly off the country in which operations were taking place, instead of spreading costs more equably through taxation. But rulers who broke their promises to pay their soldiers could not expect dependable obedience, especially in wars fought far from the seat of government.

An obvious solution was for rulers to increase their tax income; and in the first decades of the gunpowder revolution, successful monarchs did so with conspicuous success.[35] But once local rivals had been brought low and their income diverted in whole or in part to the coffers of the central government, further increases in taxation were difficult to impose. This was because until after the middle of the seventeenth century, even in the best-governed states of western Europe, subjects retained the option of armed revolt against royal tax collectors and could expect to prevail if enough of their fellows felt the same way.

Royal armies could of course be used to constrain reluctant taxpayers. That, after all, was how the Dutch wars (1568–1609) began.

---

35. Richard Bean, "War and the Birth of the Nation State," *Journal of Economic History* 33 (1973): 217, calculated that central government tax revenues in western Europe doubled in real, per capita terms between 1450 and 1500, but grew more slowly thereafter.

But such measures might severely diminish the taxpaying capacity of the population, as the wars in the Low Countries also illustrated. Thus, for example, the mutinous Spanish soldiers who sacked Antwerp in 1576 attacked the richest city in northern Europe when Philip II's bankruptcy made it clear that they would not receive the back pay the king owed them. The city never fully recovered from the "Spanish Fury," largely because the metropolitan financial and commercial role Antwerp had filled since the fifteenth century passed to Amsterdam in the rebel-held portion of the Netherlands.

This rapid relocation of financial activity resulted from the actions of innumerable private individuals who decided that their goods and money would be safer in Holland, where burghers were in political control, than in Spanish-ruled Antwerp. Private decisions of this sort meant that capital could migrate very rapidly to places where protection costs were judged to be at a minimum. Capitalists who failed to get away from heavily taxed places soon saw their resources wither to insignificance. This was the Fuggers' fate; the fortunes of that house never recovered from Philip II's bankruptcy of 1576, any more than Antwerp did. Other successful entrepreneurs (or their sons) were attracted to the display and extravagance of a nobler way of life, and either withdrew entirely from commerce or let their business affairs languish from neglect. Only in the atmosphere of a society molded around the activities of wheelers and dealers in the marketplace could the accumulation of capital and the maximization of pecuniary profit continue to flourish, year in and year out. A degree of political autonomy to assure effective insulation from confiscatory taxation was essential for the survival of such communities, even when, as in the case of London, they were mere enclaves in a larger political fabric.[36]

On the other hand, rulers and ruled had a common interest in substituting regular taxation for irregular plundering. This common interest allowed rulers to increase tax assessments in all important European states little by little, though governmental income continued to lag systematically behind military and other costs. Periodic bankruptcies resulted when rulers stopped payment on their debts, thereby precipitating a financial crisis which lasted until some settlement between creditors and the insolvent ruler could be negotiated.

36. Cf. Richard Ehrenberg, *Capital and Finance in the Age of the Renaissance* (London, n.d.); Frank J. Smoler, "Resiliency of Enterprise: Economic Crisis and Recovery in the Spanish Netherlands in the early 17th century," in Carter, *From Renaissance to Counter-Reformation,* pp. 247–68; Geoffrey Parker, "War and Economic Change: The Economic Costs of the Dutch Revolt," in Winter, *War and Economic Development,* pp. 49–71.

Thus financial limits hampered early modern European governments and sporadically paralyzed their actions for brief periods of time, without, however, effectively controlling day-by-day policy and administration, especially when it came to military affairs. Military administration proceeded convulsively—recklessly overreaching available resources, then collapsing in whole or in part, only to resume the process a few months or years later.

This was also well illustrated by the Dutch wars. In 1576, the so-called Pacification of Ghent prescribed the withdrawal of all Spanish soldiers from the Netherlands as part of the political-financial settlement Philip II had to make after his bankruptcy. Spanish forces, accordingly, disappeared from the Netherlands for most of the year 1577; and war did not begin anew on a full scale until 1583, when truce with the Turks and the successful annexation of Portugal (1680–81) made Philip believe that he now had the resources to win decisive victory in the north.[37]

At the tactical unit level, however, army administration, from the time of the Hundred Years War to the mid-seventeenth century, closely resembled the pattern of maritime commerce. A captain, often a man of local importance or military experience, was commissioned by some higher authority to recruit a company of soldiers from a loosely defined district. Such captains were semi-independent entrepreneurs, just like any other kind of government contractor. A newly commissioned captain might, for example, receive a sum of money to pay out to his recruits on enlistment; on the other hand he might have to advance recruitment bonuses from his own pocket in hope of future reimbursement. The captain was also responsible for making sure that his soldiers secured appropriate arms and armor, either by individual purchase or by buying items needed on his own account and distributing them to his soldiers either as free issue or against future stoppages of pay.

Maintenance costs were managed in the same way, with the difference that governments commonly found it easier to withhold back pay from soldiers who were already enlisted. Old soldiers responded, of course, by living off the country in which they found themselves. Sometimes their commanders organized pillage by assessing contributions upon anyone within reach. In extremity, when income from even these irregular sources fell short, the soldiers mutinied. Mutinies achieved a conventional definition in the Italian wars during the 1520s

37. Cf. Geoffrey Parker, *The Army of Flanders and the Spanish Road, 1567–1659* (Cambridge, 1972), pp. 336–41.

and became firmly institutionalized among the Spanish armies that fought in the Dutch wars (1567–1609). Sixteenth-century mutinies resembled industrial strikes of a later age and proved to be an effectual way of bringing pressure to bear on the ever impecunious Spanish court because the authorities could bring mutiny to an end only by paying up. "Loyal" troops simply would not attack their mutinous fellows; and since nearly every unit in the field had pay owing, it was dangerous even to try to coerce an unruly unit by bringing others against it.[38]

Troop training and command in the field also rested in the captain's hands. He appointed subordinate officers at his pleasure and was expected to supervise personally the apportionment of pay to his soldiers, if and when it was forthcoming from higher headquarters. Between paydays, he might advance sums of money to individual soldiers from his own pocket for purchase of necessities and collect his loans later when a payday made recovery of such debts feasible. All this much resembled the relation between captain and crew on shipboard.

The difference between armed enterprise by land and by sea was therefore one of degree. Eventually the limits of the capital market made themselves felt in land enterprise too. But a king could constrain bankers to give him loans they did not want to make—at least for a while; and the argument that one more campaigning season would bring victory and permit tax income to overtake emergency military expenditure was often persuasive—in the short run. But deficit financing had limits, as we have seen, and royal bankruptcies recurrently brought military spending back within fiscal limits.

The hope that an army might somehow manage to pay for itself by bringing new taxpayers under the victor's jurisdiction nearly always failed. European states were too evenly matched for easy conquests to bring in such windfalls. Only occasionally, and on the periphery, where European armed establishments encountered less militarily sophisticated societies, was the exercise of force at all likely to become a paying proposition. The Russians in Siberia, thanks to furs, and the Spaniards in the Americas, thanks to silver, were the two empire builders to profit conspicuously from their frontier position in the sixteenth and seventeenth centuries.

The self-supporting character of European seafaring was, in consid-

38. On mutiny in the Spanish army see the very enlightening discussion by Geoffrey Parker, "Mutiny in the Spanish Army of Flanders," *Past and Present* 58 (1973): 38–52; and his *Army of Flanders,* chap. 7. Parker counts forty-six separate mutinies by troops in the Spanish service between 1572 and 1607.

erable part, an example of pay-off resulting from collision between superior armed force and less well equipped rivals. To the land empires of Siberia and the Americas should therefore be added a sea empire of the Asian coastline, initially dominated by Portuguese and later by Dutch and English ships. It was thus not merely the financial organization of marine enterprise but also its "frontier" character that made it self-supporting. Closer to the center of European society, armed enterprise by one sovereign was sure to provoke a counter-effort by rivals; and only rarely could a ruler conquer territories from which important tax income could be garnered.

The success of the Spanish government in fashioning a vast empire in the Americas and its failure to maintain control over the Netherlands illustrate these facts very clearly. Spanish military effort in the New World paid off handsomely. Indeed it was the swelling flow of New World silver after the 1550s that made Philip think he could conduct war both in the Mediterranean against the Turks and in the north against the Dutch. Moreover, Spain's earlier experience of empire building in Europe had not been discouraging. The Spanish soldiers who conquered Naples and Milan between 1520 and 1525 and consolidated Hapsburg dominion over Italy in the following years may have come close to making war pay for itself. Long before the Spaniards appeared on the scene, the kingdom of Naples and the duchy of Milan had both developed a tax system capable of sustaining relatively large armed forces on a permanent basis. By simply substituting Spanish personnel for the Italian *condottieri* who had previously drawn pay for defending these states, the costs of empire in Europe could be met without putting much extra strain on Castilian taxpayers. This ceased to be true after 1568, when the major theater of war shifted northward to the Netherlands.

The reason for this economic reversal was largely technological. The spread of the *trace italienne* meant that the size of the Spanish army had to be increased very sharply to conduct a war of sieges. Even when victorious, the Spaniards had to build or restore fortifications in captured localities and then garrison them. Each siege, along with each fortified and garrisoned strongpoint, required gunpowder and shot in ever expanding quantities. Simultaneously, the infusion of American silver into the European economy radically raised prices for all commodities. Small wonder, therefore, that even though he tripled Castile's taxes between 1556 and 1577, Philip II had to repudiate his debts on four separate occasions (1557, 1560, 1575, 1596) and never managed to pay his soldiers on time.

A few figures will clarify the escalation of Spanish military expenditures (in millions of ducats per annum):

Before 1556	less than 2
1560s	4.5
1570s	8
1590s	13

and obligations (arrears of pay to men in service):[39]

1559	1.04
1575	2.17
1607	4.76

Philip II did not make such heroic expenditures in vain. The number of soldiers at his command in the 1550s, when he took over from his father, Charles V, has been calculated at about 150,000 men; by the 1590s at the end of his reign their number had increased to 200,000; and, when Spanish military effort reached its crest in the 1630s the king's soldiers numbered about 300,000 men.[40]

To help carry the growing burden of military expenditure, Philip II tried to apply to his vast realm the patterns of fiscal administration that had served Italian cities so well. Thus, for example, the funded debt that permitted Venetians to pay for their wars and other extraordinary public expenditures by selling bonds (often to foreigners) was duplicated in Spain. But the fiscal-mindedness that constrained Venetian magistrates to pay interest punctually on the Republic's outstanding debts, century after century, was absent from the top level of Spanish (and most other) royal governments. The result was repeated bankruptcy which raised the cost of subsequent loans to unbearable heights. By 1600 no less than 40 percent of the Spanish government's income was earmarked for the service of old debts.[41]

Taxation of Castilian peasants had reached a point at which further

39. These figures all come from the admirable book by I. A. A. Thompson, *War and Government in Hapsburg Spain, 1550–1620* (London, 1976), pp. 71, 73, 103. For year-by-year figures on the number of soldiers in Spanish service (most of them not Spaniards) in the Netherlands, 1567–1665, see Geoffrey Parker's equally admirable *Army of Flanders,* p. 28. Variations from year to year were very great, depending on what operations were planned and what money was available; but after the initial mobilization against the rebels in 1572, the Spanish forces in Flanders usually exceeded 50,000 men.

40. These figures come from Geoffrey Parker, "The 'Military Revolution' 1550–1660—a Myth?" *Journal of Modern History* 48 (1976): 206. Europe's second army, the French, was only one-third as large as the Spanish in the 1550s.

41. Thompson, *War and Government in Hapsburg Spain,* p. 72.

increases were practically impossible. Indeed, existing burdens provoked economic retrogression. Diminished royal income meant smaller and weaker armies. After the mid-seventeenth century, Spain fell behind France, where Louis XIV's intendants, presiding over a much larger population, were able to find means to pay for an army that soon outstripped anything Spanish resources could support.[42]

Eventually, therefore, fiscal limitations asserted their sovereign power over the regal majesty of even the greatest king of Europe. One may well ask why? Why should the command and will of Philip II and his ministers not have prevailed over the will of the bankers who made him loans? In Asian lands, where monarchs ruled over territories less extensive than those that obeyed Philip II's commands, no cobweb of credit spun by calculating bankers restrained the will of the rulers or limited their military initiatives. The reason was that in Asia, when goods and services were needed to put an army in the field, the rulers' commands sufficed to mobilize whatever was, or could be, mobilized. If adequate supplies were not forthcoming from taxes and free market sale to the government, officials felt free to seize the goods and money of the subject populations—insofar as agents of public authority could lay hands on such resources and convert them into forms useful for military enterprise or any other public undertaking that was in view.

Often, as we saw in the case of China, a slightly more subtle approach was preferred. By setting a "fair price" below that at which possessors of the goods in question were willing to sell, a kind of justice could be done all round—or so public authorities and the great majority of the subject population felt. An administered "just price" effectively trimmed back the "unjust" gains unscrupulous merchants and engrossers gathered into their hands. Government actions thereby effectually inhibited development of large-scale private financial and commercial activity. But under such regimes, an artisan level

---

42. According to Parker, "The 'Military Revolution' 1550–1660," p. 206, the numbers of men in the Spanish and French armies varied as follows:

	Spanish	French
1630s	300,000	150,000
1650s	100,000	100,000
1670s	70,000	120,000
1700s	50,000	400,000

Other armies lagged far behind in size even when technically abreast of French and Spanish. The Dutch army, for example, numbered only about 50,000 in the 1630s and 100,000 in the 1700s. In the north, the Swedes counted 45,000 in the 1630s, 100,000 in the 1700s; Russia, 35,000 in the 1630s, 170,000 in the 1700s. Ibid. Parker's figure for the French army in the first decade of the eighteenth century is high, however. Other authorities give Louis XIV only 300,000 men in the War of the Spanish Succession. See below, chap. 4.

of production and small-scale trading still could flourish, since confiscatory purchase or outright seizure of goods from large numbers of small people was administratively impracticable.

Rough-and-ready command mobilization of this sort had its price, of course. By making large-scale private accumulation of capital difficult and precarious, the pace of economic development and technological innovation was restricted to things that small-scale artisans could undertake. The only way larger enterprises could be sustained was by public management; and officials nearly always preferred familiar and routine methods in order to minimize risk of failure. As we have seen, in military technology after about 1500, Asian officials clung fast to gigantesque siege cannon, the sovereign weapon against town and castle walls. No one had the means or the motive for developing gunpowder weaponry in new directions; and only the Japanese redesigned their fortifications to diminish the effect of gunfire.[43] Asian regimes accordingly fell behind European military and technological development in a way that cost them dearly in the long run.

Similar conservatism or inattention prevailed in such fields as mining and shipbuilding, where European superiority to other civilizations had become apparent from the fourteenth century. This reflected the fact that private capital financed these relatively large-scale activities in Europe, and did so with the profit motive very much to the fore. Consequently, any technical change that cut costs or increased returns was eagerly sought after and rapidly propagated throughout the European world, in striking contrast to the conservatism and indifference of Asian regimes. In other fields of economic production, the contrast between European and Asian institutional patterns did not lead to equally drastic divergence until the eighteenth century, when linkage of inanimate power to industrial processes took on a new impetus in Europe and eventually left artisan and hand methods of production far behind. Nevertheless, the fundamental difference between western Europe and the rest of the civilized world

43. Cf. photos in Kiyoshi Hirai, *Feudal Architecture in Japan* (New York and Tokyo, 1973). Protection against small-arms fire was, however, more important for the Japanese than protection against cannon. This was because Japanese armies lacked logistical resources for conducting prolonged sieges where cannon would have been decisive; and the national economy, correspondingly, failed to develop a technical base for cannon manufacture on anything approaching the European scale. Samurai ideals, emphasizing hand-to-hand combat, may have inhibited efforts to develop artillery; fuel shortages were also probably important. I owe these suggestions to private correspondence with John F. Guilmartin, Jr.

had manifested itself clearly and unmistakably from the fourteenth century onward, thanks to the absence of effective inhibitions against the private accumulation of relatively large amounts of capital in Europe.

Why did not command mobilization also prevail in Europe? Certainly Philip II and his ministers would have felt far more comfortable if it had. They knew how to tax and how to confiscate just as effectively as Chinese and Islamic officials did. The fate of Castile, where restraints on royal taxation were minimal within the Spanish empire, demonstrated their ability in this direction. But alas for the command principle! Much of what Philip needed for his armies was not available within peninsular Spain. His repeated efforts to establish factories producing cannon and other needed commodities always failed to flourish. Perversely, from a Spanish official point of view, it was exactly in places where the king's will was not sovereign that economic activity and arms production concentrated. Private enterprise systematically located large-scale undertakings where taxes were low and prices could be freely adjusted to what the market would bear. Thus, for example, the bishopric of Liège, adjacent to the Spanish Netherlands but not under Spanish rule, became the major seat of armaments production for the Dutch wars, supplying a large proportion of the material needed by both the Spanish and the Dutch armies.[44]

Liège became an important armament center only after 1492 when the bishopric disarmed and officially proclaimed itself neutral. Subsequent military occupations, of which there were several, had the immediate effect of disrupting gun manufacture. Hence, if rulers wished to avail themselves of the products of Liège gunmakers' skills—which rapidly became the best and cheapest of Europe and the world—they had to withdraw their soldiers and let the market again come freely into play. Only so could the flow of goods and services required to produce thousands of guns a year resume its course. Only when the artisans and capitalists of Liège and other arms centers did not have to part with their goods at prices decreed by Spanish or any other political authority, could rulers get what they wanted in the quantities to which they had become accustomed. Their very weakness thus allowed the Liègeois to set their own prices. Even the mightiest rulers had to pay what was asked, or do without. Nor was Liège unique.

44. Cf. Jean Lejeune, *La formation du capitalism moderne dans la principauté de Liège au XVI siècle* (Liège, 1939), p. 181; Claude Gaier, *Four Centuries of Liège Gunmaking* (London, 1977), pp. 29–31.

Dozens of other refuges for entrepreneurs were scattered across the face of Europe, thanks to its peculiarly fragmented political geography.

Under these circumstances, command simply could not prevail against the market as a way to marshal men and resources. As long as no single political command structure could reach out to every corner of Latin Christendom, and so acquire the capability of nipping capitalist accumulation in the bud, the sovereignty of the market over even the greatest ruler of the age remained an ultimate reality, however muffled its actual exercise might be by the fact that states continued to be managed on a day-to-day basis by persons who utterly rejected and decried their involvement with moneylenders' calculations of profit and loss.

Philip II would have found it hard to believe, but in the long run European states actually were strengthened by their involvement in the fiscal web spun by international bankers and suppliers. First of all, the tax base grew because the scale of production in Europe as a whole tended to increase as private firms accumulated resources for large-scale trade and industrial activity. Regional specialization developed economies of scale running across political boundaries. Technological advance was hastened by the coexistence of multiple suppliers and multiple purchasers. Loans from private sources to finance extraordinary governmental expenditure, of the kind that supported all of Philip II's military campaigns, also enhanced the power of the state over men and material, and this despite the fact that paying off old debts was difficult, indeed impossible.

Paradoxically, the mix of managerial opposites—kings and ministers struggling against and collaborating with bankers and merchant suppliers—hurried along an ever deepening penetration of market relationships into European society. Each increase in taxation brought additional segments of Europe's wealth into circulation, for states spent all they received. Hence subsistence and strictly local economic patterns were continually eroded by a combination of compulsion (taxes) and attraction (cheaper or better goods, enlarged private income). War and the heavy costs of waging it accelerated the entire process. Mobilization of men and materials through the market inched its way ahead, and by degrees proved capable of integrating human effort more efficiently than command had ever been able to do.

Perhaps the fundamental contrast between European experience in the early modern centuries and that of Asia might be expressed by saying that in Asia command mobilization reinforced and was in turn sustained by the preservation of primary patterns of human interaction. Obedience, after all, is always best rendered to persons already known to the follower by long familiarity. Status relationships, traditional social structures, local hierarchies of deference and precedence; all these fitted as subordinate elements within the political command structure. Despite personal rivalries of the most diverse sort among local magnates, the principle that social behavior should conform to hierarchically patterned roles undergirded and sustained the entire system. This meant, among other things, that only a tiny fraction of the entire population could be mobilized for military action. But Asian rulers acquiesced readily enough since any more general mobilization would have put arms in the hands of persons and classes who could then be expected to challenge existing social hierarchies and patterns of government.

Market relationships, on the contrary, tended to dissolve and weaken traditional, local, and primary patterns of human interaction. Response to market incentives allowed strangers to cooperate across long distances, often without realizing it. Mobilization of a larger quantity of goods and a greater number of men became possible with the kinds of economic specialization and technological elaboration that market relationships could sustain. Power and wealth, in short, could be enhanced by reliance on market incentives to human action, however much rulers and the majority of their subjects may have deplored the greed and immorality that was thus let loose upon the world.

Breakdown of established patterns of conduct always appears deplorable to a majority of those who witness it. The European public, as much as European rulers of the early modern centuries, disliked and distrusted the handful of monied men who enriched themselves by constraining rulers and their subjects to conform to the dictates of the market. But rulers and subjects found there was little they could do about it. In Asia similar sentiments were effective because the market for goods and services remained relatively weak, being confined to an artisan level. In Europe, once a few self-governing cities in Italy and the Low Countries had demonstrated the enhanced wealth and power that a more enthusiastic unleashing of market incentives could create, market articulation of human effort gained the upper hand. By the sixteenth century, even the mightiest European command structures became dependent on an international money and credit market for organizing military and other major undertakings. Philip II's hapless financial record is proof of this proposition. As a result, the continued expansion of market relationships and their gradual penetration into remoter regions and further down the social scale became assured for several centuries to come. And during those same centuries their reluctant readiness to tolerate private pursuit of profit allowed western Europeans to dominate the rest of the earth.

Another way to describe these transactions is to speak of the rise of capitalism and the emergence of the bourgeoisie as a ruling class within European society. This has been a central concern among historians of early modern Europe ever since Marxism began to seep into intellectual and academic circles. But Marxists unfortunately share the nineteenth-century Eurocentric blinkers that inevitably limited Karl Marx's vision of human history. Among Europeans of his age, the supremacy of the market and of the pecuniary nexus seemed assured for all time—past, present, and future. From the perspective of the late twentieth century this no longer seems a self-evident truth, and historians may therefore soon become sensitive to the military-technological and political aspects of the rise of European capitalism.

We can gain a juster perspective on the remarkable European venture toward the sovereignty of the market in military as in other forms of management by recognizing it as an eccentric departure from the human norm of command behavior—the sort of behavior that dominated ancient times and has reasserted itself with remarkable power since the 1880s. The rest of this book will undertake just such a readjustment of inherited viewpoints and valuations by attempting to bridge the gap that separates military from economic history and historiography.

4

Advances in Europe's Art of War,
1600-1750

The effectiveness of commercialized war as developed in Mediterranean Europe between 1300 and 1600 was attested by the sporadic spread of what may appropriately be dubbed the "military-commercial complex" to new ground thereafter. A parallel change was the bureaucratization of military administration. By slow degrees tax collection for the support of standing armed forces began to conform to bureaucratic regularity over wider and wider areas of the European continent. The internal administration of armies and navies moved in the same direction. Then, in the seventeenth century, the Dutch pioneered important improvements in military administration and routine. In particular, they discovered that long hours of repeated drill made armies more efficient in battle. Drill also imparted a remarkable esprit de corps to the rank and file, even when the soldiers were recruited from the lowest ranks of society.

A well-drilled army, responding to a clear chain of command that reached down to every corporal and squad from a monarch claiming to rule by divine right, constituted a more obedient and efficient instrument of policy than had ever been seen on earth before. Such armies could and did establish a superior level of public peace within all the principal European states. This allowed agriculture, commerce, and industry to flourish, and, in turn, enhanced the taxable wealth that kept the armed forces in being. A self-sustaining feedback loop thus arose that raised Europe's power and wealth above levels other civilizations had attained. Relatively easy expansion at the expense of less well organized and disciplined armed establishments became assured, with the result that Europe's world-girdling imperial career extended rapidly to new areas of the globe.

Geographical Spread

As we saw in chapter 3, commercial-bureaucratic management of armed force originated in Italy and then spread to the Low Countries, France, and Spain. In the course of the seventeenth century this modern organization of war took root in the Germanies and, with interesting variations, also in Sweden, England, and even in Russia.

The beginnings of the commercialization of military enterprise in Germany went back to the fourteenth century or before, when Italian cities hired large numbers of Swiss mountaineers and other Germans to fight their wars for them. Experience of war in Italy, in turn, underlay the successful assertion of Swiss independence in the fourteenth century. By defeating a force of German knights at Sempach (1387) Swiss halberdiers and pikemen established their reputation as formidable infantry fighters; in the next century they became the wonder of all Europe by defeating Charles the Bold's technologically superior force no less than three times in 1476 and 1477. Shortly thereafter, Swiss pikemen entered French service (1479) as mercenary troops and for a brief period promised to give the French (whose native cavalry and artillery was already the best in Europe) a clear superiority over all rivals.[1]

Swiss alignment with the French monarchy induced the Hapsburgs to try to raise German foot soldiers to match the Swiss. Companies of *Landesknechten,* equipped like the Swiss but commanded by noblemen (who also fought on foot), accordingly came into existence, beginning on a significant scale in the 1490s. But since Maximilian I (emperor 1493–1519) and other German rulers were chronically impecunious, companies of *Landesknechten* could look forward to only sporadic employment. Discharge created a crisis for the soldiers and for the community in which they happened to be located at the time. The situation was quite like that which had prevailed in Italy in the early fourteenth century, before the Italian city-states learned how to weave effective political and fiscal restraints around professionalized armed forces.[2]

1. As we have already seen, technologically innovative Spanish soldiers swiftly overthrew the incipient French hegemony by relying on handguns and developing new tactics to take advantage of them. The decisive disaster to the Swiss occurred at the hands of their usual allies, the French, in the Battle of Marignano (1515), when suitably emplaced artillery fired upon the massed pikemen with devastating effect. Cf. Charles Oman, *A History of the Art of War in the Middle Ages* (London, 1898), 2:279. If Charles the Bold had been able to bring his artillery to bear against the Swiss in 1476–77, the history of Europe might have taken a very different turn.

2. On *Landesknechten* see Eugen von Frauenholz, *Das Heereswesen in die Zeit des freien*

The German situation differed from the earlier Italian experience in one important respect. Beginning in 1517, German politics came to be colored by envenomed religious controversy. Lutherans, Catholics, and various radical sects were soon challenged also by Calvinism. Each religion commanded passionate loyalties of diverse social groups, so that secular conflicts commonly found expression in theological debates. Italy, too, had experienced acute social conflicts two centuries earlier; and the lower classes regularly had met defeat wherever and whenever military force came to be professionalized and put on a permanent basis. In Germany a similar development occurred, though in its initial stages the theological diversity of the Reformation sanctified and thereby probably intensified class collisions.

At any rate, something like stability came to the Germanies only after a century and a half of widespread violence, climaxing in the brutalities of the Thirty Years War (1618–48). By the time it ended, Germany and Bohemia had been caught up with a vengeance in the European military-commercial complex; and the lower classes, along with German city-states, had been firmly subordinated to princely power based on control over standing, professional armies. As bureaucratization spread and religious fanaticism dissipated, the German lands became religiously divided according to the principle *cuius regio, eius religio.*

At the commencement of this painful process, local, ecclesiastical, princely and imperial jurisdictions overlapped in an exceedingly confused fashion. The political complexity was like that which had existed in Italy before city-states asserted their territorial sovereignty by hiring armies and garrisoning border strongpoints. In the Germanies, not cities but princely courts consolidated effective sovereignty at the expense of more local rivals as well as of pope and emperor. Mercenary armies provided them with the sinews of sovereignty, just as had happened earlier in Italy. But the atmosphere of a German princeling's court was poles apart from that of an Italian city of the renaissance era. So despite all the parallels that can be drawn between Italy from 1300 to 1500 and Germany from 1450 to 1650, the upshot of the process in the two countries was profoundly divergent.

At the beginning of this evolution the French king's recent success in centralizing the administration of his kingdom offered the German emperors a most enticing model. What a French king had done to

---

Söldnertums, 2 vols. (Munich, 1936, 1937); Fritz Redlich, *The German Military Enterpriser and His Work Force,* 2 vols. (Wiesbaden, 1964); Carl Hans Hermann, *Deutsche Militärgeschichte: Eine Einführung* (Frankfurt, 1966), pp. 58 ff.

expel the English from the land (1453), a German emperor could also attempt, by leading a crusade either against the Turks or, alternatively, against heretics within the Germanies.

But crusading against the Turks ran into what proved to be insuperable geographic obstacles. Since 1526 Hungary and Croatia had become disputed borderlands between the Ottoman and Hapsburg empires. Raiding and counter-raiding devastated the landscape, making maintenance of large field armies in the border region exceedingly difficult for either of the protagonists. As a result, building and then garrisoning a few cannon-proof forts was all the Hapsburg authorities were able to accomplish.

The alternative of turning imperial forces against German princes who had departed from the Catholic fold became more attractive as the vigor of a reformed Catholicism took hold north of the Alps. Accordingly, when Ferdinand II ascended the imperial throne in 1619, he precipitated a general war by deciding to bring Bohemia (where a Calvinist king had been elected in 1618) back to Catholic and Hapsburg obedience. His initial successes provoked a series of interventions from outside: Danish, Swedish, and eventually French. On the Catholic side, the Spaniards renewed their war with the Dutch in 1621 and with France in 1622 and sought to use their imperial position in Italy to connect all the different fronts of the war into a single, coherent Catholic counteroffensive.

The eventual outcome was stalemate in the Germanies and a peace of exhaustion (Westphalia, 1648). Before that result was attained, however, some new refinements in the art of war achieved definition; and the Germanies as a whole experienced the brutality of large-scale commercialized violence.

Three significant efforts at drastic reorganization for war came to the fore during the struggle. The first of these was the remarkable military entrepreneurship of Albrecht von Wallenstein. Starting as a petty nobleman of Bohemia, Wallenstein made soldiering into a vast speculative business. High risks were matched by extraordinary windfall profits, at least in the short run, for Wallenstein became proprietor of enormous estates in Bohemia (briefly also in Mecklenburg) and attained quasi-independent political power. But when he died in 1634 at the hands of assassins, all the lands and offices he had accumulated were confiscated. Nevertheless, for a decade Wallenstein bestrode the Germanies like a colossus, nominally a mere contractor serving the emperor but in fact almost a sovereign in his own right by virtue of the size of the military forces he commanded and supplied by improved taxation, outright plunder, and massive market transactions.

Wallenstein's business dealings were exceedingly complex. He bought products from his estates in Bohemia in his capacity as army commander at prices fixed by himself, for example, and organized arms production on those same estates with the help of capital scraped together by a Flemish businessman and speculator named Hans De-Witte. DeWitte's relation to Wallenstein was like Wallenstein's relation to the emperor. Each depended on his superior for the chance to engage in really big business. Yet in executing commissions and fulfilling contracts on a heroic scale, both Wallenstein and DeWitte pursued their own self-interest with flamboyant disregard of older standards of morality and propriety. What worked was all they cared about. Neither birth nor religion nor any of the traditional virtues governed their choice of associates and subordinates. Obedience and effectiveness in accomplishing assigned tasks was what Wallenstein and his financial counterpart demanded and got from those who served them. The result was an army of quite exceptional efficiency that for the most part lived off the country it operated in and exhibited no scruples in doing so. A more complete and grandiose merger of private commercial and military enterprise had never been seen before—nor since.

Other military middlemen played lesser roles in the Thirty Years War, but only Wallenstein succeeded in raising an army on his personal account that numbered over 50,000 men at its peak. He did so by commissioning lesser officers to form companies and regiments in the way reigning monarchs had long been accustomed to do. Towards the end of his career, Wallenstein toyed with the idea of using his army to coerce the emperor into dismissing a "Spanish" party that had gathered at court. The leading spirits of that faction vehemently distrusted the Bohemian adventurer, whose commercial virtuosity and religious ambiguity were utterly alien to their own aristocratic and Catholic ideals. It was they who arranged Wallenstein's assassination. The emperor endorsed the act only subsequently.

Ever since the sudden denouement of 1634, German nationalists have wondered what might have happened had Wallenstein prevailed. The logic of his position perhaps required him to imitate the usurpation that Sforza had carried through in Milan in 1450. Sforza had successfully melded the administration of his military following into that of the Milanese state and made Milan into a great power for the ensuing fifty years. Wallenstein's military command structure might perhaps have become the chrysalis of a new German state, greater even than the mighty kingdom of France that emerged from the Thirty Years War as hegemon of western Europe. But in fact, by 1634, Wallenstein was much enfeebled by chronic illness. Perhaps, too, even his bold entrepreneurial spirit quailed before the sacred aura that still clung to the person of the Holy Roman Emperor of the German Nation.

At any rate, the military-commercial empire he had constructed around himself collapsed. Lesser enterprisers divided his role in the imperial camp; and by the end of the war widespread devastation of some of the most fertile parts of Germany compelled armies to shrink to about half the size of those that had marched under Wallenstein's command at the peak of his power.[3]

The second remarkable power structure of the Thirty Years War was that created by the Swedish king, Gustav Adolf (r. 1611–32). What Bohemia had been for Wallenstein, Sweden was for him—a sort of personal property from which manpower and supplies could be channeled towards the war in Germany. Gustav Adolf did declare that his war would have to feed itself,[4] but he relied on public authority to conscript his soldiery from Swedish fields and forests and benefited from the fact that Swedish iron production began to boom in the 1620s, when Louis de Geer, a native of Liège and resident of Holland, dispatched Walloon ironworkers to Sweden to introduce newfangled blast furnaces to that remote land.[5]

De Geer did in Sweden what Wallenstein's agent, DeWitte, had done in Bohemia. Each of them operated on a grand scale to import new financial and technical methods into formerly backward parts of Europe—backward at least by comparison to the standard set by the Low Countries. But in other respects they were quite different. De Geer remained domiciled in Holland and prospered as an international financier and entrepreneur, dependent on Gustav Adolf only for legal permission to do business in Sweden. He worked within the relatively well-defined moral and legal framework of Dutch business

3. On Wallenstein see Golo Mann, *Wallenstein* (Frankfurt am Main, 1971); Francis Watson, *Wallenstein: Soldier under Saturn* (New York, 1938); G. Livet, *La Guerre de Trente Ans* (Paris, 1963); Redlich, *The German Military Enterpriser,* 1:229–336; Fritz Redlich, "Plan for the Establishment of a War Industry in the Imperial Dominion during the Thirty Years War," *Business History Review* 38 (1964): 123–26.

4. *Bellum se ipse alet* is the Latin phrase attributed to the Swedish king. Cf. Michael Roberts, *Essays in Swedish History* (Minneapolis, 1967), p. 73.

5. Eli Heckscher, "Un grand chapître de l'histoire de fer: le monopole suèdois," *Annales d'histoire économique et sociale* 4 (1932): 127–39.

practice and handed his business to his heirs, whereas DeWitte left nothing but the tangled accounts of a bankrupt speculator when he committed suicide in 1630. Likewise, Gustav Adolf was legal sovereign and king, and suffered from none of the moral-legal dubiousness that surrounded Wallenstein's entire career. As a result, the political and economic empires that De Geer and Gustav Adolf were able to create lasted for centuries, whereas Wallenstein's collapsed with his assassination.

The Swedish king also owed part of his success in battle to the fact that he enthusiastically imported the latest Dutch methods of waging war and training troops. But he added some touches of his own, derived from his early experience with Russian and Polish cavalry tactics (war with Russia until 1617, with Poland 1621–29). As a result, when he intervened in the German wars by landing in Pomerania in 1630, the Swedish king brought into action a battle-hardened army. It proved its formidability at the Battle of Breitenfeld in 1631 when the Swedes first exhibited their improved tactics.

Swedish tactical innovations aimed at more effective offensive action on the battlefield. Small field artillery pieces that could be maneuvered by hand added weight to volleyed small arms fire; and the shock effect of such massed fire was swiftly followed up by pike and cavalry charges. But Wallenstein adjusted his own tactics in imitation of the Swedes very promptly, as he demonstrated the very next year at the Battle of Lützen, where Gustav Adolf lost his life in winning a second victory over the imperial forces.

The rapidity with which one side reacted to any effective innovation from the other was convincingly illustrated by this episode. European kings and captains had clearly accepted the idea that improvements were always possible. An efficient information network utilizing printed texts as well as word of mouth, espionage, and commercial intelligence, spread data about enemy intentions and capabilities, new technologies, and new tactics across the length and breadth of western Europe. As a result, by the end of the Thirty Years War, European armies were no longer a mere collection of individually well-trained and bellicose persons, as early medieval armies had been, nor a mass of men acting in unison with plenty of brute ferocity but no effective control once battle had been joined, as had been true of the Swiss pikemen of the fifteenth century. Instead, a consciously cultivated and painstakingly perfected art of war allowed a commanding general, at least in principle, to control the actions of as many as 30,000 men in battle. Troops equipped in different ways and trained for different forms of combat were able to maneuver in the face of an enemy. By responding to the general's command they could take advantage of some unforeseen circumstance to turn a stubbornly contested field into lopsided victory. European armies, in other words, evolved very rapidly to the level of the higher animals by developing the equivalent of a central nervous system, capable of activating technologically differentiated claws and teeth.

The third notable military-political structure which emerged from the Thirty Years War was French. After the peace of Cateau-Cambrésis, ending the Italian wars (1559), France had fallen prey to prolonged civil disturbances, partly inspired by religious quarrels between Calvinists and Catholics, and partly precipitated by an uncertain dynastic succession to the throne. The fact that employment in Italy had come to an end for French fighting men also had something to do with the repeated outbreaks of domestic disorder, since unemployed and restless soldiers could be counted on to respond eagerly to any occasion for the exercise of their profession. Internal broils distracted the royal government as late as 1627–28, when Louis XIII's armies besieged and conquered the Calvinist stronghold of La Rochelle. Thereafter, French military resources were directed across the frontier, against the Hapsburg rulers of Spain and Germany. It was this French intervention in the Thirty Years War that finally frustrated the Catholic imperial effort to unite Germany and suppress heresy.

At first, French generals were inferior to the battle-experienced commanders of Spain and Germany; but by 1643, when the French defeated the Spaniards at Rocroi, the French too had achieved a level of skill in the art of war equivalent to the best in Europe. Thereupon the larger resources that the French king had at his command gave the Bourbon monarchy the capacity to eclipse any rivals, simply by putting larger and better-trained armies into the field. The political history of the second half of the seventeenth century turned on this elemental fact.

It hinged, also, on the fact that even after the Peace of Westphalia ended the war in Germany (1648), neither the Hapsburg emperor nor the French king found it wise or necessary to disband all the troops that had fought for them during the Thirty Years War. Indeed, since peace with Spain was not concluded until 1659, the French had to keep troops under arms until after that date; and in 1661 when the new king, Louis XIV, took power in person, he decided that glory and prudence alike required him to keep a standing army in perpetual readiness for war. The fact that civil disorder had broken out anew in

France between 1648 and 1653 made a strong impression on young Louis. His standing army was initially designed to assure the king's superiority over any and every challenge to his authority from within France, and only secondarily intended for foreign adventure.

Improvements in the Control of Armies

The successful suppression of the Fronde, as this final round of old-fashioned civil disorder in France was called, marked a significant turning-point in the history of European war and statecraft. Or perhaps it would be more accurate to say that it marked the time at which transalpine states finally caught up with the level of administrative management and control over armed force that had been attained in Venice and Milan two centuries earlier. The fact is that nearly every aspect of French and Austrian management of their armed establishments in the second half of the seventeenth century had been anticipated by Venice and Milan. Civilian control of supply, regular payment of the soldiers with money derived from tax revenues, along with differentiation and tactical coordination of infantry, cavalry, and artillery all were shared between fifteenth-century Italian city-states and seventeenth-century transalpine monarchies. Even the work of Louis XIV's famous minister, Michel Le Tellier, and his son, the Marquis de Louvois, secretary of state for war, in supplying the French army, regularizing its structure, and standardizing equipment, can be closely paralleled by the work of a little-known Venetian *provedditore,* Belpetro Masselini (in office 1418–55), who did the same for the troops that defended the Republic of St. Mark.[6]

One aspect of the new standing armies of northern Europe, however, was without clear parallel in earlier times, and its importance was such as to deserve rather special consideration here. For Louvois was assisted in his efforts to manage the royal army by an itinerant inspector, Lieutenant Colonel Martinet, whose name passed into the English language as a symbol of rigorous insistence on details of discipline. This, indeed, was what Martinet excelled in. Instructions from Louvois issued in 1668 required him to do no less.

> . . . you ought to order them [designated infantry officers] to be on hand every day when the guard changes, and, before it dis-

6. Cf. Louis André, *Michel Le Tellier et Louvois,* 2d ed. (Paris, 1943); Louis André, *Michel Le Tellier et l'organization de l'armée monarchique* (Montpelier, 1906). On Masselini and his administrative reforms, see Michael E. Mallett, *Mercenaries and Their Masters: Warfare in Renaissance Italy* (London, 1974), pp. 126–27.

Close Order Marching as Practiced in the Eighteenth Century

To march well and deploy large numbers of men swiftly into prescribed formations took endless practice. The diagram above, opposite page shows how a regiment, subdivided into two battalions and twelve platoons, ought to shift from line formation to column of attack; and the etching below shows the regiment ready to advance against the foe after completing the maneuver. Such drill had powerful psychological impact on soldiers subjected to it, creating sentiments of solidarity and esprit de corps in a fashion drillmasters only dimly comprehended.

Denis Diderot, *A Diderot Pictorial Encyclopedia of Trades and Industry*, edited by Charles Coulston Gillispie (New York: Dover Publications, 1959; vol. 1, pl. 67). Facsimile reproduction from original Paris edition of 1763.

---

perses, to exercise the soldiers in the manual of arms and various movements to the left and right and forward to teach them to march well in small units.[7]

Of course, Louvois' concern with marching well was not entirely new. But the history of drill in European armies before the turn of the seventeenth century is very obscure. Swiss and Spanish pikemen in their "hedgehogs" marched to the tap of drum,[8] and certainly strove to keep a tight formation in the field so as to leave no gaps for attacking cavalry to penetrate. Other infantry forces also marched in formation, as had been true in antiquity as far back as the Sumerians. But drill, day in and day out, practiced year round when on garrison duty, and occupying spare time even when on campaign and in the field, was something earlier armies had not, so far as one can tell, found either necessary or sensible. Yet insofar as Louvois and his agent, Colonel Martinet, were successful in making their will obeyed by French officers and troops, routine drill became the daily experience of soldiers coming off guard duty. One may well ask why.

The answer is that by Louvois' time two generations of European commanders had discovered that drill made soldiers both more obedient and more efficient in battle. The person principally responsible for developing modern routines of army drill was Maurice of Nassau, Prince of Orange (1567–1625), captain-general of Holland and Zeeland between 1585 and his death, and of the forces maintained by other Dutch provinces for varying periods of time. Maurice was a

---

7. Translated from Camille Rousset, *L'histoire de Louvois*, 4 vols. (Paris, 1862–64), 1:209. Garrison regulations settled down to a routine of drill exercises in the presence of an officer twice a week, with the entire garrison parading in battle formation once a month before a high-ranking officer or other important personage. André, *Michel Le Tellier*, pp. 399–401.

8. Roberts, *Essays in Swedish History*, p. 219.

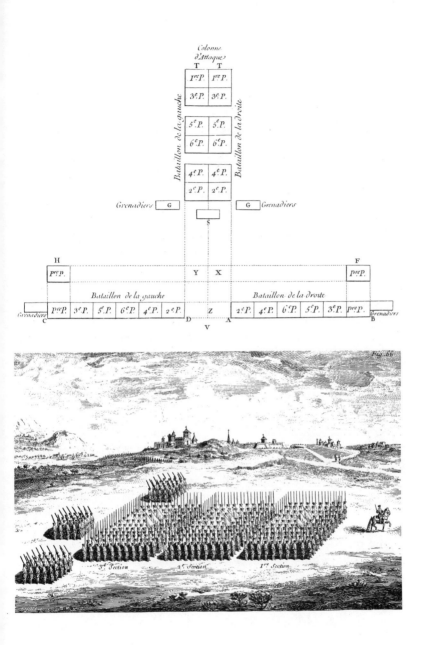

Colonne d'Attaque

T	T
1re P.	1re P.
3e P.	3e P.
5e P.	5e P.
6e P.	6e P.
4e P.	4e P.
2e P.	2e P.

Bataillon de la gauche   *Bataillon de la Droite*

Grenadiers [G]   [G] Grenadiers

S

H   F

| 1re P. | Y   X | 1re P. |

Bataillon de la gauche   *Bataillon de la droite*

Grenadiers | 1re P. | 3e P. | 5e P. | 6e P. | 4e P. | 2e P. | 2e P. | 4e P. | 6e P. | 5e P. | 3e P. | 1re P. | Grenadiers

C   D   Z   A   B

V

Fig. 66.

3e Section   2e Section   1re Section

university man, trained in mathematics and classics. Confronted by the problem of fighting the Spaniards in the Low Countries, he looked to the Roman past for models and sought to distill lessons in the art of war from the pages of Vegetius, Aelian,[9] and other classical authors.

Prince Maurice did not imitate Roman precedents slavishly; he did, however, emphasize three things that had not been common in European armies before his time. One was the spade. Roman soldiers had habitually fortified their encampments with makeshift earthen ramparts. Maurice did the same, and in particular made his soldiers dig themselves in when besieging enemy-held towns and forts. Digging had not been much emphasized by European armies before his time. To take refuge behind a wall or by burrowing in a ditch carried a taint of cowardice; and armies usually relied on conscripted laborers from the neighborhood to do most of the digging that was judged needful. For Prince Maurice's troops, however, the spade was mightier than the sword—or musket. By systematically digging ditches and erecting ramparts to defend its outer perimeter, a besieging army could protect itself against a relieving expedition while continuing to press the siege. Following this regimen, Maurice's armies suffered fewer casualties from defenders' fire, while burrowing steadily forward, closer and closer to the defended ditch and wall, until a final assault became practicable. A siege became a matter of engineering, i.e., of moving vast quantities of earth. Handling the spade became the besieging soldiers' daily occupation. Heavy work of that kind had the incidental effect of almost banishing idleness and dissipation, the usual pastime of earlier armies when besieging a strongpoint. Prince Maurice, in fact, earnestly disapproved of idleness; when his soldiers were not digging, they were kept busy drilling instead.

The development of systematic drill was the second and by far the most important innovation Maurice introduced on the basis of Roman precedents. He compelled his soldiers to practice the motions required to load and fire their matchlocks; pikemen likewise had to practice the positions in which pikes should be held when marching and in battle. This kind of instruction was not entirely new. Armies had always had to train recruits, but earlier drillmasters acted on the not unreasonable assumption that as soon as everyone knew how to use his weapon, their task had been accomplished. Maurice differed from

9. Aelian was a Greek who wrote a book on tactics in the time of Trajan, when the Roman Empire and its army were at their peak. It was translated into Latin in 1550, and so combined the authority of antiquity with an aura of novelty when Prince Maurice began his military reforms. According to Werner Halbweg, *Die Heeresreform der Oranier und die Antike* (Berlin, 1941), p. 43, Aelian provided the main inspiration for Maurice's reforms.

his predecessors in being far more systematic. He analyzed the rather complicated movements required to load and fire matchlock guns[10] into a series of forty-two separate, successive moves and gave each move a name and appropriate word of command. His soldiers could then be taught to make each movement in unison, responding to a shouted word of command. Since all the soldiers moved simultaneously and in rhythm, everyone was ready to fire at the same time. This made volleys easy and natural, creating a shock effect on enemy ranks. More important, soldiers loaded and fired their guns much faster and were much less likely to omit any of the essential steps. The result was to make handguns more efficient than ever before, and Maurice increased their number in proportion to pikes accordingly.

He also regularized marching. By keeping in step, all the men in a unit could be taught to move in prescribed patterns, forward or back, left or right, shifting from column to line and back again. The most important maneuver of Prince Maurice's drill was the countermarch, whereby, having fired their weapons, a rank of arquebusiers or musketeers marched between the files of the men standing behind them, and proceeded to reload in the rear while the men in the next rank were firing their pieces. With practice, and with an appropriate number of ranks, by the time the first rank's guns were again fully loaded, each of the other ranks had fired and retired in its turn, allowing the soldiers of the first rank to fire their second volley without obstruction or delay. In this fashion, a well-choreographed military ballet permitted a carefully drilled unit to deliver a series of volleys in rapid succession, giving an enemy no chance to recover from the shock of one burst of fire before another volley hit home. The trick was in the timing, and in preventing men from fleeing the battlefield entirely when they turned their backs on the enemy in order to reload in the rear. Oft-repeated drill, making every movement semiautomatic, minimized the possibility of breakdown. Closer supervision of the rank and file by an expanded cadre of officers and noncoms was also necessary to make the countermarch practicable. But when everything went as intended, the pay-off was spectacular.

Maurice's third reform both made drill more effective and was itself made effective by repeated drill: to wit, he divided his army into smaller tactical units than had been customary before, in imitation of

10. The gun had to be loaded with powder, followed by a wad to hold the powder in position; then a ball and a wad to hold the ball in place; then the primer pan had to be filled with a different sort of powder. The lighted match (held in the meanwhile in the left hand) was then affixed to the firing mechanism and the gun was at last ready to be aimed and fired. The match had to be detached from the gun before the cycle could be safely repeated.

the maniples of the Roman legion. Battalions of 550 men, further subdivided into companies and platoons, made convenient units for drill, since a single voice could control the movements of all the men. Primary personal ties, extending from commanding officer to newest recruit, could also establish themselves among the members of units of this size. They could move nimbly on a battlefield, acting independently yet in coordination with each other, since an unambiguous chain of command extended from the general in charge of the battle to the noncom in charge of each rank of each platoon. Commanders at each level in the hierarchy, at least in principle, responded to orders coming from above, transmitting them to appropriate subordinates with whatever additional specification the situation might require.

In this way an army became an articulated organism with a central nervous system that allowed sensitive and more or less intelligent response to unforeseen circumstances. Every movement attained a new level of exactitude and speed. The individual movements of soldiers when firing and marching as well as the movements of battalions across the battlefield could be controlled and predicted as never before. A well-drilled unit, by making every motion count, could increase the amount of lead projected against an enemy per minute of battle. The dexterity and resolution of individual infantrymen scarcely mattered any more. Prowess and personal courage all but disappeared beneath an armor-plated routine. Soldiering took on quite new dimensions and the everyday reality of army life altered profoundly. Yet troops drilled in the Maurician fashion automatically exhibited superior effectiveness in battle. As this came to be recognized, the old irregular and heroic patterns of military behavior withered and died, even among the most recalcitrant officers and gentlemen.

Efficiency in battle was important, but less significant than the improved efficiency a well-drilled army also exhibited in garrison and siege situations. Nearly all of a soldier's time, after all, was spent in anticipation of actual confrontation with an enemy. How to wait without becoming restless and unmanageable had always been a problem for earlier armies. When marching cross-country the problem solved itself. But when an army settled down in a single location, doing nothing for days or months on end, morale and discipline were very liable to break down. The fact that a few hours of daily drill were easy to organize, obviously useful, and readily enforceable made garrison discipline easy to maintain.[11]

11. On Maurice's reforms, in addition to Halbweg's previously cited work, see the provocative remarks by M. D. Feld, "Middle Class Society and the Rise of Military

Moreover, such drill, repeated day in and day out, had another important dimension which the Prince of Orange and his fellows probably understood very dimly if at all. For when a group of men move their arm and leg muscles in unison for prolonged periods of time, a primitive and very powerful social bond wells up among them. This probably results from the fact that movement of the big muscles in unison rouses echoes of the most primitive level of sociality known to humankind. Perhaps even before our prehuman ancestors could talk, they danced around camp fires, rehearsing what they had done in the hunt and what they were going to do next time. Such rhythmic movements created an intense fellow feeling that allowed even poorly armed protohumans to attack and kill big game, outstripping far more formidable rivals through efficient cooperation. By virtue of the dance, supplemented and eventually controlled by voice signals and commands, our ancestors elevated themselves to the pinnacle of the food chain, becoming the most formidable of predators.

Military drill, as developed by Maurice of Nassau and thousands of European drillmasters after him, tapped this primitive reservoir of sociality directly. Drill, dull and repetitious though it may seem, readily welded a miscellaneous collection of men, recruited often from the dregs of civil society, into a coherent community, obedient to orders even in extreme situations when life and limb were in obvious and immediate jeopardy. Hunting bands had depended for their survival on being able to sustain obedience and cooperation in the face of imminent peril. Presumably, therefore, natural selection across unnumbered generations had raised human aptitude for such behavior to a high level; and these aptitudes continued (and continue) to lurk near the surface of our subconscious psyche.

The armies of ancient Greece and Rome had also drawn on this instinctual reservoir to bind their citizen soldiers together. The peculiar intensity of city-state political life depended in no small degree on this phenomenon. So when Maurice of Nassau looked back to the practices of the Roman legions and modified their pattern of drill to fit the hand-weapons of his day, he was grafting his management of armed force onto an ancient and well-tested European tradition.

The new drill therefore drew upon literary tradition to exploit very powerful human susceptibilities. Military units became a specialized sort of community, within which new, standardized face-to-face rela-

Professionalism: The Dutch Army, 1589–1609," *Armed Forces and Society* 1 (1975): 419–42.

tionships provided a passable substitute for the customary patterns of traditional social groupings—the very groupings which were everywhere dissolving or were at least called into question by the spread of impersonal market relations. Hence, the artificial community of well-drilled platoons and companies could and did very swiftly replace the customary hierarchies of prowess and status that had given European society its form and its capacity for local self-defense in the days when knighthood had been in flower.

Social bonds among soldiers were strengthened further by the fact that from the age of Louis XIV standing armies encouraged long-term enlistment and reenlistment. Once assigned to a particular unit, a soldier might therefore spend many years in the ranks, sharing experiences with long-time comrades who disappeared more often through death than from choice. This allowed sentiments of group solidarity to become firmly fixed, and transformed small army units into effective primary communities.

As suggested above, the breakdown of primary communities as a basis for military action was what had precipitated the initial Italian venture into mercenary soldiering in the fourteenth century. Two centuries afterwards, European drillmasters managed to create artificial primary communities in the ranks of all technically proficient armies, thanks to the remarkable way in which a few weeks of drill created sentiments of solidarity, even among previously isolated individuals. The emotional tone thus aroused within the ranks of European armies in turn relieved the psychological strains and stresses that had made military management so difficult in the centuries of transition from one kind of primary community to the new one.

Well-drilled armies were usually quite insulated from the larger social context in which they found themselves. New recruits, coming directly from villages, could be fitted into the artificial community of the company and platoon with minimal psychological adjustment. For drill swiftly and dependably transformed obedience and deference defined by custom into obedience and deference defined by regulations. Armies were, therefore, readily renewable, and preserved "old-fashioned," i.e., rural, values and attitudes within an ever more drastically urbanized, monetized, commercialized, and bureaucratically rationalized world.

Such a combination of opposites, or seeming opposites, created more effective instruments of policy than the world had ever seen before. Conformity to rules laid down from above became normal, not only because men feared harsh punishments for infractions of discipline, but also because the rank and file found real psychological satisfaction in blind, unthinking obedience, and in the rituals of military routine. Prideful esprit de corps became a palpable reality for hundreds of thousands of human beings who had little else to be proud of. Human flotsam and jetsam found an honorable refuge from a world in which buying and selling had become so pervasive as to handicap severely those who lacked the necessary pecuniary self-restraint, cunning, and foresight. An artificial community bureaucratically structured and controlled, came into existence, based on deep-seated, stable, and very powerful human sentiments. What an instrument in the hands of statesmen, diplomats, and kings!

The feats of arms that European armies routinely performed, once drill had become soldiers' daily experience, were in fact quite extraordinary. Being heirs of the European past, we are likely to take their acts for granted and lose the sense of wonder they properly deserve. Yet consider how amazing it was for men to form themselves into opposing ranks a few score yards apart and fire muskets at one another, keeping it up while comrades were falling dead or wounded all around. Instinct and reason alike make such behavior unaccountable. Yet European armies of the eighteenth century did it as a matter of course.

Equally remarkable was the way in which army units obeyed the will of invisible superiors with about equal precision, whether they were located over the nearest hill crest or half the globe away. Many thousands of men who had no obvious personal stake in fighting one another and did have very obvious personal reasons for wishing to be out of the other fellows' line of fire nevertheless did what they were commanded to do—routinely. As a result, bureaucratically appointed officers, regardless of their personal competence or incompetence, expected and received automatic and obedient response to their commands, almost without fail, and regardless of what part of the globe they happened to find themselves assigned to.

The creation of such a New Leviathan—half inadvertently perhaps —was certainly one of the major achievements of the seventeenth century, as remarkable in its way as the birth of modern science or any of the other breakthroughs of that age.[12]

12. I am not aware of any really perceptive discussion of the psychological and sociological effects of close-order drill on human beings in general or within European armies in particular. My remarks are derived from reflections on personal experience—and surprise at my own response to drill during World War II.

Some military writers of the age hint at the power of drill and its relationship to dancing. Cf. Maurice de Saxe, *Reveries on the Art of War*, trans. Thomas R. Phillips

The improved efficiency aroused by drill soon became apparent to other military men of Europe. Prince Maurice's reputation rested on his recovery of dozens of fortified towns from the Spaniards through sudden strikes and obdurate sieges, each conducted with a technical precision and dispatch never attained before. Maurice's methods of training were not kept secret. In 1596 his cousin and close collaborator, Johannes II of Nassau, commissioned an artist named Jacob de Gheyn to produce drawings illustrating each of the postures that arquebusiers, musketeers, and pikemen were required to take by the new drill. These were published as a book in 1607. A full folio page was devoted to each posture, together with the appropriate word of command. An apprentice drillmaster—or common soldier—could thus see with his own eyes just how to perform the drill.[13]

Maurice organized a military academy for the training of officers in 1619—another first for Europe. A graduate of Prince Maurice's academy subsequently took service with Gustav Adolf of Sweden and brought the new Dutch drill to that army. From the Swedes the new drill (variously modified of course) spread to all the other European armies with any pretension to efficiency. Protestant states accepted the innovation first; from them it spread to the French, and last of all to the Spaniards, whose attachment to their own long-victorious tradition was naturally very great. But after the Battle of Rocroi (1643), when a French army defeated the Spanish *tercios* in open

---

(Harrisburg, Pa., 1944), pp. 30–31: "Have them march in cadence. There is the whole secret, and it is the military step of the Romans. . . . Everyone has seen people dancing all night. But take a man and make him dance for a quarter of an hour without music, and see if he can bear it. . . .

"I shall be told, perhaps that many men have no ear for music. This is false; movement to music is natural and automatic. I have often noticed while the drums were beating for the colors, that all the soldiers marched in cadence without intention and without realizing it. Nature and instinct did it for them."

The military music of Christian Europe, incidentally, derived from Ottoman fife and drum corps. These in turn were adaptations of steppe traditions of drumming which had filtered into the Moslem world via dervish communities of young men. But Ottoman troops did not drill incessantly as Christian troops started to do, nor did they march in step, thereby muting the elemental resonance that moving in unison arouses.

13. Jacob de Gheyn, *Wapenhandelinghe van Roers, Musquetten ende Spiessen, Achtervolgende de Ordre van Syn Excellentie Maurits, Prince van Orangie* (The Hague, 1607). The edition I saw was a facsimile (New York, 1971), with an informative commentary by J. B. Kist appended. According to Kist, Maurice first held a review of his troops, with field maneuvers, in 1592. At that time his battalions numbered 800 men each; later he reduced the size of the battalion—the primary unit of maneuver—to 550 to make it nimbler in the field and easier for a single voice to control. De Gheyn's book was often pirated subsequently; most significantly by Johann Jacob Wallhausen, *Kriegskunst zu Fuss* (1614), who used the same copper plates as the original work, but wrote in German.

country, informed military men of Europe all agreed that the new drill had definitely proved superior to Spanish practices.

To the east, the Russians soon took note, and in 1649, a generation after the new drill books had first appeared in German, a Russian translation came out.[14] Romanoff armies thus tried to keep step with developments in western Europe, though they still lagged noticeably behind. The Turks, however, refused to believe that infidels could improve on time-tested Moslem methods of training and deployment. Even after a long series of defeats in the field proved otherwise (1683–99, 1714–18), a belated attempt to train troops in European fashion merely provoked a successful mutiny by the janissaries in 1730. Not until after almost another century of military disaster did the sultan finally succeed in destroying the janissary corps in 1826 as a preface to modernizing training and tactics. But by that time the morale and cohesion of the Ottoman body politic had suffered irreparable damage. Consequently, efforts to catch up with European military methods could not prevent further defeat and the ultimate dissolution of the empire in 1918.[15]

Further east, the new style of training soldiers became important when European drillmasters began to create miniature armies by recruiting local manpower for the protection of French, Dutch, and English trading stations on the shores of the Indian Ocean. By the eighteenth century, such forces, however minuscule, exhibited a clear superiority over the unwieldy armies that local rulers were accustomed to bring into the field. As a result, the great European trading companies became territorial rulers over expanding areas in India and Indonesia.[16] Only the Pacific shores of Asia remained insulated from the enhanced efficiency of European troops—until 1839–41.

In earlier times one of the dilemmas that had surrounded European soldiering was the discrepancy between technical efficiency, which from the fourteenth century had favored predominantly infantry armies, and the established hierarchy of civil society. An infantry force recruited from the lower classes might be expected to challenge aristocratic dominance. The Swiss had done so, triumphantly, on their

14. Richard Hellie, *Enserfment and Military Change in Muscovy* (Chicago, 1971), pp. 187–88.

15. On Ottoman failure to respond to European drill see V. J. Parry, "La manière de combattre," in V. J. Parry and M. E. Yapp, eds., *War, Technology and Society in the Middle East* (London, 1975), pp. 218–56.

16. For details see James P. Lawford, *Britain's Army in India from Its Origins to the Conquest of Bengal* (London, 1978).

Musket Drill Devised by Maurice of Orange

*The engravings on the following pages show eight of a total of forty-three positions
prescribed for Maurice of Orange's musketeers. Getting powder, ball, and wadding
securely into place and then priming the gun while holding a lighted match in the
left hand demanded care and precision; to do it rapidly required repeated practice.
These etchings were published to help drillmasters standardize each motion and thus
speed up the soldiers' rate of fire.*

Wapenhandelinghe van Roers, Musquetten ende Spiessen, Achtervolgende de Ordre van Syn Excellentie
Maurits, Prince van Orangie . . . Figuirlyck vutgebeelt door Jacob de Gheyn (The Hague, 1607; facsimile edition, New York: McGraw Hill, 1971).

---

home ground in the fourteenth century. Egalitarian ideas also cropped
up recurrently among the German *Landesknechten*.[17]

European rulers' initial response to this dilemma had been to hire
foreign mercenaries for infantry service, since foreigners could be
expected to exhibit minimal solidarity with the lower classes over
whom the ruler in question exercised jurisdiction. The Swiss, egalitarian and self-governing at home, thus became a pillar of the French
monarchy, helping to prop up an aristocratic-bureaucratic regime for
more than three hundred years (1479–1789) against challengers both
at home and abroad.[18] Hillsmen and others coming from infertile
areas, where a distinct landowning class had never securely established
its power, played analogous roles in other parts of Europe, for example, the Albanians, Basques, and south Slavic Grenzers, together with
Celts from Wales, Scotland, and Ireland. When the Swedes intervened
in the Thirty Years War, they had something of the same character,
though, of course, they acted on behalf of their own sovereign rather
than as hirelings of a foreign ruler.[19]

17. Cf. Frauenholz, *Das Heereswesen in die Zeit des freien Söldnertums,* 1:36–39. Discharged veterans provided key manpower for the Peasants' War of 1525, for example.

18. In 1479 Louis XI of France disbanded his French infantry forces and made a
contract with the Swiss instead. The Swiss reputation as the premier pikemen of Europe
undoubtedly influenced this decision; but so did their political distance from French
social turmoils. Cf. Phillipe Contamine, *Guerre, état et société à la fin du moyen âge: Etudes
sur les armées des rois de France, 1337–1494* (Paris, 1972), p. 284. On the use of foreign
mercenaries in general see V. G. Kiernan, "Foreign Mercenaries and Absolute Monarchy," in Trevor Aston, ed., *Crisis in Europe, 1560–1660* (New York, 1967), pp. 117–40.

19. The Ottoman Empire competed with the Venetians from the 1590s for the
mercenary services of Christian infantrymen from the western Balkans. See Halil Inalcik, "Military and Fiscal Transformation in the Ottoman Empire, 1600–1700," *Ar-
chivum Ottomanicum* 6 (1980). North of the Black Sea, however, technical and geographical conditions favored cavalry for some two centuries after primacy had passed to
infantry in west European landscapes and battlefields. The cheap horses available on the
steppe allowed mounted Cossacks to play a role in the east analogous to that of the
Swiss in the west. Like the Swiss, they became military egalitarians and wavered between alternative foreign employers once their military value had been recognized

11,	12,
Hold up your musket and present	*Give fire*

Reliance on foreigners had obvious drawbacks, however. Before the eighteenth century, money was not usually available in anything like the amount needed to pay armed foreigners punctually. Chronically impecunious monarchs could not safely rely on an army that was prepared to quit the battlefield simply because its pay was overdue.[20] But from the beginning of the seventeenth century, European rulers discovered how the sweepings of city streets and sons of poverty-stricken peasants could quite literally be made into new men by repeated drilling. Egalitarian ideas lost their resonance, save on those rare occasions when the drillmasters espoused such ideals, as happened briefly in some units of the Parliamentary armies during the

among neighboring states. In the end the Cossacks affiliated with the Russian tsars but only at the price of betrayal of their earlier egalitarian tradition. Cf. William H. McNeill, *Europe's Steppe Frontier, 1500–1800* (Chicago, 1964).

20. In Islamic lands, similar difficulties had sometimes been met by reducing foreign soldiers to the status of slaves; but a slave soldier, too, was hard to control, and in several Islamic states slave captains seized power in their own right, founding "slave dynasties" in which power passed from slave captain to slave captain instead of from father to son. The Mameluke state of Egypt was the most famous of these; it lasted from the thirteenth to the nineteenth century. On slave soldiery in Islam see David Ayalon, "Preliminary Remarks on the Mamluk Military Institution in Islam," in Parry and Yapp, *War, Technology, and Society in the Middle East*, pp. 44–58; Daniel Pipes, *Slave Soldiers and Islam* (New Haven, 1981); Patricia Crone, *Slaves on Horses: The Evolution of the Islamic Polity* (New York, 1980).

13.

*Take down your musket and carry it
with your rest*

14.

Uncock your match

English civil wars (1642–49), and again, much later, in the first phases
of the French Revolution (1789–93). In more ordinary times, armies
became self-perpetuating training institutions, drilling raw recruits
until they became quite different from their former selves, that is,
until they became soldiers.[21]

Various associated behavioral traits, transmitted from soldier to soldier across the decades, grew up around the central experience of drill
to define a distinctive military style of life. Prostitutes, gambling, and
drunkenness all had a place in this way of life; so did pride, punctilio,
and prowess. European armies, in short, did not depart entirely from
older patterns and precedents. But they did relegate some of the
traditional aspects of military behavior to the margins, confining the
more disruptive of them to off-duty hours.

The new psychic character of European armies made sharp class

21. The psychic force of drill and new routines was such as to make a recruit's origins
and previous experience largely irrelevant to his behavior as a soldier. This deprives
studies of class and local origins of enlisted men of more than antiquarian interest,
despite the fact that military records sometimes lend themselves admirably to such
analysis. French historians, perhaps influenced by Marxism, have been particularly active in this endeavor, without shedding any notable light on what the French army
actually did either in war or in peace. The great monument of this genre is A. Corvisier,
L'armée française de la fin du XVIIe siècle au ministère de Choiseul, 2 vols. (Paris, 1964).

15,
*And put it again betwixt
your fingers*

16,
Blow your pan

differentiation within civil society fully compatible with domestic peace and order. Overwhelming force came to reside in the hands of soldiers obedient to the king's own bureaucratically appointed officers. Neither aristocratic challenges to royal power nor lower-class protests against perceived injustice had the slightest chance of success as long as well-drilled troops were available to defend royal prerogatives. Accordingly, Europe began to enjoy a previously unattainable level of domestic peace. This facilitated a notable increase in wealth, so that in many parts of the Continent it became feasible to support professional standing armies on tax income without straining the economic resources of the population too severely. The United Provinces, France, and Austria led the way; other European states followed close behind.

Standardization and Quasi-Stabilization of European Armed Forces

As tax income became sufficient to meet military payrolls more or less punctually, the profound disturbances that the commercialization of war had introduced into Europe in the fourteenth century seemed

24,

Charge your musket

25,

Draw out your scouring stick

finally to have been brought under control. Ravaging soldiers no longer had to sustain themselves by forcibly recirculating the movable wealth of a country. Regular, predictable taxes did the trick instead, transferring money from civilians to officials who used it to support an efficient military force as well as themselves. It seems safe to suggest that only the continuance of interstate rivalries prevented this Old Regime pattern of society and government, which emerged after 1650, from settling down to centuries of routine.

Incipient stabilization of European patterns of war and society was also forwarded by another corollary of Prince Maurice's reforms. For standardized drill presupposed standardized weapons. Maurice himself found it necessary, in 1599, to require that the armies under his command be equipped with uniform handguns. Otherwise his new system could not be made to work. Louvois did the same for the French army, and made soldiers look like soldiers as we know them in the twentieth century by presiding over the development of uniforms (which varied from regiment to regiment, however).

The short-run effect of such standardization was to reduce military costs significantly. Even artisan suppliers could cut the price of their product if assured of steady work manufacturing identical items indefinitely into the future. Supply in the field was also eased when only one caliber of musket ball was required. And since each soldier could be trained to the precise movements of standardized drill, reinforcement of the depleted personnel of any given unit became almost as simple as replacing spent musket balls. Soldiers, in short, tended to become replaceable parts of a great military machine just as much as their weaponry. Management of such an army was easier and more likely to achieve expected results than anything possible before. The cost of organized violence went down proportionally; or, perhaps it would be more accurate to say that the magnitude and controllability of such violence per tax dollar went up—spectacularly.[22]

Over a somewhat longer run, however, uniformity of weaponry among scores of thousands of soldiers introduced a new kind of rigidity into the arms market. Once an entire army had standardized its equipment, any improvement in design became far more costly to introduce than had been the case when the weapons of dozens of different designs were simultaneously in use. Military purchasers had to choose between technical improvement and the costs that would arise from loss of uniformity. Not all changes were inhibited by this new dilemma. Still, really important departures from existing designs of weapons were certain to upset established patterns of drill, training, and supply. As a result, changes in handguns, which had been very rapid from the fifteenth to seventeenth century, almost came to a halt after about 1690, when the invention of the ring bayonet made it possible to combine firepower with close-in defense against cavalry for the first time, rendering pikemen unnecessary.[23]

By that time, to be sure, the handguns in use by European armies had attained a satisfactory degree of reliability, simplicity,[24] and durability so that improvements in design were, perhaps, more difficult to

22. Standardization and routinization, applied to industrial production in the eighteenth century, were pioneered in army administration and supply in the seventeenth. Similar results—sharply enhanced productivity and lowered unit costs—occurred in both cases. This point is argued, perhaps a little too emphatically, in Jacobus A. A. van Doorn, *The Soldier and Social Change: Comparative Studies in the History and Sociology of the Military* (Beverly Hills, Calif., 1973), pp. 17–33; Lewis Mumford, *Technics and Civilization* (New York, 1934), pp. 81–106.

23. On the uncertainty surrounding the invention and introduction of the ring bayonet, see David Chandler, *The Art of War in the Age of Marlborough* (New York, 1976), pp. 67, 83.

24. Matchlocks of Prince Maurice's day gave way to flintlocks and correspondingly simplified drill by about 1710, at least in the best-managed European armies. Flintlocks had been invented as early as 1615, but were at first too expensive to displace the matchlock, despite a far higher rate of fire (about twice as fast) and superior reliability (ca. 33 percent misfire vs. 50 percent for matchlocks). I take these statistics from Chandler, *The Art of War*, pp. 76–79.

achieve than in earlier ages. But what froze infantry weapons at a given level was resistance to any change that would require a choice between the advantages of uniformity and the cost of reequipping an entire army. This rational calculation was reinforced by affectionate attachment to familiar weapons and routines. Reason and sentiment thus conspired to make the musket designed in England in 1690, and nicknamed "Brown Bess," the standard infantry weapon of the British army until 1840. It underwent only minor modification in all that time.[25] Other European armies were almost as conservative. And since foot soldiers remained decisive in battle across this entire span of time, the stabilization of infantry weapons had the effect of stabilizing tactics, training, and other aspects of army life.

Stabilization was never complete, as we will see in the next chapter; but it seems clear that as Prince Maurice's patterns of training and administration took hold across the face of Europe, the great surge of change in Europe's management of organized violence that we have considered in this and the preceding chapter came to a close.

We may sum it up as follows: things started to change in the twelfth century with the rise of infantry forces capable of challenging the supremacy of mounted knights on Italian battlefields. Town militias gave way to hired professionals in the fourteenth century, and a pattern of political management of standing armies swiftly evolved within the context of the emergent city-states of Italy during the first half of the fifteenth century, only to be upset by the irruption of French and Spanish armies after 1494. Then a reprise of the Italian development on a territorially larger scale began in transalpine Europe, achieving a pattern reminiscent of Italian city-state administration by the mid-seventeenth century, when tax income and military-naval expenditure came into more or less stable relation to each other in such countries as France, the United Provinces, and England. But the northern Europeans improved on Italian precedents in two important respects: by developing systematic, oft-repeated drill, and by constructing a clear chain of command that extended from the person of the sovereign—usually a king—to the lowliest noncommissioned officer. Jealousies within the chain of command were never completely eliminated; but the sacred aura that continued to surround royal personages made the "divide and rule" policy that Venetian magistrates and Milanese ad-

25. A stricter definition reduces the period in which the same pattern prevailed to a mere century: 1730 to 1830. For details of the many minor variations in design, and of the way the Board of Ordnance handled sudden crises when large numbers of muskets had to be procured in short periods of time, see Howard L. Blackmore, *British Military Firearms, 1670–1850* (London, 1961).

ministrators had relied on to govern military professionals un-necessary in transalpine Europe.

Stability at home meant formidability abroad. Within the cockpit of western Europe, one improved modern-style army shouldered hard against its rivals. This led to only local and temporary disturbances of the balance of power, which diplomacy proved able to contain. To-wards the margins of the European radius of action, however, the result was systematic expansion—whether in India, Siberia, or the Americas. Frontier expansion in turn sustained an expanding trade network, enhanced taxable wealth in Europe, and made support of the armed establishments less onerous than would otherwise have been the case. Europe, in short, launched itself on a self-reinforcing cycle in which its military organization sustained, and was sustained by, eco-nomic and political expansion at the expense of other peoples and polities of the earth.

The modern history of the globe registered that fact, and turned in large measure on the further fact that technical and organizational improvements in European management of organized violence did not come permanently to a halt in the seventeenth century, despite the new precision and rigidity that European armies achieved by that time. Instead, technological and organizational innovation continued, allowing Europeans to outstrip other peoples of the earth more and more emphatically until the globe-girdling imperialism of the nine-teenth century became as cheap and easy for Europeans as it was catastrophic to Asians, Africans, and the peoples of Oceania.

The succeeding chapters of the book will address themselves to these changes.

5

Strains on Europe's Bureaucratization of Violence, 1700-1789

European rulers' remarkable success in bureaucratizing organized violence and encapsulating it within civil society continued to dominate European statecraft throughout the eighteenth and well into the nineteenth century. The victories Europeans regularly achieved in conflicts with other peoples of the earth during this period attested the unusually efficient character of European military arrangements; and such successes, in turn, facilitated the steady growth of overseas trade which helped to make the costs of maintaining standing armies and navies easier for Europeans to bear. Hence European rulers, especially those located towards the frontiers of European society, were in the happy and unusual position of not having to choose between guns and butter but could instead help themselves to more of both, while their subjects—at least some of them—were also able to enrich themselves.

No doubt a long succession of good harvest years and the spread of American food crops, mainly maize and potatoes, to European soil had more to do with the prosperity of the first half of the eighteenth century than any merely governmental action. But the acceptability of Old Regime military-political patterns was surely enhanced, for all concerned, by the economic growth that set in all across the face of Europe, from Ireland in the west to the Ukrainian plains in the east, during the comparatively peaceful decades that followed the end of the War of the Spanish Succession in 1714.

Nevertheless, in the second half of the eighteenth century, sharp challenges to existing political-military patterns in Europe made themselves felt. One fundamental factor in the mounting disequilibrium was the onset of rapid population growth after about 1750. In countries like France and England this meant that rural-urban balances began to shift perceptibly, as migrants from a crowded countryside set out to make their fortunes in town, or, in a few cases, crossed the Atlantic to take up land in North America.[1] How to cope with a growing rural population when most of the readily cultivable land was already in tillage became critical throughout northwestern Europe in the second half of the eighteenth century. Only later did comparable problems confront central and eastern European societies, for when the eighteenth-century population surge set in, there was much untilled land in those parts that could be brought under cultivation by applying existing agricultural methods without resort to exceptional or costly capital improvements. By way of contrast, in England, France, Italy, the Low Countries, and Germany west of the Elbe, generally speaking, any extension of cultivation to new ground did require some sort of costly and unusual preparation of the land—fertilizing it, draining it, or altering its composition by bringing in sand or marl or some similar material to mix with the existing soil. Consequently, in eastern Europe until after the middle of the nineteenth century rising population constituted not a problem but an opportunity to make grainfields out of what had before been left as woods, wasteland, or rough pasture—without altering patterns of rural labor or customary routines and social relations in any significant degree.

Another way of describing the difference between western and eastern Europe between 1750 and 1830 is this: in the east, population growth allowed simple replication of already familiar patterns of village life. Export of local products—grain, livestock, timber, or minerals—though increasing in quantity with the growth of population was not massive enough to provoke any really new forms of social organization. In the west, however, strains were greater. The countryside could absorb only a portion of the expanding labor force. Urban occupations had to be found for a greater proportion; and insofar as this proved difficult or impossible, manpower was likely to shift towards predatory

1. Europe's population rose from about 118 million in 1700 to 187 million in 1801. The population of England and Wales grew from something like 5.8 million at the beginning of the century to 9.15 million in 1801; and French population rose from about 18 to 26 million between 1715 and 1789. Cf. Jacques Godechot, *Les revolutions, 1770–1799* (Paris, 1970), pp. 93–95; Phyllis Deane and W. A. Cole, *British Economic Growth, 1688–1959: Trends and Structure,* 2d ed. (Cambridge, 1967), p. 103; M. Reinhard and A. Armengaud, *Histoire générale de la population mondiale* (Paris, 1961), pp. 151–201. A convenient summary of demographers' opinions about the causes for population surge in the eighteenth century is to be found in Thomas McKeown, R. G. Brown, and R. G. Record, "An Interpretation of the Modern Rise of Population in Europe," *Population Studies* 26 (1972): 345–82. Perhaps the most important single factor was an altered incidence of lethal infectious disease; cf. William H. McNeill, *Plagues and Peoples* (New York, 1976), pp. 240–58.

activities, whether such predators were licensed by public authority as privateers or enlisted as soldiers, or acted without public legitimation as highwaymen, brigands, or ordinary urban thieves.

In eastern Europe, as men became more abundant, soldiers became easier for the Prussian, Russian, and Austrian governments to recruit. Armies increased in size, especially the Russian; but like the multiplying villages from whence the soldiers came, such increases in size did not involve change in structure. In western Europe, however, the mounting intensity of warfare that set in with the Seven Years War (1756–63) and rose to a crescendo in the years of the French Revolution and Napoleon (1792–1815) registered the new pressures that population growth put on older social, economic, and political institutions in far more revolutionary fashion. Divine right monarchy went down, never to be fully resurrected; but Old Regime military institutions continued to regulate even the French *levée en masse* of 1793. As a result, Napoleon's defeat in 1815 allowed the victorious powers to restore a plausible simulacrum of the Old Regime. The traditional military order did not begin to break up irretrievably until the 1840s, when new industrial techniques began to affect naval and military weaponry and organization in radical and fundamental ways. Until that time, despite the revolutionary aspiration and achievements of the French and despite technical advances in British manufactures (which we are also accustomed to call revolutionary) the organization and equipment of European armed forces remained fundamentally conservative, even when, as in France after 1792, the command structure of the army was harnessed to the accomplishment of revolutionary political purposes.

Yet even if the long-range result can be described as conservative, a closer examination of the challenges to European military establishments between 1700 and 1789 will show how the management of armed force remained persistently precarious, even when the Old Regime was apparently most secure. These challenges were of two sorts. One recurrent challenge arose from geographical expansion of the territories organized for the support of European-style armed establishments, thereby altering power balances among the European states. A second kind of challenge stemmed from technical and organizational innovations within the system itself, characteristically provoked by failure in war on the part of one or another of the European great powers. Each of these challenges requires somewhat closer consideration, as preface to a discussion of what did and did not happen to the organization and management of European armed forces during the French Revolutionary and Napoleonic periods.

Disequilibrium Arising from Frontier Expansion

Any human skill that achieves admirable results will tend to spread from its place of origin by taking root among other peoples who encounter the novelty and find it better than whatever they had previously known or done. This was conspicuously the case with the style of army organization that came into being in Holland at the close of the sixteenth century and spread, as we saw in the last chapter, to Sweden and the Germanies, to France and England, and even to Spain before the seventeenth century had come to a close. During the eighteenth century, the contagion attained far greater range: transforming Russia under Peter the Great (r. 1689–1725) with near revolutionary force; infiltrating the New World and India as a by-product of a global struggle for overseas empire in which France and Great Britain were the protagonists; and infecting even such a culturally alien polity as that of the Ottoman empire.[2]

The range of market-regulated activity which undergirded and sustained the European pattern of bureaucratized armed force expanded even more widely during the same decades, weaving the everyday activities of countless millions of Asians, Africans, Americans, and Europeans into a more and more coherent system of exchange and production. Even Australia began to enter into the European-centered and managed economy before the century closed. Only the Far East remained apart, owing to Chinese and Japanese governmental policy which deliberately restricted European trade to marginal and indeed, in the case of Japan, to economically trivial proportions.

Expansion on such a scale wrought drastic alterations in the internal

2. In 1730, Sultan Mahmud I initiated an effort to improve Ottoman defenses by imitating Christian methods. A French renegade, Claude-Alexandre, comte de Bonneval (1675–1747), played the leading role in this effort. He took the name of Achmet Pasha and was appointed commander-in-chief of Rumelia, the highest post in the Ottoman service. Ironically, real military successes against both the Austrians and Russians, 1736–39, did not prevent a sharp reversal of policy after the war. De Bonneval's ungovernable temper led to his disgrace and imprisonment in 1738 and his removal allowed pious Moslems, who preferred to rely on the will of Allah rather than on newfangled hardware, to return to power. A second abortive effort at modernization was set off by the unexpected appearance of the Russian fleet in the Aegean in 1770. A Frenchified Hungarian, Baron François de Tott (1733–93), was entrusted with emergency powers to block the Dardanelles; then he undertook a more general effort to improve the fortification of the capital and modernize the Ottoman artillery and fleet. When war ended in 1774, however, the energy behind these efforts evaporated. De Tott, who had not been required to accept Islam, as de Bonneval had done, was doubly suspect as a foreigner and an infidel; and the reforms he had introduced withered away to triviality after he returned to France in 1776. On de Bonneval see Albert Vandal, *Le pacha Bonneval* (Paris, 1885); on de Tott, see his own *Mémoires sur les Turcs et les Tartares* (Amsterdam, 1784).

European balance of power. States located towards the margins of the European world—Great Britain and Russia in particular—were able to increase their control of resources more rapidly than was possible in the more crowded center. The rise of such march states to dominance over older and smaller polities located near a center where important innovation first concentrated is one of the oldest and best-attested patterns of civilized history.[3] What happened among the great powers of Europe in the eighteenth century, therefore, ought to be understood as no more than a recent example of a very old process, a process which, of course, continued into the nineteenth century and has by no means come to any final equilibrium point in the twentieth.

European expansion in the eighteenth century, however, occurred so symmetrically that no one state achieved an overwhelming preponderance over all others. Until the 1780s, France and Britain rivaled and roughly counterbalanced each other in sharing enhanced resources from overseas expansion, while in the east Austria and Prussia disputed with Russia (though with less and less success as the century advanced) the advantages of a position on Europe's landward frontier. European political pluralism therefore survived, despite some rather sharp perturbations. The survival of a plurality of competing states, in turn, maintained Europe's uniqueness compared to the major civilizations of Asia, where gunpowder empires created in the sixteenth and seventeenth centuries continued to prevail, sometimes, as in China, in a flourishing condition, and sometimes, as in India, in increasing disarray.

The multiplicity of European states produced an enormous political confusion. Diplomatic and military alignments shifted from time to time in kaleidoscopic fashion. All the same, it seems worth suggesting that a noticeable change came to the system after 1714, when the War of the Spanish Succession ended. By that date, the coalition of states that had formed to check the preponderance of Louis XIV's armies on

3. March states conquered older, smaller polities at least three times in the ancient Near East: Akkad (ca. 2350 B.C.); Assyria (ca. 1000–612 B.C.); and Persia (550–331 B.C.). Mediterranean history offers a similar array of instances: the rise of Macedon (338 B.C.) and then of Rome (168 B.C.) in classical times followed in modern times by the Spanish domination over Italy (by 1557) which we looked at briefly in the preceding chapter. Ancient China (rise of Ch'in, 221 B.C.) and ancient India (rise of Magadha, ca. 321 B.C.) as well as Amerindian Mexico (Aztecs) and Peru (Incas) all seem to exhibit a parallel pattern. This is not surprising. A given level of organization and technique, if applied to a larger territorial base, can be expected to yield greater results. This was often possible on the margins of specially skilled centers of civilization; and whenever a ruler managed to confirm his power over a comparatively vast, marginal territory, the possibility of conquering older centers of wealth and skill with a semibarbarian force organized along civilized lines regularly arose and was often acted on.

the continent of Europe had won a qualified success. Instead of renewing full-scale combat on European soil, French energies in the relatively peaceful forty years that followed turned towards overseas enterprise in the islands of the Caribbean, in North America, in India, and in the Mediterranean Levant. Merchants and planters met with great success: French overseas trade actually increased more rapidly than that of Great Britain, though since the British started the century at a higher level, French trade never overtook British in absolute volume.[4]

National rivalries, however sharp, were effectually adjusted by monopolizing trade in particular ports and regions of America, Africa, and the Indian Ocean shorelines. Such local monopolies were sustained by local armed force—forts, garrisons, settlers—supplied and knitted together by the coming and going of ships which were themselves almost always armed with heavy cannon and could, in emergency, be supplemented by a detachment of warships sent from the home country to reinforce, protect, and extend imperial footholds overseas.

The growing French and British trade empires interpenetrated older European overseas establishments in complicated and shifting fashion. After 1715, home governments in Holland, Spain, and Portugal could no longer protect their imperial possessions against the assault of a major expeditionary force launched from Europe. Yet these older overseas empires survived precariously and without really major territorial loss. This was largely due to the fact that legally or by tacit disregard for the law Spanish, Portuguese, and Dutch imperial administrators admitted French and/or British traders to do business in the ports they controlled, thus giving the two greatest sea powers of the century the practical benefits of trade without requiring them to pay the costs of local administration. Towards the end of the century, moreover, Spanish imperial resources in the Americas began to increase. The collapse of Amerindian populations, which had provoked radical depopulation and labor shortages in the sixteenth and early seventeenth centuries, bottomed out after about 1650, at least in Mexico and Peru. Slowly, at first, and then with accelerating rapidity, population growth began to permit fuller exploitation of local resources.[5] Brazil, too, started to flourish and so did the English colonies

4. Cf. François Crouzet, "Angleterre et France au XVIIIe siècle: Essai d'analyze comparée de deux croissances économiques," *Annales: Economies, sociétés, civilisations* 21 (1966): 261–63 and passim.

5. On population phenomena in the New World see Nicholas Sanchez-Albornoz, *The Population of Latin America* (Berkeley and Los Angeles, 1974), pp. 104–29; Shelbourne

of North America. As a result, American manpower and local supplies permitted more and more significant local defense.

In this process of overseas expansion, market behavior played the
organizing role. Profits from trade supported European overseas
activity and increased its scale decade by decade. At the same time,
profits were guaranteed by ready resort to armed force. No other part
of the earth supported an armed establishment as efficient as those
which European states routinely maintained; and nowhere outside of
Europe was the management of armed force in the hands of persons
sympathetic to or much concerned about traders' profits. European
rulers, by contrast, had been accustomed since the fourteenth century
to finding themselves enmeshed in a commercial-financial system for
organizing human effort. Even when reluctant and uncomprehending,
kings and ministers depended on market-regulated behavior for the
supply and maintenance of their armed forces and of their governmental command structure in general. In England after the 1640s and
in France after the 1660s rulers ceased to struggle against the constraints of the market in the fashion Philip II of Spain and most of his
contemporary rulers had done. Instead a conscious collaboration between rulers and their officials on the one hand and capitalist entrepreneurs on the other became normal.

The rise of French and British overseas enterprise registered and
reflected the relatively smooth cooperation between business
mentality and political management that came to prevail in those
countries. Instead of looking upon private capital as a tempting and
obvious target for confiscatory taxation, as rulers in other parts of the
world regularly did, the political masters of western Europe came to
believe, and acted on the belief, that by setting precise limits to taxation and collecting designated sums equably, private wealth and total
tax receipts could both be made to grow. Wealthy merchants and
money-lenders could afford to live in London, Bristol, Bordeaux, or
Nantes under the jurisdiction of the British or French governments,
instead of seeking refuge, as in earlier centuries, in independent cities
governed by men of their own ilk.

For men of commerce the advantage of living under a militarily
formidable government was obvious: they could rely on a more efficacious and far-ranging military protection for their enterprise than

---

F. Cook and Woodrow W. Borah, *Essays in Population History: Mexico and the Caribbean,*
2 vols. (Berkeley and Los Angeles, 1971, 1974). As subsequently among Polynesians
and other island dwellers of the Pacific, the drastic population die-off that followed
initial contacts with white men was due mainly to exposure to imported infections.

when small, comparatively weak states alone permitted them free pursuit of the gains of the market. The advantage to kings and ministers of permitting a vigorous capitalist class to pursue private gain wherever a prospective profit could be discovered became equally obvious in the eighteenth century, for their activities began to swell total tax receipts and made the maintenance of standing armies and navies, which had been financially difficult in the seventeenth century, relatively easy.[6]

Cooperation between rulers and capitalists at home was matched by cooperation overseas. Indeed, the capacity to protect themselves and their goods at comparatively low cost was the central secret of European commercial expansion in the eighteenth century. It arose partly from the technical superiority of European ships and forts combined with the abundance and comparative cheapness of iron cannon. An equally critical element in European merchants' lower protection costs was the superior organization and discipline which European-trained troops, officers, and administrators commonly exhibited, even when stationed half the globe away from the seat of sovereignty and source of instruction, pay, and promotion upon which their obedience ultimately depended.

Many factors entered into this phenomenon, among them the psychological effect of repeated drill that made soldiers into obedient, replaceable parts of a military machine. However ill-supplied or poorly disciplined European troops stationed overseas may have seemed to an officer newly arrived from European parade grounds, their superiority over Asian, African, or Amerindian armed forces became apparent whenever local collisions occurred. In India, for example, when struggle for dominion over that vast land broke out between French and English military entrepreneurs, ridiculously small European contingents regularly played decisive roles, less because of their weaponry than because of their dependable obedience on the battlefield and their maneuverability in the face of an enemy.[7]

6. The Royal Navy, for example, was chronically short of funds in Samuel Pepys' time, whereas by the early decades of the eighteenth century, the financial expedients—postponement of payment and laying up of ships for part of the year which had been common practice in the late seventeenth century—ceased to be necessary. Cf. Daniel A. Baugh, *British Naval Administration in the Age of Walpole* (Princeton, 1965), p. 496 and passim; Robert G. Albion, *Forests and Sea Power: The Timber Problem of the Royal Navy, 1652–1862* (Cambridge, Mass., 1926), p. 66. For parallel improvement in the punctuality of French army pay and tightening of financial administration in the eighteenth century see A. Corvisier, *L'armée française de la fin du XVIIe siècle au ministère de Choiseul: le Soldat* (Paris, 1964), 2:822–24; Lee Kennett, *The French Armies in the Seven Years War* (Durham, N.C., 1967), p. 95.

7. Cf. James P. Lawford, *Britain's Army in India, from its Origins to the Conquest of Bengal* (London, 1978). At the Battle of Plassey (1757) Robert Clive commanded 784

The really important result of the balance between superior armed force and almost untrammeled commercial self-seeking that characterized European ventures overseas in the eighteenth century was the fact that the daily lives of hundreds of thousands, and by the end of the century of millions, of Asians, Africans, and Americans were transformed by the activity of European entrepreneurs. Market-regulated activity, managed and controlled by a handful of Europeans, began to eat into and break down older social structures in nearly all the parts of the earth that were easily accessible by sea. Africans, enslaved by raiding parties, marched to ports for shipment across the Atlantic, and consigned to work on sugar plantations, represent a brutal and extreme example of the way the profit motive could and did transform older patterns of life fundamentally. Indonesians, required to work in spice groves by local princelings who in their turn obeyed Dutch commands, were less completely abstracted from their accustomed routines and social setting; and the same was true of Indian cotton manufacturers who produced cloth for the East India Company to sell in markets hundreds or even thousands of miles removed from their spinning wheels and looms. Tobacco and cotton growers in the Mediterranean Levant and in North America represent yet another degree of personal independence vis-à-vis the merchants and brokers who put the product of their labor into international circulation. But all such people shared the fact that their daily routines of life came to depend upon a worldwide European-managed system of trade, in which the supply of goods, credit, and protection affected the livelihood, and often governed the physical survival of persons who had no understanding of, nor the slightest degree of control over, the commercial network in which they found themselves enmeshed.

No doubt Europeans gathered most of the profits into their own hands; but specialization of production also meant that wealth increased generally, even if it was very unevenly distributed among social classes and between European organizers and those who worked at their command or in response to their inducements. Even in Africa, where the devastation of slave raiding certainly crippled many communities and blasted innumerable human lives, it was also the case that new techniques and skills—most notably the spread of maize cultivation—enhanced African wealth; and the power of strategically sit-

---

European soldiers, 10 field guns, and about 2,100 Indians trained and equipped according to European methods. He routed an army of some 50,000. Cf. Mark Bence-Jones, *Clive of India* (New York, 1974), pp. 133–43.

uated African states also clearly tended to grow, thanks in part to access to weapons supplied by European traders.[8]

In the New World, as in the Old, inland regions where transport and communications were difficult remained slenderly affected by the network of trade that European enterprise wove along the shorelines of the Atlantic and Indian oceans. Yet the reach of the world market could be very long. In the frozen north, for example, the high value placed on furs led European traders to penetrate the entire breadth of North America before the eighteenth century came to its close. They entered into relations with local tribes, offering metal tools, blankets, and whiskey in exchange for furs. As a result, older Amerindian patterns of life underwent rapid and irreversible change. Russian fur traders did the same to the populations of Siberia, and in fact crossed to Alaska as early as 1741. Accordingly, in the last decades of the eighteenth century, Spanish and British claims to the Pacific coastline of North America met and collided with the expanding Russian fur trade empire, an encounter that dramatizes how Europe's overseas expansion was matched by an equally remarkable Russian eastward expansion.

Europe's land frontier was, indeed, almost as important in altering European power balances as the overseas trade empires that nourished French and British power so remarkably in the early eighteenth century. The vast Siberian wilderness—though impressive on the map —mattered less than the occupation of steppelands in the Ukraine and adjacent regions by grain farmers. Their labors increased European food production very substantially in the course of the century and provided a human and material base for the growth of the Russian empire.

Russia was not the sole power to profit from the spread of agriculture into the steppelands of eastern Europe. Indeed the seventeenth century had seen a complex struggle for dominion over the western steppes in which local polities like the principality of Transylvania as well as the Polish nobles' republic competed with the three more distant monarchies of Turkey, Austria, and Russia for control over this part of the world.[9] The upshot, by the close of the eighteenth century, definitely favored Russia, for the portions of the steppe that fell to Turkey (Rumania) and to Austria (Hungary) were much less extensive

---

8. Cf. the summing up of the impact of the slave trade on Africa in Paul Bohannan and Philip Curtin, *Africa and Africans* (New York, 1971), pp. 273–76.

9. For an account of these struggles, see William H. McNeill, *Europe's Steppe Frontier, 1500–1800* (Chicago, 1964), pp. 126–221.

than Russia's portion (the Ukraine and grasslands eastward into central Asia). As for Poland, internal quarrels so weakened that country that it disappeared entirely as a sovereign state through three successive partitions, 1773, 1793, and 1795.

Before Poland's political demise dramatized the sharp changes that had come to power-relationships in eastern Europe, another claimant to great-power status arose: the kingdom of Prussia. Like their territorially more impressive neighbors, Prussian rulers benefited from governing a march state. Prussia's comparatively large size among German principalities reflected its medieval frontier history. Even as late as the eighteenth century, by importing techniques long familiar in more westerly lands—artificial drainage and canalization above all—Prussians were able to bring considerable amounts of new land under cultivation, thereby increasing the country's wealth.[10]

But the basis of Prussia's political success was the superior rigor of its organization for war—a rigor that dated back to the seventeenth century when heartfelt local reaction against Swedish depredations found effective institutional expression within the lands of the Hohenzollern princely dynasty. After the war, the Great Elector, Frederick William (r. 1640–88), was able to beat down local opposition to centralized taxation. This allowed him and his successors to maintain an army large enough to count in European wars, despite the narrow extent and scant resources of the original domains of the electorate. The Great Elector, like many another German prince, built up his army by accepting subsidies from foreign powers to supplement local taxation. Not until the reign of Frederick William I (1713–40) did the Hohenzollerns become financially self-sufficient. This became possible only through a remarkable fusion between the nobility and the officer corps which made the king's service (the royal title dated from 1701) the normal career for rural landholders. The "king's coat" worn without badges of rank by all officers below general rank, and by Frederick William I as well, made all officers equals, and equally the servants of the house of Hohenzollern. Both officers and soldiers lived very frugal, indeed poverty-stricken lives, yet a collective spirit of "honor" and sense of duty raised the Prussian army to a level of efficiency—and cheapness—no other European force came near to equaling. As a result, a succession of canny rulers added to the size of the Prussian army and to the extent of Hohenzollern territories, but

10. Cf. Anton Zottman, *Die Wirtschaftspolitik Friedrichs des Grossen mit besondere Berücksichtigung der Kriegswirtschaft* (Leipzig, 1937); W. O. Henderson, *Studies in the Economic Policy of Frederick the Great* (London, 1963).

the leap to great-power status came only when Frederick the Great (r. 1740–86) seized the province of Silesia from Austria and made good his usurpation in the War of the Austrian Succession (1740–48).[11]

The disturbances to older balances of power within Europe which frontier expansion thus provoked were registered in the diplomatic revolution that preceded the Seven Years War (1756–63). The rivalry between the Hapsburg and French monarchies, which dated back to their quarrels over the Burgundian inheritance (1477) and around which the rivalries of lesser European states had long revolved, was replaced after 1756 by half-hearted cooperation between France and Austria aimed against their increasingly formidable respective rivals—Great Britain and Prussia. Yet despite the apparent magnitude of French and Austrian resources, it was the British and the Prussians who won the war. Great Britain's victories overseas drove the French from Canada and all but eliminated them from India as well. Recovery of French naval power, though real enough by 1788, did not suffice to repair the setback to French commerce that the defeats of 1754–63 had wrought.

Prussia's survival against the assault of the Austrian, French, and Russian armies was a tribute to the efficiency of Prussian drillmasters, to the morale of the Prussian officer corps, and to Frederick II's personal abilities as a general. Yet it is also the case that cracks in the alliance were what allowed Prussia to survive. In particular the withdrawal of Russian forces from the war when a new tsar, Peter III, came to the throne in 1762 gave Frederick a breathing space he desperately needed; and in the next year, their ill success against Great Britain persuaded the French to withdraw from the war, thus compelling the Austrians also to make peace (1763).

Prussia's military reputation rose to a pinnacle on the strength of Frederick's remarkable survival against what had appeared to be overwhelming odds. This did much to disguise from contemporaries the pivotal reality of eastern Europe, to wit, the rise of Russian power. Events in the nineteenth and twentieth centuries have likewise made Prussian (later German) history seem central to the history of Europe as a whole. Yet one can argue very plausibly that Russia was the state that profited most from Frederick's aggressive policies. (He had precipitated war in 1740 and again in 1756 by invading Hapsburg lands.) The ill-feeling that divided Austria from Prussia after 1740 meant that cooperation between those two states became next to impossible.

11. Cf. Otto Büsch, *Militarsystem und Sozialleben im alten Preussen* (Berlin, 1962), pp. 77–99 and passim; Herbert Rosinski, *The German Army* (New York, 1966), pp. 21–26.

Their mutual distrust made it easy for Russia to use the army that Peter the Great had successfully remodeled along European lines to continue expansion at the expense of weak and comparatively ill-organized polities abutting on Russia's frontiers. Thus Russia secured the lion's share of Poland, 1773–95; annexed the Crimea in 1783; extended its frontiers against the Ottoman empire into the Caucasus on the east and to the Dniester on the west by 1792; and advanced into Finland at the expense of the Swedes as well (1790). Rapid development of grain production in the Ukraine together with industrial and commercial expansion in the Urals and in central Russia supported the rise of the imperial power to unexampled heights. Under Catherine the Great (r. 1762–95) Russia was able as never before to organize its resources of manpower, raw materials, and arable land to support armed forces whose efficiency approached that of the armies and navies of western Europe. Russia, in short, was catching up to European levels of organization; as this occurred the advantages of size began to tell.

British success in the Seven Years War against France was also, in part, the result of mobilization of resources drawn from far-flung territories in North America, India, and regions in between. But whereas in the Russian case, mobilization rested ultimately on serf labor, directed by an elite of officials and officially licensed private entrepreneurs, in the British case compulsion was largely eclipsed by reliance on market incentives registered in private choices made by relatively large numbers of individuals. Yet slave labor on Caribbean plantations and press gangs for manning the navy also played prominent roles in maintaining British power. So the contrast between a frontier mobilization through command *à la russe* and mobilization through price incentives *à l'anglaise* is only a matter of degree. But the degree of compulsion mattered. Russian methods (like the slave economies of the sugar islands) were often quite wasteful of manpower, whereas private efforts to maximize profits tended to reward economies in the use of all the factors of production. Market behavior, in short, induced a level of efficiency that compulsion rarely could match.

In particular, responsiveness to a more or less free market meant that new techniques, capable of effecting real improvements in production, were sometimes able to win acceptance in the British system of economic management, whereas in Russia impulses to invent or to propagate new inventions were sporadic at best. Harassed administrators were almost always sure to decide that it was better to meet their superiors' instructions by adhering to familiar methods of work, and to increase production, if that was what was wanted, either by driving the labor force harder or by securing more workers. The alternative of trying some newfangled device that was sure to detract from short-run results and might not work in the long run either, was seldom even considered. Only when a technique had proved successful abroad was it worthwhile for Russian administrators to disrupt existing arrangements by importing the novelty—often along with foreign technicians to instruct the local work force in the use of the new methods.

At the beginning of the eighteenth century Russian armaments and Russian armies had been built up in this fashion by Peter the Great. The stability of European military organization and technique in the following decades meant that catching up and outstripping smaller powers became comparatively easy for Russian administrators and army officers to achieve. The success of Russian arms, especially in the second half of the eighteenth century, attests their ability to do so.[12]

The superior flexibility of market behavior in making room for technical innovation eventually allowed Great Britain, and western Europe generally, to steal a march on the Russians by raising economic and military efficiency to a level that eclipsed Russian and east European achievements. This did not become clear until after 1850, however. Before then, from 1736 to 1853, Russia's ambitions were only precariously contained by balance-of-power diplomacy and by the remarkable military explosion that the French Revolution generated.

The balance of power also worked to minimize the overseas preponderance that Great Britain seemed to have won in 1763. In particular, the disappearance of the French threat from Canada made British relations with the North American colonists more difficult than before; and when King George III's government sought to compel the colonists to help pay for the war, discontent turned into open rebellion. Soon France came to the aid of the American rebels (1778) and other European powers either joined the French or expressed their dislike of a British overseas trade monopoly by an "armed neu-

---

12. Naval technique was harder to master, and the Russian navy that sailed into the Mediterranean in 1770 to attack the Turks was not really up to French or British standards, though it overwhelmed the Turkish navy easily enough. By 1790, moreover, the Russian navy had won secure mastery among Baltic powers by outclassing the Swedes permanently. Cf. Nestor Monasterev and Serge Terestchenko, *Histoire de la marine russe* (Paris, 1932), pp. 75–80; Donald W. Mitchell, *A History of Russian and Soviet Sea Power* (New York, 1974), pp. 16–102.

trality" that was inimical to British interests. By 1783, Great Britain was compelled to admit defeat and recognized the independence of the United States of America.

In this way, then, the European state system partially counteracted the rise of British and of Russian power, and adjusted itself to the upheavals that resulted from the expansion of European economic-military organization to extensive new regions of the earth between 1700 and 1793.

Challenges Arising from Deliberate Reorganization

European adjustment to territorial expansion was, in a sense, quite normal—a semiautomatic consequence of balance-of-power calculations on the part of political leaders. It was a pattern that could be matched by similar behavior in other times and places—e.g., among Greek city-states responding to Athens' rise in the fifth century, or among the principalities of Italy in the fourteenth and fifteenth centuries in response to the rise of Milanese and Venetian power. On the other hand, the reorganization of political, economic, and military management that began to manifest itself as the eighteenth century neared its close was unique, not because other states in other ages had not also sought to increase their military power by internal reorganization, but because the scope and complexity of the techniques accessible to European administrators and soldiers had become enormously greater than in any earlier age. Rational calculation so enlarged the scope of deliberate action that, before the end of the century, managerial decisions began to change the lives of millions of persons.

Military manpower and materiel were clearly in the forefront of this managerial transformation. In the seventeenth century armies and navies had become, so to speak, works of art in which human lives as well as ships and guns were shaped according to preconceived plans for quite specialized uses. Results were spectacular, as we saw in the last chapter. In the early part of the eighteenth century further changes were minimal. After 1750, however, as population growth began to alter social reality everywhere, experts started to tinker with existing ways of managing and deploying armed force in the hope of escaping limits inherent in the older system. Nothing dramatic was achieved before 1792; but long before then military reformers foreshadowed the mass mobilization brought about by the French Revolution.

By the mid-eighteenth century, four limits in existing patterns of military organization had become apparent. One of these was the difficulty of controlling the movements of an army of more than about 50,000 men.[13] Even with the help of galloping aides-de-camp a general could not usually know what was happening when a battle front extended much further than a spy glass could distinguish friend from foe; and tactical control, even when bugles supplemented shouted commands, could not reach beyond the battalion level, i.e., 300–600 men. New forms of communication and accurate topographical maps were necessary before effective command of larger field armies could become possible.

Supply constituted a second and very powerful constraint on European armies. The perfection of their drill gave European armies unique formidability and flexibility at short range and for a few hours of battle. But at longer range, force could be brought to bear in a new location only by slow, sporadic stages. Available transport simply could not concentrate enough food to support thousands of horses and men if they kept on the move day after day. The Prussian army under Frederick the Great, for example, assuredly the most mobile and formidable European army of its day, could march for a maximum of ten days before a pause became necessary to bring up bake ovens and rearrange supply lines from the rear. Fodder for horses was the most difficult of all, for it was too bulky to travel far. Frederick's soldiers, indeed, sometimes stopped to cut hay for the horses even when bread supplies for their own nourishment were in hand.[14] Living off the country was possible at appropriate seasons of the year but risked loss of control over soldiers who might be expected to prefer plundering unarmed peasants to deploying against the enemy. For this reason, together with the realization that a devastated countryside could not pay taxes, eighteenth-century rulers sought to supply their armies from the rear, thereby submitting to drastic limitations on strategic mobility.

Supply of weapons, gunpowder, uniforms, and other equipment did

13. Maurice de Saxe held that no general could effectively control more than 40,000 men in the field. Cf. Eugène Carrias, *La pensée militaire française* (Paris, n.d.), p. 170. Jacques-Antoine Hypolite de Guibert, *Essai générale de tactique,* in 1772 fixed 50,000 as the ideal size of an army, and 70,000 as an absolute ceiling. Only so, he believed, could real field mobility be sustained. Cf. Robert A. Quimby, *The Background of Napoleonic Warfare: The Theory of Military Tactics in 18th Century France,* Columbia University Studies in the Social Sciences, no. 596 (New York, 1957), p. 164.

14. Christopher Duffy, *The Army of Frederick the Great* (Newton Abbot, 1974), pp. 135–36. For French supply limitations see Kennett, *French Armies in the Seven Years War,* pp. 100–111. For a general overview, Martin L. van Creveld, *Supplying War: Logistics from Wallenstein to Patton* (Cambridge, 1977) also offers interesting data.

not normally set limits on military enterprise. Costs of such items were comparatively small.[15] Food, fodder, horses, and transport were what usually ran short. All the same, the artisan production of muskets, cloth, shoes, and the like, and the manufacture of artillery pieces in state arsenals could not easily be expanded. Accordingly, wars were usually fought with stocks accumulated beforehand. When serious losses occurred, as happened to Prussian armies in the Seven Years War, purchase abroad became necessary, and this of course required money. The principal international arms market continued to center in the Low Countries, most notably at Liège and Amsterdam.[16]

A third limit was organizational and tactical. Europe's standing armies carried into the eighteenth century many traces of their origin from privately raised mercenary companies. As a result, proprietary rights often conflicted with bureaucratic rationality in matters of recruitment, appointment, and promotion. Professional skill competed with patronage and purchase as paths to advancement, while both were tempered by the principle of seniority on the one hand and by acts of valor in battle on the other. Appointments and promotion often reflected the king's personal choice or those of his minister of war.

The consequent erratic and changeable patterns of personnel administration found expression in France through heated debates over tactics. Rival groupings of officers embraced rival doctrines, and used those doctrines as tools in their struggle for places in the military hierarchy. But claim and counter claim could be settled only by experimental field maneuvers or by test firings and the like. Debate, fueled by clique rivalries for promotion, therefore, had the remarkable effect in France of opening the door on systematic testing of new materiel (especially field artillery) and tactics. Under these pressures, the fixity of Old Regime military practices had begun to crumble even before the French Revolution came along to accelerate and magnify what rivalry among professionals had already begun.

The limits of command technique, of supply, and of organization

15. According to an official reckoning made soon after the Seven Years War ended, only 13 percent of Prussia's total expenditure in that war went to pay for materiel; and weapons, powder, and lead, together, required a mere 1 percent. Paul Rehfeld, "Die preussische Rüstungsindustrie unter Friedrich dem Grossen," *Forschungen zür brandenburgischen und preussischen Geschichte* 55 (1944): 30.

16. Violet Barbour, *Capitalism in Amsterdam in the 17th Century,* reprint (Ann Arbor, Mich., 1963), pp. 36–42; J. Yerneaux, *La métallurgie liègeoise et son expansion au XVIIe siècle* (Liège, 1939); Claude Gaier, *Four Centuries of Liège Gunmaking* (London, 1977).

were all connected with and sustained by a fourth limit: the sociological and psychological restraints that went along with the professionalization of warfare. As a handful of sovereign rulers monopolized organized violence and bureaucratized its management in Europe, war became, as never before, the sport of kings. Since the sport had to be paid for by taxation, it seemed wise to leave the productive, taxpaying classes undisturbed. Peasants were needed to produce the food, and townsmen were needed to provide the money that supported governments and their armed establishments. For soldiers to interfere with their activities was to endanger the goose that laid the golden eggs. Yet the exclusion of the great majority of the population from any but a passive, taxpaying role set a ceiling upon the scale and intensity of war which the French Revolution was destined to discard.

Long before that breakthrough, however, inventions of scores of experts and technicians had prepared the way for the revolutionary expansion in the scale of warfare. Such efforts got seriously underway whenever a great power met with unexpected failure in war. Thus, for example, their lack of success first against the Turks (1736–39) and then against the Prussians and French in the War of the Austrian Succession (1740–48) led Austrian authorities to develop more mobile and accurate field guns than had been known before.[17] The improved Hapsburg artillery gave the Prussians a nasty surprise in the Seven Years War; but after its conclusion the state that had most to regret was France, whose former primacy on the battlefield had been called into question by defeats at the hands of both the Prussian (Rossbach, 1757) and English-German armies (Minden, 1759). Not surprisingly, therefore, France became the most important seat of military experimentation and technical innovation in the decades that intervened between the Peace of Paris in 1763 and the outbreak of the French Revolution in 1789.

Innovation, whether among the Austrians, French, or British (especially after their defeat in 1783), pressed hard against each of the limits to the management of war mentioned above. Thus, for example, the limits of command based on coup d'oeil and mounted reconnaisance were slowly overcome by the development of accurate mapping, changes in command organization, and resort to written orders prepared in advance by specially trained staff officers. The French began to compile the first accurately surveyed small-scale maps suitable for staff use in 1750, but it took many years before all of Europe was

---

17. I have been unable to find a copy of A. Dolleczeck, *Geschichte der österreichischen Artillerie* (Vienna, 1887) for details.

mapped on such a scale as to allow a commander in the field to plan each day's march from a map.[18] Nevertheless, as early as 1763 a French general, Pierre Bourçet, had grasped the possibility, and, in the ensuing years, actually drew up detailed plans for campaigns along French borders and for the invasion of England. He prepared a handbook in 1775 for private circulation within the French army entitled *Les principes de la guerre de montagne* in which he explained how a commander should plan troop movements and supply on a day-by-day basis from maps; and when Napoleon invaded Italy in 1797 he is said to have used Bourçet's plan for crossing the Alps and taking the Austrians by surprise.[19]

Control of army movements by means of maps required a staff of experts in map reading and logistics. Bourçet understood this and, in 1765, set up a school for training aides-de-camp in the new art. It was disbanded in 1771, reestablished in 1783, and suppressed again in 1790. This on-again off-again pattern reflected personal and doctrinal disputes within the French army that characterized the entire period between the end of the Seven Years War and the outbreak of the Revolution twenty-six years later.

Such an atmosphere proved fertile in other directions as well. High command, relying on maps and written orders prepared in advance by specially trained staff officers, could perhaps hope to control armies three or four times the size that Maurice de Saxe had judged to be the upper limit of effective command; but to do so a general needed to break his army up into parts, since existing roads and lines of supply could not possibly accommodate scores of thousands of men. Parallel lines of march undertaken by self-sufficient units that would be able to defend themselves if they stumbled on an enemy along the route of advance were what the situation required.

This was met by the invention of the division, i.e., of an army unit in

18. Use of contour lines to indicate slopes was a critical invention for making maps useful to military commanders. Symbols for marshes and other obstacles to cross-country movement were also important but far easier to devise. Topographic contour lines seem to have been first proposed in 1777 by a French lieutenant of engineers, J. B. Meusnier; but use of lines to show water depths was far older, dating back among the Dutch as far as 1584. Scarcity of data delayed resort to contour lines, which became standard on small-scale maps only after about 1810 when improved surveying instruments made gathering data far easier and more rapid. Cf. François de Dainville, "From the Depth to the Heights," *Surveying and Mapping* 30 (1970): 389–403; Pierre Chalmin, "La querelle des Bleus et des Rouges dans l'artillerie française à la fin du XVIIIe siècle," *Revue d'histoire économique et sociale* 46 (1968): 481 ff.

19. Dallas D. Irvine, "The Origins of Capital Staffs," *Journal of Modern History* 10 (1938): 166–68; Carrias, *La pensée militaire française,* pp. 176 ff.

which the deployment of infantry, cavalry, artillery, and supporting elements like engineers, medical personnel, and communications experts could be coordinated by an appropriate staff and subordinated to a single commander. Numbering up to 12,000, a division could act as an independent fighting unit, complete in itself, or, as the case might be, could combine with others, converging on an enemy or on a strategic point according to plans devised by superior headquarters. French experiments along these lines dated back to the War of the Austrian Succession (1740–48), but it was only in 1787–88 that army administration was permanently arranged along divisional lines, and in the field divisional organization did not become standard until 1796.[20]

With mapping, skilled staff officers, written orders, and a divisional structure, the French were thus in a position by 1788 to surpass older limits on the effective size of field armies. The *levée en masse* of 1793 would have been useless otherwise. Mere numbers, without effective control on the battlefield, could not have won the victories that in fact came to the revolutionary armies.

Less could be done to relieve limitations of supply. Wagons and boats could carry only so much food and fodder from here to there along existing roads, canals, or rivers. Every improvement in roads and every new canal increased the ease and rapidity with which goods could circulate; and the eighteenth century, particularly its second half, was a time when Europeans invested in roads and canals on a scale far greater than ever before. In Prussia, canal building was consciously connected with strategic planning. Canals constructed during the reign of Frederick the Great, uniting the Oder with the Elbe into a single internal waterway, were intended to assure speedy and secure movement of grain and other supplies into and out of the royal military depots. As Frederick himself remarked to his generals: "The advantage of navigation is, however, never to be neglected, for without this convenience, no army can be abundantly supplied."[21] In France and England direct linkage between communications improvements and military convenience seems not to have prevailed, with the exception of the road building through the Highlands of Scotland which British authorities undertook after the rebellion of 1745. Instead, toll roads and canals were usually built by private entrepreneurs who expected to make a profit from their investments. To

20. Stephen T. Ross, "The Development of the Combat Division in Eighteenth Century French Armies," *French Historical Studies* 1 (1965): 84–94.
21. Quoted from Geoffrey Symcox, ed., *War, Diplomacy and Imperialism, 1618–1763* (London, 1974), p. 194. Cf. also Duffy, *The Army of Frederick the Great*, p. 134.

be sure, state control and direction was far more pervasive on the Continent than in Great Britain;[22] but even when relatively short-term economic returns were what governed private as well as official action, transport improvements always had the further effect of facilitating military supply. Without such improvements, and without technical advances in road building which made possible relatively cheap construction of roads that were passable for wheeled vehicles even in wet and rainy weather,[23] the scale of armed enterprise the French revolutionaries inaugurated would have been impossible.

The armies of the French Republic were also heirs of tactical and technical advances that had been worked out in the French army after 1763. Professional pride had been badly stung by the failures and defeats of the Seven Years War. Resistance to innovation was diminished by a pervasive sense that something had to be done to regain the lead France had once enjoyed over Prussia on land and over Great Britain on the seas. But reforms inaugurated by one minister of war created a party of aggrieved officers who sought redress each time a new minister took office. Since no one could well defend a status quo which had led to failure in the Seven Years War, the rival parties instead espoused rival reforms, thus generating heated debate about tactics and army administration.

Far-reaching changes occurred rather rapidly under these circumstances. Recruitment ceased to be a responsibility of captains; instead, the king's recruiters enlisted soldiers for fixed terms of service with fixed pay and perquisites. Purchase of commissions was phased out; and the rules for promotion were made public and uniform. Regiments were made to conform to identical tables of organization; and, as we saw, the army was reorganized into divisions. Principles of bureaucratic rationality, in other words, came to assert their dominion

22. Baron Vom Stein as a relatively junior Prussian official canalized the Ruhr River, for example, in the hope of expanding coal production. Cf. W. O. Henderson, *The State and the Industrial Revolution in Prussia, 1740–1870* (Liverpool, 1958), pp. 20–41.

23. By using crushed stones of different sizes to form three distinct layers, a French engineer named Pierre Trésaguet developed a relatively cheap way to build an all-weather road. His methods were widely used in France after 1764; other European countries followed suit as far east as Russia, where a road between Moscow and St. Petersburg was built on Trésaguet's principles. In Great Britain John Loudon McAdam became interested in the problems of road building in the 1790s and developed a very similar method for making durable road surfaces. McAdam used only one size of crushed rock, thus simplifying procedures. Cf. Gösta E. Sandström, *Man the Builder* (New York, 1970), pp. 200–201; Roy Devereux, *The Colossus of Roads: A Life of John Loudon McAdam* (New York, 1936).

over more and more aspects of French military administration, even though opposition to such a transformation did not disappear.[24]

Rival tactical systems were put to the test of field maneuvers in 1778, and even though the partisans of each system disagreed about what had been proved, by degrees enough consensus was achieved to permit the French ministry of war to issue a new and more flexible tactical manual in 1791. It remained standard throughout the revolutionary wars. The new regulations authorized column, line, and skirmishers on the battlefield, according to circumstance and the judgment of the commander. Other European armies had mostly gone over to Prussian tactics after Frederick the Great's brilliant victories in the Seven Years War.[25] As a result, the French revolutionary infantry was able to move about on the battlefield faster and more freely than armies adhering to the rigid battle line favored by Frederick II, and could even operate effectively in rough and broken terrain.

Linear tactics required open fields in which to deploy; and when variegated cropping began to dictate enclosure, the landscape of western Europe became increasingly inhospitable to the old tactics. Too many fences, hedgerows, and ditches got in the way to permit a battle line two or three miles in length to form, much less to move. The French field exercises of 1778 were held in Normandy, in a region where hedgerows and open fields met and mingled. French experience thus took account of this transformation of west European landscapes, whereas further east, around Berlin or Moscow, open fields remained well suited to the old tactics.

Skirmishing had first attained prominence in European warfare thanks to the Austrian army. Maria Theresa incorporated the militia that had long guarded the Turkish border against local raiding parties into her field army during the War of the Austrian Succession. These wild "Croats," when deployed irregularly ahead of the line of battle, proved very formidable, harassing the enemy rear, interfering with supply convoys, and disturbing deployment of the enemy line with

---

24. Cf. Emile G. Leonard, *L'armée et ses problèmes au XVIIIe siècle* (Paris, 1958); Louis Mention, *Le comte de Saint-Germain et ses réformes, 1775–1777* (Paris, 1884); Albert Latreille, *L'armée et la nation à la fin de l'ancien régime: les derniers ministres de guerre de la monarchie* (Paris, 1914); Jean Lambert Alphonse Colin, *L'infanterie au XVIIIe siècle: La tactique* (Paris, 1907).

25. Great Britain set the fashion in 1757. Cf. Rex Whitworth, *Field Marshal Lord Ligonier: A Story of the British Army, 1702–1770* (Oxford, 1958), p. 218. The United States did the same by importing Baron von Steuben to drill the Continental Army in 1777.

sporadic sharpshooting before regular battle had been joined. Other armies soon began to create "light infantry" of their own to perform similar roles. French tactical improvements between 1763 and 1791 therefore drew freely on the experience of other European armies.[26]

Sometimes French innovations failed and were swiftly abandoned. This was the fate of an experiment with breech-loading muskets made in 1768.[27] After designers gave up this radical idea, a slightly modified muzzle-loader was declared standard in 1777 and remained unaltered until 1816. An old-fashioned design did not prevent upgrading of manufacture, however. Official inspectors began to insist on greater standardization of parts, with the result, presumably, that French muskets became more durable and accurate.[28]

Far more spectacular and important changes proved feasible in artillery design. Classification of cannon according to the weight of shot they could fire had been systematized in the age of Charles V in all European countries. Early in the eighteenth century, Jean-Florent de Vallière (1667–1759) reduced the number of different calibers in use in the French service. But this sort of standardization remained only approximate as long as each gun had to be cast in a unique and individual mold. It was well-nigh impossible to align the core of the mold accurately with the exterior, since at the time of casting the rush of hot metal almost always pushed the imperfectly centered and weakly supported core slightly out of position. Consequently, the chamber and barrel of the gun, which took its shape from the mold's core, usually were not perfectly parallel to the exterior of the piece; and lesser irregularities in interior dimensions were taken for granted. Cannon, as cast, were too heavy to keep up with marching troops and so seldom

---

26. On the tactical debate, cf. Colin, *L'infanterie au XVIIIe siècle;* Mention, *Le comte de Saint-Germain,* pp. 187–210; Quimby, *The Background of Napoleonic Warfare;* Robert R. Palmer, "Frederick the Great, Guibert, Bülow: From Dynastic to National War," in Edward M. Earle, ed., *Makers of Modern Strategy* (Princeton, 1943), pp. 49–74; Henry Spenser Wilkinson, *The French Army before Napoleon* (Oxford, 1915). For tactics and enclosure see Richard Glover, *Peninsular Preparation: The Reform of the British Army, 1795–1804* (Cambridge, 1963), p. 124. For skirmishing and light infantry see Gunther Rothenberg, *The Military Border in Croatia, 1740–1881: A Study of an Imperial Institution* (Chicago, 1966), pp. 18–39 and passim; Peter Paret, *Yorck and the Era of Prussian Reform, 1807–1815* (Princeton, 1966), pp. 24–42.

27. Several thousand breech-loading muskets were manufactured, but when the breech mechanism proved faulty, the inventor committed suicide, according to Kennett, *The French Armies in the Seven Years War,* pp. 116, 140.

28. After 1794, when the French annexed Liège, gunmakers of that city, the most practiced of all Europe, were compelled to upgrade their performance by the new French inspectors. For details see Gaier, *Four Centuries of Liège Gunmaking,* pp. 95 ff.

appeared on the battlefield. Their main use was to defend and attack fortresses, and on shipboard.

This situation was transformed by a Swiss engineer and gunfounder named Jean Maritz (1680–1743), who entered French employ at Lyons in 1734. He saw that it might be possible to achieve far more accurate and uniform results by casting cannon as a solid piece of metal and then boring the barrel out afterwards. It took Maritz time to develop a boring machine larger, more stable, and much more powerful than any previously known; and efforts to keep the new method secret, though not effective for long, did suffice to obscure the record of exactly when and how well he succeeded. By the 1750s, however, his son and successor, also named Jean Maritz (1711–90), had perfected the necessary machinery. In 1755 he became inspector general of gunfoundries and forges with the mission of installing his cannon-boring machines in all the royal arsenals of France.[29] Other European states soon became interested, and by the 1760s the new technique had been introduced as far afield as Russia.[30] A similar machine was set up in Great Britain by John Wilkinson in 1774.[31]

The advantages of a straight and uniform bore were enormous. Consistently true bores meant that gunners did not have to learn the vagaries of each individual weapon, and could expect to hit their target time and again. Accurately centered bores also made for safer guns since the gunmetal was of the same strength and thickness on every side of the explosion. Most important of all, guns could be made lighter and more maneuverable without losing power. These advantages arose mainly from the fact that a bored-out barrel allowed a far closer fit between cannonball and gun tube than had been considered safe hitherto, when minor irregularities in the interior walls of individual cannon, arising from variation in each mold, had required a generous space ("windage") between shot and barrel to avoid disastrous jamming. By reducing windage, a smaller powder charge could be made to accelerate a shot more rapidly than when more of the expanding gases had been free to escape around the projectile.

29. *Grande Encyclopédie,* s.v. Maritz, Jean; P. M. J. Conturie, *Histoire de la fonderie nationale de Ruelle, 1750–1940, et des anciennes fonderies de canons de fer de la Marine* (Paris, 1951), pp. 128–35.

30. In 1763 the Prussians imported a Dutch artificer to set up cannon-boring machines at the armaments works in Spandau. He was captured by the Russians when they occupied Berlin in 1760 and persuaded to perform the same service for them at Tula. Cf. Rehfeld, "Die preussische Rüstungsindustrie unter Friedrich dem Grossen," p. 11.

31. Clive Trebilcock, "Spin-off in British Economic History: Armaments and Industry, 1760–1914," *Economic History Review* 22 (1969): 477.

Cannon-Boring Machinery

This diagram shows how to bore out a cannon with machinery similar to the device invented by Jean Maritz. The secret of success lay in making the whole cannon revolve against the cutting edge, which was made to advance by weights, gears, and cogs that kept a steady pressure at the cutting face. This arrangement made it possible to hold the cutting head steady, while the cannon's bulk imparted enough inertia to the spin to prevent wobbling that might otherwise spoil the precision of the bore.

Gaspard Monge, *Description de l'art de fabriquer les canons,* Imprimée par Ordre du Comité de Salut Public, Paris, An 2 de la République française, pl. XXXXI.

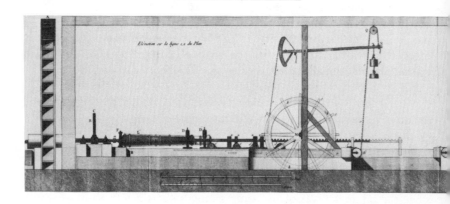

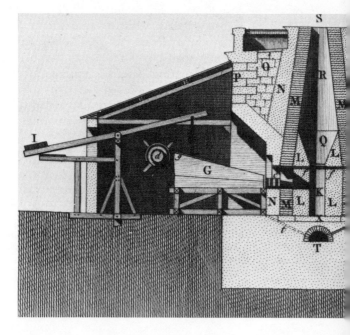

Blast Furnace Design

This diagram of blast furnaces at the French naval gunfoundry at Ruelle shows the capital plant that began to transform the ferrous metallurgical industries of Britain and France towards the end of the eighteenth century. These twin furnaces were ten meters high and could melt enough iron to cast several cannon at once. Note the power-driven bellows which intensified the fire by supplying extra oxygen to the flame.

Ibid., pl. II.

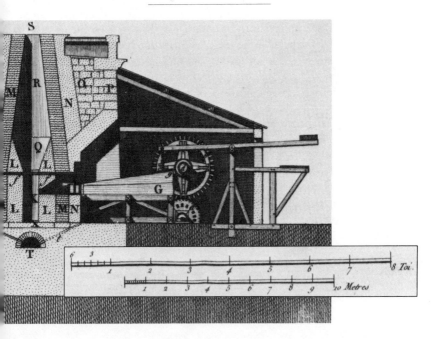

Smaller amounts of gunpowder could thus accomplish equivalent work even within a shortened gun barrel; and a smaller charge in turn made it safe to reduce the thickness of metal around the chamber where the explosion took place. Shortened barrels and thinner walls meant lighter guns, easier to move and quicker to return to firing position after recoil. Everything hinged on the accuracy of manufacture, and on systematic testing of sample weapons to find out how short the barrel and how thin the gun walls could safely be made and still achieve the desired velocity and missile throw weight.

Tests of this sort were carried through by French artillerists under the direction of Jean Baptiste Vacquette de Gribeauval between 1763 and 1767. Gribeauval also presided over similarly systematic efforts to redesign all the associated elements needed for field artillery: limbers, ammunition wagons, horse harnesses, gunsights, and the like. His idea was simple and radical: to apply reason and experiment to the task of creating a new weapons system. He succeeded in creating a powerful field artillery, able to keep up with marching infantry and capable, therefore, of playing a major role in battle.

Careful attention to detail magnified the basic improvement. Thus, for example, Gribeauval introduced a screw device for adjusting gun elevation precisely, and a new sight with an adjustable hairline made it possible to estimate accurately where a shot would hit before the gun was fired. On top of that, by combining shot and powder into a single package, rate of fire approximately doubled what had been possible when powder and shot had to be separately thrust down the cannon's throat. Finally, Gribeauval developed different kinds of shot—solid, shell, and canister—for different targets, thus assuring the guns' versatility.[32]

Sample models of Gribeauval's new artillery became available as early as 1765, but the new designs were not finally approved until 1776, owing to the quarrels and controversies which so distracted the French army in these years. Even after the new guns had been approved, manufacture to the new standards of precision was difficult, and opposition within the army to Gribeauval's artillery was not completely stilled until the divisional reorganization was decided on in 1788. Hence, new mobile field artillery was not in hand until the very eve of the Revolution. Gribeauval's guns remained standard throughout the Napoleonic wars and were phased out only in 1829. They

---

32. Very instructive diagrams illustrating how late eighteenth-century artillery worked may be found in B. P. Hughes, *Firepower Weapons' Effectiveness on the Battlefield, 1630–1850* (London, 1974), pp. 15–36.

were an important element in French victories from the Cannonade of Valmy (1792) onwards, for Gribeauval created a truly mobile field artillery, capable of reaching battlefields almost as readily as marching infantry could do and able to bombard targets at a distance of up to 1,100 yards or so.

A second aspect of Gribeauval's reforms was organizational. Transport of the new field artillery became the duty of the soldiers who fired them instead of remaining the responsibility of civilian contractors as had previously been customary. Drill on the guns, practicing motions needed to unlimber, position, aim, and fire, attained the routine precision that had long been characteristic of small-arms drill. Gribeauval also set up schools for artillery officers to teach theoretical aspects of gunnery along with how to fit the new guns to approved infantry and cavalry tactics. Rational management and design was thus extended from materiel to the human beings needed to man the redesigned weapons. As a result, the medieval craft guild heritage disappeared entirely from the French service, and artillery took its place in the new divisional structure side by side with infantry and cavalry as part of a reorganized and redesigned command structure embodying the results of rational thought and systematic testing.

Gribeauval's career is interesting not only in itself and for its contribution to French military successes after 1792, but also because what he and his associates did marked an important horizon in European management of armed force. These eighteenth-century French artillerists set out to create a weapon with performance characteristics previously unattainable, but whose use in battle could clearly be foreseen. With Gribeauval and his circle, in short, planned invention, organized and supported by public authority, becomes an unmistakable reality. Perhaps the rapid development of catapults in the Hellenistic age[33] and the remarkable design improvements that craftsmen made in cannon during the fifteenth century, when iron projectiles were first introduced, may have had something of the same character. But information about these earlier cases is scant, and the artificers who made catapults for Hellenistic rulers, as well as the bellmakers who used their art to cast guns for Charles the Bold and Louis XI may or may not have conceived in advance what better designed catapults and guns could do. The matter is simply not on record. But in the case of the French artillerists, it is perfectly clear that a reform party came

---

33: E. W. Marsden, *Greek and Roman Artillery: Historical Development* (Oxford, 1969), pp. 48–49, says that the primary loci of invention were the court of Dionysios I of Syracuse (399 B.C.) and that of Ptolemy II of Egypt (285–246 B.C.).

into being around the person of Gribeauval; that leaders of this group had clearly in mind what could be achieved by taking advantage of accurately bored gun barrels and saw their technical reforms as part of a more general rationalization of army organization and training.

The traditions of European army life, emphasizing hierarchy, obedience, and personal bravery, fitted awkwardly with Gribeauval's kind of cerebral calculation and experiment; and when technical experts sought to apply the same methods to general questions about how an army should be deployed and set out to raise the status of gunners to something like equality with infantry and cavalry, resistance was naturally intense. Sharp fluctuations of policy with respect to Gribeauval's reforms reflected this strain between an assertive rationalism and the cult of prowess (and other vested interests) within the army and within the French government as a whole.

A weapon that could be used to kill soldiers impersonally and at a distance of more than half a mile offended deep-seated notions of how a fighting man ought to behave. Gunners attacking infantry at long range were safe from direct retaliation: risk ceased to be symmetrical in such a situation, and that seemed unjust. Skill of an obscure, mathematical, and technological kind threatened to make old-fashioned courage and muscular prowess useless. The definition of what it meant to be a soldier was called into question by such a transformation, incipient and partial though it remained in the eighteenth century as compared to what was to come in the nineteenth and twentieth. The introduction of small arms in the sixteenth and seventeenth centuries had already diminished the role of direct hand-to-hand combat and muscular encounter in battle; only the cavalry, charging home with cold steel, preserved, under eighteenth-century conditions, the primitive reality of combat. This reinforced the prestige cavalry inherited in European armies from the days of knighthood. Nobles and conservatively minded soldiers in general clung energetically to the old-fashioned, muscular definition of battle. Artillerymen with their cold-blooded mathematics seemed subversive of all that made a soldier's life heroic, admirable, worthy.

This sort of heartfelt emotion seldom found clear articulation. It tapped irrational levels of human personality, and those who felt keenly the wrongness of long-range artillery were not usually gifted in the use of words. But newfangled technicians and their angriest opponents could agree on one thing: sale of commissions to the highest bidder allowed the wrong kind of men to become officers. To exclude unqualified parvenus and keep commissions in military families, the

French Ministry of War accordingly decreed in 1781 that to qualify for infantry and cavalry commissions candidates must prove four quarterings of nobility. Ambitious noncoms were the only constituency within the army displeased by this act, since the artillery remained, as before, open to commoners with suitable mathematical skills.[34]

Frederick the Great set the style for this kind of aristocratic reaction by systematically excluding commoners from the Prussian officer corps after 1763. He did so because he distrusted the calculating spirit that he associated with men of bourgeois background—exactly the traits that dominated and inspired Gribeauval and his circle. Frederick, indeed, was dismayed by the new developments in artillery, realizing that Prussia was poorly equipped to compete with Russia's great iron industry, or even with Austria and France, in a technological arms race. He reacted by downplaying artillery while emphasizing discipline and "honor," i.e., the traits that had always made Prussian officers and men ready to sacrifice their lives on behalf of the state. Frederick and his successor thus chose to rely on old-fashioned military virtues and deliberately turned their backs on rational experimentation and technical reform of the sort Gribeauval carried through. In 1806 the cost of this conservative policy became evident. At the battle of Jena, Prussian valor, obedience, and honor proved an inadequate counterweight to the new scale of war the French had meanwhile perfected, thanks, in large part, to the often reluctant hospitality French army commanders showed to the rational and experimental approach to their profession.[35]

Command technology, seeking deliberately to create a new weapons system surpassing existing capabilities, has become familiar in the twentieth century. It was profoundly new in the eighteenth; and the French artillerymen who responded so successfully to Gribeauval's lead deserve to be heralded as pioneers of today's technological arms race. Yet it is easy to exaggerate. Systematic and successful though the effort was, it remained isolated and exceptional. As had happened after 1690, when the flintlock musket and bayonet achieved

---

34. Among other factors, this "noble reaction" may have reflected population growth. With more younger sons to look after, noble families presumably looked more eagerly for army commissions and resented untitled upstarts all the more warmly.

35. On Frederick's motivation see Gordon Craig, *The Politics of the Prussian Army, 1640–1945* (Oxford, 1956), p. 16. On the aristocratic reaction in the French army see Kennett, *The French Armies in the Seven Years War,* p. 143; David Bien, "La réaction aristocratique avant 1789: L'example de l'armée," *Annales: Economies, sociétés, civilisations* 29 (1974): 23–48, 505–34; David Bien, "The Army in the French Enlightenment: Reform, Reaction and Revolution," *Past and Present,* no. 85 (1979): 68–98.

an enduring "classic" form, field artillery design reached a plateau with Gribeauval's achievement. The field guns of other European armies lagged behind the French in varying degrees when the revolutionary wars began; by the time peace returned in 1815 all the great powers had come more or less abreast of the weapons the French began with. No further fundamental change took place until breech-loaders came in after 1850.

Clearly, a sharp stimulus was required before the routines of military life could be sufficiently shaken up to allow the sort of change that French artillery achieved between 1763 and 1789. Details of Gribeauval's personal career probably mattered, for he was sent to study Prussian artillery methods in 1752 and then, in 1756, transferred to the Austrian service where he played a conspicuously successful role in the Seven Years War by first capturing a Silesian strong point with siege guns and then defending another town against Prussian attack for much longer than anyone thought possible. When he returned to France in 1762, therefore, Gribeauval was thoroughly familiar with improvements the Austrians had already made in their artillery. A vision of the possible—of how a more systematic approach could create a new kind of weapon and profoundly alter conditions on the battlefield—presumably took root in Gribeauval's mind as a result of his encounter with foreign practice.

But the will to do something drastic clearly depended also on the widespread sense among Frenchmen that something was wrong with the way their government in general and the army and navy in particular had been managed. When the vision of the possible thus united with a widely diffused dissatisfaction with existing arrangements, the kind of breakthrough that Gribeauval's reform constituted became possible. But such circumstances were unusual. The ordinary practice and routine of European military establishments were not yet systematically disturbed by research and development teams of the kind Gribeauval headed. Command technology, in short, remained exceptional, and but little noted or understood outside of a small circle of professional artillery officers. Yet as a "cloud no bigger than a man's hand" and a sign of things to come, the remarkable success achieved by Lieutenant General Gribeauval and his artillery designers deserves more attention than it has usually been accorded.[36]

36. I depend heavily on Howard Rosen, "The *Système Gribeauval:* A Study of Technological Change and Institutional Development in Eighteenth Century France" (Ph.D. diss., University of Chicago, 1981). Some of his insights are available in his "Le système Gribeauval et la guerre moderne," *Revue historique des armées* 1–2 (1975):

Nevertheless, though the development of an efficient field artillery was certainly significant for the future of European warfare, it remained true that siege guns, fortress guns, and naval guns consumed far more metal and were numerically far more important than newfangled and, to begin with, quite untested field artillery.[37] Yet here, too, the French began to probe hitherto established limits on the eve of the Revolution. The problem, from a French point of view, was that new and superior techniques for smelting iron developed in Great Britain during the 1780s. The key change was Henry Cort's invention in 1783 of what was known as "puddling." This referred to the possibility of melting pig iron inside a coke-fired reverberatory furnace that reflected heat from its roof in such a way that the iron need not be in direct contact with the fuel at the bottom. By stirring the molten metal while it was in the furnace, various contaminants could be vaporized and thus removed from the iron. Then when the metal had been allowed to cool to red-hot viscosity, British ironmasters discovered that they could pass the metal through heavy rollers and thereby extrude additional impurities by mechanical force while shaping the metal to any desired thickness by adjusting the space between rollers. The end product was cheaply made, conveniently shaped wrought iron that was suitable for use in cannon, as well as for innumerable other purposes. But it took some twenty years of trial and error (i.e., until the first decade of the nineteenth century) to overcome all the difficulties in designing suitable furnaces and getting rid of damaging contaminants.[38]

Long before then, French entrepreneurs and officials recognized the potential value of the new method of iron manufacture for armaments production. By using coke, a relatively cheap and potentially abundant fuel, costs could be sharply reduced; by using rollers, relatively vast amounts of iron could be wrought without the expensive hammering which had previously been necessary. Accordingly, French promoters hatched a grand scheme for building a smelting plant at Le Creusot in eastern France, where the latest British technology for coke firing would be used. This was to be linked by canal and navigable rivers to a

---

29–36. For details see Jean Baptiste Brunet, *L'artillerie française au XVIIIe siècle* (Paris, 1906); and for the internal struggle in the army, Chalmin, "La querelle des Bleus et des Rouges," pp. 490–505.

37. In 1791 the French field artillery totaled only 1,300 guns according to Gunther Rothenberg, *The Art of Warfare in the Age of Napoleon* (Bloomington, Ind., 1978), p. 122.

38. Charles K. Hyde, *Technological Change and the British Iron Industry, 1700–1870* (Princeton, 1977), pp. 194–96.

naval gunfoundry at Indret, an island at the mouth of the Loire. In this way, French planners hoped that the French navy could secure large numbers of cheap guns for its ships and for harbor defense. An English technician and entrepreneur, William Wilkinson, joined forces with a French captain of industry, Baron François Ignace de Wendel, and Parisian financiers to promote this scheme. Interest-free loans from the French government helped with initial expenses and Louis XVI personally subscribed to 333 of the 4,000 shares. With this august backing, Le Creusot began production in 1785, but met with severe and persistent technical difficulties of the same sort that were plaguing British ironmasters in these years. The grandiose enterprise in fact went bankrupt in 1787–88, and after years of unsatisfactory production the scheme was abandoned in 1807 because the poor quality of iron from Le Creusot produced too many defective cannon.[39]

Despite its ultimate failure, this grand plan clearly adumbrated nationwide mobilization for large-scale arms production of a kind that became important only in the twentieth century. Such plans were not entirely without precedent. In the seventeenth century, Colbert imported considerable numbers of Liègeois arms makers to staff royal arsenals in France.[40] Even earlier than this, import of technology from abroad, and its application on a grand scale to armaments production, had helped the Russian state outstrip its rivals and neighbors. Thus, the establishment of a Dutch-managed arms plant at Tula in 1632 was followed by Peter the Great's successful efforts to build up ferrous metallurgy in the Urals.[41] Moreover, the transfer of Flemish metallurgical technique to Sweden in the early part of the seventeenth century had a very similar character,[42] and Prussian efforts to establish an arms

39. Bertrand Gille, *Les origines de la grande industrie métallurgique en France* (Paris, 1947), pp. 131–35 and passim; Conturie, *Histoire de la fonderie nationale de Ruelle,* pp. 248–80; Theodore Wertime, *The Coming of Age of Steel* (Leiden, 1961), pp. 131–32; Joseph Antoine Roy, *Histoire de la famille Schneider et du Creusot* (Paris, 1962), pp. 11–15.

40. Gaier, *Four Centuries of Liège Gunmaking,* p. 60.

41. Most of the labor needed was provided by ascribing serfs to the new enterprises. Much of the work was done in winter when there was nothing to do in the fields; hence the extra burden on the serfs cut into their agricultural productivity only slightly. By generous resort to compulsion, in other words, the Russian government instituted a far more efficient distribution of labor through the year—and acquired an iron industry, basic for armaments, for little more than the cost of supporting supervisory personnel and a few imported master workmen. Cf. James Mavor, *An Economic History of Russia,* 2d ed. (New York, 1925), 1:437–38. By 1715 Peter's factories had produced no fewer than 13,000 cannons; in 1720 the annual production of muskets reached 20,000—fully equivalent to French production. Cf. Arcadius Kahan, "Continuity in Economic Activity and Policy during the Post-Petrine Period in Russia," in William L. Blackwell, ed., *Russian Economic Development from Peter the Great to Stalin* (New York, 1974), p. 57.

42. See above, p. 122.

industry in the neighborhood of Berlin, by importing skilled personnel from Liège (1772), though on a relatively modest scale,[43] also involved strategic planning like the French scheme of the 1780s.

What made the Le Creusot–Indret plan different was that Baron de Wendel and his associates were exploring the potentialities of new, large-scale industrial methods for the manufacture of armaments. In this they anticipated developments of the second half of the nineteenth century, when private entrepreneurs successfully sold big guns and other weapons to the governments of Europe and the world. De Wendel's connections with the government were rather more intimate than the later relations between private armaments makers and governments in the nineteenth century. Close collaboration between public authority and private entrepreneurs for arms manufacture had Colbertian roots in France; on a mass industrial scale, however, of the sort attempted by Baron de Wendel, such collaboration was lastingly achieved only after 1885.

The fact was that in the 1780s, if French entrepreneurs were to catch up with British advances in ferrous metallurgy, the navy offered the only readily apparent consumer for a vastly increased scale of production. To transplant the new technology, with its expensive capital installations, to French soil required an assured outlet for the product. Otherwise no sensible investor would even consider the idea, since internal tariffs and the high cost of overland transport had inhibited the development of a national market in France. In Britain, by contrast, a nationwide civilian market had already appeared by the 1780s, offering the new ironmasters of Wales, and soon also of Scotland, a variety of outlets for their goods. Yet even in Great Britain, Henry Cort justified his patent for the puddling process by claiming that he could thereby lower the price of guns for the navy;[44] and during the critical years of take-off, between 1794 and 1805, the British government purchased about a fifth of the ironmasters' product, nearly all of which was used for armaments.[45]

---

43. W. O. Henderson, *Studies in the Economic Policy of Frederick the Great* (London, 1963), p. 6.

44. Trebilcock, "Spin-off in British Economic History," p. 477.

45. Hyde, *Technological Change and the British Iron Industry,* p. 115. Inasmuch as some of the iron sold privately ended up in muskets purchased by the government in a finished or semifinished state from private producers, Hyde's estimate of 17–25 percent as the government's share of the total production of iron is, presumably, minimal; indeed it seems to me that he systematically underrates the importance of armaments and state purchasing in the rise of the British iron industry, despite, or perhaps because of, his sophisticated use of economic measures and concepts. For example: the pioneer iron foundries in Wales and then in Scotland both started up on the strength of contracts with the navy to manufacture cannon. Cf. Harry Scrivenor, *History of the Iron*

The grandiose character and ultimate failure of the Le Creusot–Indret plan for supplying the French navy with cheap and numerous heavy guns was entirely characteristic of the way things went in the French navy during the seventeenth and eighteenth centuries. The difficulty was that the army came first. Only sporadically did French policy put major effort into building up a great navy. Colbert had done so between 1662 and 1683 in order to defeat the Dutch. He succeeded so well that even when England joined Holland against the French in 1689, the French navy initially proved itself superior to the combined Dutch and English fleets. But French naval resources were stretched close to their limits when the war began. It therefore proved impossible to increase the size of the navy very much in the course of hostilities, whereas in England both the means and will to outbuild the French were present. After 1692, when fifteen French ships of the line were destroyed at the Battle of La Hogue, English-Dutch naval superiority to the French became unmistakable.

Two years later the French turned to a cheaper (for the government) form of naval war, i.e., to privateering. This was a fateful decision. The English, in effect, went the opposite way, inventing an efficient centralized credit mechanism for financing war by founding the Bank of England in 1694. At exactly the same time, under the pressure of a financial crisis provoked by bad harvests, the French government assigned the financing of naval enterprise to private investors, i.e., to privateers. Continued state expenditure on the navy had come to seem impossibly costly. The result was to assure Great Britain of relatively easy naval superiority throughout the early eighteenth century. This allowed Great Britain to come close to sweeping French commerce from the seas during the Seven Years War. English victories, in turn, drastically reduced the resources available within France to finance privateering, whereas within England commercial interests gained such a strategic position in Parliament that resistance to naval appropriations was effectually blunted.[46]

Trade, 2d ed. (London, 1854), pp. 122–23; Arthur Henry John, *The Industrial Development of South Wales* (Cardiff, 1950), pp. 24–36, 99 ff. An assured large-scale market helped entrepreneurs to overcome the start-up costs in what, to begin with, was almost uninhabited country. It offers on British soil an example of a much wider phenomenon: for, as we have just seen, state arms contracts often provided a basis for establishing new and relatively expensive technology on new ground: Russia's Urals, Prussia's Spandau, France's Le Creusot, are parallel examples of this same phenomenon.

46. Two excellent books cast much light on this fateful turn in state policy and power balances: John Ehrman, *The Navy in the War of William III, 1689–1697: Its State and Direction* (Cambridge, 1953), and Geoffrey Symcox, *The Crisis of French Sea Power, 1688–1697: From the Guerre d'Escadre to the Guerre de Course* (The Hague, 1974).

After the disasters of the Seven Years War, French ministers drew the conclusion that they needed a navy as good as or better than the British, in order to reverse the verdict of 1763. But French naval architects were not so fortunate as Gribeauval, inasmuch as no important technical improvements came within their reach that might have permitted them to leave the British behind. Bored-out cannon improved naval gunfire too, but the British kept pace with this change; and the difficulties of aiming heavy cannon from a pitching ship made the refinements in aiming, which were so important for field artillery, ineffective on shipboard. French warships were nearly always better built than their British counterparts, but in the last decades of the eighteenth century, the Royal Navy pioneered two important technical advances—copper sheathing for ships' bottoms, and the use of short-barreled, large caliber guns, known as carronades.[47]

Throughout the century, the shape and strength of oak timbers set a definite limit to the size of warships. Improvements of design that did prove feasible, such as the use of a steering wheel to give mechanical advantage to the steersman, the use of reef points to adjust the area of canvas to variations in the strength of the wind, and the use of copper sheathing to prevent fouling the bottom, although they cumulatively did much to improve the maneuverability of heavy warships, never established a clear break with older performance levels of the kind Gribeauval's field guns enjoyed.[48]

Numbers, therefore, were what mattered, and between 1763 and 1778 the French succeeded in building enough new ships of the line to be able to confront Great Britain on almost even terms at sea. Indeed, when war broke out again and Spain allied herself with France, the combined French and Spanish fleets briefly dominated the English channel. Later in the war, however, the British recovered their tradi-

---

47. To accommodate these large caliber (and thin-walled) guns on shipboard, it was necessary to lessen the charge, since otherwise recoil became too great for wooden construction to withstand. This meant lesser muzzle velocity and shorter range; but the projectiles' extra weight nevertheless proved more destructive than standard cannon fire. First manufactured in 1774, carronades were initially sold to merchant vessels and then in 1779 the Royal Navy accepted them as supplementary armament. The carronade thereafter provided the technological basis for Nelson's famous injunction to lie close alongside the foe, since its fire became effective only at short ranges.

48. On the technical constraints of seventeenth- and eighteenth-century naval vessels, see the very instructive pages in Ehrman, *The Navy in the War of William III,* pp. 3–37; G. J. Marcus, *Heart of Oak: A Survey of British Seapower in the Georgian Era* (London, 1975), pp. 8–9, 39, and passim. Shipbuilding remained an affair of artisan skill, fitting odd-shaped timbers to the curves of the hull, etc. Efforts to bring theory to bear on how best to proportion hull and sails made little difference, though the French began such attempts as early as 1681.

tional naval preponderance so that peace, when it came in 1783, secured American independence without overthrowing Britain's naval primacy.

Two factors continually hampered French naval efforts. One was the way in which land operations took precedence in French strategic planning. Against England, as earlier against Holland, the master scheme was to mount an invasion by land forces. The navy was therefore expected to escort the invading force either directly across the Channel or to the coast of Ireland or Scotland rather than to act independently and on its own. Repeatedly, invasion plans were prepared, only to break down because of difficulties of coordination. The fact was that in the eighteenth century staff work and technology were inadequate to sustain a successful landing on a defended coast, as the failure of several British efforts to land troops on the French coast amply demonstrated. But when overambitious plans for invasion of England or Ireland aborted, French policy makers were almost driven to conclude that money spent on the navy was a waste and should be cut back drastically.[49] Such a policy was doubly tempting when privateering constituted a cheap and popular alternative way of harassing enemy commerce at no cost to the government whatever.

The impulse abruptly to turn off naval expenditure was reinforced by the second persistent weakness the French navy confronted: inadequate finance. The collapse of John Law's schemes in 1720 meant that throughout the rest of the eighteenth century the French government lacked a central bank and source of credit analogous to the Bank of England. Costs for building, equipping, and manning warships were very great. With only short-term credit from suppliers and contractors to rely upon, any significant increase in naval expenditures, responding to sudden changes in circumstances—repairs after a storm or battle, commissioning ships from the reserve, moving a squadron from Brest to Toulon or back again—immediately created severe financial problems.

Command mobilization could only carry so far. Compelling sailors to man naval vessels was feasible. Both France and Britain regularly resorted to force to fill out naval ranks. Against victuallers and timber merchants, however, compulsion was almost wholly ineffective. Failure to pay promptly raised prices and choked off supplies.[50] Early in

---

49. Cf. Vauban's memorandum of 1695 to Louis XIV: "... fitting out fleets has cost enormous sums; and these expenses have been a complete loss." Quoted from Symcox, *War, Diplomacy and Imperialism,* p. 240.

50. Timber suppliers in the Baltic preferred the English to the French because French

the eighteenth century, when British naval administration started to pay its bills with reasonable regularity, thanks to credits available to the government through the Bank of England, British superiority to the French in this respect became very marked. Easy credit made it possible to expand the scale of British naval effort quite rapidly whenever a war emergency required such action. Lacking comparable credit arrangements, French administrators were completely unable to match the remarkable elasticity that made naval power a particularly supple and effective instrument of policy for eighteenth-century British governments.[51]

It is worth pointing out that contracts for supplying the British navy with all the thousands of items that fighting ships and men required tended to reinforce and expand the market mobilization of resources within the British Isles, as well as in such outlying regions as New England and the Canadian Maritimes where, from an early period, big timber for masts had to be sought. The victuallers, who provided meat, beer, and biscuit for the Royal Navy, had to feed a population of anywhere from 10,000 to 60,000 men by buying provisions inland and delivering them to naval storehouses on the coast. In Ireland and other remote parts of Great Britain, the navy victuallers did much to stimulate the rise of commercial agriculture, while the spread of market relations into new regions and down the social scale within Great Britain, in turn, sustained the tax and credit system that allowed the navy to pay its bills more or less punctually.[52]

The French navy never established such a feedback loop within France as a whole. In and around the chief naval ports local suppliers and contractors no doubt benefited from naval expenditures; but no centralized source of credit gave naval expenditure the nationwide force it acquired in Great Britain after 1694. High policy in the days of Colbert and again between 1763 and 1789 might decide that a naval buildup was called for. But general support for the heavy expenditures such a program involved was not usually to be found among the

---

payment procedures were undependable. This reinforced strategical difficulties the French faced in getting timber from the Baltic past their Dutch and British foes. Cf. Paul Walden Bamford, *Forests and French Sea Power, 1660–1789* (Toronto, 1956).

51. In the War of Jenkins' Ear, for example, British naval manpower rose from just under 10,000 in 1738 to over 40,000 in 1741 and reached a peak of 60,000 in 1748. After the war, in turn, naval personnel was cut back to 20,000 by 1749. Daniel A. Baugh, *British Naval Administration in the Age of Walpole* (Princeton, 1965), p. 205.

52. Cf. Ehrman, *The Navy in the War of William III*, p. 171: "Maritime war did not merely help her [Great Britain] to gain wealth, its progress directly increased wealth, and the expensive fleet did not exhaust trade and industry. . . . Power and wealth reacted upon each other, and increasing costs were met with increasing resources."

French,[53] whereas whenever a crisis arose, the British Parliament could be counted on to authorize extra taxes, as might be needed, to pay off indebtedness the Admiralty incurred in the course of naval operations.

This difference reflected and also confirmed the fact that French commercial interests remained politically muffled, if not handcuffed, by the command structure of the royal administration. Lacking nationwide cohesion, French merchants tended to support decentralized finance and management of armed force at sea—privateering—if only because it put decisions as to the scale and incidence of such enterprise into their own hands. But the *guerre de course,* seeking prizes and avoiding encounters with enemy warships whenever possible, was not amenable to strategic direction. Each captain and crew did what seemed advantageous to themselves. In time of war, therefore, the French commercial empire overseas was at the mercy of the British navy, whose ships acted in response to governmental decisions about when, where, and how they should act.[54]

It might be supposed that the tasks of supplying the French army with bread and other necessities might have served as a substitute for the business of naval contracting. Assuredly, supplying the army was a considerable business in eighteenth-century France, and private contractors were in charge of the supply of muskets[55] as well as of nearly everything else soldiers needed. But most such items had to be procured within a rather short radius because they were bulky and therefore costly to transport overland. Bread and fodder far outweighed all other army needs; and even when the bread contractors lived in Paris, grain supplies were nearly always purchased locally. No nationwide commercial network analogous to that stimulated by British naval

53. Public reaction to naval defeats in the Seven Years War allowed the duc de Choiseul, minister of marine 1761–66, to pay for sixteen new warships by subscriptions, more or less voluntary, from various monied groups—tax farmers, provincial estates, country gentlemen, Paris merchants, etc. Cf. the list of ships built by subscription in E. H. Jenkins, *A History of the French Navy* (London, 1973), p. 142.

54. Symcox, *The Crisis of French Sea Power,* pp. 221 ff., argues this point convincingly.

55. Musket manufacture was organized at four centers where a handful of "entrepreneurs" contracted with the government for the delivery of specified numbers of guns each year. The muskets were actually manufactured by artisans who worked at the order of the entrepreneurs; and the whole process was supervised by a government officer, whose duty it was to make sure that each musket came up to official specifications. The best account of French gunmaking I have found is Louis Joseph Gras, *Historique de l'armurerie stéphanoise* (St. Etienne, 1905), pp. 36–40, 59, and passim. Production fluctuated between 10,000 and 26,000 muskets per annum in the second half of the eighteenth century—a not inconsiderable figure but falling far short of the scale of manufacture at Liège, where about 200,000 muskets were produced yearly, according to Gaier, *Four Centuries of Liège Gun Making,* p. 42.

contracting and sustained by the Bank of England's credit therefore arose in France; or, more accurately, nationwide markets remained slender and weak—something to be planned for, as in the Le Creusot–Indret scheme, but not yet firmly and routinely in being.[56]

These structural weaknesses meant that the French never caught up with the Royal Navy, even though in the second half of the eighteenth century French warships were usually better designed than their British equivalents, and the government continued to aspire to naval parity or predominance.

Great Britain, for its part, reacted to its defeats of 1776–83 by improving the financial, administrative, and supply organization of the Royal Navy.[57] Even though unsuccessful, the fact that in the War of American Independence the British government maintained up to 90,000 soldiers overseas, most of whom were fed and supplied entirely from Great Britain, was a remarkable administrative feat. In effect, the army and its supply needs were superimposed upon the navy's already considerable wartime demands upon the British economy. After intense administrative friction, the Navy Board took responsibility in 1779 for delivering army supplies to America. Despite shipping shortages it thereafter managed to prevent the army from running out of food or other necessities, though persistent uncertainty and long delays in communication and the even longer delays in delivery drastically hampered all the strategic moves planned in New York and London.

Earlier in the century, British wars had been fought under circumstances that permitted army units sent overseas to procure food, horses, and transport on the spot, whether in America, India, or on the European continent. After 1775, however, the American patriots were able to prevent British troops from having more than sporadic access to local supplies. This took the authorities in London completely aback. But they had at their disposal a relatively efficient naval procurement system which, in a pinch, could be expanded to accommodate the requirements of thousands of soldiers. This saved the

---

56. For army bread contractors and their tendency to dictate troop movements in the field, see Kennett, *The French Armies in the Seven Years War,* pp. 97–104. On the absence of a nationwide commercial integration in France, see Edward Fox, *History in Geographic Perspective: The Other France* (New York, 1971).

57. P. K. Crimmin, "Admiralty Relations with the Treasury, 1783–1806: The Preparation of Naval Estimates and the Beginnings of Treasury Control," *Mariner's Mirror* 53 (1967): 63–72; Bernard Pool, *Navy Board Contracts, 1660–1832* (Hamden, Conn., 1966), pp. 111–15; Albion, *Forests and Sea Power,* pp. 45 ff. British army reform, for the most part, waited until after 1795. See Richard Glover, *Peninsular Preparation, 1795–1809* (Cambridge, 1963).

redcoats from complete disaster, though barely, for in January 1779, the British army in New York had only four days' rations in hand when a relieving fleet arrived.[58]

The strain, nevertheless, was considerable. Earlier in the century, wars appear to have been economically beneficial to Great Britain. Stepped-up government purchases provided a tonic to the market; technological advances in the metal trades were hastened; and chronic underemployment was reduced. Subsidies to foreign governments were easily recouped by the export of commodities from overseas. But the war of 1776–83 brought economic setback: loss of trade with the rebellious colonies as well as contraction of investment at home.[59] In other words, with the War of American Independence, Great Britain began to run up against limits to the ninety-year-old feedback pattern whereby naval power and expenditure reinforced commercial expansion while commercial expansion simultaneously made naval expenditures easier to bear.

In France, too, in the 1780s the government was also running up against the limits of its fiscal resources. The costs of the American war put what proved to be an unmanageable strain upon existing forms of government credit and tax income. The effort to meet resulting financial shortfall led, as is well known, to the summoning of the Estates General in May 1789 and to the outbreak of the French Revolution. Drastic political and social changes precipitated by the Revolution soon had the effect of unleashing hitherto unimagined military force. But in Great Britain, too, a different kind of revolution—technological and industrial—simultaneously raised the limits of the possible beyond men's earlier dreams, in matters military as well as civil. Other countries of Europe and the world were left behind by the remarkable transformations that came to France and Great Britain between 1789 and 1815. Indeed all humankind is still reeling from the impact of the democratic and industrial revolutions, triggered so unexpectedly in the last decades of the eighteenth century. We must therefore consider these twin mutations of humanity's social organization in the next chapter.

58. Three fine books discuss details of the British logistical effort during the War of American Independence: Piers Mackesy, *The War for America, 1775–1783* (Cambridge, Mass., 1964); David Syrett, *Shipping and the American War, 1775–1783: A Study of British Transport Organization* (London, 1970); R. Arthur Bowler, *Logistics and the Failure of the British Army in America, 1775–1783* (Princeton, 1975). Norman Baker, *Government and Contractors: The British Treasury and War Suppliers, 1775–1783* (London, 1971) is also informative.

59. A. H. John, "War and the English Economy, 1700–1763," *Economic History Review*, 2d ser. 7 (1954–55): 329–44.

6

The Military Impact of the French Political and the British Industrial Revolutions, 1789-1840

The French Revolution amazed contemporaries as time after time angry and excited crowds succeeded in overturning governments and other constituted authorities that had seemed sacrosanct and inexpugnable. The industrial revolution, though little noticed at the time, amazes modern historians who seek to understand how it happened and why. Ideas and aspirations, self-interest, hunger and fear played their roles in both revolutions; so did group, class, and national attachments. This chapter will focus attention in military aspects of these twin upheavals, but in doing so I do not mean to imply, nor do I believe, that organized force was all that mattered.

On the contrary, the fundamental disturber of Old Regime patterns in both France and England in the last years of the eighteenth century was probably population growth, which in China as well as in Europe seems to have depended mainly on a changing incidence of lethal infections.[1] Whatever the causes, population growth in the later eighteenth century undoubtedly occurred, manifesting itself both in rural underemployment in many parts of France and Great Britain and in the growth of city populations, especially in the two capitals. London grew from something like 575,000 in 1750 to no less than 900,000 by 1801; Paris attained a total of from 600,000 to 700,000 in 1789, of whom up to 100,000 constituted a floating population that had not succeeded in rooting itself securely enough in the urban environment to figure in the official numeration of the inhabitants made in that year.[2]

---

1. This argument is developed as fully as sketchy data allow in W. H. McNeill, *Plagues and Peoples* (New York, 1976), pp. 240–56.
2. George Rudé, *Paris and London in the Eighteenth Century: Studies in Popular Protest*

Serious problems arose in fitting so many new citizens into society. Urban employment and food supplies did not automatically increase to accommodate the newcomers. Economic cycles of boom and bust put urban workers and hangers-on into serious jeopardy, for as the mass of people and their mobility within the cities increased, older methods of social control and poor relief, usually tied to parish organizations, became completely inadequate.[3] In Strasbourg, for example, where the officially enumerated population rose from 26,481 in 1697 to 49,948 in 1789, no less than 20 percent of the population was indigent by the later date. The always precarious local balance between population and means of subsistence within the city had been seriously upset.[4]

Crowd action of the kind so decisive for the early course of the French revolution became possible under these circumstances. London had seen the like in the so-called Gordon riots (1780); and it may have been more by accident than design that London crowds chose to rally to a reactionary cause—opposition to Catholic emancipation —rather than championing change in the existing legal order. That was what happened in Paris in 1789, leading, within a few months, to full-throated assault upon aristocrats and other enemies of the people.[5]

Yet however slender the stimuli that made London crowds reactionary while Paris crowds became revolutionary, this divergence turned out to be indicative of a persistent difference between French and British reaction to the new problems that population growth and urban expansion had created in the two countries. To put matters in a nutshell: France exported armed men and created an empire over much of Europe, whereas Great Britain exported goods as well as men (armed and unarmed) and thereby contrived to establish a market-supported system of power that proved more durable than anything the French achieved, despite their many victories. No one planned

---

(New York, 1971), pp. 35–36; Jacques Godechot, *La prise de la Bastille* (Paris, 1965), p. 75.

3. Oliven F. Hufton, *The Poor of Eighteenth Century France, 1750–1789* (Oxford, 1974) provides a masterful overview.

4. Y. LeMoigne, "Population et subsistence à Strasbourg au XVIIIe siècle," in M. Bouloiseau et al., *Contributions à l'histoire démographique de la révolution française,* Commission d'histoire économique et sociale de la révolution, no. 14 (Paris, 1962), pp. 15, 44.

5. On the Gordon riots cf. Rudé, *Paris and London,* pp. 268–92. As Rudé is at pains to point out, the London crowds attacked established figures—those who had advocated Catholic emancipation—rather than assaulting the poor Irish of London; hence the social character of the rioting was not so very different from that of revolutionary Paris.

this divergence; it developed as a result of hasty improvisation and desperate actions in the face of overwhelming emergency.

Yet it is also the case that the market basis of British power, both economic and military, reflected a bias apparent from Elizabethan times or even earlier. As for the French, their revolutionary resort to command mobilization was never complete, despite the rhetoric of 1793. The French revolutionary governments' mix between compulsion and reliance upon a more or less free market for mobilizing resources for state purposes was, in fact, a fairly faithful replica of similar mixes the royal governments of Louis XIV and earlier French kings had resorted to in time of foreign war and internal crisis. The British-French divergence unquestionably had geographic roots and reflected a recurrent difference between island and continental states that can be traced as far back as the second millennium B.C.[6] But in the late eighteenth century, the divergence became especially marked, presumably because of the new horizons of the possible that accumulating skills and a growing population created for both countries.

The French Formula for Relieving Population Pressure

The French revolutionary solution to an excess of manpower and a deficiency of economically productive jobs did not emerge clearly until 1794 and became firmly established only with the rise of Napoleon. Between the initial defiance of royal authority in June 1789, when the National Assembly constituted itself from the Estates General, and the victorious advance of French armies into Belgium and the Rhinelands in 1793–94, important changes came to the army and navy inherited from the Old Regime.

The first such change was absolutely critical to the success of the revolutionary cause, for it made the army unwilling to defend the Old Regime against its assailants.[7] In ways largely untraceable, soldiers of

6. The Minoan civilization of Crete appears to have concentrated resources at Knossos more by trade than by raid. Sea empires of Java and Sumatra did the same in the first millenium A.D. But islands divided among rival political masters, as Japan was through most of its history, characteristically conform to continental patterns of mobilization, in which command plays a more prominent part and the market remains subordinate.

7. Use of regular troops against civilian crowds was an awkward matter for eighteenth-century armies. Cf. Tony Haytor, *The Army and the Crowd in Mid-Georgian England* (London, 1978). A volley of muskets at close range was murderous; yet no other tactics were available. Crowd control was not systematically developed by European police forces until the 1880s. The London dock strike (1889) established the principles of "Keep moving, please," i.e., of allowing marches and peaceful demonstra-

the French army, especially those stationed in and near Paris, became affected by the revolutionary agitation that boiled up so suddenly among the inhabitants of the capital.

In view of remarks in the preceding chapter about the insulation of Old Regime armies from civil society—in but not of the civilians' world—this wind of change within the ranks of the French army calls for special explanation. Two circumstances clearly facilitated the infiltration of new ideas among the soldiery. One was the fact that under normal garrison conditions French officers, even junior officers, spent little time with their men, and left daily drill and other routines largely in the hands of noncoms. Practical, day-to-day command therefore rested in the hands of persons who were predisposed to be sympathetic to the revolutionary assault on aristocracy, since aristocratic privilege blocked any hope of their achieving commissioned rank. Earlier, sergeants did sometimes become officers, though few ever got beyond the rank of lieutenant.[8] The regulation of 1781 reserving commissions to noblemen therefore rankled, and was still, in 1789, a fresh and remembered grievance.

Moreover, many of the aggrieved noncoms were literate. Schools to teach corporals and sergeants to read and write had been decreed in 1787, since the growing importance of written orders and records required that even the most junior levels of command be filled by literate persons.[9] Hence, the written propaganda revolutionary journalists and pamphleteers put into circulation could, and presumably did, affect the minds of the men who commanded the rank and file. By the time regimental officers realized what was happening, it was too late to reverse the trend of opinion within the ranks, and efforts to isolate soldiers from the populace, especially in and around Paris, proved ineffectual.

Revolutionary sympathies within the army were dramatically demonstrated on 14 July 1789 when the Paris crowd attacked the Bastille.

---

tions to pass through designated streets by arrangement. This marks the dawn of modern techniques for allowing an angry crowd to expend its energy harmlessly with hours of muscular exertion and shouting, without having to disperse it by brute force. But such sophistication was far in the future in 1789; so, for that matter, were disciplined civil police forces. On the police of Paris see Godechot, *La prise de la Bastille*, pp. 95–115.

8. A. Corvisier, *L'armée française de la fin du XVIIe siècle au ministère de Choiseul* (Paris, 1964), pp. 784–90.

9. Samuel F. Scott, *The Response of the Royal Army to the French Revolution, 1787–1793* (New York, 1978), pp. 26, 34. Most of what follows about how the army responded to the first years of the revolution derives from this excellent book.

To be able to prevail on that famous day, the attackers required the tacit acquiescence of the soldiers, some 7,000 strong, who were stationed in Paris to guard the royal palaces and perform other duties for the king. Detachments of the French Guard actually joined the crowd, and by bringing artillery pieces up against the Bastille played an important role in its capture.[10] In the aftermath, Louis XVI promised to withdraw his soldiers from Paris and Versailles so as to quiet fears of armed counterrevolution. The king's decision (or indecision, for he wavered often enough in private) blunted the plots and plans army officers and other aristocrats harbored for using the royal army to repress the revolutionaries by force; and such plans became more and more illusory as time passed, since the processes that had led soldiers of the French Guard to support the revolution swiftly undermined the loyalty of the army's rank and file to the Old Regime in other parts of France. The noncoms thus made the army revolutionary by almost imperceptible degrees, and deprived the Old Regime of its ultimate basis for survival before officers and ministers really noticed what was occurring.

The second circumstance that facilitated the merger of army opinion with public opinion was that army units did not usually reside in separate barracks but were quartered in towns and lived amidst the humbler ranks of urban society when off duty—sometimes indeed engaging in handicraft work to supplement their pay. Most of the soldiers were townsmen when they enlisted,[11] and the experience and discipline of military life did not suffice to cut them off from ordinary contacts with the urban populace whence they had come; whereas, by way of contrast, rural recruits were effectually severed from their village ties in those armies (Prussian and Russian) that depended on peasant manpower.

In the field French soldiers could, like the Old Regime armies, become an encapsulated, autonomous society, only slenderly connected with civil society back home. This is what happened after 1794 and made Napoleon's career possible. But under the circumstances of 1789–92 the distance between soldiery and urban revolutionaries was reduced to the disappearing point, with results fatal to Louis XVI's monarchy.

The Paris National Guard was the revolutionaries' first effort to create an armed force of their own. Volunteers came from the house-

10. Godechot, *La prise de la Bastille,* pp. 289 ff.
11. Scott, *Response of the Royal Army,* pp. 17, 45.

holders of Paris, who had to be well enough off to buy their own uniforms and weapons. But, from its inception, the Paris National Guard also included a core of sixty paid professional companies which enrolled many former members of the king's French Guards, as well as some veterans and deserters from line units of the army. Election of officers by voters of the district of the city where each National Guard company was stationed represented a radical change from old principles of army administration. Yet in practice the Marquis de Lafayette, duly elected as commander of the Paris National Guard at its very inception, played a large role in deciding who got elected, even though his command over the Parisian Guard remained open to challenge, whenever popular excitement again rose to fever pitch.[12]

Veterans of the royal army became drillmasters for the new volunteer units. They played an important role in making the National Guard a significant military force in Paris and, on occasion, also outside the city boundaries, as when the Guard marched to Versailles on 5–6 October 1789 along with other angry Parisians and brought the king back with them as a kind of hostage to the revolution. Assuredly revolutionary ideals and popular insurgency strained older military institutions in Paris to the breaking point. But the paid core units of the National Guard together with the drillmasters assigned to the volunteer battalions maintained real continuities between old and new armed establishments. At the top a few individuals like Lafayette, who had held the rank of major general in the king's service in 1789, also provided a patina of legitimacy to the changes that came thick and fast.

Outside of Paris, a parallel transformation spread throughout the whole of the French army. Continuities were stronger than in the capital since only a few of the Old Regime units, mostly foreign regiments, were suppressed. Between 1789 and 1791 relations between officers and men grew tense as revolutionary ideas and sympathies began to filter into provincial garrisons. Different units accepted revolutionary notions at different times and with different degrees of warmth, depending in part on the political tone of the towns in which they were stationed, and in part on internal dynamics among officers, noncoms, and the rank and file within particular units. At first, the soldiers expressed their alienation from their officers by deserting, often seeking to join the National Guard in Paris. When this was prohibited, acts of overt insubordination began to multiply.

---

12. Louis Gottschalk and Margaret Maddox, *Lafayette in the French Revolution: Through the October Days* (Chicago, 1969), pp. 159–90, 256–340.

A tip point came after June 1791 when the king's attempted flight from Paris ended ignominiously in his capture at Varennes. That event damped aristocratic hopes of being able to rally the army behind the king for an attack upon the revolutionaries of Paris, whereupon multiplying signs of revolutionary sympathies among the soldiers led increasing numbers of French army officers to throw up their commissions and flee the country. By the end of 1791 more than half of the French officer corps had gone into exile. Their place was taken by sergeants and corporals promoted to commissioned ranks. As a result, in the course of 1792 outbreaks of insubordination dwindled to insignificance and the army achieved a far greater internal cohesion than it had known in the three preceding years.[13]

The new officers were professionally competent and experienced men. They proved numerous enough and hardbitten enough to transmit old army ways to the horde of newcomers who poured into the ranks in 1792 and 1793 when foreign and domestic enemies began to threaten the revolution. This upshot was not, however, immediately apparent. In 1791, even before war with Austria and Prussia broke out, the Legislative Assembly decreed a new volunteer army, enlisted initially for only six months. In 1792 volunteers were again enrolled, this time for a year's service; and since quotas were assigned to each *département*, an element of compulsion was added to the voluntary principle. One result was to bring significant numbers of peasants' sons into the ranks of the revolutionary armies for the first time.

In the first phases of the revolution, the new armed forces were aimed at domestic enemies. When, however, after April 1792, Austrians and Prussians joined the domestic foes of the revolution, the role and character of the French armed forces underwent yet another rapid transformation. On the one hand, the recruitment of bourgeois volunteers into the National Guard had to yield to a policy of arming a broader segment of the population. As the leaders of the revolution became more dependent on the lower classes of Paris, this seemed no more than a prudent guarantee of their continuance in power. On the other hand, it also seemed necessary to rally the whole nation against the foreign enemy. The awkward distinction between the regular army, inherited from the Old Regime, and the separate revolutionary armed force of volunteers became meaningless when a foreign rather than a domestic foe had to be met. Accordingly, in February 1793, the Convention decreed an amalgamation between the regulars and the

13. Scott, *Response of the Royal Army,* pp. 98–120; Henry S. Wilkinson, *The French Army before Napoleon* (Oxford, 1915), pp. 99–143.

volunteers. Despite certain gestures in the direction of revolutionary ideals,[14] it seems fair to say that the regular army dominated the amalgamation less because of numbers than because experience in the field put new recruits into situations in which the lore of the old army was useful and meaningful, whereas the liberal, egalitarian elements of the revolutionary aspiration found little chance for practical expression.[15]

Basic continuity between the old army and the armies of the revolution was thus assured. The army even survived the famous *levée en masse* of 1793. In August of that year the Convention decreed:

> ...all Frenchmen are permanently requisitioned for service into the armies. Young men will go forth to battle; married men will forge weapons and transport munitions; women will make tents and clothing and serve in hospitals; children will make lint from old linen; and old men will be brought to the public squares to arouse the courage of the soldiers, while preaching the unity of the Republic and hatred against Kings.[16]

The revolutionary principle that everyone owed military service to the nation could scarcely have been more emphatically proclaimed; and the effort to implement the high rhetoric of the decree, while often chaotic, was also energetic and remarkably successful.[17]

Political ideals surely mattered and so did the legal forms of conscription. But what made the *levée en masse* work as well as it did was the distress and disorganization which had descended on civil society, thanks to poor harvests, catastrophic inflation, and general economic disruption. Unemployment was widespread, and when young men were summoned to enlist in the army, the poorest of them did so willingly enough. Military service offered an escape from frustrating idleness and gave them a legitimate claim to a livelihood at others' expense. The new armies were only occasionally provided through bureaucratic channels with what they needed to keep themselves going; instead they had to depend on their own efforts to find food

14. The elective principle for appointment to junior officer ranks was not entirely given up; but the right to vote on a new appointment was limited to holders of the rank to be filled. In addition, 33 percent of all vacancies was to be filled by promotion based on seniority in length of service. Scott, *Response of the Royal Army*, pp. 157, 165, 180. In 1795, election of officers was discontinued.

15. Jean-Paul Bertaud, "Voies nouvelles pour l'histoire militaire de la révolution," *Annales historiques de la révolution française* 47 (1975): 83.

16. This is the translation of Crane Brinton et al., in Edward Mead Earle, *Makers of Modern Strategy* (Princeton, 1941), p. 77.

17. Richard Cobb, *Les armées révolutionaires: Instrument de la Terreur dans les départements, avril 1793–floreal an II,* 2 vols. (Paris, 1961), offers enormous detail.

and other necessities, and often added to the prevailing economic disorder by seizing goods without regard to competing claims, e.g., for the provisioning of Paris and other cities.

As long as the armies remained on French soil, such behavior made civilian life in the towns precarious, and the precariousness of civilian life in turn encouraged young men to submit to enlistment.[18] Such feedback made the Convention's degree of August 1793 a living reality in the months that followed; and provided the revolutionary armies with the numbers and enthusiasm needed to put down all the pockets of counterrevolutionary action inside France. This was achieved by the end of 1793, whereupon it became possible to concentrate superior numbers against the revolution's foreign foes. After their first victories, the armies then moved onto foreign soil. From that time onward, the costs of their support devolved largely upon populations outside French borders; economic recovery within France and return to a market system for supplying urban centers with food became possible once again.

This, by and large, was the situation by 1794;[19] and as return to more normal conditions began to seem feasible, a powerful reaction gained headway against revolutionary terror, price fixing, and the armed infringement of property rights which had occurred so generally at the height of the crisis. Simultaneously, the mass and energy went out of city crowds, even in Paris, for most of the young and unemployed males were miles away in the ranks of the army. Hence, even when discomfited politicians attempted to summon the genie of crowd action once again in order to prevail against their foes, the former force and fervor were no more. Robespierre's friends vainly summoned the sections of Paris to his rescue in July 1794; and about a year later, on 3 June 1795, after another angry crowd had tried to cow the Convention as aforetime, army units were called in to subdue the Faubourg St. Antoine, whence the crowd had come. "This is the date which should be taken as the end of the Revolution" says Georges Lefebvre;[20] and not without reason.

18. It also encouraged counter-revolution, as at Lyons, Toulon, and in the Vendée. For a while in 1793 it was unclear which reaction would prevail. By the end of that year, the superior organizational effort from Paris, centering in the famous Committee of Public Safety, and the appeal of liberty, even when paradoxically it meant conscription, combined to tip the balance.

19. In June 1794 an official rapporteur told the Convention that the French army was three times as large as a year before yet cost only half as much. S. J. Watson, *Carnot* (London, 1954), p. 88. On military service and the poor see Alan Forrest, *The French Revolution and the Poor* (Oxford, 1981), pp. 138–67.

20. Georges Lefebvre, *The French Revolution from 1793 to 1799* (London, 1964),

Urban unrest and distress, which had done so much to set the revolution in motion, did not disappear; but the fighting manpower that could make the anger of the crowd effective was missing from the streets after 1794, making repression relatively easy. Something like 600,000 French soldiers died between 1792 and 1799;[21] the survivors, stationed outside France for the most part, lived on plunder and forced contributions from the "liberated" people of Belgium, Germany, and Italy. When that did not suffice, supplies could come from within France itself, where, after 1794, a rapid recovery of market-regulated economic activity took place. As purchase replaced forcible requisition a new clique of war profiteers grew rich by supplying the armies, and French military administration at home again conformed to Old Regime patterns, despite the substantial increase in numbers that the *levée en masse* made possible.

French victories amazed contemporaries, but in retrospect the revolutionary success in creating vast armies seems relatively simple and straightforward, given the dynamic of expanding population and economic dislocation from which France both profited and suffered. The parallel task of creating enough arms to make French numbers meaningful on the battlefield was, on the whole, far more remarkable, for when the war began, royal arsenals were depleted as a result of deliveries to the American forces during the War of Independence.[22] In the six years between the victorious conclusion of that war and the outbreak of the revolution, the fiscal embarrassments of the government had been such as to prevent any significant build-up of reserve stocks. Hence the revolutionaries found the cupboard almost bare,[23] and current production was entirely inadequate to equip the hundreds of thousands of new soldiers called up by the mobilizations of 1791 and the following years.

The general disruption of orderly administration and the prevalence of local self-help in the first days of the new revolutionary armies means that no very plausible statistics about arms production can be discovered. In the white heat of the "revolution in danger" arms fac-

p. 145. On the weakening of crowd action by withdrawal of young men into the armies see his remarks, ibid., p. 70. Jacques Godechot, *Les revolutions, 1770–1799* (Paris, 1970), pp. 94–95.

21. Lefebvre, *French Revolution,* p. 315.

22. One hundred thousand muskets had been sent from French armories to the Americans between 1778 and 1783, according to Gunther Rothenberg, *The Art of Warfare in the Age of Napoleon* (Bloomington, Ind., 1978), pp. 120–21.

23. In 1789 the French army possessed only 1,300 pieces of Gribeauval's new field artillery; by 1795 the number almost doubled, thanks to an intense revolutionary effort, using melted-down church bells as the prime source of metal. Ibid., p. 123.

tories were improvised in Paris and other cities.[24] Something like the program envisioned by the *levée en masse* was, at least temporarily, realized. The decree had declared that married men would "forge weapons and tranport munitions." Clearly, not all of them did so, or could have produced a worthwhile musket had they tried. But many did, and muskets were produced in improvised workshops—often former convents and other religious buildings.

Arms supply problems were accentuated by the fact that the main royal arsenals were located far from Paris, in parts of France where revolutionary sentiment was not always strong. In the area around Lyons, for example, a bitter revolt broke out against Paris in the autumn of 1793, disrupting arms manufacture at nearby St. Etienne, where by far the largest French armory was located. When new supplies of metal were delivered to the gunsmiths of St. Etienne, however, production picked up again rapidly and soon exceeded older ceilings. Under the Old Regime, for example, St. Etienne's annual production of handguns had oscillated between 10,000 and 26,000; in 1792–93 production plummeted, but since records were not kept, exactly what happened is unknowable. Then, between 1794 and 1796 production rose above prewar levels, averaging 56,600 per annum. Output slacked off subsequently, varying from year to year according to the demand. The peak came in 1810 when Napoleon's officials procured no fewer than 97,000 handguns from the artisan producers of St. Etienne.[25] Other Old Regime arsenals, like Charleville near the Belgian frontier, were occupied by invading armies at the height of the crisis in 1792–93 and only began to serve the revolution after the French had driven back the foe.

Improvisation and reliance on inexperienced labor was, therefore, the norm at the height of the revolutionary crisis, from August 1793 to July 1794. During those months, the principles of a command economy were blended in remarkable fashion with voluntary and semivoluntary behavior. When the army needed something badly, representatives on mission, as well as army personnel and other agents of the government, tried desperately to find the needed items. Louis Antoine de St. Just, a member of the Committee of Public Safety, for example, managed to collect 20,000 pairs of shoes from the citizens of Strasbourg by demanding that they contribute to the army's urgent

24. Theodore Wertime, *The Coming of Age of Steel* (Leiden, 1961), p. 249, says that Paris produced 1,100 muskets a day under the Committee of Public Safety.

25. These figures come from Louis Joseph Gras, *Historique de l'armurerie stéphanoise* (St. Etienne, 1905), pp. 99, 225–27.

need. His imperious demand was, of course, backed by an implicit threat: whoever did not contribute was in danger of being recognized as an enemy of the people and therefore liable to arrest and execution. Yet to many, and probably to most, Frenchmen the cause seemed just and the sacrifices, whether of personal possessions or of time and effort, were deemed tolerable.

In some instances new techniques were invented or applied on an industrial scale for the first time. For example, two chemists devised a way of manufacturing saltpeter instead of depending for this critical ingredient of gunpowder on scrapings from the walls of stables and latrines.[26] This invention freed France from dependence on imports —a matter of no small significance when the British navy controlled the seas. Other technical novelties included a balloon corps, to permit aerial observation of enemy troop dispositions, and a semaphore telegraph, connecting Paris with the front.[27]

The main problem for the new army, as for older and much smaller armies, was to assure an adequate supply of food and fodder. Supplying the capital and other cities with enough grain to keep the poor from starving was a second critical problem for a government that depended in large degree on the support of the Paris populace. The revolutionary regime met this problem by decreeing the Law of the Maximum, which set fixed prices for grain and other articles of common consumption. Since the legal maximum fell far below the price market speculators defined, producers and dealers often held back their goods, refusing to offer them for sale at the prescribed figure. Then it was up to agents of the government, often accompanied by detachments of armed men, to search out hoarders and appropriate what they found for public use, paying, if at all, only the legal maximum.

Local initiative in these matters was everything: no real control from Paris or any other single center was possible. Statistical data were lacking for anything resembling a planned mobilization of national resources. Instead, what was accomplished rested on actions of innumerable individuals and local groups, each interpreting the will of the people and the welfare of the revolution in its own way. Nevertheless, by a combination of exhortation, compulsion, and payment at fixed prices, millions of men and women were induced to contribute to the tasks of national defense. Measured by ordinary economic yard-

---

26. *Grande Encyclopédie,* s.v. LeBlanc, Carny.
27. Lefebvre, *French Revolution,* pp. 101–3; Shepard B. Clough, *France: A History of National Economics* (New York, 1939), p. 51.

sticks, much of the effort was undoubtedly inefficient. But all the same, things got done, and on a mass scale. Men joined the army, and food and supplies were found for their support, even when the size of the army swelled to about 650,000 by July 1793. This figure was more than twice what Louis XIV had ever been able to put into uniform. Doubling of the army's size (on the basis of a population only about 30 percent greater in 1789 than in 1700) offers a rough measure of the intensification of mobilization for war that the revolution wrought in France.[28]

The revolutionary war effort of 1793–94 was like a breaking wave: it rose very high but could not be long sustained. Once Maximilien Robespierre had been overthrown and the Terror relaxed, hectoring methods of wringing further supplies from the French public met with mounting resistance. The Law of the Maximum was repealed and the government fell back (willingly enough) on private contractors who had to pay inflated prices for the commodities they gathered for the army and other government uses, and added a handsome profit for themselves. Rampant inflation and the rise of a class of *nouveaux riches* resulted, giving a character of its own to the years of the Directory (1795–99).

But as the government fell back on market incentives to manage the French economy, it, in effect, exported the emergency command economy to neighboring lands—Belgium, the Rhinelands, and, after 1797, to Italy as well. To do so, of course, it was first necessary to win victories over the republic's enemies. The first success came in September 1792, at Valmy, when forty of Gribeauval's artillery pieces, firing at extreme range, so discomfited the Prussians as to persuade them to withdraw from French soil.[29]

In subsequent battles, revolutionary ardor and numbers played a more conspicuous role than any kind of expertise. Yet here, too,

28. In 1694 Louis XIV's army totaled about 300,000 men, the highest figure of his reign according to David Chandler, *The Art of War in the Age of Marlborough* (New York, 1976), p. 65. I take the figure for the size of the revolutionary army from Lefebvre, *French Revolution*, p. 81.

29. Other considerations, notably widespread illness in the Prussian army, also affected this decision. Curt Jany, *Geschichte der Königlich Preussischen Armee* (Berlin, 1928–37), 3:257 says that, on 20 October 1792, 12,864 men out of 15,068 reported in sick! In general, Prussia and Austria found it impossible to concentrate attention on France when the final partitioning of Poland was still in process (1793, 1795). Nonetheless, it is symbolic of the continuity in matters military between the Old Regime and the revolutionary management of armed force that this initial success against the vaunted Prussian army depended on superior weaponry, inherited from Gribeauval's reforms. The recovery of Toulon (1793), where Napoleon played his first conspicuous role, also turned upon the accuracy and rate of fire of the new French field artillery.

revolutionary performance conformed roughly to new tactical ideas developed in the French army after 1763. At Hondeshoote (September 1793) for example, skirmishers firing at the enemy line from behind hedgerows played an important role in compelling the English-German force to withdraw; and at Wattignies (October 1793), sustained only by revolutionary enthusiasm and by whatever they could pick up along the way, French soldiers proved able to move cross-country at something like twice the accustomed rate. They were therefore able to concentrate vastly superior numbers on the field of battle and, by enveloping the Austrian line, counteracted the fire superiority of professional troops by coming at them from front, flank, and rear.

This was the first time the revolutionary recipe for decisive victory came clearly into focus. Lazare Carnot, the "organizer of victory," was present at the Battle of Wattignies, representing the supreme authority of the Committee of Public Safety. Perhaps he deserves the main credit for taking the risks inherent in radically aggressive strategic and tactical moves. But if the French soldiers had refused their utmost effort in the approach march, or if their morale had wavered in battle, defeat would surely have followed. Instead, a new confidence in the might of the revolution flowed deep and strong through the ranks and began to inspire most of the French officers as well.[30]

Speed of march, strategic concentration, and aggressive tactics on the battlefield became the hallmarks of the French armies thereafter. By using skirmishers more freely than armies whose discipline was less spontaneous could afford to do, the French were able to attack through rough or wooded landscapes where the old-fashioned battle line was quite unable to form.[31] Impassable terrain could no longer be counted on to safeguard the flanks of a deployed infantry line, as in the days of Frederick II, and numbers (of artillery pieces as well as of men) attained a decisiveness that lasted throughout the Napoleonic period.

Victories, in turn, allowed the French armies to invade Belgium and the Rhinelands, carrying into those fertile and populous regions the principles of command economy which were about to disappear from France itself as the Terror wound down. Food and fodder, the perpetual needs of all armies, were too bulky to travel far. In any case, the victorious French had no desire to supply their troops from their own

30. Marcel Reinhard, *Le grand Carnot* (Paris, 1952), 2:81–82.
31. The superiority of the Roman legions over the Greek-Macedonian phalanx rested on a similar adaptability of Roman cohorts to hilly ground. In this as in other respects, the French revolutionaries consciously identified themselves with Roman republican models.

meager stores when forced contributions and outright plunder of the newly occupied lands could serve the purpose.

In this simple but effective fashion the French government went far towards relieving the social instability that had triggered revolution in the first place. Under the Directory, the mass of young men who had been unable to find satisfactory careers in civil occupations before the revolution were either successfully absorbed into the work force at home or living as soldiers at the expense of neighboring peoples, or else more or less gloriously dead.[32]

Until 1800 the revolutionary solution to the demographic-economic crisis that had done so much to overthrow Louis XVI remained precarious. But when Napoleon came to power (1799) and once again sent enemy armies reeling backward in defeat, the French government became able to impose an effective tax system upon its citizens. Thereafter, inflation was checked, and Napoleon distributed the costs of supporting his armies more equably than the revolutionary regimes had ever managed to do. In 1804–5, when he assembled the cream of the French armed forces at Boulogne to prepare for invasion of England, the maintenance of the army devolved again mainly on France, although neighboring lands continued to provide significant contributions—more or less forced—to the French war effort.[33]

Recruitment into the French armies had been regularized somewhat earlier. The men called up in the general mobilization of 1793–94 remained under arms indefinitely. Subsequent call-ups were erratic and partial—applied often to territories newly annexed to France—until in 1798 the Directory passed a law requiring all men between the ages of twenty and twenty-five to enroll with the Ministry of War. They were classed according to the year of their birth; and the legislature was then supposed to decide, each year, just how many new recruits were needed. The Ministry of War then assigned quotas to each *département,* and local authorities chose the persons who would serve, beginning with those of the youngest eligible age class. In time,

32. As always before the twentieth century, disease killed far more soldiers than enemy action; but statistics as to disease deaths were not kept and cannot be reconstructed.

33. These were sometimes in kind, i.e., an armed contingent, and sometimes in cash. In 1804, for example, Napoleon wrested 16,000 soldiers from Holland as well as having Dutch shipyards build many of the invasion barges intended to carry his troops across the Channel. From Spain he extracted a heavy money payment, though it required an ultimatum to persuade the Spanish government to pay up. Georges Lefebvre, *Napoleon* (Paris, 1947), p. 165.

it became standard to draw lots to determine who would march off to the army; but revolutionary equality was modified after 1799 by making it legal for a man whose number had been called to find a substitute by paying whatever sum of money the two could agree upon. In this fashion the military draft was modulated by resort to the market, so as to allow the rich to escape the burden and risk of personal service. This system remained in force in France until after 1871, though in most years after 1815, when few or none were called up, the draft affected only a small portion of the eligible male population.

No one, of course, conceived of the annual draft as a way of exporting surplus young Frenchmen to foreign lands and thereby ameliorating social frictions arising from rapid population growth. All the same, it had that effect throughout the Napoleonic years; and, conversely, the success of the draft depended on the annual maturation of enough young men to fill the ranks of the army and also perform essential tasks at home. By 1814 Napoleon was scraping the bottom of the barrel; but until 1812 his ever renewed demands on the French nation for more recruits did not disrupt civil life very noticeably. For twenty years the surge in population dating from the mid-eighteenth century continued to supply sufficient numbers of able-bodied young men to meet both military and civil demands for manpower.

Within France itself, the demographic impact of the draft was diminished by expanding the geographic area to which it was applied. Annexations to France almost doubled the number of "Frenchmen"—from about 25 million in 1789 to 44 million in 1810—and these new citizens under Napoleon's jurisdiction supplied their share of the 1.3 million conscripts Napoleon enrolled between 1800 and 1812. In addition, allied states were induced or compelled to contribute armed contingents to the *Grande Armée* of 1812, so that only a minority of the forces invading Russia in 1812 actually spoke French.[34]

In effect, therefore, Napoleon applied the revolutionary device for defusing social tensions arising from rapid population growth to all the

---

34. Ibid., pp. 191, 195, 379, 513–14. According to Lefebvre, the *Grande Armée* totaled 700,000, of whom 611,000 crossed the Russian frontier. Of this number, only 300,000 were French and 230,000 were from "old France." The really heavy draft hit France only in 1812–13 when Napoleon called up more than 1 million new soldiers, and succeeded in mobilizing about 41 percent of all the men registered with the Ministry of War. On population pressure in Germany and its political expression see Karl H. Wegert, "Patrimonial Rule, Popular Self-Interest and Jacobinism in Germany, 1763–1800," *Journal of Modern History* 53 (1981): 450 ff.

more densely populated parts of western Europe where it was difficult to meet the problem by simply extending tillage to new ground. Within the Austrian and Russian borders, the Hapsburg and Romanov regimes also built up the size of their armies and replaced losses by heavy drafts upon the peasantry. Their situation differed inasmuch as nothing prevented economically useful engagement of the growing work force in agriculture, whereas in more densely populated parts of western Europe this was difficult or impossible. In other words, political-diplomatic and military factors accounted for the growth of east European armies; no internal social dynamic pushed in that direction, although the growth of population made it relatively easy for the recruiters to fill their quotas from the villages.

Prussia constituted something of an exception, for after 1808 the terms of the treaty Napoleon imposed on Frederick William III limited the size of the Prussian army to 42,000 men. But this compulsory demobilization, and the economic distresses arising from years of French occupation and requisitioning, provided a store of men and emotion for the *Befreiungskrieg* of 1813, when Prussian manpower, summoned to the colors en masse, responded willingly.

Within the bounds of continental Europe, therefore, the revolutionary response to the demographic crisis of the Old Regime proved generally effective, at least until 1810. Napoleon's repeated victories over Austria (1797, 1800, 1805, 1809) and the crushing blow he gave to Prussian power in 1806 dismayed and discredited the Old Regime everywhere except in Great Britain. There popular feeling tended instead to harden against the French and rally behind the aristocratic-oligarchic leadership which managed the British economy and polity throughout the war with considerable success, as we shall soon see. Russian elites were ambivalent, both admiring and fearing the revolutionary upheaval. Given such hesitancy, nearly everyone was content to take his cue from the quirks of the reigning autocrat, first the angry eccentric Paul I (1795–1801) and then the guilt-ridden ideologue, Alexander I (1801–25).[35]

Neither a British-directed commercial integration of all Europe nor a French-dominated military consolidation of western Europe was truly compatible with Russian Orthodox feeling nor in accord with

35. Alexander was implicated in the murder of his father, Paul; and soon after his accession to the throne enthusiasm for enlightened French ideas competed in his mind with mystical pursuit of communion with God. His flip-flops from a French to a British alliance and back again were often associated with shifts in his intellectual posture, before as well as after his well-known conversion by Mme. de Krüdener to Christian ideals in 1815. Cf. Alan Palmer, *Alexander I: Tsar of War and Peace* (New York, 1974).

Russian state interests. But this, in effect, was the choice that the sudden upthrust of French and British power presented to the tsars and the Russian ruling elite. It was a dilemma less acute than those faced by rulers further west inasmuch as the Russian peasantry and lower classes of the towns were almost unaware of the winds of change blowing so powerfully in western Europe. The tsars therefore remained free to shift back and forth between a British and a French alliance, finding no real satisfaction in either. The Hapsburg rulers of Austria did the same, though when, in 1810, Klemens von Metternich arranged the marriage of Napoleon to a daughter of the emperor, Francis II, it looked as though a permanent reconciliation according to the ancient pattern of dynastic alliance had been achieved. The upstart emperor of the French valued the legitimation imparted by his marriage into the ancient house that claimed the headship of Christendom, and the Hapsburg emperor valued the immunity from further defeats that having Napoleon for a son-in-law seemed to guarantee.

From a military and diplomatic point of view, therefore, it surely seemed by 1810 that the French hegemony over western and central Europe was secure. Far-reaching legal changes followed in the wake of French conquests. Vested interests in the new regime, within France and beyond its borders, came swiftly into existence and grew stronger year by year.

Nevertheless, Britain's antagonism remained formidable, and the French effort to bring Great Britain to bay by cutting off all British trade with the Continent—a policy Napoleon announced in 1806— ended by putting his authority on a collision course with the interests of a considerable proportion of the European population, for whom cheap cotton cloth and other British manufactures as well as colonial goods available only through British entrepôts had become important. Had France been able to deliver equivalent goods from factories within her own borders, the continental blockade would surely have worked; but that was not the case. French manufactures had suffered severe dislocation between 1789 and 1800, and even though there was a recovery under Napoleon so that by 1811 the value of production surpassed that of the prerevolutionary period by as much as 40 percent[36] this rate of growth lagged far enough behind the British to make it difficult for articles of French manufacture to compete in quantity and price with British products.[37] More important, there was

36. L. Bergeron, "Problèmes économiques de la France Napoléonienne," *Annales historiques de la révolution française* 42 (1970): 89.

37. The gap was easy to exaggerate. Napoleon had no difficulty in supplying his armies with all the military hardware they could carry. Annual production of iron cannon

no way in which satisfactory substitutes for tea, coffee, sugar, raw cotton, and similar goods from overseas could be found within the limits of continental Europe—at least not in the short run.[38]

A fundamental French weakness was their dependence on costly overland transport, both for distribution of goods to civilian markets and, more decisively, for military supply as well. The catastrophes to Napoleon's power, in Spain and in Russia, arose from the fact that in both these theaters of war his enemies were able to avail themselves of water transport for supplying their armies, whereas the French had to rely mainly on overland haulage for whatever they could not find by plundering the countryside along the way. In rich enough rural landscapes, such as those of Italy and Germany, and for a period of a few weeks in summer time, the French reliance on overland haulage for whatever could not be seized along the line of march worked well enough, as Napoleon's earlier victorious campaigns attested. But when a single year's operations proved indecisive—as in Spain—and when the poverty of the landscape made living off the country difficult, then the formula for military success which French armies had followed since 1793 lost its potency. Plundering to make good de-

---

grew from 900 to 13,000 a year, and seventeen new foundries turned out no fewer than 14,000 bronze guns per annum, according to Clough, *France,* p. 49. One near-contemporary calculation held that between 1803 and 1815 the French produced 3.9 million muskets, rifles, carbines, and pistols, whereas Great Britain turned out only 3.1 million in the same period. F. R. C. Dupin, *Military Force of Great Britain* (London, 1822), quoted in Richard Glover, *Peninsular Preparation in 1795–1809* (Cambridge, 1963), p. 47. This may understate British production: Birmingham alone turned over 1,743,383 handguns and 3,037,644 gun barrels to the Board of Ordnance between 1804 and 1815, according to William Page, ed., *The Victoria History of the County of Warwick* II (London, 1908), "The Gun Trade of Birmingham," pp. 226–32.

France and French-controlled regions of Europe also saw spurts of entrepreneurship into new branches like cotton-spinning. Cf. Fernand Lelux, *A l'aube du capitalisme et de la révolution industrielle: Lieven Bauwens, industriel Gaulois* (Paris, 1969). Irregularities in access to raw cotton hurt the latter venture, however; and, in general, industries dependent on goods imported from overseas languished. Indeed the main effect of the war years was to choke off the Atlantic face of France and build up industry in the Rhine-Rhone valleys. Cf. François Crouzet, "Wars, Blockade and Economic Change in Europe, 1792–1815," *Journal of Economic History* 24 (1964): 567–88; Bertrand Gille, *Les origines de la grande industrie métallurgique en France* (Paris, 1947), pp. 206 ff.

38. Experiments, later to be important, were made with sugar beets; likewise cotton-growing in the Po valley was initiated; but these never came near filling the gap created by the cutoff of colonial goods. Realizing this weakness of his position, Napoleon kept hoping to be able to challenge Britain on the seas once again. After Trafalgar (1805) reduced the French army to a mere 30 ships of the line, he set about rebuilding. By 1814 103 ships of the line and 65 frigates were ready for sea. But the new vessels huddled uselessly in port, and in 1812 Napoleon took many of their crew members into the army for the invasion of Russia, thus tacitly admitting his inability, for the time being, to challenge his rival effectively. Cf. Joannes Tramond, *Manuel d'histoire maritime de la France: Des origines à 1815* (Paris, 1947), pp. 772 ff.

ficiencies of supply from the rear simply intensified the hostility of the local population, whether in East Prussia, Spain, or Russia; and means for increasing the flow from a distant rear by overland haulage were lacking.

By contrast, the British expeditionary force in Portugal and Spain (1808–12) relied largely upon supplies delivered by sea from Great Britain. Administrative means for performing this feat had been developed during the American War of Independence, and the effort in 1808–12 did not unduly strain British home resources. Moreover, in the poverty-stricken Iberian landscapes, the British paid negotiated prices to the local inhabitants for the goods and services (overland transport above all) that they needed. This meant that the British had preferential access to whatever the Spanish and Portuguese peasants had to spare whenever the hostile armies approached one another closely. Hence the French starved while British troops were more or less adequately nourished during the critical confrontation outside Lisbon in 1810–11 at Torres Vedras. The size of the French armies in Spain (up to 250,000) was no compensation; on the contrary numbers intensified their dilemma.

Spain, in short, remained a country of the Old Regime in many senses; its open wheat fields and pastures accorded well with old-fashioned British line tactics; and its poverty made a highly trained, relatively small force of the sort Wellington led a match and more than a match for the far more numerous French.[39]

Napoleon's invasion of Russia in 1812 confronted almost exactly the same difficulty. Earlier campaigns against the Russians in East Prussian and Polish territory in 1807–8 had shown the French how difficult it was to live off a country where marsh and forest occupied far more acreage than grainfields did. Napoleon therefore made unusually careful preparations to feed the *Grande Armée* from the rear; but transport overland by cart was slow and expensive and restricted the speed of march to a pace that Russian troops could easily match. Moreover, the whole supply system broke down utterly during the retreat from Moscow with the result that all but a few of the men who had accompanied Napoleon died or were captured.[40]

39. The Spanish guerrillas, together with Spanish and Portuguese regular troops who served under Wellington's command, did much to supplement the action of the British army. Without them, the old-fashioned tactics Wellington used so successfully would perhaps not have won so many victories. On the Peninsular War see Charles W. C. Oman, *A History of the Peninsular War,* 3 vols. (Oxford, 1902–08).

40. On Napoleon's supply arrangements for 1812 see David G. Chandler, *The Campaigns of Napoleon* (New York, 1966), pp. 757–59.

The Old Regime at Sea

The ships portrayed here show how warship design altered from the seventeenth to the nineteenth century in Europe. The ship above was built in Holland in 1626; the ship below was built in France in 1847. The number of guns carried more than doubled in this span of time, but the fundamental idea of lining up tiers of heavy cannon along the sides of a stoutly built ship remained unchanged.

E. Van Konijnenburg, *Shipbuilding from Its Beginnings* (Brussels: Permanent International Association of Congresses of Navigation, n.d.), figs. 146, 173.

In relying on carts to supply his army, Napoleon was, in effect, pitting them against water transport, for the tsar's control of the river and canal system of Russia meant that his forces could hope to benefit from supplies of grain and other necessities delivered by barge and riverboat in summer and by sleigh in winter. Since it was easy to move even heavy cargoes up and down stream—for many miles if need be—the Russians were in a position to supply their soldiers more abundantly than was possible for the invaders, whose carts moved lesser weights with much greater effort.[41]

The British Variant

Before considering the consequences of Napoleon's defeat in Russia, it seems wise to shift attention across the channel and inquire briefly how the British government managed its war effort against France in the revolutionary years. No sudden breaks and no violent domestic upheavals accompanied the mobilization of British resources for war, though changes in British society were in the long run quite as revolutionary as anything that transpired in France, as our accustomed use of the phrase "industrial revolution" attests.

The thesis that population growth was an important and perhaps the principal factor upsetting older economic equilibriums in Great Britain is a familiar one among historians who have tried to explain how and why that island became the seat of the industrial revolution.[42] An abundant labor force on the one hand and an expanding domestic market on the other made economies of scale through use of newly invented machinery feasible, whether it was a spinning mule for making cotton thread or a blast furnace for smelting iron. Cheap water

41. At least in principle. I have not been able to find any discussion of how the Russian troops were actually supplied in 1812; but an examination of the map shows that the line of their retreat and advance crossed a series of river lines whose banks, on either side of the route of march, were securely controlled by the Russian government. I assume, therefore, that supplies came along the rivers; and even if deliveries were ill organized, as is probable, they clearly surpassed French arrangements. The fact that the Russian army remained in being and was able to harass the retreating *Grande Armée* throughout the winter months stands as proof of this elementary fact.

42. This was the central thesis of Phyllis Deane and W. A. Cole, *British Economic Growth, 1688–1959* (Cambridge, 1962) and, ten years later, W. A. Cole, "Eighteenth Century Economic Growth Revisited," *Explorations in Economic History* 10 (1973): 327–48, reaffirmed the idea. Cf. also H. J. Habakkuk, *Population Growth and Economic Development since 1750* (New York, 1971), p. 48 and passim; D. E. C. Eversley, "The Home Market and Economic Growth in England, 1750–1780," in E. L. Jones and G. E. Mingay, eds., *Land, Labour and Population in the Industrial Revolution* (London, 1967), pp. 206–59.

transport was essential to the whole development, both for importing raw materials like cotton from overseas and for distributing and redistributing commodities within and beyond the British isles. The duke of Bridgewater's canal (opened in 1761) that brought coal to the burgeoning cotton mills of Manchester made that town's spectacular development possible; and the canal's no less spectacular financial success triggered a canal-building mania in Great Britain that lasted into the 1790s. Together with improvements in existing riverbeds, the result was to give England an effective system of inland waterways that greatly cheapened the movement of heavy goods by reducing overland haulage almost everywhere to a matter of a few miles at most.[43]

Yet, as in France, nothing assured satisfactory relationships between population, food supply, and opportunities for gainful employment; and in parts of the British Isles intense rural poverty failed to provoke any sort of commercial and industrial growth. This was conspicuously the case in Ireland and in the Scottish Highlands. Even London, for all its exuberant commercial and industrial expansion, also housed a volatile, poverty-stricken multitude, some of whom scraped a living by beggary and thievery even in good times. London's potential for crowd violence was equal to anything Paris had to offer; and leaders like John Wilkes (1725–97) were in ready supply to provide an aroused populace with political goals and causes to espouse, as happened so spectacularly in Paris, 1789–94.

Nevertheless, the aristocratic-oligarchic leadership of England was not seriously challenged within the country even in the first days of the revolution when the French version of liberty gleamed most brightly across the channel, as it did also among France's other near neighbors.[44] One reason was that challenge to the prevailing governmental regime became hard to distinguish from treason once war against France had been joined. But in addition, the British government found effective ways of coping with a rapidly growing population and therefore managed to keep discontent from assuming the explosive force that Louis XVI had encountered in Paris.

As in France, recruitment into the army and navy played a significant role. At the peak of mobilization in 1814, some half a million

---

43. It is worth noting, perhaps, how closely this development, along with the simultaneous rise of the coke and iron technology in Great Britain, paralleled the much earlier Chinese developments discussed above in chapter 2.

44. Robert R. Palmer, *The Age of the Democratic Revolution: A Political History of Europe and America, 1760–1800,* 2 vols. (Princeton, 1959, 1964).

men were carried on the rolls of the two armed services,[45] i.e., nearly 4 percent of the entire active work force of Great Britain. Recruitment into the army came disproportionately from the impoverished Scottish Highlands, and to the navy from seaport towns where press gangs picked up any ablebodied man they encountered who did not have a fixed abode and settled employment. This meant that two localities whose eighteenth-century record showed them particularly responsive to political discontent were drained of unemployed and underemployed young men, just as happened in Paris and the rest of France after 1794–95.

In Ireland, the other long-standing ulcer of British society and politics, response to rural impoverishment and population growth followed two divergent paths. In Ulster among Scots-Irish Protestants, emigration to America had become a tradition since the famine years of 1717–18; and after interruption during the War of American Independence, 1775–83, a trickle of emigration from the north of Ireland resumed until interrupted again in 1812–14 by a new American war.[46] This outflow, averaging something like 2,000–3,000 per annum, was large enough to make a difference to the province of Ulster and seems to have provided an effective safety valve for social discontent in that part of the British Isles. In the south of Ireland, a different stream of migration temporarily relieved the rural overcrowding from which Catholic Irish had long suffered, when landlords in Leinster and Munster discovered that instead of using their estates for grazing, as had been usual before 1793, the rising price of grain made it worthwhile to break the sod and sow wheat or oats. This required manpower for plowing and harvest; and by offering the poor Irish an acre on which to grow potatoes for the support of their families, the necessary manpower could be found. As a result, Connaught, where the Cromwellian settlement of 1650 had confined the Catholic poor, par-

45. This figure is from Glenn Hueckel, "War and the British Economy, 1793–1815: A General Equilibrium Analysis," *Explorations in Economic History* 10 (1972): 371. Patrick Colquhoun, *A Treatise on the Wealth, Power and Resources of the British Empire* (London, 1814), p. 47, gives figures that add up to 511,679.

46. Official statistics were not kept on either side of the Atlantic, but historians are of the opinion that a total of about 225,000 Ulstermen arrived in America between 1718 and 1775, and that when emigration resumed after 1783 the flow was somewhat smaller than it had been before the War of Independence. Cf. H. J. M. Johnston, *British Emigration Policy, 1815–1830* (Oxford, 1972), pp. 6–7. The beginnings of emigration to Canada and the Carolinas from the Scottish Highlands dates from after the Seven Years War, when discharged veterans were offered land in the New World. Cf. Helen I. Cowan, *British Emigration to British North America: The First Hundred Years,* rev. ed. (Toronto, 1961), pp. 3–64. But the numerical scale of this movement was too slight to have much demographic effect back home.

tially emptied out during the war years, and for a decade or so southern Ireland enjoyed something approaching full employment.

Thus the most impacted regions of the British Isles each found a
reasonably effective solution to the problem of growing rural populations: the Highlands by enlisting in the army, Ulster by sending a
proportion of its workforce overseas, and southern Ireland by shifting
from pasture to tillage. In England itself, where commercial agriculture and "high farming" were far more fully developed, the most
significant response to the growth of population was modification of
poor law administration. After 1795 more and more parishes authorized outdoor relief for the indigent, tying amounts disbursed to
the applicants' wage income, to the size of his family and—significantly—to the price of bread. Administrative practices varied from
place to place, but this so-called "Speenhamland" system[47] assured a
minimal subsistence to everyone. It meant that even in bad years,
when partial crop failures pushed the price of bread to great heights,
the poor could count on escaping outright starvation. In the absence
of the poor law help, rural laborers in time of dearth and in the seasons
of the year when work on the land was slackest, would have had no
choice but to flee into town, hoping against hope to find employment
there or survive on charity unavailable within their hard-pressed rural
community. Crowds of just such desperate people had flooded into
Paris because of bad harvests in 1788–89. After 1795, however, the
like could scarcely occur in England. The new pattern of poor law
administration allowed rural laborers to survive seasons of dearth simply by remaining where they were. As a result, the Speenhamland
system of outdoor relief went a long way towards stabilizing English
society.

Thereafter, migration within England was governed by response to
economic opportunities and wage differentials; and such migration in
turn contributed to the distinctive and fundamentally important way
in which British society adjusted itself to the population growth of the
late eighteenth century, that is, by expanding opportunities for economically productive work in commerce and industry. New technologies lowered prices; lowered prices expanded markets; expanded
markets increased the scale of production, which in turn required
more and more factory hands, transport workers, and service per-

47. Named for the place where justices of the peace from Berkshire met in 1795 to
set up a schedule for outdoor relief payments which became a model, widely imitated, in
the following years. See Michael E. Rose, *The English Poor Laws, 1780–1930* (New
York, 1971), pp. 18–20.

sonnel of the most diverse sort to keep the exchange economy running as smoothly as it did. No one planned this growth, and several sharp crises during the war years made the whole system waver. But in each case the British government and British owners and managers resumed activity, and the crisis passed. Three times, in particular, the national phlegm and ingenuity combined to surmount incipient disaster, for the public accepted an unbacked paper currency in 1797, submitted to an income tax in 1799, and exporters found new markets in Latin America and in the Levant when sales of British goods on the continent of Europe were seriously restricted after 1806.

Most historians of the industrial revolution pay little attention to the war. Those who do notice it usually argue either that the war hindered rather than promoted British industrial development or that it made little difference one way or the other.[48] This is a questionable proposition. The vast increase in governmental expenditures, nearly all for war purposes, surely affected supply and demand for every article exchanged within the British economy.[49] Only if one assumes that some other stimulus would have put the entire labor force to work and endowed the formerly underemployed portion of the British public with an effective purchasing power equivalent to that exercised by the British army and navy, does it seem plausible to assume that in the absence of the war the pace of British industrialization would have equaled or exceeded that which actually occurred. Abroad, also, government expenditures paved the way for British exports. Subsidies to allied governments, totaling 65.8 million pounds in all,[50] allowed continental officials to buy British goods to equip their armies; and that portion of the subsidies spent within Russian, Austrian, or Prussian territory distributed foreign exchange against London to Berlin, St. Petersburg, and Vienna, thus allowing civilians to purchase colonial goods and other commodities, most of which passed through or originated in the British Isles. Without these gov-

48. John U. Nef, *War and Human Progress* (Cambridge, Mass., 1950) perhaps expresses an extreme view, but W. W. Rostow, "War and Economic Change: The British Experience," *The Process of Economic Growth,* 2d ed. (Oxford, 1960), pp. 144–67, comes to a similar conclusion. Phyllis Deane, "War and Industrialization," in J. M. Winter, ed., *War and Economic Development* (Cambridge, 1975), p. 101, concludes that the war of 1793–1815 "does not seem to have caused more than superficial fluctuations in the pace and content of the British Industrial revolution."

49. Government expenditure in 1814 was no less that 29 percent of the estimated GNP, according to Alan T. Peacock and Jack Wiseman, *The Growth of Public Expenditure in the United Kingdom* (Princeton, 1961), p. 37.

50. John T. Sherwig, *Guineas and Gunpowder: British Foreign Aid 1793–1815* (Cambridge, Mass., 1969), p. 345.

ernmental subsidies to continental allies, and without the transfer of effective purchasing power to the half a million otherwise indigent and underemployed men who wound up in the ranks of the army and navy, it seems impossible to believe that British industrial production would have increased at anything like the actual rate.[51]

Not only that. Government intervention also altered the mix of commodities coming from the expanding industrial plant of Great Britain, mainly by putting a special premium on iron. Indigent and underemployed men do not buy cannon and other expensive industrial products. But by putting indigent thousands into the army and navy and then supplying them with the tools of their new trade, effective demand was displaced from articles of personal consumption towards items useful to big organizations—armies and navies in the first place, but factories, railroads, and other such enterprises in times to come. Moreover, the men who built the new coke-fired blast furnaces in previously desolate regions of Wales and Scotland would probably not have undertaken such risky and expensive investments without an assured market for cannon. At any rate, their initial markets were largely military.[52]

Thus both the absolute volume of production and the mix of products that came from British factories and forges, 1793–1815, was profoundly affected by government expenditures for war purposes. In particular, government demand created a precocious iron industry, with a capacity in excess of peacetime needs, as the postwar depression 1816–20 showed. But it also created the condition for future growth by giving British ironmasters extraordinary incentives for finding new uses for the cheaper product their new, large-scale furnaces were able to turn out. Military demands on the British economy

51. This was not lost on contemporaries. Joseph Lowe, *The Present State of England in Regard to Agriculture, Trade and Finance* (London, 1833), pp. 29 ff., attributes Britain's wartime prosperity to full employment resulting from taxation and government borrowing, whose tonic effect was "distributed over the country, for . . . our total expenditure . . . with trifling exception, was circulated at home" (p. 33).

52. J. L. Anderson, "Aspects of the Effects on the British Economy of the War against France, 1793–1815," *Australian Economic History Review* 12 (1972): 1–20. The short-barreled, extra-large gun used with greater effect aboard Nelson's ships at Trafalgar, the carronade, was named for the Carron works in Scotland where it was first designed; and the wharf in Cardiff where the products of the South Wales ironworks were loaded is still known as Cannon Wharf. Popular speech in this fashion recorded the importance of armaments for the new iron industry of Great Britain. Even the Quaker firm founded by Abraham Darby at Coalbrookdale made cannon in the mid-eighteenth century, but discontinued the practice before 1792. Cf. Arthur Raistrick, *The Coalbrookdale Ironworks: A Short History* (Telford, 1975), p. 5.

thus went far to shape the subsequent phases of the industrial revolution, allowing the improvement of steam engines[53] and making such critical innovations as the iron railway and iron ships possible at a time and under conditions which simply would not have existed without the wartime impetus to iron production. To dismiss this feature of British economic history as "abnormal"[54] surely betrays a remarkable bias that seems to be widespread among economic historians.

On yet another front: enclosure acts peaked in Britain during the first fifteen years of the nineteenth century when grain prices put a premium on high farming. Parliament's readiness to override the interest of the poorer agricultural classes in passing enclosure acts is well known; but even a Parliament of landlords and merchants would probably not have passed so many acts with so little deliberation about the social consequences of enclosure, had wartime conditions not provided adequate alternatives to the dispossessed, who could join the army, go on relief, or find employment in the booming civilian economy, stimulated as it was by wartime demands. If enclosure acts had instead provided recruits for angry city crowds of unemployed and underemployed laborers, the enclosures would surely not have proceeded as they did, and, once again, British economic history would have taken a different path, rather more like that which France experienced in the nineteenth century.

Counterfactual history is useful only to stimulate the imagination; what matters for the argument of this book is the assertion that massive governmental intervention in the marketplace[55] had the effect, only half recognized or intended at the time, of hurrying on the industrial revolution in Great Britain and helping to define its path. Thanks to government expenditure, prosperity and full employment predominated during the wartime years even as the population of the United

53. Wilkinson's cannon-boring machine allowed Watt's steam engine to become efficient by making possible a close fit between piston and cylinder. Cf. Clive Trebilcock, "Spin-off in British Economic History: Armaments and Industry, 1760–1914," *Economic History Review* 22 (1969): 477.

54. As Phyllis Deane, *The First Industrial Revolution* (Cambridge, 1965), p. 110, does. Cf. also the otherwise admirable work, Charles K. Hyde, *Technological Change and the British Iron Industry, 1700–1870* (Princeton, 1970), p. 129: "In the absence of fighting, overall demand for iron might have been higher." Hyde offers no explanation for this surprising judgment; he just tosses it off as an aside. The most careful assessment of the impact of war on the British iron industry I have seen is Alan Birch, *The Economic History of the British Iron and Steel Industry, 1784–1879: Essays in Industrial and Economic History with Special Reference to the Development of Technology* (London, 1967), pp. 47–56.

55. Public expenditure increased from £22 million in 1792 to £123 million in 1815, or almost six times.

Kingdom leaped upward from 14.5 million in 1791 to 18.1 million in 1811.[56]

In France, government policy was no less successful in coping with the problem presented by unemployed and underemployed manpower; but the mix was different. A larger proportion of young Frenchmen went into the armies, while industrial-commercial growth, though real enough, went more slowly, partly because, as the territorial base of French power expanded, it brought new industrial regions under the jurisdiction of the government in Paris, so that Liège and Turin as well as older armaments centers in France proper began to contribute to the French war effort. Similarly, cotton mills and other new industries, when they sprang up, clustered in Belgium and Alsace on the borders of historic France.

The different balances of military as against commercial-industrial occupations that divergent government policies opened up for previously underemployed young men in France and Britain had long-range consequences of great importance. French war losses, totaling between 1.3 and 1.5 million between 1792 and 1815,[57] together with the notable drop in birthrates in France that became manifest with the new century, meant that the stimulus (and problem) of rapid population growth disappeared permanently from French soil with the restoration of the Bourbons, whereas Great Britain and Ireland, as well as Germany and the rest of continental Europe, continued to exhibit a rate of population growth throughout the nineteenth century that left the French far behind.[58]

56. Figures from Deane and Cole, *British Economic Growth,* p. 8.

57. Jacques Dupaquier and Christine Berg-Hamon, "Voies nouvelles pour l'histoire démographique de la révolution française: Le mouvement de population de 1795 à 1800," *Annales historiques de la Révolution française* 47 (1975): 8, offer a total for French war losses of 1.3 million; but by adding Lefebvre's total of 600,000 war losses for the years 1792–99, cited in n. 21 above, to a new total of 900,000 for losses under the empire worked out by J. Houdaille, "Pertes de l'armée de terre sous le premier Empire," *Population* 27 (1972): 42, one gets a total of 1.5 million. Inasmuch as Houdaille's data and methods are clearly superior to previous calculations, the larger figure is likely to be correct. Houdaille calculates that no less than 20.5 percent of all French males born between 1790 and 1795 inclusive died before 1816 from war-related causes. These were the age classes most severely affected. Ibid., p. 50.

58. What happened to French birthrates to set them off from the rest of Europe is a capital question of historical demography. The prevalence of peasant property in land must have mattered; postponing marriage until inheritance of land was in sight for the newlyweds could have a powerful effect in slowing population growth, as the history of Ireland after the famine of 1845 proves. But the French must also have resorted to deliberate birth control on a scale other European peoples did not approach until the twentieth century. It seems possible that French soldiers' experiences with prostitutes in the wars may have spread familiarity with birth control methods among the French,

Thus it appears that the French learned to control births and the British learned how to employ a growing population in industry and trade largely as unintended by-products of the actions of their respective governments between 1792 and 1815. British technological advantage lasted for half a century or so as a result of being first in the field; the French moved far more slowly towards industrialization and urbanism, retaining a numerical preponderance of peasants in their society until after 1914.

Overall, one should recognize that both countries were strikingly successful in coping with the crisis presented in the late eighteenth century by unprecedented population growth occurring in a landscape where uncultivated land was already in short supply. For in the tumultuous years from 1789 to 1815 both France and Britain raised their national wealth and power to new heights, whereas eastern Europe lagged behind, even though, by any other standard, the economic and military growth of Russia and Austria was spectacular. But increase in population and in army size did not require new forms of human cooperation and management in the parts of Europe where new hands could readily be put to work turning woods and wasteland into fields. Extensive development of this sort was less valuable to governments than the French-British pattern of exploring more intensive forms of integrating human effort on a mass scale, whether principally through command, as in France, or primarily through the market as in Great Britain. This was so because new settlement on former wasteland quickly ran into the law of diminishing returns. Cultivators occupying less and less fertile soil could only put a shrinking surplus of agricultural products at the disposal of governmental and other urban authorities. Ireland went the same way after 1815, in stark contrast to the continued urban and industrial development of Great Britain. Like eastern Europeans during the latter part of the nineteenth century, the Irish had to resort to emigration as an escape from rural impoverishment, when the brutal force of famine did not supervene.

The precarious and spectacular success of French policy between 1792 and 1812 disguised a weakness that became flamingly apparent

---

and this, with the general secularization and break with Catholic teachings that the revolution brought, may explain what happened to French birthrates. Jacques Dupaquier, "Problèmes démographiques de la France napoléonienne," *Annales historiques de la Révolution française* 42 (1970): 21, is the only authority I have seen who recognizes the possible importance of wartime military experiences of sex as affecting French family patterns after 1800; but any veteran of twentieth-century wars can confirm the plausibility of this suggestion—and the improbability of finding written sources as evidence.

after Napoleon's defeat in Russia. For however unpopular British financial and commercial superiority became among the peoples of the European continent, it was resented far less sharply than French military superiority and economic exploitation were by those compelled to support and obey French armies of occupation. When British subsidies and British arms became available to supply shortfalls in the equipment of Prussian, Russian, and Austrian armies in 1813, therefore, the material means and the will to overthrow Napoleon came together. The combination proved overwhelming. Napoleon's prefects performed prodigies in raising new armies to meet the enemy, and the emperor's battles and maneuvers against the advancing allied forces have won the admiration of military historians. But French resources were inadequate and much of the *élan* of the first revolutionary days had long since evaporated from the army and from French civil society as well. Once Napoleon was out of the way, therefore, a negotiated peace, in which traditional calculations of balance of power played the decisive role, proved possible, and France was able to rejoin the concert of Europe in a remarkably short time.

Postwar Settlement, 1815–40

Yet the marks of the revolution could not be erased from the face of Europe, and even the most reactionary of the restored regimes scarcely made the attempt. In military matters, changes pregnant for the future concentrated chiefly in Prussia. The British and Russian armies remained entirely of the Old Regime, despite the wartime increases in their size. Elsewhere, the effort of rulers and aristocrats to summon the people to arms against the French was very much muted by traditional social hierarchies and residual distrust between noble and commoner, rich and poor, ruler and subject. Austrian action against the French was qualified by the fact that Napoleon was, after all, the emperor's son-in-law; and after 1812, Prince Klemens von Metternich, the architect of Hapsburg foreign policy, recognized that if France were eliminated as a military power, the Russian tsar would be able to dominate all of the continent, eclipsing Hapsburg pretensions to primacy within Latin Christendom and undermining Austria's headship of the Germanies by throwing tidbits to his Prussian jackal. Metternich's style of diplomacy and war thus conformed to Old Regime standards as completely as the British and Russian armies did.

But in Prussia, the very unexpectedness and completeness of the military collapse in 1806 opened the way for energetic reform of society and government as well as of the army. A Hanoverian upstart, Gerhard Johann David von Scharnhorst (1755–1813), won remarkable ascendancy among the military reformers, thanks to his personal qualities and to halfhearted support from Frederick William III. The Prussian king felt that he had been betrayed by incompetent and even cowardly aristocratic officers. So after Jena he turned to Scharnhorst and his fellow reformers, but only in a mood of desperation, for he mistrusted their faith in the revival of Prussian greatness through partnership with the people. Active alliance between ruler and ruled, Scharnhorst believed, was the real secret of French successes. Time and again ordinary Frenchmen had proved themselves willing to fight bravely on behalf of their nation and its rulers. Germans would do the same for the king of Prussia but only if they were given a proper stake in the country. King Frederick William acceded to such ideas reluctantly, for he remembered what had happened to Louis XVI when he had tried to ride the tiger of the popular will. Abolition of serfdom and establishment of limited local self-government were about all that the Prussian king was prepared to approve in the way of social and political reform.

In strictly military matters, however, Scharnhorst's ideas met with fuller success. Until 1813, French policy made implementation of the ideal of a people in arms plainly impossible. But in the meantime, improvement in military efficiency, skill, and level of training seemed attainable. Accordingly, Scharnhorst's idea that officers should be appointed and promoted only on the basis of demonstrated capacity was officially decreed by royal proclamation in 1808, as follows:

> A claim to the position of officer shall from now on be warranted in peace-time by knowledge and education, in time of war by exceptional bravery and quickness of perception. From the whole nation, therefore, all individuals who possess these qualities can lay title to the highest positions of honor in the military establishment. All social preference which has hitherto existed is herewith terminated in the military establishment, and everyone, without regard for his background, has the same duties and the same rights.[59]

To implement this declaration, schools were established in which cadets might qualify for commissions and in which serving officers might qualify for promotion to higher rank. Schooling for artillerymen

59. Translation by Gordon A. Craig in *The Politics of the Prussian Army, 1640–1945* (Oxford, 1955), p. 43.

had been of long standing in every European army, since the technicalities of gunnery were complex enough to require it.[60] But to make schooling general for all officers, and to require examinations to test what had been learned before certifying that the individual in question was qualified for appointment or promotion, was a new idea.[61] The French army had briefly experimented with a similar regulation in 1790, but in the heat of revolutionary enthusiasm a system that reserved officer rank for educated men smacked too much of class privilege. Accordingly, educational requirements validated by written examinations were abolished in 1791 and promotion to officer rank was made to depend on seniority and selection.[62] Napoleon continued this policy, so that the French officer corps became a group of hard-bitten veterans, among whom a disdain for book learning and ideas of any sort prevailed. Anti-intellectualism in the Russian, British, and Austrian armies was almost as intense, for in those armies ideas and ideologies tended to be identified with the revolutionary French.

Amongst the Prussian officer corps, anti-intellectualism did not vanish simply because new regulations required officers to go to school and pass examinations. Indeed after 1819 the principle of the 1808 ordinance was modified and often betrayed by giving special privileges to noble candidates for commissions. But a residue of the reformers' ideals persisted, and from 1808 onwards some Prussian officers owed their position to their intellectual attainments. Such persons encouraged one another to apply their minds to professional questions as new problems and possibilities arose, much in the style and spirit of General Gribeauval.

The creation of the Great General Staff between 1803 and 1809 provided an organizational stronghold within the Prussian army for intellectually vigorous officers. Appointment came only after a man had distinguished himself in the advanced school for officers seeking to qualify for higher commands. The General Staff was responsible for planning possible future campaigns in peacetime—a radical and dubiously moral step when first proposed. For that purpose it was neces-

---

60. Scharnhorst's ideas reflected the fact that he was both a gunner and a commoner born.

61. Civil officials in Prussia had, since the seventeenth century, been recruited from the universities of Germany, and from 1770 had to validate their studies by passing an examination. Hence the 1808 ordinance concerning Prussian officer recruitment simply assimilated army management to that of the civilian state.

62. Samuel F. Scott, *The Response of the Royal Army to the French Revolution, 1787–1793* (Oxford, 1978), pp. 153, 161. Examinations continued for the artillery and engineers as in the days of the Old Regime.

sary to collect topographical and other intelligence, to study what had
been done well or badly in campaigns of former times, and to
criticize tactics and strategy as simulated in peacetime maneuvers. The
staff officers thus became a kind of collective brain for the Prussian
army, seeking systematically to apply reason and calculation to all
aspects of army administration and operations. Links with regular
units and troop commanders were assured by the practice of attaching
members of the General Staff to every general headquarters, where
they were expected to use their specialized knowledge of technical
and logistical matters to advise the commander about how best to
implement his will.

The rewards for collaboration between trained expertise and a resolute commander had been amply demonstrated in 1813–15. For
General Gebhard Leberecht von Blücher (1742–1819), a man of the
old Prussian school, found first in Scharnhorst (until his death from a
wound in 1813) and then in Scharnhorst's close collaborator, August
Count Niethardt von Gneisenau (1760–1831), a chief of staff who
could translate his intentions into detailed operational orders that
foresaw and forestalled many of the factors which would otherwise
have made punctual obedience impossible. Knowing ahead of time
from maps what local topography was like, a competent staff officer
could calculate from past experience and codified rules of thumb what
rate of march a baggage train, artillery park, or infantry unit could
sustain across the terrain in question. This allowed him to foretell
what length of time would be required to complete the movements to
be performed. When to start each unit off on its march and which lines
of advance to follow could then be specified with such exactness that
the field commander could exercise far greater real control over his
troops than was possible without such staff work.

Blücher, more than most other Prussian commanders, recognized
this fact and came to respect and depend on the expertise around him
in a way that Napoleon and other generals of the era were not prepared to do. Blücher's relationship to Scharnhorst and Gneisenau
continued to affect Prussian military practice in the years after 1815,
though the prestige of staff officers was not completely secure until
after midcentury, when Helmut von Moltke (1800–91) showed in the
Austro-Prussian war of 1866 precisely how General Staff planners
could speed up and control strategic deployment of vast numbers of
men by calculating everything carefully ahead of time.

The Prussians also preserved the ideal of universal military obliga-
tion into peacetime. This was partly because of the emotional residue

of 1813–14, when a hastily raised army, in which civilians in uniform far outnumbered regular soldiers, participated in notable Allied victories over the French.[63] But sentiment was not alone in sustaining the ideal of a people in arms. The budgetary weakness of the postwar Prussian state made it impossible to maintain a long-term service army of a size to match what the Austrians, Russians, and French were able to support. To count as a great power, even *in potentia,* the Prussians had to rely on reserves, the *Landwehr.* This army of civilians had been called suddenly into existence in 1813 to fight against Napoleon. Subsequently, in peacetime, it was replenished by assigning to it men who had completed a three-year term of duty with the army. Reserve officers came to be recruited from among students at the universities who, by volunteering for a year's active service in the regular army, qualified as *Landwehr* lieutenants.

Even in its most reactionary moments, therefore, the Prussian army managed to preserve into peacetime some of the revolutionary traits that had surged to the fore in 1813–14. Although a strongly aristocratic bias again became dominant among the Prussian officers after 1819, a heightened professional competence, especially among staff officers, and residual reliance on a civilian reserve remained as heritages from the age of reform when, for a while, partnership of king and people had become a reality and the might of the Prussian state had again ranked with that of the greatest powers of Europe, as in the glorious days of Frederick the Great.[64]

In other European armies, return to the principles of the Old Regime was much more thorough. Long-service professional troops were everywhere preferred. France, Austria, and Russia kept armies of several hundred thousand men under arms in regular garrison duty. Education and learning were not in favor in these armies. Staff work was held in comparatively low esteem. Technical branches—artillery and engineers—continued to require a modicum of intellectual competence, but retrenchment after the extraordinary military expenditures

63. The Prussian army had been limited to 42,000 men by Napoleon's fiat in 1808. In 1814 its field strength was 358,000 men with an additional 30,000 or so in the rear to perform various service and supporting roles. Figures from Jany, *Geschichte der Königlich Preussischen Armee,* 4:114.

64. The era of Prussian reform was long a favorite field for German patriots. The little essay by Friedrich Meinecke, *The Age of German Liberation, 1795–1815* (Berkeley and Los Angeles, 1977; originally published 1906) is an elegant summary of mainstream opinion. On military matters, in addition to Gordon Craig's magistral book, already referred to, William Shanahan, *Prussian Military Reforms, 1786–1813* (New York, 1945) and Peter Paret, *Yorck and the Era of Prussian Reform, 1807–1815* (Princeton, 1966), which corrects Shanahan on some minor details, are especially informative.

of the war years was everywhere the order of the day, and no one supposed that industrial technology could be harnessed to the task of producing radically new sorts of weapons capable of upsetting the traditional routines and patterns of military and naval life. No one wanted such a revolutionary break either, and when it came, after 1840, nearly all professional officers were opponents of change, not its proponents.

To sum up: despite the new power that revolutionary idealism and the administrative implementation of liberty and equality had conferred upon the French between 1792 and 1815, the rulers and military men of Europe clearly and emphatically preferred the security of old routines. Consequently, the traditions and patterns of Old Regime armies and navies survived the storm of the revolutionary years essentially intact. Weaponry changed little. Promising innovations met short shrift from conservatively minded commanders. Thus Napoleon disbanded the balloon observation corps that had been introduced into the French army in 1793, and Wellington flatly refused to employ the new "Congreve" rockets which, despite difficulty in controlling their flight accurately, had proved quite effective in attacking large targets such as towns and forts.[65]

"Tried and true," seemed a far safer policy to the rulers of Europe and their military advisers after 1815. Some residues of the wars remained: divisional and corps organization, still a novelty in the 1790s, had become normal by 1815. Increased reliance on maps and on staff work was also pretty much taken for granted, since the great escalation in the size of armies that had taken place between 1792 and 1815 was by no means entirely reversed in the demobilization that

65. These weapons were invented by an Englishman, William Congreve (1772–1828), in the first decade of the nineteenth century. He was stimulated by reports of how the Indian prince, Tipoo Sahib, had used rockets against British soldiers in 1792 and 1799. His rockets attained a range about twice that of contemporary field artillery; they were used with considerable effect against Boulogne in 1806 (after a failure the year before), and in subsequent attacks against Copenhagen (1807), Danzig (1813) and at the battle of Leipzig (1813). Congreve rockets also played a conspicuous part in the War of 1812, a fact commemorated in "The Star-Spangled Banner." They may indeed have allowed the British to reach and burn the new American capital of Washington.
Rocket corps were set up in most European armies after 1813; but after the 1840s spectacular new developments in artillery made rockets seem too inaccurate to be worthwhile. They disappeared from war towards the end of the nineteenth century, to be revived in a big way only in World War II. Cf. Willy Ley, *Rockets, Missiles, and Men in Space* (New York, 1968), pp. 61–75; Wernher von Braun and Frederick I. Ordway III, *Rocketry and Space Travel*, 3d ed. (New York, 1975), pp. 30–34. On Wellington's rejection of Congreve's rockets, see Glover, *Peninsular Preparation,* pp. 68–73.

followed the peace. Russia, for example, scarcely demobilized at all, maintaining an army of about 600,000 men ten years after the end of hostilities against France.[66] Technically improved field artillery also had become standard in every European army.

But after 1815 it seemed self-evident to those in charge of public policy that the fierce energy of the French conscripts in 1793–95, and the nationalistic fervor of some German citizen-soldiers in 1813–14, could challenge constituted authority as readily as it could confirm and strengthen it. Like the warheads of Congreve's rockets, armed man-ifestations of popular will were hard to control. The people in arms might turn against any ruler so incautious as to summon help from the depths of society, just as an experimental firing of Congreve's rockets, put on for Wellington's benefit in 1810, had in fact endangered the men who launched them, thus discrediting the new weapon in the duke's eyes forever after.

Not without reason, therefore, Europe's rulers agreed that further military experimentation was unwise. Armies and navies, disciplined and equipped in the style of the Old Regime, were what they wanted and what they got. If, thereby, they refrained from tapping depths of national energies that the revolutionary years had unveiled, what matter, so long as the victors could agree among themselves and keep the specter of revolutionary disorder at bay?

For a quarter of a century after 1815, therefore, it seemed that Old Regime patterns of military management had survived the untoward combination of crowd violence and political idealism that had triggered the revolution in France. To be sure, the restored Bourbon kings faced a few sporadic manifestations of political disaffection on the part of French soldiers. Drab routine and low pay were a poor substitute for the excitement of a career open to talent that had pre-vailed in Napoleon's day. But campaigning in Algeria, begun in 1830, opened a safety valve for such discontents, and thereafter memories of republican and Napoleonic glories faded fast. In the 1840s an apoliti-cal army, ready to obey constituted public authority, whether royalist, republican, or Napoleonic, took form on French soil; and with that

66. The Russian tsar, in effect, sought to match the British "two power" naval stan-dard by maintaining an army equal in size to the forces of any two other European powers. To lessen the cost, Alexander resorted to so-called military colonies which put about a third of his peacetime army on a life-routine close to that of the peasantry. On the Russian military colonies see Alan Palmer, *Alexander: Tsar of War and Peace* (New York, 1974), pp. 344–48.

change the last military residue of the revolution seemed safely buried.[67] The other armies of Europe were already pillars of conservatism, and remained so throughout the nineteenth century. The same was true of the only navy that mattered, the British.

Thus political revolution had been successfully turned back. Industrial revolution had yet to assail military routine and tradition. It began to do so in the 1840s. Consideration of this transformation of European ways of war will be the subject of the next chapters.

67. Douglas Porch, *Army and Revolution: France, 1815–1848* (London, 1974), pp. 138–39 and passim.

7

The Initial Industrialization of War, 1840-84

In the 1840s the Prussian army and the French and British navies broke away from the weapons pattern that had served European governments of the Old Regime so well. These changes prefigured the industrialization of war, but the transformation of weapons manufacture did not get into high gear until the next decade, when the Crimean War (1854–56) highlighted the deficiencies of traditional methods of supply and presented British and French inventors with an opportunity to apply civil engineering to military problems of every sort. The pace of change in weaponry and in methods of management of armed force continued to accelerate thereafter, so that by the 1880s, military engineering had begun to forge ahead of civil engineering, reversing the relationship of thirty years before.

New weapons changed warfare, of course, but they were less important during the first phase of the industrialization of war than changes in transport resulting from the application of fossil fuels to the age-old problem of supplying and deploying armed forces. Steamships and railroads proved capable of moving men, weapons, and supplies on an entirely unprecedented scale. This in turn meant that most of the male population of European countries could be trained for war and actually delivered to the battlefield. The ideal of every man a soldier, characteristic only of barbarian societies in time past, became almost capable of realization in the technologically most sophisticated countries of the earth. Accordingly, armies began to count their soldiers by the million.

Simultaneously, cheaper transport and accelerated communications allowed Europeans to unify the surface of the globe, bringing weaker Asian and African polities into a European-centered and managed market system. Relatively minor resort to military force sufficed to open China, Japan, inner Asia, and Africa to European (especially British) trade. Europeans' vulnerability to tropical diseases remained an obstacle, especially in Africa; but even this barrier to the expansion of world market relationships began to fall after about 1850 when European doctors developed effective prophylaxis against malaria.

Until the mid-1870s the triumph of a world market, with its most active center firmly planted in London, seemed unmistakable. Yet the depression that began in 1873 marked a turning point. Britain's industrial primacy began to be challenged by countries that sheltered behind protective tariffs. Such demonstrations of the effectiveness of administrative action in economic matters was followed by a veritable avalanche of managerial intervention aimed at altering patterns of supply and demand by deliberate policy. The pioneers sometimes sought private profit,[1] sometimes the welfare of the poor, and sometimes more efficient warfare. But all three pursuits ran parallel and with increasing power to affect human behavior.

This constituted a remarkable change in the organization of society. In retrospect one can see that the industrialization of war, so casually launched in the 1840s, played a leading role in forwarding the transition to managed economies. But this denouement was hidden from the actors of the age itself by the fact that before the 1880s initiative for technical change nearly always rested with private inventors who hoped to make money by persuading the authorities to change some aspect of existing weaponry or production methods. Plenty of cranks and crackpots competed with those who did have a technically sound innovation to peddle; and until the 1880s the prevailing attitude among officers charged with deciding whether to approve technical change was one of extreme skepticism toward the claims that eager salesmen made for their new gadgets.

Commercial and National Armaments Rivalries

The ritual routine of army and navy life as developed across centuries discouraged innovation of any kind. Only when civilian techniques had advanced clearly and unmistakably beyond levels already incorporated into military and naval practice, did it become possible to overcome official inertia and conservatism. About midcentury this situation presented itself more dramatically in maritime than in mili-

---

1. Cf. Alfred D. Chandler, *The Visible Hand: The Managerial Revolution in American Business* (Cambridge, Mass., 1977).

tary matters. The reason was that from the 1830s private firms vigorously set about the task of building steam vessels that would be capable of crossing the Atlantic. Hope of profit and prestige rivalry that pitted one group of financial entrepreneurs against another in order to build bigger, better, faster, and more beautiful vessels hastened the process forward; governmental subsidies for carrying the mail, initiated by Great Britain in 1839, helped defray costs of developing new designs without completely committing naval authorities to the new steam and iron technology.[2]

The pace of development was very rapid. Robert Fulton had demonstrated one of the first successful steam-drive vessels on the Hudson River in 1807. Thirty years later the paddle wheeler *Sirius* crossed the Atlantic under sustained steam power (assisted by sails to be sure) in a mere eighteen days. Two years later, crossing time was reduced to fourteen days and eight hours. In the 1840s propellers began to replace the clumsy paddle wheels of the earliest successful steamships, and in the same decade iron hulls supplanted wooden construction for large, oceangoing steamships. Engines grew from the 320 horsepower that impelled the *Sirius* across the Atlantic in 1837 to the 1,600 horsepower that propelled the vast bulk (680 feet long) of the *Great Eastern* just twenty-one years later.[3]

The pell-mell development of steamships did not at once alter the way navies were managed. The principal seat of the new steamship technology was in Great Britain; but the world supremacy of the British navy, assured since Trafalgar (1805), depended on sails and the skills required to fight in ships whose design had not fundamentally altered since the 1670s. Under the circumstances, the British Admiralty was perfectly justified in standing pat. Timber supply, naval shipyard facilities for building and repairing warships, for casting of cannon and for preserving victuals: in short, all that was needed to keep

2. British mail subsidies, administered by the Admiralty between 1839 and 1860, were given only to ships deemed potentially useful in war. Specifications required, for example, that the mail carriers be capable of mounting heavy guns in case of need. Until experiences of the Crimean War proved differently, commercial steamships were presumed to be capable of swift conversion into warships. This recapitulated the situation that prevailed from 1300 to 1600, when stoutly built commercial vessels doubled as warships as a matter of course. In the nineteenth century the presumed convertibility of the new steamers lasted less than two decades—a measure of the heightened pace of technical change after 1800. On steamers as reserve ships of war see David B. Tyler, *Steam Conquers the Atlantic* (London, 1939), pp. 77–81, 170–72, 231–32.

3. These statistics come from W. A. Baker, *From Paddle Steamer to Nuclear Ship: A History of the Engine-Powered Vessel* (London, 1965), pp. 41–58. Cf. Francis E. Hyde, *Cunard and the North Atlantic: A History of Shipping and Financial Management* (London, 1975); Tyler, *Steam Conquers the Atlantic.*

the British navy supreme on the seas was firmly in place and functioning. Why, then, embrace untried devices? Why indeed? The Admiralty's oft-quoted memorandum of 1828, though radically wrong in
its view of the future, nevertheless expressed an entirely rational ap-
preciation of the circumstances British naval authorities confronted.
The memorandum read as follows:

> Their Lordships feel it is their bounden duty to discourage to the
> utmost of their ability the employment of steam vessels, as they
> consider that the introduction of steam is calculated to strike a
> fatal blow at the naval supremacy of the Empire.[4]

The Royal Navy's conservatism, however, constituted an opportunity for any rival who might choose to build technologically more
modern ships. The French saw the possibility very quickly. In 1822,
for example, General Henri J. Paixhans published a book entitled
Nouvelle force maritime, in which he argued that ships protected by
armor plate and carrying large-caliber guns capable of firing explosive
shells could break up and destroy wooden warships with complete
impunity. Paixhans had just developed a shell gun when he wrote his
book. Tests against an old hulk in 1824 showed that his claims were
well founded, so the French navy officially adopted Paixhans' shell
guns in 1837. The Royal Navy followed suit in the very next year, and
other European navies soon did likewise. From that time onward,
everyone was aware that if it ever came to battle, wooden warships
were critically vulnerable to the new explosive shells.[5] This was demonstrated in 1853 at the Battle of Sinope in the Black Sea when
Russian shells swiftly destroyed the Turkish fleet. This Russian victory
did much to precipitate British entry into the Crimean War
(1854–56), for it seemed in London that Constantinople now lay
within the Russians' reach, unless British (and French) warships sailed
into the Black Sea to bar the way.
    Experience during the Crimean War set French and British naval
designers off on a new tack, seeking security against increasingly pow-

4. Quoted from Michael Lewis, *The History of the British Navy* (Baltimore, 1957),
p. 224.
5. As early as 1827, private initiative and British philhellenism had in fact armed a
steamship with one of Paixhans' shell guns for use in the Greek War of Independence
against the Turks. This ship, the *Karteria,* gave sovereignty over the Aegean to the
Greek insurgents; but it never really was tested, since British, French, and Russian
warships of the old design had already destroyed the only important Moslem counter-
force at the Battle of Navarino (1827), before the *Karteria* came on the scene. Cf.
Christopher J. Bartlett, *Great Britain and Sea Power, 1815–1853* (Oxford, 1963),
p. 200.

erful guns by armoring their ships of war. This in turn required more and more powerful steam engines to drive what soon amounted to floating citadels through the water.

Use of steam engines in naval vessels had started a decade earlier. The French were provoked to this particular technological adventure by their humiliation at the hands of the Royal Navy during the Near Eastern crisis of 1839–41, when a British squadron compelled the French navy to withdraw support from Mehmet Ali of Egypt in his quarrel with the Ottoman sultan. An influential faction within the French navy reacted by seeking to find new technological means wherewith to challenge British supremacy at sea. Steam-powered ships of war, able to cross the Channel regardless of how the wind was blowing seemed especially promising. French efforts to equip some ships of war with steam engines soon provoked an invasion scare in England and hastened the installation of auxiliary steam engines in the Royal Navy's ships of the line.[6]

For the next twenty years, important technical advances continued to come from the French side of the Channel. Repeatedly, French engineers and politicians were lured by the hope of overturning British naval hegemony with epoch-making new ship designs. Twice they were able to outstrip the Royal Navy: once in 1850, when the warship *Napoleon* was launched, capable of steaming at thirteen knots with a 950 horsepower engine; and again in 1858, when four and a half inches of iron plate made *La Gloire* proof against shot from any existing gun.[7]

Each French breakthrough provoked immediate countermoves in Great Britain, accompanied by public agitation for larger naval appropriations and dire predictions of disaster if the French should decide to invade across the Channel. But Great Britain's greatly superior industrial capacity made it relatively easy for the Royal Navy to catch up technically and surpass the French numerically each time the French changed the basis of competition.

Financial restraints were always important in this, the heyday of European liberalism. As in the eighteenth century, British public sentiment supported the costs of maintaining naval superiority cheerfully enough. In France, on the contrary, periods of naval buildup

6. Cf. Stephen S. Roberts, "The Introduction of Steam Technology in the French Navy, 1818–1852" (Ph.D. diss., University of Chicago, 1976).

7. On the technical revolution provoked by the *Gloire* see Paul Gille, "Le premier navire cuirassé: La *Gloire*" in Michel Mollat, ed., *Les origines de la navigation à vapeur* (Paris, 1970), pp. 43–57.

Industrial Revolution on the Sea

These illustrations register the onset of the age of steam and iron in naval design.
Above, opposite page, H.M.S. St. George has a funnel obtruding among its sails.
But the steam engine in its bowels involved minimal alteration in overall design.
This sort of compromise between old and new became obsolete in 1861 when the
French navy launched La Gloire, *pictured below. Its ironclad hull was proof*
against all existing naval guns, but instead of remaining a sovereign and invulner-
able weapon, La Gloire *soon became obsolete in its turn as new and more powerful*
guns carried by more and more heavily armored warships came off rival designers'
drawing boards.
Illustrated London News 38 (January–June, 1861): 78, 227.

---

alternated, as before, with periods of dearth when the government decided that outstripping Great Britain at sea was impractical and cut back on naval appropriations accordingly.[8]

Ups and downs in expenditure for the French navy reflected, in part, Louis Napoleon's view that his uncle's great mistake had been to antagonize Great Britain. From the time that he became emperor of the French in 1851, therefore, he sought not only to win glory on the battlefield and to topple the settlement of 1815, as befitted the heir of the great Napoleon, but also to cooperate with Great Britain, or at least to refrain from open quarrel. Frictions and rivalries between the two governments did not entirely disappear during the 1850s and 1860s when Napoleon III ruled France. Far from it. But even a sporadic and imperfect cooperation between France and Great Britain sufficed to upset the European balance of power as defined in 1815.

The Crimean War made this apparent. Russia had emerged in 1815 as the greatest land power of the European continent, and the Russian army remained by far the largest of Europe in the years that followed.[9] Its efficiency had been tested repeatedly in numerous wars on differ-ent fronts and diverse terrains: in Central Asia (1839–43 and 1847–53); in the Caucasus (1829–64); against Persia and Turkey (1826–29); and against Polish (1830–31) and Magyar (1849) rebels.

---

8. In addition to works already cited on the mid-nineteenth-century French-British naval rivalry see James Phinney Baxter, *The Introduction of the Ironclad Warship* (Cam-bridge, Mass., 1933); Bartlett, *Great Britain and Sea Power;* Oscar Parkes, *British Battleships, "Warrior" to "Valiant,"* rev. ed. (London, 1970), pp. 2–217; Bernard Brodie, *Sea Power in the Machine Age,* 2d ed. (Princeton, 1942); Wilhelm Treue, *Der Krimkrieg und die Entstehung der modernen Flotten* (Göttingen, 1954); William Hovgaard, *Modern History of Battleships* (London, 1920).

9. Its manpower totaled 980,000 before hostilities began in 1853, and by the war's end had expanded to a total of no less than 1,802,500 men, despite some 450,000 casualties. John Shelton Curtiss, *Russia's Crimean War* (Durham, N.C., 1979), p. 470.

Little changed technically; but then, other European armies also remained generally content with the weapons and organization perfected during the Napoleonic Wars. The Russian navy was the third largest of the world, lagging behind the British and French in technical change, but not by much, as the dramatic destruction of the Turkish fleet at Sinope in 1853 attested.

To take on such a behemoth and yet prevail was quite a feat for the French and British expeditionary forces in the Crimea. Their success depended on superior supply. The Russians had great difficulty delivering powder and other necessities to the forces defending Sevastopol. Access by sea was cut off by the Allies, and the Russians found it all but impossible to traverse the empty steppeland to the north of their Crimean naval base. Though something like 125,000 peasant carts were requisitioned for the purpose, deliveries could never attain a satisfactory scale. Animals needed to eat, and forage could not be found along the way after initial roadside stocks had been depleted. But to carry enough forage to keep the draft animals in shape en route meant that payloads dropped almost to nothing. By comparison, the French and British expeditionary forces, supplied by ship, were able to command a vast flow of supplies. To be sure, there were initial disasters and mismanagement, and it took a while for deliveries to get properly organized. Yet in the final days of the siege the allies were able, in a single day, to fire as many as 52,000 cannonballs against Sevastopol's fortifications, whereas the Russians had to ration their guns for lack of sufficient powder and shot.[10]

The Crimean War, in other words, reversed the supply situation of 1812, when Russian armies had profited from access to water transportation while the invaders had been compelled to rely on overland cartage. As a result, Russia's big naval guns, however numerous and however skillfully mounted in defense of Sevastopol, eventually proved insufficient to counterbalance allied materiel superiority. After a heroic defense, the garrison withdrew, thereby ending active hostilities, since the Allies were quite unable to go in pursuit, and, by capturing Sevastopol and destroying the Russian Black Sea fleet, they had in fact achieved the goal of their campaign by making Constantinople safe against naval attack from the north.

The siege of Sevastopol was a rehearsal in miniature for the Western Front of World War I. Trench systems, field fortifications, and artillery barrages became decisive. Only the machine gun was missing. On the

---

10. I take these figures from Curtiss, ibid., pp. 339–40, 448.

other hand, the three initial battles of Alma, Balaclava, and Inkerman, which cooped the Russians up in Sevastopol, were rehearsals for the Prussian victory over Austria at Königgrätz (1866) in the sense that superior rifled handguns, newly issued to French and British infantry, gave them a decisive edge over the Russians, who still carried old-fashioned muskets. The difference boiled down to this: the new rifles had an effective range of about 1,000 yards as against the 200 yards within which smoothbore muskets could fire effectively.

The advantages of rifles had long been familiar to European gunsmiths, who discovered as early as the end of the fifteenth century that a rifled gunbarrel, by imparting spin to the bullet, could assure a smooth flight through the air. Smooth flight, in turn, gave superior range and accuracy. But rifles cost more to make and were slow to fire, since it was necessary to force the soft lead to shape itself tightly to the rifling by hammering the bullet down through the barrel. This took both time and care and was unsuited to the confusion of battle. A few specialized sharpshooters, used mainly as skirmishers, had been equipped with rifles in European armies since the sixteenth century. But since victory and defeat depended on the rate of fire, the main body of infantry could not take advantage of rifles' superior range.

This long-standing technical situation was transformed in 1849 when a French army officer, Captain Claude Etienne Minié, patented an elongated bullet with a hollowed-out base that could be dropped through the bore (just as spherical musket balls had been dropped for centuries) but which nevertheless expanded to take the rifling when the force of gases from the exploding powder spread the flanged base tightly against the inside of the gun barrel. The Minié bullet had to be inserted into the rifle barrel with its nose pointing upward. But except for this refinement, the procedure for loading and firing was the same as for the old smoothbores. Minimal change in routine made the improvement easy to adopt. Accordingly, the French experimented with the captain's invention at once, and made it standard in 1857 after it had proved its value in the Crimea. The British, for their part, bought patent rights in 1851 and equipped their Crimean regiments with rifles, thereby assuring superiority even against the vaunted Russian army.[11]

The lesson was not lost on other European armies. The Prussians,

11. Howard L. Blackmore, *British Military Fire-arms, 1650–1850* (London, 1961), pp. 229–33; O. F. G. Hogg, *The Royal Arsenal: Its Background, Origin and Subsequent History* (London, 1963), 2:736–40; James E. Hicks, *Notes on French Ordnance, 1717–1936* (Mt. Vernon, N.Y., 1938), p. 24.

who ever since 1840 had been secretly building up stocks of a breech-loading rifle, took the precaution of converting their old muskets to the Minié system between 1854 and 1856;[12] and across the Atlantic the United States Army went over to the Minié bullet and rifling in 1855.

From the mid-fifties onward, therefore, patterns of both naval and land armament that had remained almost stable since the seventeenth century began to crumble away, exposing admirals, generals, and statesmen to the acute discomfort of having to face the possibility of war under conditions and with weapons of which they had no direct experience. This put a premium on imagination and intelligence among naval and military leaders and drastically penalized the old bluff disregard for anything that smacked of thinking. The consequences were greatest on land. Troops that had attained the highest levels of drill and mindlessness, i.e., the best armies of Europe, were the most vulnerable to the strains that new technology imposed. Conversely, from the 1860s the weakest army among the great powers, the Prussian, found itself in a position to capitalize on what had hitherto seemed crushing disadvantages.

Before exploring how Prussia achieved military primacy on land, two other by-products of the Crimean War experience with new weaponry deserve attention. The first of these was the application of mass production techniques to the gun trade. It all started because the artisanal organization of manufacture in Birmingham and London proved notably inelastic when war with Russia suddenly created a new demand. Making handguns had long been a craft, subdivided among numerous specialists. Each artisan worked as a subcontractor for entrepreneurs who in turn contracted with the government for a stated number of finished guns. Government inspectors checked along the way to make sure that each part met specifications; and sometimes the arsenal at Woolwich made the final assembly on its own account. The system had borne the strain of the Napoleonic Wars successfully enough, even though it took two decades for British (and French) gunmakers to reach peak rates of production in response to the wartime demand.

In 1854–56 no one was willing to wait for decades while thousands of artisans adjusted to a new level of demand. The problem was exacerbated in England by the fact that manufacture was already in the throes of adjustment to the new Minié design. Old habits and methods

---

12. Dennis Showalter, *Railroads and Rifles: Soldiers, Technology and the Unification of Germany* (Hamden, Conn., 1975), pp. 81, 96–98.

of ironworking attuned to the manufacture of the Brown Bess (almost unchanged since Marlborough's day) did not readily achieve the accuracy needed for the new rifles. But when inspectors sought to enforce narrower tolerances by rejecting badly made parts, they provoked bitter quarrels with the artisans. On top of this, the sudden upsurge of demand when the Crimean War broke out offered the workmen what looked like a golden opportunity to cash in by holding out for higher wage rates. Consequently, with long-standing routines and expectations already in radical flux, the gun trade suffered innumerable stoppages at every stage of the production process. Instead of turning out more and better guns on demand, output actually fell in the country's hour of need.

Resulting indignation both within and outside government circles persuaded the responsible authorities that something drastic would have to be done to accelerate and improve rifle manufacture. As it happened, an alternative scheme was already familiar to officials of the Woolwich arsenal. They called it the "American system of manufacture" because it had been developed in the United States arsenal at Springfield, Massachusetts, and among private manufacturers of small arms in the Connecticut River Valley between 1820 and 1850. The key principle was the use of automatic or semiautomatic milling machines to cut component parts to prescribed shapes.[13] These machines produced interchangeable parts, so that a gun could be assembled without the delicate filing and adjustment which the less exact hand methods of manufacture required. Milling machines were costly, of course, and wasteful of material as well, for they produced more scrap than a skilled man with a hammer and file would do. But if a large number of guns were needed, automation paid for itself many times over through the economies of mass production.

Englishmen had become aware of the American methods of gun-making at the Great Exhibition of 1851, where Samuel Colt put his revolvers on display and demonstrated the interchangeability of parts

---

13. Such machines were not particularly difficult to design. The principle was the same as that used to make extra keys from an original today: that is, mechanical linkages forced a cutting tool to follow a path defined by a tracer that moved along the contours of an original master shape or jig. This pantograph principle had been known since Hellenistic times, when such machines had been used to mass-produce statuary for export from Alexandria. Cf. Gisela M. A. Richter, *The Sculpture and Sculptors of the Greeks*, 4th ed. (New Haven, 1970), p. 246. Americans developed these machines partly because skilled gunsmiths were in short supply; partly because after the War of 1812, U.S. government policy, by giving long-range contracts to suppliers, encouraged heavier capital investment. Cf. Felicia Johnson Deyrup, *Arms Makers in the Connecticut Valley*, Smith College Studies in History, No. 33 (Northhampton, Mass., 1948).

by disassembling a number of pistols, jumbling the parts and then reassembling them into workable revolvers once again.

Hence when production bottlenecks and frictions multiplied in the early months of the Crimean War, enough persons in Great Britain knew about American achievements to make it possible for a special Committee on Small Arms to recommend the establishment of a new plant at Enfield, using the American system of manufacture. Work began in 1855 but the necessary machinery, imported from the United States, was not fully installed until 1859—three years after the Crimean War had ended.[14]

Automation did not stop with the import of American machinery to manufacture standard rifles. New machines, invented for the purpose, began to spew forth Minié bullets at a rate of 250,000 a day in the Woolwich arsenal, for example; and another machine turned out 200,000 completed cartridges a day, combining bullet and charge into one simple package.[15] Nor did mass production long remain a monopoly of government arsenals. The private gun trade was swiftly compelled to follow suit. To pay for the expensive new machinery, previously independent contractors merged to form the Birmingham Small Arms Company in 1861, and a similar merger led to the foundation of the London Small Arms Company six years later. Thereafter, government contracts were divided between Enfield and the two new, modernized private arms manufacturers in proportions dictated partly by political lobbying and partly by public officials' desire to maintain a suitable reserve capacity in case some new war should suddenly require rapid escalation of rifle production. The two private firms maintained themselves largely by sales of sporting weapons to private persons in Great Britain and abroad, but also undertook contracts for foreign governments.[16]

Other European governments, too, took note of how machines

14. On American arms-making, in addition to Deyrup, see Merritt Roe Smith, *Harpers Ferry Armory and the New Technology* (Ithaca, N.Y., 1977); Robert J. Woodbury, "The Legend of Eli Whitney and the Interchangeability of Parts," *Technology and Culture* 1 (1960): 235–51. For British arms trade and the revolution brought to it in the 1850s, see Nathan Rosenberg, ed., *The American System of Manufactures: The Report of the Committee on the Machinery of the United States, 1855, and the Special Reports of George Wallis and Joseph Whitworth, 1854* (Edinburgh, 1969), Introduction; H. J. Habakkuk, *American and British Technology in the Nineteenth Century* (Cambridge, 1962); A. Ames and Nathan Rosenberg, "Enfield Arsenal in Theory and History," *Economic Journal* 78 (1968):825–42; Russell I. Fries, "British Response to the American System: The Case of the Small Arms Industry after 1850," *Technology and Culture* 16 (1975): 377–403.

15. O. F. G. Hogg, *Royal Arsenal* 2:783, 792.

16. S. B. Saul, "The Market and the Development of the Mechanical Engineering Industries in Britain," *Economic History Review* 20 (1967): 111–30; Fries, "British Re-

could produce handguns en masse and on demand. By 1870, Russia, Spain, Turkey, Sweden, Denmark, and Egypt had all followed the British example by importing American milling machinery for gun-making.[17] In Belgium, Liège gunmakers formed a new company to import American machinery. It seemed the only way to satisfy a British order for 150,000 rifles, which was lodged in 1854 when British home production was lagging.[18]

The result was to alter the European gun trade profoundly. Artisan methods faded away; and as new machines were installed in government arsenals, the international trade in small arms, focused on Liège for centuries past, shrank back to relatively trivial proportions.[19]

Another consequence was this. Before the 1850s, change in the design of small arms issued to hundreds of thousands of soldiers had been a long-drawn-out and inherently awkward enterprise. That was why European muskets had remained so nearly the same for 150 years. With automatic machinery, however, once new jigs had been made, hundreds of thousands of guns of a brand new design could be produced in a single year. An entire army could be reequipped about as quickly as soldiers could be familiarized with the new weapon. The door was thus opened wide for further improvements in the design of small arms, but only at the cost of upsetting all existing tactical rules and infantry drill regulations.

The difficulties of altering small-arms designs when production remained artisanal had been made painfully obvious to the Prussians after 1840, when King Frederick William decided to begin equipping his army with breech-loading rifles. The initial order was for 60,000 such weapons. Seven years later, in 1847, Johann Nicholas von Dreyse, the inventor, was able to turn out only 10,000 guns a year from his workshops and found it difficult to maintain quality control at that scale of production. Since the Prussian army numbered something like 320,000 with its reserves, it would have taken more than thirty years to complete the changeover from muskets to breech-loaders at such a rate of manufacture. No wonder the Prussians in

sponse to the American System"; Conrad Gill, *History of Birmingham: Manor and Borough to 1865* (London, 1952), p. 295.

17. This, at any rate, was the proud boast of Charles H. Fitch, "Report on the Manufacture of Interchangeable Mechanisms," U.S. Congress, *Miscellaneous Documents of the House of Representatives,* 4th Cong., 2d sess. 1882–82, 13, pt. 2: 613–14. Unfortunately, Fitch gives no details and I have not found confirmatory evidence from all of the purchasers.

18. Cf. Claude Gaier, *Four Centuries of Liège Gunmaking* (London, 1977), p. 122.

19. Ibid., pp. 190–95.

1854 decided to rebore their existing stock of muskets to make them rifles and invest in Minié bullets—a shift that required a mere two years to complete!

Yet the Prussian king and his military advisers were sufficiently convinced of the superiority of the breech-loading design to persevere. Efforts to hasten the rate of manufacture by converting three state arsenals to the production of the new guns increased output to about 22,000 per annum. As a result, in 1866, when Dreyse's "needle guns," as they are often called, met their first and spectacular test in battle against the Austrians, the new weapons had only just become available to each and every unit of the Prussian army. It had taken a total of twenty-six years to complete the change from muzzle-loaders. No wonder, under such circumstances, that governments had left handgun designs unchanged, save for trivial details, since the seventeenth century.[20] By comparison, in 1863, four years after it had started production, the Enfield arsenal turned out 100,370 rifles at a time when no special emergency required extra effort;[21] and when France (1866) and Prussia (1869) decided to reequip their armies with new rifles, it took each government a mere four years to complete the process, despite the long months needed to design and install the necessary new machines.[22]

Mass production thus came to Europe's small arms business be-

20. Dennis Showalter, *Railroads and Rifles,* pp. 81–82, 95–98; Curt Jany, *Geschichte der Königlich Preussischen Armee* (Berlin, 1928–37) 4:199–202.

21. John D. Goodman, "The Birmingham Gun Trade," in Samuel Timmins, ed., *History of Birmingham and the Midland Hardware District* (London, 1866), p. 415. In that same year, the "trade" produced 460,140 gun barrels in Birmingham and 210,181 in London, of which most were sold overseas and only 19,263 were proved and accepted for government use.

22. Napoleon III reacted to Prussia's victory over Austria by ordering a new arsenal built at Puteaux in August 1866, capable of making 360,000 new chassepôt rifles annually. By 1870 over a million of the new rifles were in stock, according to Louis César Alexandre Randon, *Mémoires* (Paris, 1877), 2:236–42. This extraordinary feat was, however, only achieved by calling on gunmakers in Birmingham, Liège, and Brescia to supplement Puteaux's output. Cf. François Crouzet, "Recherches sur la production d'armement en France, 1815–1913," *Révue historique* 251 (1974): 54. Prussia fixed on a new rifle model, the Mauser, in 1869. It could not be manufactured before the war with France broke out. Nevertheless, the new weapon was ready for issue to the now much enlarged German army in 1873. For the acceptance of American machines in Germany after 1869 see Ernst Barth, *Entwicklungslinien der deutschen Maschinenbauindustrie von 1870 bis 1914* (Berlin, 1973), pp. 48–49. The Austrians went over to the "American system" of automated manufacture of small arms after 1862, according to Gunther Rothenberg, *The Army of Francis Joseph* (West Lafayette, Ind., 1976), p. 43. For Russia see J. G. Purves, "Nineteenth-Century Russia and the Revolution in Military Technology," in J. G. Purves and D. A. West, eds., *War and Society in the Nineteenth-Century Russian Empire* (Toronto, 1972), pp. 7–22.

tween 1855 and 1870 as a direct by-product of the Crimean War. The new machinery remained, for the most part, safely inside arsenal walls. Indeed, public management of small-arms design and manufacture became far more exact and pervasive than had been possible when the work of artisans had been subject only to crude official inspections. Quite the opposite happened to the manufacture of artillery. This was partly due to bitter competition in Great Britain among would-be gun manufacturers. But a new factor confirmed and stabilized what began as a merely accidental result of personal rivalries, to wit, the emergence of a new gunmetal—steel—whose manufacture required resources that lay beyond the reach of all existing government arsenals.

As with small-arms manufacture, the decisive stimulus to new departures in artillery came from the Crimean War. British and French difficulties in the Crimea achieved unprecedented publicity through newspapers; and the detailed accounts of military actions that war correspondents sent back to Paris and London provoked, among other things, a remarkable outburst of warlike inventiveness.[23] Only a few ideas for new weapons ever got past the drawing boards. Those that did often proved abortive, like the forty-two-ton mortars, completed a year after the fighting had ended, which subsequently became heraldic guardians of the Woolwich arsenal's main gate, offering an oddly apt symbol—too clumsy and too late—of the arsenal's nineteenth-century role in artillery design and production.[24]

But some of the new ideas and inventions had far-ranging and enduring consequences. Most important of all, probably, was the discovery of the "Bessemer process" for making steel. Henry Bessemer was one of England's busy inventors, whose experiments with artillery of novel design led him to discover a method for refining steel by blowing air through molten ore. This permitted large-scale steel production and more exact regulation of its chemical content and structure than had been possible before. Consequently, patents issued to Bessemer in 1857 inaugurated a new metallurgical era. Within twenty years, older methods for gun-casting became hopelessly obsolete even though efforts by arsenal officials to cling to traditional gunmetals did not completely cease until 1890.[25]

23. The Patent Office in Great Britain issued a total of about 300 patents for inventions pertaining to firearms between 1617 and 1850, but approved more than 600 such patents in the single decade beginning in 1850, according to Rosenberg, *American System of Manufactures*, p. 29.

24. Hogg, *Royal Arsenal* 2:756–60.

25. Sir Henry Bessemer, *An Autobiography* (London, 1905), pp. 130–42, gives a

In 1850s and 1860s, imperfect knowledge of the molecular structures of steel made it impossible to cast guns that were uniform and unflawed. The German steelmaker, Alfred Krupp of Essen, the first to make the attempt, met with many disappointments and obstacles along the way before the quality of his guns achieved its decisive vindication in the Franco-Prussian War of 1870–71. Before then, the greatest private gunmaker of Europe was William Armstrong. He was a Newcastle manufacturer of hydraulic machinery before the Crimean War and got into the armaments business almost as casually as Bessemer had discovered his process for making steel.

Reading in a London club about how British troops had saved the day at the Battle of Inkerman by bringing two field artillery pieces to bear on the enemy after overcoming enormous difficulties in getting their ponderous pieces into firing position, Armstrong is said to have remarked that it was "time military engineering was brought up to the level of current engineering practice."[26] He promptly sketched the design of a breech-loading artillery piece and proceeded to manufacture a prototype.[27] Tests in 1857 showed its superior accuracy to muzzle-loading smoothbores.

By this time the Crimean War was over, but the Mutiny in India (1857–58) commanded so much public attention in Great Britain that a sense of urgency about technological improvements in weaponry continued to prevail. Armstrong's gun was, accordingly, approved by appropriate authorities. Through a deal arranged in 1859 he gave his patents to the government and accepted appointment as "Engineer for Rifled Ordnance," with a salary of £2,000 per annum and a knight-

---

vivid if perhaps incomplete and self-serving account of how he made his discovery. Theodore A. Wertime, *The Coming of Age of Steel* (London, 1961) offers an excellent account of metallurgical history, blessedly accessible to nontechnical readers. For resistance to the use of steel guns, the Prussian case is the most telling. Cf. W. A. Boelke, *Krupp und die Hohenzollern in Dokumenten* (Frankfurt am Main, 1970), pp. 106, 123.

26. J. D. Scott, *Vickers: A History* (London, 1962), p. 25.

27. Instead of being cast in one piece, as big guns had been since the fifteenth century, Armstrong's gun was built around a core, either by winding iron strips (eventually steel wire) around the barrel lining, usually of steel, or by "sweating" hoops of iron around the core, to build the gun up in a series of layers. "Sweating" refers to the practice of heating a hoop of metal to make it expand, and then slipping it over the already assembled parts of the gun. The hot hoop shrank as it cooled, but not back to its room temperature dimensions. Instead, a lasting internal tension squeezed the exterior band tightly against the interior layers, thus creating a force to oppose the expansive force of a powder explosion inside the gun. In this ingenious way a gun could be made stronger for a given weight than anything that could be fashioned out of a homogeneously cast block of metal. Armstrong's method of gunmaking had the additional advantage of allowing a rapid increase in size, since it was feasible to manufacture and assemble component parts of guns much too big to cast in a single piece.

hood in return. From his official position Armstrong proceeded to organize the Elswick Ordnance Company, located just outside Newcastle. This private company then entered into a contract with the War Department to manufacture the guns Armstrong had just designed, and agreed to supply no one else. By 1861, Elswick had produced some 1,600 guns of varying sizes. But there were difficulties with the breech mechanism, which was liable to jam, and on the larger calibers, Armstrong's breeches required so much strength to operate that ordinary men could not serve the guns.

Critics claimed that Sir William was using his official position to channel contracts towards the Elswick company while preventing other designs from having a fair trial. Argument waxed very hot. Joseph Whitworth, a Manchester manufacturer and personal rival to Armstrong, exhibited muzzle-loading guns which he claimed, with justification, were superior to Armstrong's both in accuracy and armor-piercing capacity.[28] Half a dozen other inventors were loudly touting other designs, though none of them had Armstrong's and Whitworth's capacity to build and test prototypes without government funding.

The navy's dislike of the Armstrong guns soon added weight to private criticism. In 1859 the French launched *La Gloire,* which carried armor proof against anything that existing British warships could bring against it. It therefore became a matter of urgency for British gunmakers to come up with a weapon that could smash through *La Gloire's* armor. Armstrong's biggest breech-loaders proved incapable of doing so; and official tests, painstakingly conducted in 1863–64, convinced the committee in charge that muzzle-loading guns were safer, simpler, and more effective against armor than breech-loaders. Whitworth's guns were deemed too difficult to make since they required a closer fit between projectile and bore than prevailing methods of manufacture could readily attain.[29] Distrusting the truthfulness of profit-seeking private armsmakers to begin with, and caught

---

28. Whitworth combined scientific and technical with pecuniary entrepreneurship in quite extraordinary degree, and developed connections with Liberal as Armstrong did with Conservative politicians. Whitworth tested different forms of rifling and projectile shapes more systematically than others had done and was able to develop a flat-nosed, elongated, armor-piercing projectile that was indeed superior to all others. Cf. James E. Tennant, *The Story of the Guns* (London, 1864), for Whitworth's side of the story, and David Dougan, *The Great Gunmaker: The Story of Lord Armstrong* (Newcastle-on-Tyne, n.d.) for Armstrong's.

29. Whitworth's guns had oval or polygonal bores, twisted in such a way as to impart rotation to an elongated projectile, shaped to fit the bore. To manufacture such complex planes precisely enough to assure a smooth passage in loading and firing was a formidable assignment for the metalworking methods of the age. Whitworth's lasting claim to

in a noisy crossfire of rival claims, the committee recommended that the government terminate the contract with Elswick and again procure artillery exclusively from the Woolwich arsenal, as had been the practice before 1859. The arsenal staff was instructed to develop new gun designs, using the best features of the dozen or so diverse types that had been presented in the competition.[30]

In the event, Woolwich experts opted for a French design that sought to combine the advantages of rifling with those of muzzle-loading by fitting lugs attached to the sides of the projectile into spiral grooves cut into the gun barrel. As with the Minié rifles, this had the great advantage of requiring minimal change in existing guns and drill. A cannon needed only an inner lining, grooved to fit the lugs of the new projectiles, to be converted from an old-fashioned smoothbore into the new rifled artillery. The French and British armies accordingly retained their muzzle-loaders for a full decade after the Prussian artillery began to use Krupp's breech-loading steel guns. On the other hand, the two western powers engaged in a strenuous effort to build bigger and more powerful naval guns. State monopoly of manufacture for the armed forces in France and Britain did not, therefore, lead to stability in heavy weaponry. Their rivalry at sea and the restless seesaw between gunfire and ships' armor saw to that.

Moreover, though France prohibited private manufacture of artillery for export until 1885,[31] in Great Britain, after he resigned from his official post in 1863, Armstrong, like his rival Whitworth, was entirely at liberty to offer Elswick's wares to anyone who could afford to pay for them. Krupp, whose breech-loading steel artillery design had been unveiled to an admiring world at the Great Exhibition in London (1851), competed with the two English gunmakers. Krupp sold his first guns to Egypt in 1855. An order from the Prussian War Ministry for three hundred steel breech-loaders followed in 1858; but he really began to cash in only after 1863, when large Russian orders came his way. Armstrong and Whitworth, for their part, profited handsomely by selling guns to the Americans during the Civil War.

---

fame was the invention of ways to shape metal far more accurately than had been possible before. But his prototype guns achieved their high performance only by straining the technical proficiency of his shop to the limit.

30. Cf. Peter Padfield, *Guns at Sea* (New York, 1973), pp. 174–76; Ian V. Hogg, *A History of Artillery* (London, 1974), pp. 59–70; O. F. G. Hogg, *Royal Arsenal* 2:773–78, 812–14; Charles E. Caldwell and John Headlam, *The History of the Royal Artillery from the Indian Mutiny to the Great War,* 2 vols. (Woolwich, n.d.), 1:151 ff.

31. Comité des Forges de France, *La sidérurgie française, 1864–1914* (Paris, n.d.), p. 310.

Nor did the Union's victory blight their prosperity for long. Lesser countries of Europe and governments in distant parts, like those of Japan and China in the Far East and Chile and Argentina in South America, proved able and willing to purchase privately manufactured big guns and soon began to buy the warships to carry them as well.

A global, industrialized armaments business thus emerged in the 1860s. It quite eclipsed the artisanal manufacture of arms for international sale that had been centered in the Low Countries ever since the fifteenth century. Even technically proficient government arsenals like the French, British, and Prussian, faced persistent challenge from private manufacturers, who were never loath to point out the ways in which their products surpassed government-made weaponry. Commercial competition thus added its force to national rivalry in forwarding improvements in artillery design.

The effect was felt first and most radically in naval artillery. Giant guns needed to puncture armor that got thicker and thicker with each new ironclad design made the old principle of mounting rows of cannon along a warship's sides impractical. The new guns were so ponderous that they had to be installed amidships to assure stability. Inboard mounting, in turn, meant that masts and sails had to go, since otherwise the big guns could not command a free field of fire. Radical improvements in steam engine efficiency and power made this feasible by the 1880s. Protection from enemy fire likewise dictated the construction of armored turrets to house the big guns; but the turrets had to be capable of revolving so as to bring the gun on target. Heavy hydraulic machinery able to perform this task in turn required additional steam power; and as though these complications were not enough, electrical ignition, introduced as early as 1868, added still another dimension to the art of naval gunfire and gunlaying. Yet in the only European naval combat of the period, which occurred in the Adriatic between Austria and Italy in 1866, gunfire proved indecisive. But one warship sank after being rammed. For a generation thereafter ramming rivaled gunfire in the esteem of naval officers as the key to victory. Everyone assumed that sea battles would continue to be fought as in Nelson's day by laying close alongside. Ship design therefore concentrated on achieving maximal power to penetrate armor at pointblank range.[32]

32. Stanley Sandler, *The Emergence of the Modern Capital Ship* (Newark, 1979) gives a clear narrative of these developments; Parkes, *British Battleships, "Warrior" to "Vanguard"* is the standard authority for Royal Navy ships and provides very full technical details. Brodie, *Sea Power in the Machine Age* offers a briefer, more incisive account.

A New Paradigm: The Prussian Way of War

Armies, on the other hand, were insulated from the initial impact of the mid-nineteenth century mutation in methods of gunmaking by the simple fact that anything too heavy for horses to pull across open country was ruled out for field artillery. But after the Franco-Prussian War of 1870–71, armies too found themselves swept into the vortex of a rapidly evolving artillery technology. In that war, Prussian breech-loading steel guns outclassed the bronze muzzle-loaders with which the French entered the fray. After 1871, European armies therefore rapidly changed over to guns of the new design. Even more important, Prussian models of army management and mobilization became normative. Only insular Britain held back. To understand how this happened, we must review European and American experience of war in the second half of the nineteenth century.

The greatest armed struggle of the period, the American Civil War, had little impact across the Atlantic. Europe's soldiers were unimpressed by the scale and intensity of mobilization Americans attained. On the surface, the Civil War was sloppy and unprofessional. Spit and polish were conspicuously absent. Battles were untidy and confused; campaigns bogged down; no ruling class existed, even in the South, with which European officers felt much rapport. For all these reasons, together with the general sense that their skills were superior to those of the United States, European military professionals felt that they could safely disregard the American experience of war. Only later, in the 1920s, did it become possible to recognize in the bitter struggle between North and South a presage of World War I. The American Civil War then took on a new significance as the first full-fledged example of an industrialized war, in which machine-made arms dictated new, defensive tactics, while railroads competed with waterways as arteries of supply for millions of armed men.

After initial setbacks, the Union generals, being unable to overcome the superiority that rifled small arms gave to the defense, turned the struggle into a war of attrition. Decisions in the field came to depend on the ability to threaten the enemy's flow of supplies. Final victory required disruption of the transport and administrative systems by virtue of which the Confederacy had supported its armies from far in the rear.

At the siege of Sevastopol, less than a decade before, peasant carts had vainly sought to match deliveries by ship. But both the Union and the Confederacy had railroads at their disposal. Not surprisingly, therefore, the struggle turned out to be more nearly equal than it had been in the Crimea. What tipped the balance decisively against the Confederacy was the South's weakness on the sea and along inland waterways. By blockading the southern states, the United States Navy made it impossible for the Confederacy freely to remedy deficiencies of its own production by importing arms and supplies from Europe. In addition, strategic mobility along the coasts and navigable rivers was of key importance in many of the Union's offensive campaigns. These critical roles for water transport in war were nothing new. The fact that warships were sometimes steam-propelled and even armored, as in the famous encounter between the *Merrimac* and the *Monitor* in 1862, gave the naval actions of the Civil War a novel character and underlined the importance of newfangled industrial capacities that alone could produce such complicated instruments of war.

Railroads were a far greater novelty. The mechanical power of locomotives radically transcended older limitations on land transport. A hundred miles by rail became easier to traverse than ten by cart; and a single train could carry as much as thousands of horse-drawn wagons. Railroads, in fact, allowed armies of a hundred thousand and more to fight for years while drawing supplies from hundreds of miles away. Such feats, quite impossible in any earlier age, demonstrated once again the vital importance of industrial capacity for waging a new kind of war.

By 1865, the president of the United States, like Cromwell some two centuries earlier, found himself in command of formidable armed force. But instead of trying to maintain its newly won armed might, as Cromwell had done, the United States vigorously dismantled its military establishment, treating the war, in effect, as an aberration. This made it all the easier for Europeans to regard what had happened in northern Virginia and at Vicksburg and Chattanooga not as an intelligent response to changing technology, but as a clumsy failure to achieve a professionally efficient management of war.

This judgment was sustained by the brisk tempo of the wars that broke out on the European continent (not to mention a number of colonial campaigns) between 1859 and 1870. The principal disturber of the peace was Napoleon III, who saw it as his historic role to assure the grandeur of France by supporting national aspirations for liberty. Success in the Crimea simply whetted his appetite, so he lent himself gladly to schemes for driving the Austrians from Italy, expecting the grateful Italians to look to France as their patron. The result was a short, sharp war in 1859. French armies defeated the Austrians in two pitched battles, though not without heavy losses. In the political reorganization that followed, all of Italy except Venetia and the Papal States united with Piedmont to form the kingdom of Italy.

The War of 1859 was less important in itself than for the lessons the participants drew from it. Austrian troops had been partially reequipped with new, muzzle-loading rifles, yet the French attacked in columns and broke the Austrian line. This seemed to prove that well-drilled troops could advance through rifle fire and win victory in the good old Napoleonic way.[33] Having defeated first the Russians and then the Austrians, the French army seemed to have shown itself, as in the great Napoleon's day, to be the best in Europe. It was an army that held fast to Napoleonic models, believing that the key to victory lay in élan and courage rather than in staff work or any other form of cerebration. Promotion from the ranks was far more frequent than in other European armies and gave the French officer corps a hard-bitten, professional character that aristocratic officers of other armies often lacked.[34] As for the rank and file, it came only from the lower classes of French society, for the law allowed anyone who drew a "bad number" in the conscription lottery to pay someone else to serve as a substitute. Time-expired veterans made the best and most available substitutes. Conscription therefore did not prevent the French army from relying on long-term service troops, whose professionalism complemented that of the officer corps.

Minié rifles and the muzzle-loading rifled field artillery, upon which Napoleon III lavished personal attention, demonstrated that the French army was not indifferent to improvement of materiel. Use of newly built railroads to get to Italy in 1859 showed a similar spirit of technical venturesomeness. Yet experience in Algeria, Mexico, and Asia against poorly armed opponents, and the glorious tradition of Napoleonic battles, kept the French army loyal to tactics that took no account of the enhanced firepower of the newer weapons with which European armies were beginning to equip themselves. These tactics, nevertheless, brought victory over the Austrians, whose political will to resist the new ideas of nationalism, liberalism, and progress—which the French claimed to represent—was somewhat shaky.

33. The Austrians, eager to exploit the power of their new rifles, fired at extreme range, with little effect. Their subsequent volleys mostly passed over the heads of the charging French, owing to inadequate instruction in aiming. Even so, French losses at Solferino and Magenta were heavy; and Napoleon's taste for war was permanently dampened by his personal inspection of the two battlefields. On the Austrian army in 1859, see Rothenberg, *The Army of Francis Joseph,* pp. 43–84.
34. Pierre Chalmin, *L'officier français de 1815 à 1870* (Paris, 1957).

Napoleon III's powerful, "progressive" ideology combined with a fully professional army and an innovative technology of war made a formidable combination indeed. For all these reasons, the French appeared in 1860 to be the greatest power of the European continent, in their own eyes and in those of expert foreign observers.[35]

The Austrians, for their part, concluded from their defeat in Italy that they needed to emulate French infantry tactics and invest in rifled field artillery. By 1866 new field guns did, in fact, give the Austrian artillery a distinct edge over the Prussians;[36] but the emphasis they put on retraining their infantry to charge the foe in dense columnar formations cost them the Battle of Königgrätz.

The reason was that the Prussian army had taken a different path from its rivals in trying to keep up with technological changes, opting, as we saw above, for a rifled breech-loader as its fundamental infantry weapon. The great advantage of breech-loading was that a soldier could shoot crouching or lying down, taking cover wherever it was to be found. This tactic made troops far less of a target for enemy fire than when they had to stand erect for muzzle-loading. A second advantage of breech-loaders was a far higher rate of fire.[37]

Yet there were drawbacks that persuaded other European armies to look askance at the Prussian army and its equipment. The breech of the Dreyse gun was not perfectly tight and its firing pin was liable to break. It also had a shorter range and less accuracy than Minié rifles. These technical weaknesses were matched by problems of control and tactical mobility that seemed implicit in any shift away from the ancient patterns of drill built around the motions needed to load infantry weapons from the muzzle. Lining men up and teaching them to load, aim, and fire "by the numbers" had proved its value since the time of

35. For the French army under Napoleon III see Ludovic Jablonsky, *L'armée française à travers les âges* (Paris, n.d.), vols. 4, 5; Chalmin, *L'officier français de 1815 à 1870;* David B. Ralston, *The Army of the Republic: The Place of the Military in the Political Evolution of France, 1871–1914* (Cambridge, Mass., 1967), chap. 1; Alphonse Favé, *The Emperor Napoleon's New System of Field Artillery,* trans. William H. Cox (London, 1854); Raoul Girardet, *La société militaire dans la France contemporaine, 1815–1939* (Paris 1953); and Joseph Montheilhet, *Les institutions militaires de la France, 1814–1924* (Paris, 1932).

36. The Austrians had 736 new rifled cannon and 58 old smooth-bores to the Prussian 492 rifled and 306 smoothbores, according to Gordon A. Craig, *The Battle of Königgrätz* (Philadelphia, 1964), p. 8.

37. The Dreyse needle gun could be fired five to seven times a minute, more than twice as rapidly as the Minié rifle. This was because the needle gun relied on "bolt action" to open the breech, allowing ball and cartridge to be inserted, after which the reverse motion closed the breech and locked the bolt into firing position. The firing pin was automatically drawn back and cocked by the movement of the bolt. Cf. Peter Young, *The Machinery of War* (New York, 1973), pp. 73–76.

Maurice of Orange. With a breech-loader, what would prevent an excited or frightened soldier from wasting his bullets by firing indiscriminately and at top speed until his ammunition was exhausted? Conversely, what could persuade men lying upon the ground under enemy fire to get up on their feet again and move about the field of battle?

Such questions seemed all the more pointed when applied to the Prussian army, whose rank and file comprised short-term recruits and whose reserve units—needed to flesh out numbers and bring the Prussian army up to Great Power scale—were no more than civilians in uniform. But reservists' training and discipline could not possibly come up to the levels of long-term service troops like those of the French, Austrian, and Russian armies.

Moreover, the Prussian army of the 1840s and 1850s suffered from an acutely ambiguous relationship with civil society. The officer corps, recruited mainly from the trans-Elban aristocracy, was politically reactionary. It disliked and distrusted the middle-class entrepreneurs who had begun to make the Rhinelands and cities like Berlin and Hamburg into seats of machine production and technical innovation. The revolution of 1848 had left a bitter residue. The crowds' initial successes in winning control of the streets of Berlin offended and humiliated the Prussian officer corps, while the unwillingness of the government to capitalize on its chance to unite Germany alienated all those who looked to national unification as a panacea for the difficulties and disappointments of everyday life. Prussian officers feared renewal of revolution and strove to make the army an effective bulwark of the hierarchic principle of society upon which their own way of life and, as they thought, the greatness of the Prussian state depended. Political reformers, for their part, believed that the Prussian army was readier to oppose revolution at home than to create the great Germany of which they dreamed.

Yet the memory of the *Befreiungskrieg* of 1813–14 haunted both sides. Patriotic Germans remembered how their fathers and grandfathers had rallied as a people's army under the Prussian king's banners to fight against the French. Prussian officers, too, were well aware that an effective civilian reserve was essential if Prussia were to play the role of a great power in war.

In 1858 a new reign began when Wilhelm I became regent for his demented brother. In the next year, the unification of Italy intensified nationalist discontent in the Germanies. Wilhelm (king in his own right, 1861–88) responded by seeking bigger appropriations for the army, but the elected representatives gathered in the *Landtag* refused to approve the necessary law. Both sides appealed to English precedents from the seventeenth century, for the Stuart kings' struggles with Parliament seemed precisely parallel. But the outcome in Prussia was different. In 1862 King Wilhelm found in Otto von Bismarck a minister and politician whose thirst for power, skill in using it, and readiness to wage war in pursuit of policy soon left all rivals far behind.

To begin with, Bismarck and the king simply pushed ahead with army reforms and continued to collect taxes as usual. The *Landtag's* right to ratify governmental expenditures had been granted in 1848 and enshrined in a constitution handed down by the king as part of the settlement of the revolutionary upheavals of that year. But what one king had given, another could take back, or so it seemed to many Prussians; and habits of obedience were far too deeply engrained to make refusal to obey seem plausible, even for those who most bitterly opposed Bismarck and the king.

Aside from such expensive moves as completing the manufacture of enough needle guns to equip the whole army, and the purchase of three hundred steel breech-loading cannon from Alfred Krupp, the main thrust of King Wilhelm's reforms was to increase the size of the army by drafting a larger proportion of the eligible age classes. He also sought to improve the efficiency of the reserves by putting units designed for active field service in time of war under the command of regular officers.[38]

Military reform took on new urgency in 1864, when Bismarck allied Prussia with Austria in a war against Denmark. At first, the Austrian troops performed better against the Danes than the Prussians, whose soldiers, after all, had seen no action against a foreign foe since 1815. But in April 1865 the Prussians successfully assaulted a fortified position at Düppel—the most significant action of the war—and sent a wave of patriotic excitement across the Germanies. Thereupon, the Danes sued for peace, ceding Schleswig and Holstein to the victors. This in turn allowed Bismarck to pick a quarrel with Austria over how to divide the spoils and reorganize the German constitution.

An important aspect of the Danish war was that it allowed the General Staff and its chief, General Helmut von Moltke, to attain

---

38. This aspect of the reformers' plans was particularly offensive to the *Landtag*. Liberals suspected that the real motive was simply to capture the *Landwehr* for the forces of reaction so that the Prussian army could safely be used for suppression of revolution at home. Cf. Gordon A. Craig, *The Politics of the Prussian Army, 1640–1945* (New York, 1964), pp. 138–48.

unprecedented prestige and authority. The General Staff, it will be remembered, had been established by Scharnhorst as part of the reforms that followed the collapse of the Prussian army in 1806. Professional training of staff officers had continued thereafter in the Prussian service, and a small group of planners, accustomed to calculate carefully all the factors affecting an army's mobility, maintained a level of expertise other armies seldom equaled. But whether or nor a Prussian general chose to act on advice coming from staff officers assigned to his headquarters depended on the personalities involved, and varied from case to case. In Berlin, the chief of the General Staff remained relatively obscure. He did not even report directly to the minister of war, but was subordinated to the General War Department.

Soon after he became regent, Wilhelm, who took a lively interest in all military matters, appointed Moltke chief of the General Staff. The new chief's prestige became firmly established during the Danish war when he was called from Berlin to become senior staff officer to Crown Prince Frederick, who, when placed in command of the Prussian forces at Düppel, relied completely on Moltke's advice. The king thenceforward added Moltke to the group of councillors who advised him about questions of military importance. Then, when war with Austria drew near, King Wilhelm decided not to delegate full authority to army commanders, as had become customary, but to revive the glorious tradition of Frederick the Great and exercise command himself. He did so by relying on advice and plans prepared by the General Staff. To make Moltke's new authority effective, the king decreed that the chief of the General Staff had the right to issue orders in the field without going through the Ministry of War or any other intermediary. Thus, in military matters, Wilhelm's sovereign authority for all practical purposes became Moltke's, though of course the king had to be consulted about each important move and approve it before orders went out.

Effective centralized command depended on new means of transport and communication. The electromagnetic telegraph, developed in the 1840s, allowed an advancing army to keep contact with a distant headquarters simply by paying out wire as it advanced. In this fashion Moltke and the king could maintain accurate check on large-scale strategic movements. Instructions could be sent instantaneously to any subordinate headquarters that remained within reach of a telegraph wire. To be sure, keeping many miles of wires in working order was no simple matter, especially in an age when few understood the mysteries of electricity. Periodic breakdowns and unexpected delays continued to occur.[39] But in principle, and to a considerable degree also in practice, the development of an effective field telegraph meant that Moltke and the king could exercise control of the strategic deployment of Prussian armies day by day and even hour by hour.

The General Staff's other great instrument was the railroad. Use of railroads to move large bodies of troops into battle was not new. But detailed advance planning had never been done in the way that Moltke and his subordinates prepared for the invasion of Bohemia in 1866. Schedules of troop movements, drawn up carefully beforehand, maximized speed and mass. Calculating exactly how many locomotives and railroad cars each move required, meant that rail transport could be used to full capacity.[40]

All the same, the Prussian campaign of 1866 involved great risks. But the outcome was a Prussian victory, swiftly followed by a peace that permitted the Prussians to begin the political reorganization of the Germanies. Bismarck and Moltke shared the glory with King Wilhelm, while the Austrians attributed their defeat to the needle gun and, quite unfairly, to the incompetence of their commander.

Such a brisk, decisive campaign stood in dramatic contrast to the indecisive, long-drawn-out military actions of the American Civil War and seemed convincing evidence of the superiority of European—or at least of Prussian—military expertise. Yet in retrospect it is clear that a large part of the secret of Prussian success in 1866, like that of the French in 1859, rested on the political traditions of the Hapsburg Empire that persuaded the Austrian government to conclude peace after one or two lost battles. The Hapsburgs had survived Napoleon

39. Moltke was fearful of inhibiting his commanders in the field by issuing too many commands from the rear and so intervened only sparingly. Cf. Dennis Showalter, "Soldiers into Postmasters? The Electric Telegraph as an Instrument of Command in the Prussian Army," *Military Affairs* 27 (1973): 48–51. In any case, Moltke lost telegraph contact with the crown prince's army just before the Battle of Königgrätz began, and had to fall back on a dispatch rider to summon the prince's army to the place of battle. Craig, *Königgrätz*, p. 98.

40. Systematic use of available means at full capacity was the main secret of successful industrial management in the 1880s, according to Chandler, *The Visible Hand*, pp. 259 ff. Military staff officers and captains of industry had more in common than either party recognized when, in the second half of the nineteenth century, they were learning how to apply managerial techniques to the parallel problems of destruction and production. In this connection it is worth noting that production of anything involved destruction of something else. The consumption of fuel and raw materials in heavy industry bears detailed comparison with the consumption of resources in war; even the fate of the labor forces involved offer interesting parallels.

and many an earlier rival by making peace after defeat, the better to fight again another day. War, conceived as the sport of kings and an affair of professional armies, was best managed in such a way. Austria's great misfortune after 1848 lay in the fact that the Hapsburg monarchy and the Hapsburg traditions of statecraft were becoming archaic, quite unable to tap the deeper springs of human action and passion which more popular governments could command.

Assuredly, the national pride and yearnings for collective greatness that the Prussians unleashed by their reorganization of the Germanies in 1866 had no place in the Hapsburg scheme of things. Bismarck, however, skillfully contrived a partnership of state and people, such as Scharnhorst and his fellow reformers of the early nineteenth century had envisioned. Indeed, Bismarck's feat of political prestidigitation, linking reaction to revolution within the framework of the Prussian state, was quite as critical for Prussian victories as Moltke's professionalism.

As a matter of fact, once the advancing Prussian armies marched into Bohemia, their supply system fell into considerable disarray. Capacity to ship by rail far exceeded the capacity to deliver food and ammunition from the railheads by road and wagon. Despite Moltke's best efforts, an enormous confusion prevailed along the roads the Prussians used for their advance. Only by driving ahead as fast as men and horses could go, leaving supply trains behind and accepting severe shortages of food and fodder, did the Prussians succeed in carrying through their concentration at Königgrätz. The Austrians suffered from similar difficulties of course, even though they moved more slowly. But had the war lasted longer, and had the Hapsburg regime not been ready to negotiate peace after its initial defeat, supply difficulties would have caught up with the advancing Prussians and might well have brought their swift and dramatic success to a halt.[41]

No such limitation on Prussian war-making capacity was evident in the first weeks of the Franco-Prussian War of 1870–71, for it began with even more spectacular victories than those of 1866. Moreover in 1870 the Prussians overwhelmed an army deemed the best in Europe; and one which had reacted to the news of 1866 by reequipping itself with breech-loading rifles superior in performance to Prussia's needle guns. Napoleon III intervened personally to hasten production of the new rifles, which were based on a design developed by a French lieutenant as far back as 1858. Fittingly the new gun was named *chas-*

---

41. Martin Van Creveld, *Supplying War: Logistics from Wallenstein to Patton* (Cambridge, 1977), pp. 79–82; Craig, *Königgrätz,* p. 49.

sepôt, after its designer. The French also had high hopes for a machine gun, the *mitrailleuse;* but only 144 of these secret weapons were on hand when war broke out in 1870,[42] and no effort was made to teach the French soldiers how best to use their new weaponry. In fact, French army leaders did not believe that any change in tactics would be needed. Instead the mitrailleuse was treated like an artillery piece, in which role it proved ineffective. As in 1859, they expected the climax and crisis of battle to be a bayonet charge delivered by columns of infantry.

In speed of supply and deployment, the French fell far behind the Prussians—a weakness that proved irremediable. So Prussian planning defeated French élan and, as a result, citizen-soldiers easily overwhelmed Europe's best professionals, to the amazement of all the world. Instead of taking the offensive and fighting on German soil, as everyone, including Moltke, had expected, the French had to improvise a defense against the advancing Prussians. Napoleon III and an entire French army soon found themselves surrounded at Sedan. After watching his troops take a fearful pounding from Prussian artillery, the emperor surrendered, just six weeks after hostilities had begun. Eight weeks later the principal French field army, besieged at Metz, also capitulated.

An important factor in this surprising victory was the way Prussian staff officers had profited from their experience against the Austrians. Prussian field artillery, for example, had fallen distinctly short of Austrian levels of performance in 1866. Designing and manufacturing new and better guns took time, and little was done in that respect before 1870. But the manner in which the Prussians deployed their artillery in battle could be and was radically altered. As a result French troops found themselves distracted by long-range bombardment as they were trying to form into columns for the attack. Such formations, of course, offered easy artillery targets, whereas the more open order favored by the Prussian infantry gave the French gunners nothing comparable to shoot at. Moreover, since Prussian guns outranged the French, their most punishing attacks were often delivered without any French riposte whatever.

The Prussian's capacity to learn from deficiencies in their past per-

---

42. On chassepôt and mitrailleuse, see Maréchal Randon, *Mémoires,* 2:234–36; E. Ann Pottinger, *Napoleon III and the German Crisis, 1865–66* (Cambridge, Mass., 1966), pp. 94–97; G. S. Hutchison, *Machine Guns: Their History and Tactical Employment* (London, 1938), pp. 9–15; Louis Etienne Dussieux, *L'Armée en France: histoire et organization* (Versailles, 1884), 3:233; Michael Howard, *The Franco-Prussian War: The German Invasion of France* (London, 1961), p. 56.

formance was, perhaps, the master key to their dazzling succession of victories. The application of reason and intelligence to the waging of war was not in the least new in nineteenth-century Europe; but seldom had it been carried out so systematically by a circle of men with the authority to put their ideas for change into practice without delay. The prestige that Moltke and the General Staff had won in 1865 and the authority King Wilhelm had conferred upon the chief of the General Staff in 1866 were what made Prussian reaction to the experience of war so much more rapid, rational, and thorough than anything other European armies were able to achieve.

Another example may reinforce this point. From the time they went over to the breech-loading needle gun, Prussian staff officers had recognized that such a change in weaponry called for a new drill; and a new drill called for retraining of the noncoms and junior officers who actually commanded troops in the field. This was an enormous undertaking. A special six-month training course was therefore set up to teach the new tactics. Each regiment was required to send a quota of noncoms and junior officers to this school; and its graduates, in turn, were responsible for teaching what they had learned to the rest of the regiment. The result was truly remarkable. The twin problems that had seemed insuperable to other armies—conservation of ammunition and maintenance of tactical mobility under fire even when individual soldiers were free to take cover and shoot from crouching or prone positions—were triumphantly overcome. Indeed, extension of radical rationality towards the bottom of the chain of command was just as important for Prussian successes as was the strategic control from the top that Moltke, Bismarck, and the king exercised with the help of the telegraph and railroads.

Yet there were limits to what advance planning and rational administration could accomplish. This was illustrated by the sequel to the Prussian victories at Sedan and Metz. French resistance did not end. An insurrectionary government, established as soon as the news of Napoleon III's surrender reached Paris, attempted to summon the spirit of 1793 from the depths and did succeed in making life uncomfortable for the invading German armies by guerrilla attacks on their lengthening lines of communication. A siege of Paris culminated in the surrender of the city to the Germans in January 1871, ten days after the establishment of the Second German Empire had been formally proclaimed in the Hall of Mirrors at Versailles. Peace, transferring Alsace and most of Lorraine to the new German empire, was signed in May, but not before violent revolution in the capital led to a brief but bloody civil war between a newly elected French government and the Commune of Paris. A more inauspicious beginning for the Third Republic could scarcely have been imagined.[43]

By 1871, therefore, the Prussians had twice demonstrated how to win a war against a great power in jig time. It had taken them just three weeks to defeat the Austrians and only six weeks to capture Napoleon III. It was impossible not to prefer such a model to the bumbling agony of the American Civil War or the year-long standstill at Sevastopol. Prussian military prestige rocketed accordingly. From being the least regarded of the European great powers, the new masters of Germany became pacesetters for all the world in matters military.

Obviously mass mobilization was the basis of Moltke's success. His victories had been won by getting Prussian armies into motion before their opponents were ready. Speed, mass, and momentum, in turn, depended on skillful use of railroads to assemble and deploy troops and their equipment. Numbers required an army of conscripts reinforced in time of war by reservists. Since conscripts were paid the merest pittance, a conscript army was also the only way European governments could afford to field a force big enough for the first critical encounters of this new style of war. Simultaneously, machinery for the mass production of small arms had made the cost of equipping vast citizen armies affordable. Every continental European army therefore sought to imitate the Prussians in the decades that followed. The British alone held back.

The art of war that thus defined itself in Europe from the 1870s onward fitted well with both Napoleonic and older chivalric notions. Reservists called back to duty for a few weeks or months found something enormously exhilarating about leaving ordinary routines of life behind, running risks, experiencing hardship, and testing personal prowess, while also winning victories and writing another glorious page in the national history that every child learned in school from patriotic and enthusiastic teachers. In retrospect, at least, the wars of 1866 and 1870–71 were indeed "Frisch und Fröhlich" for nearly all the Prussians who took part. Consequently, warfare shed most of its sinister meanings among the immediately ensuing generations, especially in Germany.

43. Howard, *The Franco-Prussian War* is by far the best military narrative and analysis of the subject. Alistair Horne, *The Fall of Paris* (New York, 1961) provides a vivid account of the Paris Commune. Cf. also Melvin Kranzberg, *The Siege of Paris* (Ithaca, N.Y., 1950).

The Prussian victories of 1866 and 1870–71 gave army officers, in Germany and other leading continental states, a Janus-like role in society. On the one hand, they were the spiritual and often the bodily heirs of rural estate owners, accustomed to giving orders to the laborers who cultivated their fields. Yet these landlords-in-uniform also required up-to-date industrial machinery for successful war. For some forty years this symbiosis of opposites seemed a happy one. In all of central and eastern Europe—and to some degree also in France—the military chain of command preserved a human pattern of unquestioning submission to a social superior which was fast disappearing from civil society as market relationships multiplied and freedom to choose which job to take and what to buy extended further and further down the social hierarchy, from cities to towns, and from towns to villages, across the face of Europe. Even Russia abolished serfdom in 1861!

Armies therefore acquired an archaic flavor. This was especially true of the Prussian pacesetter, for the Prussian officer corps took its coloration from the Junkers of the east, among whom residues of the old master-serf relationship lingered long after most of Germany had left the rural simplicity of a bipolar pattern of society behind. Yet part of the efficiency of European armies in general, and of the German army in particular, rested on this archaism. Individuals drafted into the army found themselves in a simpler society than the one they knew in civil life. The private soldier lost almost all personal responsibility. Ritual and routine took care of nearly every waking hour. Simple obedience to the orders that punctuated that routine from time to time, and set activity off in some new direction, offered release from the anxieties inherent in personal decision-making—anxieties that multiplied incontinently in urban society, where rival leaders, rival loyalties, and practical alternatives as to how to spend at least a part of one's time competed insistently for attention. Paradoxical as it may sound, escape from freedom was often a real liberation, especially among young men living under very rapidly changing conditions, who had not yet been able to assume fully adult roles.

From about the middle of the nineteenth century, an officer class that aped the manners of aristocrats even when of bourgeois birth coexisted in most of Europe with a rank and file of young draftees who found obedience an attractive solution to some of the dilemmas of life in an urbanizing society. This sort of escape from troubling ambiguity, superimposed on the atavistic resonance with hunting band sociability that close-order drill continued to arouse, gave continental armies after 1870 a character of their own, noticeably offset from the ethos of long-service troops, who had dominated the scene before the Germans showed what citizen-soldiers, commanded by professional officers, could do.[44]

All this accorded oddly with the changeability and growing mechanical complexity of industrial society. The routine simplicity of army life dictated standardized weaponry and ritualized drill. Even the expertness of the General Staff, which had brought the Prussians such striking rewards between 1864 and 1871, began to exhibit technological rigidity in the aftermath of their triumph over the French. Other European armies equaled, or in Britain's case exceeded, the Germans in resisting technical change. Though private arms makers did all they could to peddle heavy artillery and machine guns to the world's armies, they met with slow and reluctant response. What use were guns too heavy for horses to pull? How could machine guns, spitting hundreds of bullets a minute, find an adequate diet of ammunition on the battlefield? Delivery systems from the railhead were already inadequate, after all, as the Franco-Prussian War had demonstrated anew. Adding to the strain seemed senseless, and justified stalwart resistance to the wiles of arms salesmen who kept on proffering new and expensive weapons to reluctant officers and officials.

Cordial dislike prevailed between private arms makers and their official customers in every country of Europe. Yet, after 1870, each needed the other: arsenals were simply not equipped to produce steel guns, and the costs of fitting them out to do so were politically unacceptable. Hence, even in countries with the most technically proficient state arsenals, weapons made of steel had to be purchased from private manufacturers. The French had paid the price of relying on arsenal-made bronze artillery in 1870; the British, too, saw the giant muzzle-loading guns produced at the Woolwich arsenal fall decisively behind the performance of breech-loading models available from

44. I have not found a persuasive analysis of European armies' sociopsychological pattern in the pre–World War I era. The above remarks derive largely from personal experience of the American army in World War II, where, of course, an aristocratic officer corps was lacking. But cf. Martin Kitchen, *The German Officer Corps, 1890–1914* (Oxford, 1968); Girardet, *La société militaire*, pp. 198–291. The fact that both the German and British armies were organized into territorially based regiments gave regimental esprit de corps a remarkable importance in civil society. Draftees and volunteers often made lifelong friends during their military service, and renewed contact at regimental reunions throughout their adult lives. The cameraderie of army life, prolonged in this way, colored and often dominated local male society, especially in the countryside, since no other linkages united so many men so strongly. I owe this insight to personal communication from Professor Michael Howard.

Krupp and Armstrong. By the 1880s this technical gap had become
glaring, and when the Royal Navy managed to break away from the
tutelage of the Board of Ordnance (1886), its procurement officers
embarked on a far more intimate alliance with private arms makers
than European armies and navies had ever been ready to contemplate
previously. But before exploring the intensified patterns of military-
industrial interdependence that this breakaway inaugurated, it seems
well to pause a moment to survey the global impact of the European
art of war as it had evolved by 1880 or thereabouts.

Global Repercussions

A striking discrepancy at once leaps to the eye when one turns attention from the European continent itself to the military experience of
states and peoples in Africa and Asia during the period from 1840 to
1880. Larger and larger armies, built around a system of short-term
conscription followed by a period of service in the reserves, came to
dominate the scene on the continent of Europe. Such armies, however, were not for export. Asian and African rulers could not create
mass armies of conscripts. They lacked the needful administrative
structure, not to mention an officer corps, an arms supply, or even, in
many cases, a citizenry which could be trusted not to attack its rulers if
it had the chance. Only in Japan did the European pattern of a conscript army prove feasible—and that only after provoking a brief but
brutal civil war in 1877.

Conversely, European governments could not readily use short-
term conscripts for service overseas, since getting them to and from
the scene of action would consume most of the conscript's legal term
of service. What Europeans needed for action at a distance were long-
service troops. Great Britain maintained such an army in India until
1947, and in fact most of Britain's military engagements in the
nineteenth century were fought by troops of the Indian army.[45] The
other great imperial powers of the age, France and Russia, lacked such
a distinct instrument as the Indian army gave to Great Britain;
although the French, even after going over to a conscript short-term

---

45. Cf. Brian Bond, ed., *Victorian Military Campaigns* (London, 1967), pp. 7–8;
Philip Mason, *A Matter of Honour: An Account of the Indian Army, Its Officers and Men*
(London, 1974). The Cardwell reforms of the British army, 1870–74, constituted a kind
of halfway house between the Old Regime patterns of long-term service that had
prevailed until that time and the continental conscript and reservist system that Prussia
had made *de rigueur*.

service army in 1889, maintained volunteer units in their African and Asian colonies, including the famed Foreign Legion.

An amazing fact of world history is that in the nineteenth century even small detachments of troops, equipped in up-to-date European fashion, could defeat African and Asian states with ease. As steam-ships and railroads supplemented animal packtrains, natural obstacles of geography and distance became increasingly trivial. European ar-mies and navies therefore acquired the capacity to bring their re-sources to bear at will even in remote and previously impenetrable places. As this occurred, the drastic discrepancy between European and local organization for war became apparent in one part of the world after another.

The most important demonstration of the newly effective margin of armed superiority Europeans came to enjoy over other peoples oc-curred in 1839–42 on the coast of China, when small British detach-ments defeated the forces available to the Chinese Empire in the Opium War. Throughout Queen Victoria's long reign (1837–1901) a series of similar wars—some almost unnoticed by the public in England—kept British arms almost continuously engaged.[46] The re-sulting expansion of the British Empire, formal and informal, was matched by more sporadic but no less successful military action by France and Russia in Africa and Asia.

All three of the imperial powers found that armed actions along the periphery of their respective empires cost them next to nothing. For example, the Opium War, so fateful for China and Japan, lasted from November 1839 to August 1842. Yet British military appropriations actually decreased in 1841 below prewar levels, as the following figures (in millions) show:[47]

Year	Army and Ordnance	Navy	Total
1838	£8.0	£4.8	£12.8
1839	8.2	4.4	12.6
1840	8.5	5.3	13.8
1841	8.5	3.9	12.3
1842	8.2	6.2	14.4
1843	8.2	6.2	14.4

46. Bond, *Victorian Military Campaigns,* pp. 309–11, counts no fewer than seventy-two separate British campaigns during Victoria's reign, or more than one per year.

47. B. R. Mitchell, *Abstract of British Historical Statistics* (Cambridge, 1971), pp. 396–97.

The fact was that army and navy detachments did not cost much more when they went into the field than when they remained quietly in garrison. Payrolls did not alter and the cost of supplies did not rise much so long as only small detachments were engaged. Ammunition expended scarcely made any difference, for powder did not store well for long periods of time, and when not used in active combat had to be discarded after a few years because of chemical deterioration. The loss of a few European lives seemed of no great importance either in an age of rapidly expanding populations, and when opportunities for heroism in civil society were few and far between. Thus from the 1840s onward, far more drastically than in any earlier age, Europeans' near monopoly of strategic communication and transportation, together with a rapidly evolving weaponry that remained always far in advance of anything local fighting men could lay hands on, made imperial expansion cheap—so cheap that the famous phrase to the effect that Britain acquired its empire in a fit of absence of mind is a caricature rather than a falsehood.[48]

At the same time, there were real limits to European power. The explicit policy and potential military might of the United States, briefly apparent during and at the close of the Civil War, warned European powers away from military adventure in the New World. The French withdrawal from Mexico in 1867, and British deference to American interests in such matters as the *Alabama* claims (1872) and the Venezuelan (1895–99) and Alaskan (1903) boundary disputes, demonstrated this fundamental fact. Without bothering to maintain an army or navy of European scale, the United States still was able to stop European imperial expansion in the Caribbean and Latin America. Similarly, as soon as Japan proved capable of organizing an army and navy of European type, that nation, too, carved out a sphere of influence of its own within which European power could not prevail. This, however, did not become evident until the very end of the nineteenth century, and Japan had to show its might in war with Russia, 1904–5, before this second limit upon European military superiority was universally recognized.

In a sense, too, Russian withdrew within its own vast boundaries after the Crimean War and constituted yet another separate world within which western European industrial and military superiority could not penetrate. Indeed, military failure against the West found compensation in Central Asia, where Russian expeditionary forces

48. Cf. Daniel R. Headrick, *The Tools of Empire: Technology and European Imperialism in the Nineteenth Century* (New York, 1981).

conquered Moslem tribes and states with ease. The tsar's soldiers found scope for old-fashioned heroism in these campaigns just as French colonial troops were simultaneously doing in Africa and Indochina. Successes of this sort helped to disguise from both armies their failure to keep pace with German organization and planning.

Nevertheless, the Russians could not forget their Crimean humiliation. But efforts to overcome the backwardness that had permitted a French and British expeditionary force to defeat the Russian army on its own ground merely opened painful rents in the social fabric without altering the peasant base upon which the army rested or restoring Russia to the military primacy it had enjoyed from 1815 to 1853. Nevertheless, Russian state power remained formidable, and official policy devoted great effort to the task of equipping the tsar's army and navy with the latest and most efficient weapons, even when they had to be purchased abroad from Krupp or Armstrong. Russia, in fact, ranked among the very best customers for both these firms from the 1860s onwards.[49]

Within Russia, powerful residues of older command structures of society remained apparent, even after compulsory state service was legally abolished in the eighteenth century for nobles and for peasants in 1861. Japan's society, too, carried forward into the twentieth century strong traces of older "feudal" forms of human relationships. These aspects of Russian and Japanese society were profoundly alien to the liberal, individualistic and market-regulated patterns of behavior that achieved such remarkably broad scope in Britain and France in the nineteenth century. Until after World War II, however, these heritages from the past seemed handicaps, not strengths, destined to decay and disappear sooner or later. Indeed, British and French success and self-confidence were so great that their brands of liberalism exercised a powerful attraction upon the rest of Europe and the world, at least until economic depression, setting in after 1873, invited more active state intervention in economic matters.

Both France and Britain had been able to solve the problems each had confronted in the late eighteenth century when rapidly growing populations pressed hard against the limits of an already well-cultivated countryside. The French had done so by lowering birthrates and attuning population growth to expanding economic opportunities

49. Cf. John Bushnell, "Peasants in Uniform: The Tsarist Army as a Peasant Society," *Journal of Social History* 13 (1980): 565–76; John Bushnell, "The Tsarist Officer Corps 1881–1914: Customs, Duties, Inefficiency," *American Historical Review* 86 (1981): 753–80.

arising from their steady development of new industrial and commercial activities. Great Britain, on the contrary, maintained a high birthrate until the end of the century but from the 1850s found it possible to export those who could not find suitable employment at home as settlers in distant lands overseas.[50] The Germanies, too, found the British recipe for coping with population growth—i.e., rapid industrialization supplemented by emigration—generally effective; and by the 1880s, lands farther east in Europe began to react in similar fashion to overcrowding in peasant villages.[51]

As far as western Europe was concerned, therefore, by about 1850 the factor that had been so unsettling to Old Regime institutions and governments a century earlier seemed to have come under satisfactory control at last. The stormy passage of the French revolutionary wars and the first onset of the industrial revolution had begun to recede into the past. For the next ten decades, liberal ideas of peace, prosperity, free trade, and private property attained greater plausibility than before or since.

After a lapse of more than a century, it is easy to find fault with the narrow sympathies and ethnocentric outlook of nineteenth-century liberals, whether in Britain, France, Germany, or America. Yet even if the tide of social change since the 1870s has turned towards collective forms of human action and seems to have reinstated the primacy of the command principle in human affairs, it still seems appropriate to emphasize the truly extraordinary character of the world dominance Britain and France briefly exercised in the period between 1840 and 1880. Cheap machine-made goods and cheap machine-based superiority of armed force were both available for export, and exported they were. As a result, the world was united into a single interacting whole as

50. Overseas settlement as a safety valve for British and other European populations was enormously facilitated by the fact that vast and fertile regions of the earth were drastically depopulated when diseases of civilization attacked the native populations of such places as Australia, South Africa, North and South America. It consequently became possible to settle and develop these half-emptied lands without using any but the most trifling military force. Russian expansion into central Asia required rather more resort to force because it impinged on populations already inured to civilised diseases; the same was true in other Moslem lands, whether of Africa or the Middle East. On disease and European expansion, cf. W. H. McNeill, *Plagues and Peoples* (New York, 1976), chap. 5.

51. An adequate account of nineteenth-century European migration—both of industrial techniques and of population—remains to be written, but cf. D. F. Macdonald, "The Great Migration," in C. J. Bartlett, ed., *Britain Pre-eminent: Studies of British World Influence in the Nineteenth Century* (New York, 1969), pp. 54–75 for a brief conspectus of one half of the phenomenon. He estimates that 23 million persons left Europe for overseas destinations between 1750 and 1900, of whom 10 million came from the British Isles.

never before. World markets reached across all existing political boundaries, though tariffs in the United States and Russia, as well as natural obstacles to transport in the continental interiors of Africa and Asia, blunted the globalization of economic relationships.

All the same, the transcontinental integration of human effort attained by the 1870s constituted a landmark of world history comparable to the commercial integration of Sung China that had occurred some nine hundred years before. As argued in chapter 2, the Chinese achievement of the eleventh century probably played a key role in launching an ecumenical upsurge of market relationships of which the nineteenth-century global trade patterns were the apogee. The commercialization of diverse landscapes within China under the Sung had permitted more people to survive and productivity to increase far above earlier ceilings. So, too, the global integration of market-regulated human effort in the nineteenth century allowed the earth to accommodate a rapidly rising population by increasing human productivity enormously. More than a century later we remain the heirs of this achievement, in spite of all the obstacles to the free flow of goods and services that the twin considerations of welfare and warfare have since introduced into the world market system.

8

Intensified Military-Industrial Interaction, 1884-1914

Just as the industrialization of war can be dated to the 1840s, when railroads and semiautomated mass production together with Prussian breech-loaders and French efforts to exploit steam to the detriment of British naval supremacy began to transform preexisting military establishments, so, too, one can date the intensification of interaction between the industrial and military sectors of European society to a naval scare promulgated in Great Britain in 1884. A clever journalist, W. T. Stead, and an ambitious naval officer, Captain John Arbuthnot Fisher, were the protagonists of this affair, though other men also played a part in manipulating British public opinion from behind the scenes.

Decay of Britain's Strategic Position

Their success depended on the fundamental fact that British strategic security underwent systematic erosion from the 1870s onward. At bottom lay the diffusion of industrial techniques from the British Isles to other lands. This process went into high gear from about 1850, as Germany and the United States began to compete with, and in some lines of production to excel, British capacities and skill. In the narrower field of naval armament, too, Britain's superiority was endangered by the export of high technology to other navies. Private shipyards and armament manufacturers based in Britain played an active role in this process. It was, indeed, only on the strength of foreign sales that Armstrong and other British firms were able to stay in business after the decision of 1864 had entrusted the production of artillery for the British services to the Woolwich arsenal. But when, in 1882, Armstrong's built a cruiser for Chile, fast enough to outrun all existing capital ships, yet heavily enough gunned to overpower any lesser target, their technical expertise and readiness to sell to any comer who could pay the price began to bring British naval security into question.[1]

Swift cruisers were particularly menacing to Britain at a time when the nation had come to depend on food coming from across the Atlantic. From the mid-1870s, cheaper transportation made it possible to ship wheat and other foodstuffs to Liverpool and London from the distant plains of North America (and soon also from Argentina and Australia) at prices below those which British farmers could match. As a result, in the absence of tariffs of the kind that protected other European nations from the full force of overseas agricultural competition, crop farming in Great Britain decayed drastically.[2] Cheaper bread for consumers, however beneficial to the urban working classes, also meant a radically increased vulnerability. By the 1880s, when 65 percent of Britain's grain came from overseas, a fleet of enemy cruisers capable of intercepting grain shipments from the other side of the Atlantic could be expected to bring Great Britain face to face with starvation in a matter of months.

This possibility invited French politicians and naval officers to renew their long-standing rivalry with Britain at sea. A group of naval theorists, the so-called *jeune école,* argued that specialized gunboats for shore bombardment, plus fast cruisers and even faster torpedo boats, were all that France needed to nullify Britain's naval preeminence. Such vessels had the enormous attraction of being cheap. One armored warship cost as much as sixty torpedo boats; yet one torpedo could sink any existing warship if its warhead hit below the water line. After the French disaster of 1870–71, reequipment of the army had to take precedence. Hence, a plan that promised to diminish the cost of

1. Fast, heavily gunned cruisers proved very salable. Altogether, Armstrong's built no fewer than eighty-four warships for twelve different foreign governments between 1884 and 1914. More than once in the course of these thirty years, a technical advance introduced on behalf of a foreign customer compelled the Royal Navy to tag along and order equivalent improvements in its warships. In addition to the Chilean cruiser of 1882, the eight-inch guns Armstrong's provided for the Russian cruiser *Rurik* (launched 1890) is the best-known instance of this kind of whipsaw. Cf. David Dougan, *The Great Gunmaker: The Story of Lord Armstrong* (Newcastle-on-Tyne, n.d.), pp. 138–44; Donald W. Mitchell, *A History of Russian and Soviet Sea Power* (New York, 1974), p. 193.

2. Wheat prices fell from 56s. 9d. a quarter in 1877 to a nadir of 22s. 10d. in 1894. Acreage under wheat dropped by about 50 percent between 1872 and the end of the century; rents declined, though not as much; emigration from the countryside assumed almost catastrophic proportions. Yet real wages rose by something like 77 percent between 1860 and 1900. These statistics are from R. C. K. Ensor, *England, 1870–1914* (Oxford, 1936), pp. 115–16, 275, 284–86.

the navy and still compel British warships to withdraw from the Mediterrannean and retire from the Atlantic coasts of France seemed irresistible. Accordingly, in 1881, the Chamber of Deputies voted funds for seventy torpedo boats and halted construction of armored warships. Five years later, when the protagonist of the *jeune école,* Admiral H. L. T. Aube, became minister of marine (1886–87), he persuaded the Chamber to approve a program for constructing fourteen commerce-raiding cruisers and an additional one hundred torpedo boats. Although battleship admirals continued to exist in France and indeed regained ascendancy over the French navy in 1887, it certainly seemed by the mid-1880s that Britain's traditional rival had pinned its faith on a radically new weapons system for close-in operations, while falling back on the age-old strategy of commerce-raiding for action at longer distances.[3]

Such a strategy seemed genuinely threatening to the small group of technically minded British officers who had followed the development of self-propelled torpedos since their invention at Fiume in 1866 by a British emigrant, Robert Whitehead.[4] Small, fast torpedo boats of the sort the French proposed to build had little to fear from existing capital ships in 1881. British warships carried ponderous muzzle-loaders, weighing up to eighty tons. Such monsters might have a devastating effect when fired at stationary objects from close range. That was what they had been designed to do, on the assumption that future naval battles would be fought yardarm to yardarm, as in Nelson's day. But their slow rate of fire and inaccuracy of aim at long ranges meant that fast, maneuverable boats could dart in, release their torpedoes, and be off and away before the Royal Navy's guns could catch up with such

---

3. Volkmar Bueb, *Die "Junge Schule" der französischen Marine: Strategie und Politik, 1875–1900* (Boppard am Rhein, 1971) gives the best account I have seen. For a French point of view, see Henri Salaun, *La marine française* (Paris, 1932), pp. 18 ff. The shift of naval policy between 1881 and 1887 in France duplicated earlier turns away from all-out competition with England, and largely for similar reasons: French taxpayers' resistance to the excessive cost of naval armament (cf. chap. 5 above). For British responses see Brian Ranft, "The Protection of British Seaborne Trade and the Development of Systematic Planning for War, 1860–1906," in Brian Ranft, ed., *Technical Change and British Naval Policy, 1860–1939* (London, 1977), pp. 1–22.

4. "Torpedo" initially referred to any explosive package designed to strike a ship under the water line. Water being far denser than air, such an explosion could exercise a much greater force against the ship's side than a similar one occurring in thin air. This made torpedoes particularly lethal. The problem of bringing a charge up against an enemy ship's side was first resolved by towing torpedoes from projecting spars. But as self-propelled torpedoes began to achieve a degree of accuracy, weapons of this design supplanted all others. On the history of torpedoes see Edwin A. Gray, *The Devil's Device* (London, 1975).

quick-moving targets. In short, Goliath confronted David over again—this time on the sea.

Torpedoes, lethal to armored ships at ranges of 500 to 600 yards, were bad enough, but the embarrassments of the Royal Navy were rendered even more acute by a simultaneous revolution in gunnery which made muzzle-loading hopelessly inefficient. The most important change was in the propellant. By shaping grains of powder with interior hollows so that each grain could burn simultaneously from inside out as well as from outside in, it proved possible to equalize the rate of chemical change that occurred within a gun barrel from first ignition to the end of the burn. This improvement, mainly the work of an American army officer, Thomas J. Rodman (d. 1871), was combined in the 1880s with the invention of new nitrocellulose explosives (here the French took the lead) to produce much more powerful, smokeless propellants.

The sustained push that a well-regulated explosion could communicate to a projectile increased muzzle velocities very greatly. It also made longer gun barrels necessary, since the expanding gases of the regulated explosion could continue to accelerate the projectile for a far longer time than had been possible when a sharp initial impetus petered out as the powder grains burned down to nothingness, diminishing the rate of gas generation as the burning surfaces shrank in area. Longer barrels, in turn, made muzzle-loading impossible; and in 1879 the British officially decided that the navy had to have breech-loading guns. What finally persuaded the Admiralty that muzzle-loaders were hopeless was Krupp's spectacular demonstration of what his big guns could do. He set up a special firing range for the purpose at Meppen (see plate *b* on p. 266) and in 1878 and 1879 conducted a series of test firings that showed foreign and German observers, invited as potential customers, how vastly superior long-barreled, breech-loading steel guns had become.[5]

Decision to abandon muzzle-loaders, the sole form of gun approved by the British Board of Ordnance since 1864, presented the Woolwich arsenal with a crisis it was ill prepared to meet. Conversion to breech-loading was expensive and difficult in itself; but costs were enormously increased by the fact that simultaneously the arsenal would have to convert from wrought iron to steel as the basic gun-

5. R. F. Mackay, *Fisher of Kilverstone* (Oxford, 1973), pp. 144–45; William Manchester, *The Arms of Krupp* (Boston, 1964), pp. 176–77; Ian V. Hogg, *A History of Artillery* (London, 1974), pp. 82–92.

Steel Technology and Mass Production of Armaments

These four photographs show how the firm of Krupp used a head start in steel technology to develop armaments production on a really large scale by the 1890s. The exterior views show (a) *blast furnaces where the steel was smelted and* (b) *the firing range at Meppen where finished guns were tested. The interior views show* (c) *a machine shop for making gun carriage parts and* (d) *the shop where gun tubes were given their final machining, inside and out. These photographs formed part of a promotional collection distributed by the firm in 1892.*

Reproduced from copies in the University of Chicago Library.

a

b

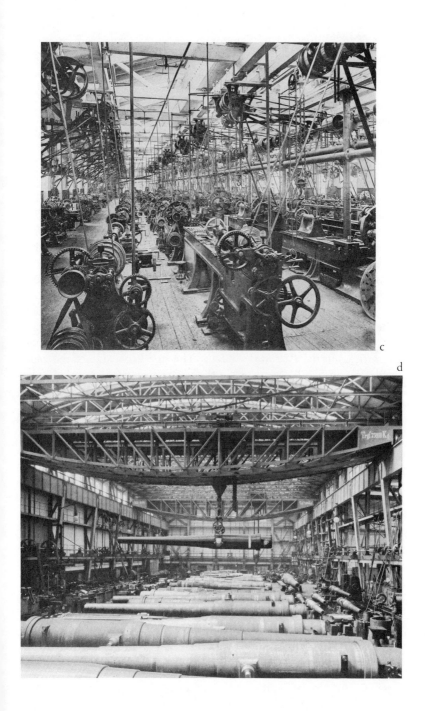

c

d

metal. This required a fundamentally different plant from anything Woolwich had in hand. No matter how fast changes were made, waiting for officials of the arsenal and of the Board of Ordnance to take the necessary steps to convert their establishment to the new requirements was bound to strain the navy's patience.

Long-standing army-navy frictions here came into play, for the Board of Ordnance was under army control and responded sluggishly to demands and initiatives coming from the navy. Or so it seemed to naval gunnery officers. In particular, they chafed at the fact that in the years 1881–87 the board authorized only one-third of the expenditure necessary to meet the navy's program for conversion to breech-loading.[6] Such a pace, however revolutionary in itself, seemed wholly inadequate at a time when the French and Germans as well as private gun manufacturers in England were already turning out steel guns that made all the Royal Navy's existing armament hopelessly obsolete.

Bureaucratic infighting against cheeseparing army officers and unsympathetic arsenal officials seemed an inadequate response to such a critical technical situation. This was what persuaded Captain John Fisher to leak information surreptitiously to the journalist W. T. Stead, with the knowledge that he intended to publish a series of inflammatory articles in the *Pall Mall Gazette*. The first broadside of the campaign came in September 1884 in the form of an article entitled "The Truth about the Navy," portentously attributed to "One Who Knows the Facts." It provoked widespread concern, for it argued, with abundant substantiating detail, that "the truth about the Navy is that our naval supremacy has almost ceased to exist."[7] Other articles followed, climaxing in a detailed account of "What Ought to Be Done for the Navy." This article appeared on 13 November, shortly after Parliament had reconvened and two weeks before the government got round to responding to the agitation which had swept the country in the wake of the *Pall Mall Gazette* revelations. The official response was to recommend an increase in naval appropriations of £5.5 million, to be spread over five years' time. Since the regular appropriation for the navy in 1883 was £10.3 million, this increase, unsatisfactory though it seemed to "One Who Knows the Facts,"[8] represented a very considerable victory for the alarmists.

By going public, even if surreptitiously, Fisher had forced decisions that the Liberal government and indeed Fisher's own naval superiors

6. Cf. Mackay, *Fisher of Kilverstone,* p. 187.
7. *Pall Mall Gazette,* 18 September 1884, p. 6.
8. Ibid., 8 December 1884, p. 1.

had been loath to make. The First Sea Lord of the time, Sir Astley Cooper Key, did not approve of such tactics. Indeed, he detested public agitation and distrusted the stategy of increasing naval appropriations dramatically, believing that such a policy would merely provoke other nations to increase their naval expenditures, thus hastening instead of heading off the decline of British naval preponderance.[9] As the senior officer of the navy he held that his proper role was to do the best he could with what the government of the day provided in the way of funds. Naval discipline forbade entry into the political process by which such sums were determined. But Fisher was prepared to violate this long-standing code to get his way, impelled partly by personal ambition and partly by a sense of technological urgency which more senior naval officers, immersed in paper work, did not share.

Emergence of the Military-Industrial Complex in Great Britain

Needless to say, Fisher did not act alone. The year 1884 was a time of depression. Idle shipyards were eager for work and journalists did not hesitate to point out that "it might be possible at the present time to kill two birds with one stone—to find ships for our fleet and employment for starving artisans by applying to private dockyards for aid which the Government yards cannot supply."[10] A question in Parliament raised the issue of aid to the unemployed on 25 October, as the government prepared its revised naval estimates; and when the First Lord of the Admiralty disclosed his supplementary program to the House of Lords he declared: "if we are to spend money on the increase of the Navy, it is desirable in consequence of the stagnation in the great shipbuilding yards of this country, that the extra expenditure should go . . . to increase the work by contract in the private yards."[11]

In earlier decades, when Parliament had represented property owners and taxpayers, a depression of trade could be counted on to provoke a demand for corresponding reduction in government expenditure. But just two weeks before that upward revision of the naval estimates in 1884, William E. Gladstone's Liberal government brought

---

9. For Cooper Key's views see Richard Hough, *First Sea Lord: An Authorized Biography of Admiral Lord Fisher* (London, 1969), p. 83.

10. The *Daily Telegraph,* as quoted in the *Pall Mall Gazette,* 11 October 1884.

11. *Hansard,* 2 December 1884, col. 410. The Earl of Northbrook referred to the letting of private contracts four separate times in his speech, and in rebuttal mentioned the government's intention of encouraging "the great manufacturers of steel" by refraining from giving Woolwich the capacity to produce the new gunmetal.

in a bill that widened the franchise substantially. Thereafter, the income tax affected only a small proportion of the electorate.[12] On the other hand, no parliament could long resist pressures from unemployed voters, backed up by entrepreneurs eager for government contracts.

The new suffrage, therefore, altered the dynamics of politics. Trade depressions, instead of making costly naval bills more difficult to get through Parliament, made extra expenditures more urgent and attractive than in times of prosperity. Arms contracts, after all, could restore both wages and profits and strengthen Britain's international position, all at the same time. Taxpayers' reluctance to pay for it all was no longer decisive in politics, especially since more and more voters came to believe that the rich could and should be made to foot the bill.[13]

This vague and general, yet decisive, realignment of political and economic interests achieved a cutting edge when a handful of technically proficient naval officers inaugurated intimate collaboration with private manufacturers of arms. Captain Fisher played a key role in this change too. In 1883 he had become commander of the naval gunnery school at Portsmouth—the vantage point from which he launched his venture into high politics in 1884. Being responsible for improving naval gunnery, Fisher made it his business to find out all he could about every available model of big gun, including those being manufactured privately. He believed fervently in competition, and his idea in 1884 was to stimulate rivalry between the Woolwich arsenal and private manufacturers in order to assure an optimal result for the navy.

In practice, however, Fisher's ideal was not realized. The Woolwich arsenal never got the necessary plant to allow it to compete with private firms on anything like equal terms. Ironically, Fisher's own actions and characteristic impatience with the bureaucratic delays that army officers interposed between his wishes and their realization at the arsenal helped to assure this result. What happened was this: in 1886, when Fisher became director of naval ordnance, he demanded and was accorded the legal right to purchase from private firms any ar-

12. In 1914 less than one-seventh of the work force in Britain paid income tax, according to Arthur Marwick, *The Deluge: British Society and the First World War* (London, 1965), p. 21.

13. Conservatives, who supported defense expenditures more warmly than the Liberals, were nonetheless troubled by the drift towards graduated taxation as the way to pay for more ships and guns. In 1889, for example, Lord Salisbury wrote confidentially to the Chancellor of the Exchequer urging him to meet the increased naval appropriations of that year by raising excise as well as property taxes, since "it is dangerous to recur to realized property alone in difficulties because the holders of it are politically so weak that the pernicious financial habit is sure to grow." Quoted from Gwendolyn Cecil, *Life of Robert, Marquis of Salisbury* (London, 1932), 4:192.

ticle that the arsenal could not supply quickly or more cheaply. Though no one realized it at the time, this decision soon gave private arms makers an effective monopoly on the manufacture of naval heavy weapons. The reason was simple. Woolwich never caught up with the grandiose scale of capital investment needed to turn out giant steel guns, turrets, and other complicated devices with which warships came to be armed. Armstrong, on the other hand, recognized immediately after Krupp's demonstrations of 1878 and 1879 that to compete successfully his firm must at once install the machinery needed to produce large steel breech-loaders. Sir William therefore reacted to Krupp's threatened invasion of a field in which he had hitherto held undisputed pride of place—the building of big guns for coast artillery and naval use—by investing in a brand new steel mill and ship yard.[14] By 1886, therefore, Armstrong was ready and eager to add the Royal Navy to his already distinguished list of foreign customers at a time when Woolwich had only begun to convert to the manufacture of breech-loaders.

For the next thirty years the gap proved quite unbridgeable because of economies of scale. It had long been true that international sales were needed to keep gunmaking capital equipment in continual—or nearly continual—use. Such a regime cheapened production drastically, which was why Liège had played such a dominating role in the European gun trade between the 15th and 19th centuries. Still, in the course of the eighteenth century, Europe's leading states all set up arsenals where guncasting machinery stood idle most of the time. Only so could they enjoy full sovereign power over the manufacture of their artillery. Then in the middle years of the nineteenth century Prussia, the poorest of the great powers, and Russia, the least industrialized, had supplemented arsenal production with purchases from Krupp. But in France and Britain (with the exception of William Armstrong's years of official recognition, 1859–63) state arsenals retained their official monopoly until the 1880s. Woolwich had invested in new machinery for producing larger and larger wrought iron guns for the Royal Navy ever since the 1860s. But the shift to steel escalated costs so suddenly and drastically that the responsible authorities balked at installing the necessary new facilities at Woolwich.

If they had done so, a very expensive capital plant would have stood

14. J. D. Scott, *Vickers: A History* (London, 1962), pp. 34–44. Before 1878 Krupp had concentrated on field artillery and tacitly left the manufacture of naval artillery to the British. His big guns of 1878–79 threatened to overturn that division of the market. Hence the energy of Armstrong's reaction.

idle much of the time, because the demands of the Royal Navy did not suffice to keep such an installation busy—or anything near. International sales, of the kind Krupp and Armstrong had learned to thrive on, were the only way in which a new capital plant could come close to full utilization. This meant, in turn, that arsenal costs of production would certainly exceed those of private companies so long as Woolwich only served the British government.

Thus the ground rules agreed to in 1886 had the effect of allowing Armstrong and, after 1888, Vickers as well, to undercut the arsenal systematically. Woolwich simply could not compete; and in fact the officers in charge never wanted and never got the enormous expansion of capital plant that would have been needed to keep up with the explosive pace of technical change resulting from the new form of naval-industrial collaboration that prevailed throughout the thirty years between 1884 and 1914.

Woolwich and the Royal Naval Dockyards continued to do a great deal of work for the navy,[15] but they did not, as a rule, introduce important innovation. Woolwich did sometimes take on new weapons after initial development work had been done elsewhere. This was the case with self-propelled torpedoes, for example, which were built at Woolwich after 1871. The fact that Robert Whitehead, the inventor, was willing to sell his patents to the Admiralty made room for the arsenal in this instance.[16] When, however, an inventor preferred to set up a new company, as Hiram Maxim did in 1884 to make his newly invented machine guns, the law did not permit Woolwich to infringe patents.

The army rather than the navy was, of course, the principal British purchaser for Maxim's machine guns; and the fact that truly efficient designs could be secured only from private manufacturers after 1884 probably reinforced professional suspicion of the new weapon. At any rate the War Office purchased very few Maxims despite the fact that their lethal efficiency was demonstrated repeatedly in colonial campaigns.[17] Before the Boer War (1899–1902) the British army re-

15. Private firms handled only 35.7 percent of the navy's total expenditure for munitions between 1881 and 1890, but the proportion of contracts let to private firms steadily increased, to 46.1 percent in 1890–1900 and 58.5 percent in 1900–1910. Clive Trebilcock, "Spin-off in British Economic History: Armaments and Industry, 1760–1914," *Economic History Review* 22 (1969): 480.

16. Gray, *The Devil's Device,* pp. 71, 88. Whitehead did subsequently set up a private company in England to manufacture torpedoes for sale to foreign countries. It merged into Vickers in 1906.

17. Cf. John Ellis, *The Social History of the Machine Gun* (London, 1975), pp. 79–109. Mockery is easy in view of what happened in 1914–18; but an army that sought to

mained generally satisfied with what the arsenal could supply and avoided contracts with private firms on principle whenever possible. This was facilitated by the fact that technical changes in land armament remained comparatively modest.[18] Everyone assumed that field weapons would always have to be light enough for horses to pull. The potentialities of internal combustion motors (developed from the 1880s for private automobiles) were left unexplored. Such technical conservatism made it easier for soldiers to preserve their traditional affection for horses and their no less traditional suspicion of profit-seeking businessmen and inventors. This was true on the Continent as well as in Great Britain. Even the Germans, who had to deal with Krupp rather than with arsenal personnel for their field artillery after 1871, nurtured a deep repugnance towards the self-seeking and greed that they felt to be intrinsic to commerce; and the few army officers who lent themselves to Krupp's blandishments remained an isolated handful, more or less suspect among their fellows.[19] Conversely, the preservation of such attitudes in all European armies after the 1880s held back the pace of technical change to no more than a snail's pace in comparison to what was happening simultaneously to European navies.

The very complexity of naval construction dictated a quite different attitude as soon as the Royal Navy began buying guns and other heavy equipment from private manufacturers. Inevitably, personal links between the circle of technically responsible naval officers and the managers of private firms became very close. William White, for

achieve mobility in the field, as all European armies did before 1914, simply lacked the transport capacity to supply more than a token population of guns that spat forth bullets at the rate of 600 a minute.

18. Change, radical enough measured against older standards, was modest only by comparison to the galloping transformation in naval armament. Brass cartridges (1867 onwards), steel artillery (1883), magazine rifles (1888), and control and communications devices to allow accurate indirect artillery fire (from 1906) added up to a revolution in tactics and fire power. Cf. Arthur Forbes, *A History of the Army Ordnance Services* (London, 1929), 3:112–34; Charles E. Caldwell and John Headlam, *The History of the Royal Artillery from the Indian Mutiny to the Great War*, 2 vols. (Woolwich, n.d.), 2:105 and passim.

19. Documents reproduced in W. A. Boelke, *Krupp und die Hohenzollern in Dokumenten* (Frankfurt-am-Main, 1970), pp. 104–6, 123, show how stubbornly the German army officers held aloof from collaboration with private arms makers, despite the fact that both Wilhelm I and Wilhelm II entered into personal relations with Alfred Krupp and his heir. Oddly, admirers and critics of the house of Krupp agree in distorting the relationship between German army officers and the firm. Cf. Wilhelm Berdrow, *The Krupps: 150 Years of Krupp History, 1787–1937* (Berlin, 1937), and William Manchester, *The Arms of Krupp* (Boston, 1964). Gert von Klass, *Krupps: The Story of an Industrial Empire* (London, 1954) does better justice to the social distance and mutual distrust that prevailed between buyer and seller.

example, who became chief naval designer in 1885, had worked at Armstrong's for a two-year spell immediately before assuming his new post. He became perhaps the principal link between the Royal Navy and private industry thereafter.[20] Captain Andrew Noble moved the other way. He abandoned a career in the navy to work for Armstrong and rose to become head of the firm in 1900 when the founder died. It was also possible to start at the top, as Admiral Sir Astley Cooper Key did in 1886 by becoming chairman of the board of a newly established armaments firm, the Nordenfeldt Gun and Ammunition Company. By the first decade of the twentieth century, it was even possible for Admiral Sir Percy Scott to enter into royalty contracts with Vickers for inventions he made "on the side" in the course of his professional work.[21]

Pecuniary self-aggrandizement did not become really respectable in the navy any more than in the army; and Admiral Scott was greedy rather than businesslike. Nevertheless, extensive dealings with one another and continual consultation over technical and financial questions between private businessmen and naval officers went a long way to break down older mistrust.

Friction and subterfuge were never entirely eliminated from the relationship, which revolved, after all, around the ancient ambivalences between buyer and seller. But in spite of occasional accusations of bad faith, collaboration in the myriad problems of how to design new and better warships prevailed. In effect, a small company of technocrats constructed a slender bridge across the chasm which had previously divided naval officers from the manufacturing and business world. In doing so, they provided a means whereby the new potentialities of democratic and parliamentary politics could be realized in the form of successive generations of new weaponry, each more formidable, more costly, and more important for the national economy as a whole than its predecessor.

The bridge between the navy and the arms industry was still weak and carried relatively little traffic in 1889, when the building program of 1884 ran out. A Naval Defence Act was duly brought in by the government. It cost £21.5 million, nearly four times the supplementary appropriation in 1884; and the number of ships to be built, half of them in private shipyards, reached the impressive total of seventy.

---

20. Cf. Frederic Manning, *The Life of Sir William White* (London, 1923).

21. A notably cantankerous and inventive naval officer, he successfully sued Vickers in 1920 for withholding some of his royalties. Cf. Peter Padfield, *Aim Straight: A Biography of Admiral Sir Percy Scott* (London, 1966), pp. 262–68.

The scale of the program was officially justified by proclamation of a "two-power standard." This meant that the Royal Navy ought always to be equal or superior to the combined forces of the next two largest navies in the world. Only so, it was argued, could Britain's security be guaranteed against any and all contingencies.[22]

A striking fact about 1889 program was that it exceeded what the Admiralty had asked for. Personal initiative and purpose no longer controlled what happened. Instead, organized groups interacted with one another, creating a process more complicated than any of the participants could fully comprehend. But the upshot was unidirectional, propelling the government to increased investment in armaments.

As in 1884, there were plenty of viewers-with-alarm on the English side of the Channel. The French cooperated magnificently, partly by themselves embarking in 1888 on a large-scale naval building campaign no longer limited to torpedo boats and cruisers; and partly by unleashing a surge of jingoism focused upon the mock heroic figure of General Boulanger. French jingoism wakened an answering note across the channel. Britain's most respected soldier, Lord Wolseley, announced in the House of Lords that "so long as the Navy is as weak as it is at the moment her Majesty's army cannot . . . guarantee even the safety of the capital in which we are at this moment."[23] And the prime minister, Lord Salisbury, convinced himself that "there are circumstances under which a French invasion may be possible."[24]

The fact that even in a time of general prosperity the steel business and shipbuilding were in difficulty added fuel to the fires of agitation. But what most affected government thinking was the strategic calculation that the French and Russian fleets, acting in concert, might be able to drive the Royal Navy from the Mediterranean. In addition, Conservative politicians like Lord George Hamilton, First Lord of the Admiralty in 1889, recognized that naval appropriations were popular and might help the party at the polls.[25]

With party advantage, national interest, and popular enthusiasm all

22. The two-power standard was attributed to William Pitt the Elder and thus acquired a respectable ancestry. But it had not been a guiding principle of British naval policy throughout the intervening years as its proponents in 1889 declared to be the case. Cf. Arthur Marder, *British Naval Policy, 1880–1905: The Anatomy of British Sea Power* (London, n.d.), pp. 105–16.

23. *Hansard,* 14 May 1888, vol. 326, col. 100.

24. Cecil, *Life of Robert, Marquis of Salisbury,* 4:186.

25. In memoirs written after World War I, Lord George remarked: "The great additions to the electorate by the Reform Bill of 1884 had, to a large extent, swamped the old niggardly and skinflint policy of the Manchester School. It is true that the mass of the recently enfranchised escaped direct taxation out of which new burdens of expen-

pulling in the same direction as the special interest of private arms makers and the steel and shipbuilding industries, it is not so surprising that the Admiralty got more money to spend for new ships in 1889 than it had asked for or expected. The effect within British society, clearly, was to confirm and strengthen vested interests in continued, indeed expanded, naval appropriations.[26]

This became obvious as the five-year plan of 1889 neared its end. In 1893, a general trade depression hit; Gladstone was back in office and earnestly opposed the idea of increasing taxes to pay for more warships in a time of economic downswing. But when it came to the pinch, no other member of the Cabinet agreed with his views. After tense weeks of debate, Gladstone resigned rather than endorse the naval building plan which his ministerial colleague, Lord Spencer, brought in as First Lord of the Admiralty. Once Gladstone was out of the way, the program, requiring a five-year expenditure of £21.2 million, passed through Parliament with ease. Publicists aroused support for the bill swiftly and skillfully. Indeed such agitation became fully institutionalized with the establishment of the Navy League in 1894.

New crises were swift in coming, for by the 1890s other nations had caught the naval fever, including such industrial giants as the United States and Germany. An American naval officer, Alfred Thayer Mahan, published his famous volumes, *The Influence of Sea Power on History,* in 1890 and 1892 in an effort to persuade Americans of the importance of building a new, modern navy. His success at home in the United States as well as abroad, especially in Germany, was phenomenal. As a result, with the new century, the two-power standard became impractical for Britain at a time when the outbreak of the Boer War dramatized the country's isolation. The unexpectedly long and difficult character of that war raised military and naval expenditures to hitherto unequaled levels, so it was not until 1905, when a new Liberal government took office, that an opportunity to bring military expenditure under stricter control again seemed to present itself.

By that time Admiral Fisher had become First Sea Lord, remaining

---

diture were mainly defrayed; but independently of this personal consideration, the wage earning classes are very proud of the Navy." Lord George Hamilton, *Parliamentary Reflections 1886–1906* (London, 1922), pp. 220–21.

26. Arthur J. Marder, "The English Armaments Industry and Navalism in the Nineties," *Pacific Historical Review* 7 (1938): 241–53, cites industrial spokesmen on this point. It is worth noting, perhaps, that Royal Navy ships built under the 1889 bill were the first to use nickel steel armor and to rely wholly on steam propulsion. Remodeling older ships to remove masts and rigging was an important (and expensive) part of the 1889 naval building program.

in office from 1904 to 1910. He reacted to demands for economy by reforming personnel policies at home while closing down naval stations overseas and ruthlessly retiring obsolescent warships.[27] At the same time, he concentrated much of his enormous energy on building a new super battleship, H.M.S. *Dreadnought.* This formidable vessel, launched in 1906, made it necessary for rival navies—the German above all—to suspend building programs until vessels comparable to the *Dreadnought* could be designed. Liberal politicians believed that this would allow the government to cut back the pace of naval building. Only so could projected reductions in the naval estimates be sustained.

But such a policy meant unemployment and loss of business for shipbuilders and other contractors who had become dependent on naval construction. It was one thing when naval cutbacks worked harm to overseas communities like Halifax, Nova Scotia, or the Bahamas, which lacked parliamentary representation; it was quite another when British constituencies were about to be affected.[28] Conservatives seized upon the issue fervently and launched a noisy agitation for more, not fewer, warships. The Germans tipped the balance decisively by announcing a new and enlarged building program in 1908; and as a result, the Liberal government, which had proposed to build only four dreadnought-type ships in 1909, ended by authorizing the construction of eight such ships. In Winston Churchill's words: "In the end a curious and characteristic solution was reached. The Admiralty had demanded six ships: the economists [of whom he was one] offered four: and we finally compromised on eight."[29]

This long series of political decisions, trending always towards larger naval expenditures, was fueled by a runaway technological revolution as well as by international rivalries and the changed structure of Great Britain's domestic politics. A powerful feedback loop established itself, for technological transformations could not have proceeded nearly so rapidly if economic interest groups favoring enlarged public expenditure had not come into existence to facilitate the pas-

27. Naval appropriations were substantially cut back from £36.8 million in 1905 to £31.1 million in 1908. B. R. Mitchell, *British Historical Statistics* (Cambridge, 1971), pp. 397–98.

28. Cf. Philip Noel-Baker, *The Private Manufacture of Armaments* (London, 1936), 1:449–51 for details of how threatened idleness at Coventry Ordnance Works provoked the manager to launch a campaign of scare publicity and political wire-pulling with the result that the eight-dreadnought program did indeed provide his company with the new business it needed.

29. Winston S. Churchill, *The World Crisis,* abridged and rev. ed. (London, 1931), p. 39.

sage of bigger and bigger naval bills. Each naval building program, in turn, opened the path for further technological change, making older ships obsolete and requiring still larger appropriations for the next round of building.

How much weight to assign technological innovation as an autonomous element in this pattern of escalating expenditure is impossible to say. What one can discern, however, is a change in its character. Before the 1880s, invention had nearly always been the work of individuals, sometimes with the help of a supporting cast of technicians and skilled mechanics who built prototypes and otherwise assisted the inventor himself in embodying his idea in material form. Armstrong and Whitworth had both worked on these lines, using the resources of their respective firms to develop new models for guns and other kinds of machinery as they personally saw fit. Development costs, such as they were, had to be borne by the entrepreneur, and his only prospect of recovering them and making a profit depended on being able to sell his invention to skeptical buyers—whether these were private consumers in civil life or officers of the armed forces. Risks in the armaments field were very great. As Whitworth discovered in 1863–64, even a definitely superior product might not be accepted by fiscally and technically conservative officers and officials.

Under these circumstances, investment in arms research and development was sure to remain comparatively modest. Even so, as we have seen in the preceding chapter, a few innovators—Armstrong, Dreyse, Krupp, and their like—were able to revolutionize armaments simply by bringing military technology to the level of civil engineering. But this mid-nineteenth-century style of private invention was quite incapable of carrying naval engineering to the heights actually attained between 1884 and 1914. Even big and successful firms, like Krupp and Armstrong, could not risk the ballooning costs of experiment and development, had they not been assured of a purchaser ahead of time.

From the 1880s onward, however, the Admiralty routinely provided the assurance private firms required. Navy technicians set out to specify the desirable performance characteristics for a new gun, engine, or ship, and, in effect, challenged engineers to come up with appropriate designs. Invention thus became deliberate. Within limits, tactical and strategic planning began to shape warships instead of the other way around. Above all, Admiralty officials ceased to set brakes on innovation by sitting in judgment on novelties proposed by the trade. Instead, technically proficient officers clustered around the dynamic figure of Admiral Fisher to hurry innovations on. With the new century, the Admiralty even began to ease the tribulations that had always before beset inventors by paying at least some of the costs for testing new devices that seemed particularly promising.

One of the first triumphs of this "command technology" was the development of quick-firing guns. In 1881, when the torpedo-boat threat was new, the Admiralty defined the characteristics of a quick-firing gun needed to combat the danger. What the Admiralty wanted was a gun capable of firing at least twelve times a minute and powerful enough to blow an approaching torpedo boat out of the water long before it got within the 600 yards which then represented the effective range for self-propelled torpedoes.[30]

By 1886, when Admiral Fisher was at last authorized to turn to private firms for weapons the arsenal could not supply, two different designs already existed which met the Admiralty's 1881 specification. The one actually chosen was the work of a Swedish engineer named Nordenfeldt. He promptly set up a new company, with retired Admiral Sir Astley Cooper Key as chairman, to manufacture it. Armstrong simultaneously developed large-caliber quick-firing guns whose power much exceeded the specifications of 1881. The largest of these used hydraulic recoil cylinders to return the gun automatically to firing position after each discharge. This, together with radically improved breech mechanisms and a simple device for sealing the chamber at the moment of ignition—both borrowed from French artillery designs—made the Armstrong quick-firing guns of 1887 profoundly revolutionary. All subsequent artillery, indeed, derives basically from this combination of features which allowed the gun to fire several times a minute and still remain almost on target, round after round. The man mainly responsible for the new recoil system was Joseph Vavasseur. His personal and professional association with Admiral Fisher became so close that he made Fisher's son the heir to his fortune, having no children of his own.[31]

Command technology was not entirely new in 1881, of course. As we saw in chapter 4 sporadic instances of similar relationships between officials and inventors appeared in the eighteenth century, and perhaps even earlier. Indeed, from the 1860s, as warship design began to alter rapidly, it became usual for the Admiralty to specify the basic characteristics a new ship should have—speed, size, armor, and arma-

---

30. Full specifications included: a three-man crew, six-pound projectile, overall weight of not more than a thousand pounds, etc. See William Laird Clowes, *The Royal Navy: A History from Earliest Times to the Death of Queen Victoria* (London, 1903), 7:48.

31. Mackay, *Fisher of Kilverstone*, p. 252.

ment. Sometimes more specific requirements were set forth, e.g., with respect to all-round fire from turrets when they were first introduced.[32]

What distinguished the situation that developed after 1884 was not so much any absolute novelty as the range, breadth, and constantly expanding ramifications of the new naval version of command technology.[33] Indeed, for thirty years, 1884–1914, it grew like a cancer within the tissues of the world's market economy which earlier had seemed immortal as well as invincible.

Even a hasty review of the major landmarks of naval technological change between 1884 and 1914 will demonstrate the enlarged scope command technology attained in these years. After quick-firing guns—which rapidly escalated in size with only a modest diminution in rate of fire[34]—came the escalation of ships' speed. The initial departure lay in the development of a new "tube boiler" design, pioneered by a boat builder named Alfred Yarrow. He won an Admiralty contract to build a new type of vessel first called "torpedo boat destroyers" but soon known simply as destroyers. Their task was to intercept torpedo boats before they could get dangerously close to capital ships. This required destroyers to be faster than their prey and also seaworthy. It was a tall order, yet the first destroyer, launched in 1893, attained a speed of over 26 knots—some two to three knots faster than contemporary torpedo boats. Four years afterwards, when Yarrow's boilers were hitched up to steam turbines (patented by Charles Parsons in 1884), the result was a ship capable of over 36 knots—more than twice the speed warships of a decade earlier had been able to attain.[35]

In 1898 and again in 1905 actual sea battles in distant waters gave naval designers a better idea of what their new warships could achieve in combat. The Spanish-American War of 1898 showed the penalty of lagging behind technically, for obsolete Spanish vessels were no match for the newer American ships. Yet United States naval bombardments

32. Cf. Stanley Sandler, *The Emergence of the Modern Capital Ship* (Newark, N.J., 1979), pp. 306–13.

33. Hugh Lyon, "The Relations between the Admiralty and Private Industry in the Development of Warships" in Ranft, *Technical Change and British Naval Policy*, pp. 37–64, offers a useful conspectus.

34. Very elaborate and powerful machinery for pointing and loading the big guns had also to be developed—and constantly improved. By 1914, enormous revolving turrets descended deep into the bowels of the ship. Inside each turret loading machinery moved with the guns so as always to be able to serve them, no matter what their azimuth and elevation.

35. Oscar Parkes, *British Battleships: "Warrior" to Vanguard,"* rev. ed., (London, 1970), p. 377; Clowes, *The Royal Navy,* 7:39, 54.

in Manila Bay, under calm conditions, and at Santiago Bay in a rougher sea, proved embarrassingly inaccurate.[36] Subsequent efforts to improve aiming methods met with such success, that when the Japanese defeated and destroyed the Russian navy in Tsushima Straits (1905), they were able to deliver punishing fire at up to 13,000 yards. This was about twice the range that had baffled American marksmen in Manila Bay seven years before.[37]

H.M.S. *Dreadnought* was the Royal Navy's answer to these developments. Designed for long-range gunnery, it outclassed all existing warships, thanks to a combination of superior speed and firepower. At 21 knots, the *Dreadnought* could outstrip all other capital ships by some two to three knots; and its broadside of ten twelve-inch rifles far exceeded the throw weight attainable by older battleships. Oil fuel and turbine engines of unprecedented size gave the *Dreadnought* an impressive range on top of its other characteristics. Its comparatively light armor scarcely mattered, if accurate gunnery at long ranges could be achieved, since its speed would permit the captain to choose when and where and at what range to engage an enemy.[38]

In 1906, however, the Royal Navy's ability to hit a moving target from the deck of a pitching ship that was itself moving at speed and might be obliged to change course while engaged against a foe was very much in question. Intense efforts to solve the problem extended naval guns' effective range spectacularly, but when war broke out in 1914, most Royal Navy ships were not yet equipped with the improved range finders and centralized fire control apparatus which experts had developed. Moreover, British range finders were inferior to comparable German equipment and the whole system fell short of making the guns carried by the newer ships effective at anything like their full range. In 1912, for example, fifteen-inch guns, capable of lofting a shell 35,000 yards (20 miles), were ordered from Armstrong, but the Royal Navy's range finders were inadequate at 16,000 yards.[39]

36. At Manila Bay, 5,895 shots resulted in only 142 hits; at Santiago, 8,000 shots achieved only 121 hits, according to official reckoning afterwards. Donald W. Mitchell, *History of the Modern American Navy from 1883 through Pearl Harbor* (London, 1947), pp. 73, 105.

37. Parkes, *British Battleships*, p. 461.

38. On the dreadnought revolution in naval architecture see ibid., pp. 466–86; Arthur Marder, *The Anatomy of British Sea Power: A History of British Naval Policy in the Pre-Dreadnought Era, 1880–1905* (New York, 1940), pp. 505–43; Arthur Marder, *From Dreadnought to Scapa Flow*, vol. 1, *The Road to War, 1905–1914* (London, 1961), pp. 43–70; Mackay, *Fisher of Kilverstone*, pp. 293 ff.; Richard Hough, *First Sea Lord: An Authorized Biography of Admiral Lord Fisher* (London, 1969), pp. 252 ff.

39. Parkes, *British Battleships*, pp. 560, 592; Peter Padfield, *Guns at Sea* (New York, 1974), pp. 195–252. Elting E. Morison, *Men, Machines and Modern Times* (Cambridge,

Technology Takes Command

The photograph on the left shows H.M.S. Dreadnought, *the speedy, heavy-gunned battleship that altered the basis of naval competition between Britain and Germany when it was launched in 1906. Insets show views from bow and stern. But submarines already constituted a threat to even the most heavily armed and armored battleships, as the artist's drawing (upper right) suggests. Note the periscope, invented only three years before. Airplanes were also developing rapidly as shown in the 1906 photograph of a French aviator (lower right) who seems to be flying backward in his push-prop plane.*

Illustrated London News, 1906, pp. 548 (20 Oct.), 301 (1 Sept.), and 841 (8 Dec.)

Torpedo ranges, meanwhile, spurted upward,[40] and improved torpedo-carrying submarines made them far more of a threat to the Royal Navy than the torpedo boats of the 1880s had ever been. As before, the French took the lead when Gustave Zédé designed the first practicable seagoing submersible in 1887. In 1903, periscopes gave submarines eyes with which to aim torpedoes at their targets while remaining submerged. This imparted fresh substance to the long-standing French dream of finding a new weapon with which to destroy British sovereignty of the seas. But the Franco-British naval race, briefly reinvigorated by Fashoda (1898), soon dwindled to insignificance. The diplomatic entente of 1904 made nonsense of the French plan to build submarines for use against Great Britain. Resources were concentrated instead on outbuilding France's Mediterranean rivals—Italy, Austria, and Turkey.[41]

Anglo-German rivalry, however, which set in seriously only after 1898, concentrated almost exclusively on capital ships because Admiral Tirpitz and his colleagues accepted Mahan's teachings wholeheartedly. Submarines seemed to him no more than minor adjuncts to the battleships which alone could exercise command of the sea. As a result of such single-mindedness, in the decade after the *Dreadnought* revolution of 1906 battleship design showed signs of approaching a limit set by the physical characteristics of the alloyed steel used in engines, guns and armor.

Any such incipient stabilization was destined to be upset by the rise of air power, a possibility clearly foreseen before 1914. The Royal Navy, for instance, conducted successful experiments with torpedo-carrying airplanes in 1913, though difficulties in making a torpedo

---

Mass., 1966) has some perceptive things to say about the strains that the first phase of this revolution in naval gunnery put on older patterns of shipboard relationships.

40. A table of guaranteed performance levels supplied by the Whitehead torpedo factory for its longest-range models in successive years show highlights:

Year	Torpedo Range (in yards)
1866	220
1876	600
1905	2,190
1906	6,560
1913	18,590

These figures come from Gray, *The Devil's Device*, Appendix.

41. I have not found any really satisfactory account of French naval policy between 1884 and 1914, but see Ernest H. Jenkins, *A History of the French Navy* (London, 1973), pp. 303 ff.; Bueb, *Die "Junge Schule" der französischen Marine;* Joannès Tramond and André Reussner, *Eléments d'histoire maritime et coloniale contemporaine, 1815–1914,* new ed. (Paris, 1947), pp. 652 ff.; Salaun, *La marine française,* pp. 1–75.

establish an appropriate path through the water after being dropped from the air were not entirely solved when the war began.[42]

As of 1914, the British Admiralty had developed no technical riposte to these new underwater and airborne challenges to capital ships. The fears that had been played upon in 1884 to mobilize support for the technical modernization of the Royal Navy were as lively as ever and rather better based in technical fact. Like the Red Queen in *Through the Looking Glass* Britain and all the other naval powers had to run ever faster just to stay in the same place. Indeed, thanks to the German naval building program, after 1898 the Royal Navy faced a more serious challenge at sea than at any time since the 1770s. But before considering this vindication of Admiral Sir Astley Cooper Key's foresight concerning the consequences of Fisher's initiative of 1884, it seems well to consider how the naval race affected British society in the decades before World War I, for this was the time when the modern military-industrial complex suddenly came of age and began, in the very citadel of European liberalism, to exhibit a wayward will of its own.

Naval Armament and the Politicization of Economics

First of all, naval construction and the manufacture of the diverse kinds of machinery that went into warships became really big business. Instead of lagging behind civil engineering, as had been the case in 1855 when William Armstrong decided it was time to bring gun-making abreast of contemporary standards, military technology came to constitute the leading edge of British (and world) engineering and technical development.[43] According to one calculation, about a quarter of a million civilians, or 2.5 percent of the entire male work force of Great Britain, was employed by the navy or by prime naval contractors in 1897;[44] and by 1913 when naval appropriations had doubled the figure for 1897, estimates make as much as one-sixth of Britain's work force dependent on naval contracting.[45]

The process through which welfare and warfare linked together to

---

42. Gray, *The Devil's Device,* p. 206.

43. Trebilcock, "Spin-off in British Economic History," pp. 474–80.

44. W. Ashworth, "Economic Aspects of Late Victorian Naval Administration," *Economic History Review* 22 (1969): 492.

45. Marder, *Anatomy of British Sea Power,* pp. 25–37. This is probably an exaggeration, but I have not found a responsible econometric calculation. See also William Ashworth, *An Economic History of England, 1870–1939* (London, 1960), pp. 236–37 for remarks on the navy's economic role.

support the naval race had its shady side. Outright bribery and corruption played a lesser role than half-truths and deliberate deceptions. Businessmen seeking contracts found support from their local MPs helpful in persuading Admiralty officers to incline in their direction; and candidates for Parliament found contributions from grateful or merely hopeful constituents useful in meeting election expenses. Newspaper agitation, too, could be arranged by giving cooperative journalists inside information, or by entertaining them lavishly while hinting at secrets they were expected to trumpet to the world the next day.

Using these techniques, naval officers began to fight battles among themselves through calculated and uncalculated leaks to the press, exacerbated, as often as not, by journalists' speculation and plain rumor-mongering. In particular, a personal vendetta between Admiral Fisher and Admiral Charles Beresford, conducted largely through the press and in Parliament, came to involve almost every aspect of Admiralty affairs. Naval officers achieved star billing in the popular press, much as movie actors were later to do, and sometimes behaved like spoiled children.

Rules of the game were unclear. Muckraking journalism dated back only to the scandals of the Crimean War, and all who undertook to manipulate public affairs through newspapers faced awkward tensions between personal advantage and presumed public good. A journalist who built up circulation at the expense of truth was on morally dubious ground. So was the manufacturer who set out to influence a naval contract by contributing to politicians' election funds. The morals of naval officers who resorted to the press as a means of criticizing their superiors or who tried to influence public policies by divulging secret information were also questionable, since their private sense of "higher duty" to the nation collided with long-standing rules of obedience and discipline. Yet personal careers were made and broken by such gambits, as Admiral Sir John Fisher's example so conspicuously demonstrated.

Any important change in society is likely to entail disturbances in prevailing moral codes and patterns of conduct. The moral ambiguities inherent in the new way of mobilizing resources, so flamboyantly inaugurated in 1884, perhaps only registered the importance of this new path for getting things done.

How powerfully it operated is best summed up by the figures in table 1. Thus we see that while army costs fell short of doubling, navy costs multiplied almost five times in thirty years, and this in an age of

Table 1. Authorized Expenditures (£ million)

Year	Army and Ordnance	Navy
1884	16.1	10.7
1889	16.0	13.0
1894	17.9	15.5
1899	20.0	24.1
1904	36.7	35.5
1909	26.8	32.3
1914	28.3	48.8

Source: B. R. Mitchell, *Abstracts of British Statistics* (Cambridge, 1971), pp. 397–98.

almost stable price levels. Clearly, by embracing new technology and the private sector as suppliers of armaments, the Royal Navy succeeded in capturing a larger slice of public appropriations in a time when the army, remaining loyal to older forms of management and relying almost wholly on arsenal production and design for its weapons, lagged far behind.

Intensified interaction between industry and the navy brought serious new pressures on two other facets of public management, the one financial, the other technical.

Financial problems became especially acute because of the unpredictability of costs. This in turn arose out of the very rapidity with which new devices and processes were introduced. Over and over again, a promising new idea proved far more expensive than it first appeared would be the case; yet to halt in midstream or refuse to try something new until its feasibility had been thoroughly tested meant handing over technical leadership to someone else's navy.

The Royal Navy, of course, was not supposed to spend more than Parliament authorized. But from the time of Samuel Pepys and before, the Admiralty had been in the habit of borrowing money from London bankers to meet current expenses whenever outgo ran ahead of parliamentary grants. As long as ships and guns changed slowly, if at all, costs were quite predictable. A prudent Board of Admiralty could therefore borrow in emergency and then repay when Parliament saw fit to cover past deficits without piling up dangerously heavy debt. The system gave Parliament more or less what it paid for, while the Admiralty had a useful flexibility in managing its affairs.

But when technology began to change as rapidly as it did after 1880, predictable limits to expenditures faded from sight. Borrowing to cover cost overruns became irresistible. Not to borrow might hold up completion of a new ship or allow the Germans to outstrip the Royal

Navy in some important technical development. Yet if borrowing to cover excess costs went too far, interest payments alone would soon eat seriously into current appropriations. In pursuing a go-for-broke policy in technical matters, the Admiralty therefore found itself heading straight towards what would be bankruptcy for any private firm, and that despite the upward curve of parliamentary appropriations.

Under the circumstances, parliamentary control over naval expenditure began to dissolve. Ordinary members of Parliament knew little or nothing about Admiralty borrowing, and, like the general public, assumed that annual appropriations registered and regulated what was actually spent. By 1909, the situaion had got so far out of hand that it became necessary to find new sources of tax money to pay off past indebtedness while simultaneously expanding the scale of naval building. Lloyd George's famous budget of 1909, with its soak-the-rich and social welfare provisions, was the government's answer to the problem. It showed, clearly enough, that an all-out arms race could be conducted only by a government prepared to intervene drastically in prevailing socioeconomic relationships. In particular, progressive taxes, heavy enough to effect perceptible redistribution of wealth within society, were needed to mobilize resources for public purposes on the necessary scale. The House of Lords' effort to block the new taxes imposed by Lloyd George's budget, and the quasi-revolutionary atmosphere that resulted from the government's determination to override the peers and nullify their veto, was an important element in the general breakup of liberal nineteenth-century society and institutions that came to a head during World War I.

Financial uncertainty and disordering of accustomed patterns of management were not confined to the Admiralty and Treasury. On the contrary, the new arms technology also presented private armaments firms with extremely difficult managerial problems. Feast or famine was the usual alternative they faced. Some firms' fat profits (Vickers averaged at 13.3 percent dividend on its capital in the first decade of the twentieth century)[46] were matched by the bankruptcy or threatened bankruptcy of others. Admiralty policy in awarding contracts, a policy that itself wavered between narrowly pecuniary and broader political considerations, played the decisive role more often than not in determining which firms flourished and which would go under.

Ordinary market behavior had only limited scope in such an envi-

46. Scott, *Vickers,* p. 81.

ronment. Special relationships with procurement officials and with technically innovative officers often mattered more than prices in deciding who got a contract and who was passed over. Yet this cozy relationship among experts was also subject to jarring disturbance from outside when overtly political pressures to economize, or to spread the work by helping some depressed region or firm, were brought to bear.

Conventional cost accounting was an imperfect instrument for anyone trying to manage an arms firm under these circumstances. A contract to built a piece of machinery that had never been seen on earth before commonly required capital investment of a substantial sort. But whether the new facility would continue to be used or would instead have to be discarded after the completion of a single contract because some new device or design had come along in the meanwhile and rendered it obsolete—this no one could ever know for certain. What then was the proper cost to assign to such an undertaking? Could and should a firm expect to recover its entire capital costs from a single contract? If so, the price would have to be very high; and any subsequent utilization of the new capital plant would be sure to bring in those swollen profits of which armaments producers were later to be so vigorously accused. But if capital costs were instead amortized over a longer period of time, what guarantee was there that fresh contracts would be forthcoming so that the new plant would not simply stand idle after the initial contract had been fulfilled? Neither Admiralty officials nor private entrepreneurs could answer such questions with any kind of precision in a world of rapidly changing techniques. It was, therefore, a high risk business—inevitably.

To be sure, foreign sales could make such problems far less acute for the private firm, but only as long as the Admiralty did not impose restrictions upon letting foreigners share technical secrets that derived from research and development which had been funded, at least in part, by public monies.[47] Collusive bidding among competing firms was an even more obvious way to reduce risks. The Admiralty countered by looking around for new firms and inducing them to enter the arms trade as a way of expanding supply, lowering prices, and forestalling monopoly. This was how Vickers entered the arms business in

47. Restrictions of this kind became increasingly important. Secrecy, indeed, tended to supplant patents as a mode of protecting new technology, if only because the public deposit of plans and drawings required to support a patent allowed rival firms and countries to borrow what they liked (perhaps with minor variations to make patent infringement legally debatable), or to develop a superior device with full knowledge of the performance characteristics of the rival product.

1888, for example, responding to urgent solicitation from the Admiralty to bid on a contract for armor plate. But Vickers' decision also reflected the firm's mounting difficulty in matching American and German steel prices on the civilian market. By moving into armaments production, Vickers successfully insulated itself from foreign cost competition, since the Admiralty was not interested in buying armaments from any but British suppliers.[48]

With costs so unpredictable on both the private and the public side, the reality of competition and open bidding diminished rapidly. New firms like Vickers quickly learned how to cooperate with Armstrong and other established arms makers. To be sure, a new patent might permit the entry of another firm into the arms trade; but such companies regularly confronted financial crisis once initial contracts had been fulfilled since new orders were usually not forthcoming on a scale to keep their capital plant busy. Under such conditions, the universal response was to amalgamate with older arms makers and form corporations whose financial and technical resources then would allow managers to spread risks within the firm by shifting men and machinery from one to another contract as the needs of the Admiralty (and foreign sales) might dictate.

Such firms, when they became big enough, assumed many of the characteristics of a government bureaucracy. Being in a monopolistic or at least quasi-monopolistic position with respect to capacity for making complex armament items, they could bargain on more or less even terms with Admiralty purchasing agents, who, increasingly, had nowhere else to turn when they sought to buy highly specialized (and often secret) new kinds of equipment. Private arms makers, in other words, came more and more to resemble the Woolwich arsenal, with the difference that the navy and their suppliers were accustomed to live with far more radical technical changeability than anything that had yet descended upon the army and the arsenal.

How rapidly amalgamation of British arms firms occurred may be illustrated from the history of the Maxim Gun Company. Having been established to make machine guns in 1884, it merged, just four years later, with the Nordenfeldt Company. Then the Maxim-Nordenfeldt Company was bought out by Vickers in 1897. Armstrong, too, entered upon a series of mergers, the most important of which was the acquisition of Whitworth's, its long-standing rival, in 1897. By 1900, therefore, two big firms, Vickers and Armstrong, dominated the business of heavy armaments in Great Britain. Each dealt with the Admi-

48. Scott, *Vickers,* pp. 20, 42.

ralty on a quasi-public basis. That is to say, considerations of the political and economic consequences of how any big new contract was to be shared out between the two great firms and their lesser rivals came to be an important consideration in Admiralty decision-making, competing with and sometimes overriding simple pecuniary calculation.[49]

In the foreign field, where competition with Krupp and the principal French arms manufacturer, Schneider-Creusot, became intense after 1885, considerations of national prestige, diplomatic alignments, and outright bribery frequently entered into deciding what kind of guns or warships a technically backward country would purchase. Credit arrangements, often at least partly inspired by foreign offices' representations to private bankers, were even more decisive, since few of the arms-purchasing countries could come across with cash to pay for the weaponry they wanted.

Once they had consolidated their position in the home market, Vickers and Armstrong found it imprudent to compete against each other abroad. By 1906, they had, in effect, achieved market-sharing agreements covering most of the globe. In addition, patent and royalty arrangements with Krupp gave the two British firms access to some of Krupp's metallurgical inventions, while Krupp got rights to certain British patents in return. Schneider had similar arrangements too. In this way an international arms ring, which became the object of intense opprobrium after World War I, came into existence. Pecuniary considerations ordinarily dictated cooperation and collusive bidding among the leading firms. On the other hand, political rivalries and national pride made for cutthroat competition and sometimes set prices at uneconomic levels. What really happened depended on how these contrary forces interacted in each particular case.

Ever since the technological breakaway of the 1850s, private arms manufacturers had prospered by entering the foreign market as a way of increasing their income and smoothing out peaks and valleys created by fluctuating home demand for their products. As long as invention and costs of development were met entirely by private firms, this did not raise any particularly delicate moral questions; but after

49. Two excellent books, Scott, *Vickers*, and Clive A. Trebilcock, *The Vickers Brothers: Armaments and Enterprise, 1854–1914* (London, 1977) provide the main basis for these remarks. Noel-Baker, *Private Manufacture of Armaments*, vol. 1, and Helmut Carl Engelbrecht and F. C. Hanighen, *Merchants of Death: A Study of the International Armaments Industry* (New York, 1934) express the hostile, scandal-mongering outlook that prevailed in the 1930s; Dougan, *The Great Gunmaker: The Story of Lord Armstrong* partakes of the apologetic tradition instead, though all contain relevant if sometimes unreliable information.

the 1880s, when intimate collaboration between navy officers and private engineers and production experts entered into the development of every important new device, foreign sales did begin to raise serious questions about who had the right to sell what, and to whom. National loyalty obstructed profitable dealing with potential enemies. By operating in lands allied or aligned with the home country, this dilemma could be sidestepped, at least as long as the diplomatic constellation remained unchanged. But patent-sharing agreements between British arms firms and Krupp, some of which were honored even during World War I years, raised the issue of which came first —the nation or the firm, public good or private enrichment—and in especially poignant fashion.[50]

Overall, it seems clear that as arms firms became pioneers of one new technology after another—steel metallurgy, industrial chemistry, electrical machinery, radio communications, turbines, diesels, optics, calculators (for fire control), hydraulic machinery, and the like—they evolved quickly into vast bureaucratic structures of a quasi-public character. Technical and financial decisions made within the big firms began to have public importance. The actual quality of their weapons mattered vitally to the rival states and armed services of Europe. After 1866 and 1870, everyone recognized that some newly won technical superiority might bring decisive advantage in war. Each technical option in arms design therefore carried a heavy freight of political and military implications and had to be taken with an eye both to the national interest and to the financial future of the firm within which the new device was being developed.

Fast acting feedback loops thus arose whereby financial and man-

50. Trebilcock, *The Vickers Brothers* is especially perceptive in treating the way private managers strove to minimize risks and react rationally to the market they served. In a series of articles he discussed these same issues more concisely and more generally. All by Clive A. Trebilcock, they are: "Legends of the British Armaments Industry: A Revision," *Journal of Contemporary History* 5 (1970): 2–19; "A 'Special Relationship'— Government, Rearmament and the Cordite Firms," *Economic History Review* 19 (1966): 364–79; and "British Armaments and European Industrialization, 1890–1914," *Economic History Review* 26 (1973): 254–72. The last is an especially striking article. Trebilcock argues that the scale and economic importance of public investment in arms manufacture between 1890 and 1914 deserve comparison with the earlier effort governments made to build railroads. Both strategies for modernization used public credit to channel massive investment along new lines where private capital would not, by itself, have gone. He even argues that spin off from armaments affected local economies at large almost as much as railroads had done earlier. At the peak of the official effort to import new arms technologies, he calculates that Spain spent 2 percent of its national income on the task (in 1906) while Japan devoted no less than 10.3 percent of its national income to the same purpose in 1903. Other countries that went along this path fell between these extremes; but in each case the effort was massive and made a major

agerial decisions in the Admiralty meshed into financial and managerial decisions made within what were still ostensibly private firms. Public and private policy became irremediably intertwined. Liberal critics of the 1920s and 1930s and Marxist or quasi-Marxist historians since the 1950s assert that the dominating element in this mix was the private one. The pursuit of profit, according to this view, provided the energizing force. Everything else was derivative, manipulated by clever and greedy men who wished to enrich themselves and the stockholders they served.

This seems a distorted vision of human motivation and behavior. No doubt when patriotism and profit were seen to coincide, the response was so much the more electric; and this was the way private managers of arms firms usually viewed their roles. But the abstract challenge of problem-solving has its part in governing human actions, and the arms trade attracted more than its share of technically innovative minds in the pre–World War I period simply because it was there that industrial research was most vigorously underway.[51] One innovator attracted others in chain-reaction fashion.

Moreover, concepts of technical efficiency, public service, and advancing a career by making the right decisions clearly dominated the minds of the naval officers who played such a large role in the entire process. The power of promotion in rank to focus ambition and inspire men to strenuous effort is very great indeed, as anyone who has served in a modern army or navy can attest. Promotion carried economic perquisites, to be sure; but what really mattered was the deference and precedence over others that advance in rank entailed. If the profit motive had really dominated behavior, Admiral Fisher would not have turned down a job offer he got from Whitworth's in 1887, for example, nor would the naval designer William White have returned to the Admiralty at one-third of the salary he had received during his two years at Armstrong's.

The public interest, as colored by careerism within the naval command hierarchy, together with overtly political pressures coming from the Cabinet and through Parliament, probably did more to control the overall direction of technical change than did private considerations of profit. But it is really unhistorical to ask which of a complex of motives

difference to the national economy as a whole by establishing new skills, new demands, and a new flow of public credit and taxes.

51. The personality of Tom Vickers, the engineering enterpriser behind the rise of Vickers, illustrates how technology can become an end in itself. Tom Vickers lived wholly for his work. Wealth, ownership, and the trappings of property meant little or nothing to him. Cf. Trebilcock, *The Vickers Brothers,* p. 33.

dominated decision-making. The important thing was how closely public and private motives intertwined. Market and pecuniary considerations were not firmly subordinated to political command before 1914; but then, political and military decisions were not subordinated to profit maximizing by private manufacturers either.[52]

The push towards making political decisions into the critical basis of economic innovation was clearly apparent in the weaker and less industrialized countries of Europe before 1914; and in Japan it was unmistakable. But Britain and Germany, too, were moving rapidly in that direction from the 1880s onward. In the politicization of the decision-making by which they lived, as in high technology, the great arms firms were far in the lead of other industrial sectors. The arms firms and the armed forces that dealt with them thus became the primary shapers of the twin processes that constitute a distinctive hallmark of the twentieth century: the industrialization of war and the politicization of economics.

The Limits of Rational Design and Management

The rush of new technology that cascaded upon the Royal Navy after 1884 not only put strains on morals, money, and managerial organization; it also began to get out of control itself. By the eve of World War I, fire control devices had become so complex that the admirals who had to decide what to approve and what to reject no longer understood what was at issue when rival designs were offered to them. The mathematical principles involved and the mechanical linkages fire control devices relied upon were simply too much for harassed and busy men to master. Decisions were therefore made in ignorance, often for financial or personal or political reasons.

The secrets of steel metallurgy, too, are exceedingly complex, and admirals presumably never understood the chemistry behind each of the new alloys that revolutionized guns and armor time and again. But the tests to be applied to guns and armor were fairly obvious,[53] and after a test anyone could tell which gun or sample piece of armor plate was superior. When it came to fire control devices, similar tests could perhaps have been devised. But there was much room for difference of opinion about what suitable conditions for trials should be: parallel

52. Cf. the acerbic iconoclasm of Peter Wiles, "War and Economic Systems," in *Science et conscience de la société: Mélanges en honneur de Raymond Aron* (Paris, 1971), 2:269–97.

53. Even here, the British Admiralty found to its regret at Jutland in 1916 that shells hitting an armored surface at an acute angle behave differently from shells that hit head on. Tests had always been conducted for right-angled hits only; as a result many British

courses for both the target and the test ship presented entirely different problems from zigzag courses, while high speed made a ship toss differently from what it did at low speed, and a rough day made more difference still. Moreover, it was an expensive thing to hitch up the guns of a battleship to a machine capable of pointing every gun of the ship at a target. Such an installation had to be made by experts who thereby learned even the most secret inner workings of the ship.

The most fundamental issue, perhaps, was how to define the desired level of performance for fire control devices. This depended, in turn, on what kind of future battle was envisaged. If the Germans planned to come out and fight in Nelsonian fashion by laying alongside, then equipment that could pick up an enemy at 20,000 yards in poor light and drop the first salvo of shells in his vicinity was not critically important. Yet if a machine capable of such refinement could be invented, what navy could safely be without it?

This became a real dilemma for the Royal Navy when an ingenious private citizen named A. J. H. Pollen claimed to have solved the mathematical and mechanical problems inherent in accurate aiming at long range even from a moving and tossing ship. When he approached the Admiralty with drawings of his device in 1906, Admiral Fisher responded with enthusiasm, and declared that the navy should stop at nothing to get exclusive rights to the invention. Within a month, Pollen signed a contract guaranteeing him £100,000 and a handsome royalty on future sales if tests showed that his machine could do what he claimed. On the strength of this contract, Pollen set up a new company to manufacture his invention. He soon got into financial trouble, for there were all the usual complications in actually building a working model. Meanwhile, the Admiralty also was facing financial difficulties; and when a technically proficient officer decided that he could design a machine just as good as Pollen's, the Admiralty saw a way of saving the promised £100,000. It took four years for the navy's own machine to achieve a workable form, and that only after plagiarizing from a Pollen prototype in 1911.[54] Nonetheless by 1913, Winston Churchill, then First Lord of the Admiralty, could say in Parliament:

"It is not intended to adopt the Pollen system, but to rely on a more satisfactory one which has been developed by service ex-

---

armor-piercing shells, striking German vessels at far greater range than had been anticipated, simply glanced off or exploded before penetrating the armor. German shells had been tested for glancing fire and behaved more effectively, thanks to an appropriate design.

54. A Royal Commission in 1926 officially recognized this infringement of patent rights, awarding Pollen a sum of £30,000 in compensation. Cf. Anthony Pollen, *The*

perts. . . . I have been guided by the representations of my naval
colleagues and the advice of experts on whom the Admiralty must
rely."[55]

Yet the machine "developed by service experts" could only work if
a ship followed a straight-line course while firing its guns, whereas Pollen's device could adjust for a changing course as well. There were
other defects in the fire control system installed on British ships from
1913 onwards. In particular, the Royal Navy's optical range finders
gave far less accurate results than those the Germans used at Jutland.
Tests which might have shown the superiority of Pollen's system were
never held. To have done so would have cost large sums, risked having
to pay the £100,000 the Admiralty had promised Pollen in case of success, and discredited an influential coterie of experts inside the Admiralty as well.[56]

One may argue, of course, that a machine capable of working under
limited conditions and costing a good deal less was indeed, as
Churchill said in Parliament, "more satisfactory" than the more expensive private design. Given the financial pressures that the navy had
begun to experience, reasonable men might so decide. Moreover,
firing from line-ahead formation was traditional. How else could an
admiral keep control of a fleet and bring maximum firepower to bear?
How else could naval tradition be upheld in a desperately confusing
world? If it made range-finding for the enemy easier than firing from a
zigzag pattern would do, what matter? The preferred tactic among
British admirals was to fall back on the Nelsonian formula and close
the range as fast as possible so as to achieve a decisive victory. To alter
fleet management and tactical doctrine in deference to a piece of machinery few besides its inventor really understood—that was too
much.

It seems clear that the angry cross-purposes that came to bear upon
the controversy quite obscured the technical matters at issue. Few

---

Great Gunnery Scandal: The Mystery of Jutland (London, 1980), p. 145. This book,
written by the inventor's son, polemically corrects earlier misinformation about Pollen's
work. Playing fast and loose with private patent rights was not unprecedented. In a
famous instance, Admiral Fisher himself sent copies of Alfred Yarrow's boiler designs
for the new destroyers to rival shipbuilders. Yarrow advertised publicly for information
that might lead to the discovery of the culprit; and a public apology was made by the
navy, but without ever openly implicating Fisher. Hough, *First Sea Lord,* p. 101; Eleanor
C. Barnes, *Alfred Yarrow, His Life and Work* (London, 1923), pp. 102–5.

55. *Parliamentary Debates,* Commons, 30 June 1913, vol. 54, col. 1478.
56. Pollen was a friend of Admiral Beresford. This made him *persona non grata* to
Fisher and his followers, who remained in control of the Admiralty after 1906.

understood fully what was at stake. The whole question was supposed to be secret, and was in fact secret from all but a small number of insiders. But the men who had to decide were not themselves technically well informed and relied on what others told them. Under such circumstances Pollen's status as a civilian, tainted with greed,[57] put his salesmanship at a hopeless disadvantage against the advocacy of "service experts" for their own, technically inferior, invention. As an angry admiral wrote in 1912:

> By placing Mr Pollen in the position of a favoured inventor we have put him in possession of the most complicated items of our Fire Control system and we are being constantly pressed by Mr Pollen to pay him large sums of money to keep that information for our exclusive use. Each time we pay him thus (monopoly rights) he gains more confidential information. . . . . it is a chain around our necks being forged more and more relentlessly.[58]

The decision to settle for an inferior system of fire control was particularly ill advised inasmuch as the Royal Navy seemed committed to bombardment at extreme range. The so-called battle cruisers (under construction 1905–10) had guns of the very largest size and could move at the highest speeds, but lacked more than rudimentary armor.[59] They could hope to confront enemy battleships with impunity only by using their speed to hover just out of reach, while pounding their opponent to pieces by outranging his fire. Fisher conceived these super ships as constituting a second revolution in ship design, comparable to the famous *Dreadnought* revolution with which he had inaugurated his regime at the Admiralty. But without fire control machinery capable of exploiting the superior range of their heavy guns, such vessels were death traps, or close to it.

Oddly, no one seemed to care, not even Admiral Fisher, whose ini-

---

57. After deciding against Pollen's fire control devices in 1912 the company he had founded was stricken from the list of contractors with whom the Admiralty was authorized to do business. Like Armstrong in 1863, Pollen then proceeded to try to sell his product to other navies, and did so to the Russians. As his son points out, however, he patriotically did not offer his know-how to the Germans. On the other hand, negotiations with the United States Navy, and with Brazil, Chile, Austria, and Italy must have made the principles of Pollen's fire control devices readily accessible to German naval experts, if they had been interested. Pollen, *The Great Gunnery Scandal*, pp. 96, 108, 114. Pollen's company was in dire financial straits once Admiralty advances were turned off—a history that illustrates the perils of armaments business for a small company attempting to enter it.

58. Ibid., p. 116.

59. Parkes, *British Battleships*, p. 486.

tial enthusiasm for Pollen's invention evaporated when his subordinates told him that their cheaper device would do. Fisher's tactial conception for the new battle cruisers was never even established as doctrine. Instead, Admiral Lord Beatty, who took command of the battle cruiser squadron in 1913, regarded his ships as a kind of sea cavalry whose superior speed should be used in reconnaissance and to lead the charge in battle. Traditionally minded naval officers, perhaps, felt that there was something sneaky and un-Nelsonian about trying to hover beyond the enemy's reach while pounding him at extreme range. It could not be done anyway with the navy's existing fire control devices. Hence, regulations prescribing target practice at 9,000 yards—a distance likely to be suicidal for thinly armored battle cruisers—remained in force. Bureaucratic inertia, however irrational, prevailed.[60]

In retrospect, at least, it seems clear that factional infighting and technical illiteracy combined with penny-pinching (what was Pollen's £100,000 compared to the cost of a battle cruiser?) to make a botch of things. The Royal Navy paid for these errors at Jutland, where the long range at which the battle was fought, and the changes of course that took place during the encounter, diminished British chances of winning decisive victory of the kind they had counted on.[61]

Thus it seems correct to say that technical questions got out of control on the eve of World War I in the sense that established ways of handling them no longer assured reasonably rational or practically satisfactory choices. Secrecy obstructed wisdom; so did clique rivalries and suspicion of self-seeking. Most of all, the mathematical complexity of the problem—a complexity which clearly surpassed the comprehension of many of the men most intimately concerned—deprived policy of even residual rationality.

The technical revolution so brashly unleashed in 1884 could scarcely have had a more ironical outcome. Like so many other aspects of the naval race of the first years of the century, this, too, was a foretaste of things to come, anticipating the technologically uncontrolled and uncontrollable age in which we currently find ourselves. A colossal paradox lay in the fact that energetic effort to rationalize

60. Stephen Roskill, *Admiral of the Fleet Lord Beatty: The Last Naval Hero* (London, 1980), pp. 59–72.

61. My understanding of these fire control controversies depends on Jon T. Sumida, "British Capital Ships and Fire Control in the *Dreadnought* Era: Sir John Fisher, Arthur Hungerford Pollen and the Battle Cruiser," *Journal of Modern History* 51 (1979): 205–30, and on his remarkable Ph.D. dissertation "Financial Limitation, Technological Innovation and British Naval Policy, 1904–1910" (University of Chicago, 1982).

management, having won enormous and impressive victories on every front,[62] nevertheless acted to put the social system as a whole out of control. As its parts became more rational, more manageable, more predictable, the general human context in which the Royal Navy and its rivals existed became more disordered and more unmanageable.[63]

International Repercussions

The international side of this paradox is its most obvious aspect, for, as is well-known, military-industrial complexes spread swiftly from Great Britain to other industrial lands. Up to the 1890s, France had constituted the only plausible naval rival Great Britain had to face; but French taxpayers continued to resist the scale of naval appropriations needed to develop a self-sustaining feedback loop of the kind that arose in Great Britain after 1884. Even such a notable French technical breakthrough as the invention in 1875 of production methods capable of supplying the first uniform and dependable alloy steel for naval use, [64] did not suffice to make the French navy a reliable ongoing market for French metallurgists. Instead, as we saw above, the French Chamber of Deputies suspended the building of battleships completely between 1881 and 1888.

This coincided with intensified price competition from German steelmakers. The French government reacted by imposing a protective tariff in 1881, and then in 1885 removed the ban on the sale of weapons to foreigners which had hitherto prevented French manufacturers from competing with Krupp, Armstrong, and Vickers in the international arms business. Response on the part of French arms makers was spectacular.[65] During the 1890s, Schneider-Creusot, the leading French arms firm, squeezed Krupp out of the Russian market.

62. Personnel selection, training, and promotion underwent systematic rationalization in the same tumultuous decades when naval material was being radically transformed. Cf. Paul M. Kennedy, *The Rise and Fall of British Naval Mastery* (New York, 1976), and Michael A. Lewis, *The History of the British Navy* (Harmondsworth, 1957).

63. A similar paradox inhered in the chronologically parallel triumphs of industrial management. From the 1880s, big corporations could plan production and achieve enormous economies by nursing a smooth flow of appropriate factors of production through shop floors, steel mills and assembly lines; but before World War II, their capacity to manage their own internal affairs did not extend to the economy as a whole, where, indeed "sticky" administered prices for industrial products probably began to accentuate the dysfunctional effect of the business cycle from the 1873 crash onwards.

64. Duncan L. Burn, *The Economic History of Steel Making, 1867–1939: A Study in Competition* (Cambridge, 1940), pp. 52–53.

65. James Dredge, *Modern French Artillery* (London, 1892) trumpeted French technical virtuosity to the English-speaking world.

French field artillery was, in fact, of superior design;[66] but what sewed up the Russian market for the French was the political rapprochement of 1891–94, by which France became Russia's ally against the Germans. Generous loans floated by French banks in response to hints from the Quai d'Orsay kept the tsar's government solvent and allowed it to pay for strategically valuable imports from France. Steel for railroads was as important as weapons, and especially so for French steelmakers, who, thanks to their new foreign markets, were at last able to achieve a scale of production large enough to make technologically efficient, completely up-to-date mills profitable. As a result, the growth rate of French ferrous metallurgy in the twenty years before 1914 far outstripped even Germany's.[67] Their new technical efficiency, plus the financial recklessness of French banks in extending loans to dubiously credit-worthy governments, allowed French firms to invade German markets for arms and rails in such diverse places as China, Italy, the Balkans, and Latin America as well as Russia.

Export of arms and steel rails was matched by export of know-how. French and British arms firms energetically set out to help the Russians by building new and expanding old arms factories on a massive scale, especially after 1906. Soon the specter of a rearmed, technically modernized Russia, with a rail net that would permit rapid mobilization of its vast manpower, began to haunt German General Staff planners with ever increasing poignancy. The financial-technical linkup between France and Russia, with some British assistance, gave tangible reality to the German fear of encirclement.[68]

66. In 1893 Schneider-Creusot introduced the famous French 75mm quick-firing field gun. It revolutionized artillery design because of its unprecedented stability. Despite its lightness, which allowed easy and rapid deployment and redeployment in battle, the 75mm, perfected in 1898, remained on target shot after shot without needing any adjustment whatsoever, and consequently could fire about four times as fast as other guns—up to twenty rounds a minute—with no loss of accuracy. The secret was an exact equilibrium between the energy of recoil and the force of the compressed air that returned the gun to firing position. Krupp designs did not catch up for several years. Cf. Bernhard Menne, *Krupp, or the Lords of Essen* (London, 1937), p. 237. British artillery remained inferior throughout World War I. Cf. O. G. F. Hogg, *The Royal Arsenal,* (London, 1963), 2:1421; I. V. Hogg, *A History of Artillery,* pp. 95–97.

67. Joseph A. Roy, *Histoire de la famille Schneider et du Creusot* (Paris, 1962), pp. 88–89, says that Schneider sold half of its guns and nearly half of its armor plate abroad between 1885 and 1914. Fifteen countries bought armor plate. Italy, Spain, and Russia were the leading customers. Twenty-three countries bought artillery, with Russia by far the most important buyer, Spain and Portugal next. For statistics on the growth of French metallurgical output see Comité des Forges, *La sidérurgie française, 1864–1914* (Paris, n.d.). Newly opened coalfields at Briey near the German border contributed to the spectacular rise of French steelmaking.

68. Raymond Poidevin, *Les relations économiques et financières entre la France et l'Allemagne de 1898 à 1914* (Paris, 1969), pp. 290–98, 709–11, 811; René Girault, *Em-*

The French invasion of foreign arms markets was of serious concern to Krupp and to the German government, for economic as well as for military-strategic reasons. Krupp had always depended on foreign sales to keep its machine shops and arms manufactories busy. In the year 1890–91, for example, before French competition had begun to affect sales significantly, no less than 86.4 percent of Krupp's armaments were sold abroad, whereas the German government took only 13.6 percent.[69] After that date, the published figures for foreign sales break off, but it is certain that new French (and British) arms sales to foreign powers came largely at Krupp's expense. As a result, Krupp's foreign sales shrank to less than half the firm's total output of armaments by 1914. Schneider likewise exported about half of its arms production on the eve of the war, whereas Vickers sold less than a third of its output abroad.[70]

In case after case, price competition, in which Krupp excelled, gave way to political economics. After 1903, Krupp could no longer finance sale of its arms by inducing French banks to subscribe to new loans to Russia and other impecunious governments. This had previously been possible, owing to the way investment capital traditionally pursued maximal returns, regardless of political frontiers or alliances. But after 1904 French lenders required borrowers to buy French arms and other goods more and more strictly.[71] As a spokesman for Schneider-Creusot put it some years later: "We consider ourselves collaborators with the Government and we engage in no negotiations and follow up no business which has not received its concurrence."[72] This sort of collaboration allowed French arms exports almost to double in less than twenty years, from 6.6 million francs annual average

prunts russes et investissements français en Russie, 1887–1914 (Paris, 1973), pp. 435–44, 536–40; Herbert Feis, *Europe, the World's Banker, 1870–1914* (New Haven, 1930), pp. 212–31; Rondo E. Cameron, *France and the Economic Development of Europe, 1800–1914: Conquests of Peace and Seeds of War* (Princeton, 1961), pp. 494–501; Trebilcock, "British Armaments and European Industrialization," pp. 254–72.

69. W. A. Boelcke, *Krupp und die Hohenzollern in Dokumenten,* (Frankfurt am Main, 1970), Appendix.

70. Hartmut Pogge von Strandmann, *Vita Rathenau, Grand Master of Capitalism* (forthcoming) corrects looser estimates of Krupp's export of arms in the prewar decades to be found in Gert von Klass, *Krupps,* p. 308, and Boelke, *Krupp und die Hohenzollern,* pp. 178–84. For Schneider's foreign sales see Roy, *Histoire de la famille Schneider et du Creusot,* p. 89; for Vickers see Trebilcock, *The Vickers Brothers,* pp. 20–22.

71. Cf. the excellent and detailed study by Poidevin, *Les relations économiques et financières entre la France et l'Allemagne de 1898 à 1914,* which dates the definitive expiry of the apolitical market in international loans to 1911.

72. Paul Allard as quoted by Noel-Baker, *The Private Manufacture of Armaments,* 1:57.

value in the decade from 1895 to 1904, to 12.8 million francs annual average value in the years 1905 to 1913.[73] Obviously, as Krupp's foreign markets shrank back, the firm needed a politically assured substitute outlet. As is well known, Krupp's managers found a solution in the form of the German naval building programs, launched in 1898 and periodically renewed thereafter at an ever escalating scale until 1914.

At first the German naval program appeared as only one of several similar challenges to the Royal Navy's supremacy. Japan's rise as a naval power in the Far East was a good deal more urgent, in that it decisively altered the balance of forces in Chinese waters. The British reacted by making Japan an ally in 1902. In addition, the rise of the United States Navy,[74] registered by the defeat of Spain in 1898, assured an American sphere of influence in the Caribbean and Pacific. In 1901 the First Lord of the Admiralty informed his Cabinet colleagues that a two-power standard that counted the Americans among potential enemies was beyond Great Britain's means.[75] Ostentatious cordiality between British and American naval detachments in American waters soon was followed by wholesale withdrawal of Royal Navy squadrons and drastic cutbacks, amounting almost to closure, of Britain's naval bases in Nova Scotia, British Columbia, and the Caribbean. This helped Admiral Fisher save money for H.M.S. *Dreadnought* and, with the Japanese alliance, permitted him to concentrate British naval units in home waters. Then, after 1904, rivalry with France, whose submarines had begun to pose a nasty threat, gave way to entente; and Russia's defeat by Japan, 1904–5, erased the Russian navy as a serious factor in the balance of power. This left Germany as Britain's only remaining rival.

Admiral Tirpitz and his colleagues were, however, quite formidable enough. As a faithful disciple of Mahan and a believer in decisive victory as the ultimate goal of all naval policy, Admiral Tirpitz concentrated on building battleships. This made the threat to Britain unmistakable. Yet the German government was unwilling to state publicly that the new navy was designed to drive the Royal Navy from the nar-

73. François Crouzet, "Recherches sur la production d'armements en France, 1815–1913," *Révue historique* 251 (1974): 50. Alan S. Milward and S. B. Saul, *The Development of the Economies of Continental Europe, 1850–1914* (London, 1977), pp. 79, 86–89, note the importance of armaments in French metallurgical expansion just before World War I.

74. For details, see Donald W. Mitchell, *History of the Modern American Navy from 1883 through Pearl Harbor* (London, 1947).

75. Cf. Cabinet memorandum reproduced in Kenneth Bourne, *The Foreign Policy of Victorian Britain, 1830–1902* (Oxford, 1970), p. 461.

row seas. Instead, Tirpitz proclaimed a "risk" theory, to the effect that when the German fleet became sufficiently formidable to constitute a real risk to British naval supremacy, then Great Britain would have to respect Germany's interests as a world power. Then, and only then, would the danger of being cut off by the British from access to overseas markets and raw materials cease to hang over German businessmen and strategists.[76]

In 1898, Tirpitz had difficulty in rallying the necessary votes in the Reichstag and had to promise that the naval building program would not require new taxation. Then, in 1906, Fisher's *Dreadnought* upset everything, since if they were to keep up, the Germans would have to build far more expensive ships than had been contemplated before. In addition, widening the Kiel Canal (opened 1885) to permit bigger warships to move freely between the Baltic and the North Sea became necessary, and dredging to assure access to Wilhelmshafen and other North Sea ports had also to be undertaken.

To go before the Reichstag and ask for new taxes threatened to upset the delicate alliance between conservative agrarian interests and those urban elements that provided the main support for Tirpitz' plans. Even with the protection of high tariffs on imported grain, the estate-owners of Prussia—the class from which army officers traditionally came—were hard pressed to make ends meet, and they were resolutely opposed to paying heavier taxes in any form. The fact that three battleships cost as much as five army corps was not lost upon the agrarians; and yet the public support that Tirpitz and his assistants had mobilized behind the naval program was too great to be checked, even by representatives of Prussia's old ruling class.[77]

When the German Admiralty had first begun to aspire towards building a fleet to rival Britain's, Tirpitz knew he would have to

76. A convenient, and I think judicious, summary of the German naval program is offered by Volker R. Berghahn, *Die Tirpitzplan: Genesis und Verfall einer innerpolitischen Krisenstrategie unter Wilhelm II* (Düsseldorf, 1971). Berghahn also published a summary of his views in Geoffrey Best and Anthony Wheatcroft, eds., *War, Economy and the Military Mind* (London, 1976), pp. 61–88. Holger H. Herwig *"Luxury Fleet": The Imperial German Navy, 1888–1918* (London, 1980) is excellent for the technical side of German naval administration.

77. The idea that the German naval program reflected internal political strains was first propounded by Eckhardt Kehr, *Schlachtflottenbau und Parteipolitik, 1894–1901* (Berlin, 1930). Anathema under the Nazis, Kehr's ideas have become normative among German historians since World War II. But it seems to me that German scholarship, reacting against older idealist traditions, has gone to an opposite extreme by emphasizing interests more exclusively than they deserve. The belief that national greatness and prosperity could only be won by war narrowed public choices in all European countries before 1914. When pecuniary self-interest attached itself to such an idea, it made a heady brew; but the idea surely continued to have a semiautonomous life of its own, and

mobilize potential supporters. He did so systematically and thoroughly. Newspapers and journalists, industrialists and university professors, politicians and clergymen: no one who could exercise influence on the political process within Germany was overlooked. Success of the propaganda effort was attested by the size of the Navy League, founded with Krupp's financial support in 1898. By the next year it counted no fewer than 250,000 members,[78] far exceeding anything the British ever managed to attract into their parallel organization, established three years previously.

As a result, when H.M.S. *Dreadnought* upset Tirpitz' original plans, he still was able to get another, enlarged naval bill through the Reichstag in 1908—just in time, as we saw, to trigger the British decision to raise the pace of their building to eight dreadnought-type ships a year in 1909.

All the same, Chancellor von Bülow's support in the Reichstag was shattered by quarrels over what and whom to tax in order to pay for the enlarged naval program. He left office in 1909 as a result. This was the year when Great Britain began to be convulsed by the dispute over Lloyd George's budget, which also hinged on paying for the expanded British naval building program. Clearly both countries found it hard to apportion the costs of their rivalry. Yet efforts to call a halt failed, even when the two governments expressed an interest in doing so, as happened, for example, in 1912.

Though shipbuilding continued, after 1909 Admiral Tirpitz' plan to create a fleet strong enough to defeat the Royal Navy in the North Sea was in disarray. His initial assumptions had proved false. Instead of being distracted by imperial conflicts with France and Russia, Great Britain had established a diplomatic entente with Germany's enemies. And in 1910, the British government showed its mettle by imposing graduated new taxes to pay for the navy and for social welfare in a way the imperial German government was unable to do.

Moreover, by 1912 Tirpitz and the German navy had to face a formidable new rival at home in the form of the army. Anxiety over risks of revolution had haunted Prussian officers ever since 1848. Even

---

affected the behavior of millions of Germans who had no clear or immediate personal interest in making the navy strong. Jonathan Steinberg, *Yesterday's Deterrent: Tirpitz and the Birth of the German Battle Fleet* (New York, 1965) emphasizes the deliberate manipulation of public opinon more than German historians seem to do; but he also puts greater weight on economic self-interest and pecuniary rationality than I think the circumstances truly warrant.

78. Kehr, *Schlachtflottenbau und Parteipolitik*, p. 101. Cf. Wilhelm Diest, *Flottenpolitik und Flottenpropaganda: Das Nachrichtenbureau des Reichsmarineamptes, 1897–1914* (Stuttgart, 1976).

after the triumph of 1870–71, fear of what a truly mass army might do to the privileges of the propertied classes made it easy for the army's leaders to acquiesce in a system that, as population grew, called up only a diminishing proportion of eligible young men to military service. By limiting the army to a size acceptable to penny-pinchers in the Reichstag, it was possible to keep the officer corps more nearly homogeneous and aristocratic in background—a safe bulwark against potential revolution as preached by socialists.

This policy was called into question towards the end of the first decade of the twentieth century by the accelerated pace of Russian rearmament, financed largely by France. When Germany's protégé, Turkey, went down in swift defeat in the first Balkan War (1912) to states whose armies had been reequiped by the French, Germany's sense of beleaguerment intensified. The kaiser's military advisers concluded that, despite the risk of revolution, the army would have to be enlarged by training a larger proportion of the eligible age classes each year. They also decided to equip the army with heavier field artillery. Costs of such a program were significant and competed directly with naval expenditures. Indeed, the new chancellor, Theobald von Bethman-Hollweg, actively encouraged the army program as a way of checking Admiral Tirpitz' demands for funds.[79]

Russia's apparent recovery from the revolutionary disturbances that followed the defeat of 1905–6 even called the feasibility of the famous Schlieffen plan into question. If Russia could develop a dense enough rail net to mobilize its vast manpower quickly, the Germans might not have the time needed to defeat France before suffering unacceptable disaster at the hands of invading Russian hordes. Yet ever since 1893 it had been an article of faith in the Great General Staff (as the Prussian General Staff had been rechristened after 1871) that the only way to fight a two-front war was to strike first against France by marching through Belgium while the Russians were still in process of mobilization. This was what Alfred von Schlieffen, the chief of the Great General Staff, 1891–1905, had concluded when first he faced the problem of what to do about the French-Russian rapprochement of 1891–94.

The Schlieffen plan was carefully revised each year to take account of changes in German and enemy resources as reported by the latest

79. Fritz Fischer, *War of Illusions: German Policies from 1911 to 1914* (London, 1975), pp. 116 ff. Cf. the interesting analysis of the German army's dilemma in Bernd F. Schulte, *Die deutsche Armee, 1900–1914, zwischen Beharren und Verandern* (University of Hamburg dissertation, 1976).

military intelligence. But from 1893, when it was first devised, until 1914, when it was acted upon, the basic idea never altered. The fact that Belgium's neutrality was guaranteed by an international treaty to which Prussia had been a signatory in 1839 did not seem important to the German planners. It might assure Great Britain's belligerency, for the independence of Belgium (against France) was a long-standing British commitment. But after the entente between France and Britain (1904) was supplemented by a similar arrangement with Russia (1907), the Germans assumed that the British would link up with their enemies in the event of war—sooner or later, if not at the outset. To precipitate the confrontation by invading Belgium seemed worth the price, if by that means a quick, crushing victory over France could be assured.[80]

A more important consequence of the meticulous detail with which the German plan of attack was worked out between 1893 and 1914 was that once the order for mobilization had been issued, there was no drawing back. Everything had to go like clockwork. Any effort to interfere would jam the works at once and substitute paralyzing confusion for the smooth shuffling of men and supplies dictated by the plan. Hence, subordination of military action to political considerations, which Bismarck had already found difficult in 1866 and 1870–71,[81] became completely impossible. No one, not even the kaiser, could change the plan once war had been decided on. Similar rigidities also arose in France, Russia, and Austria, though the lesser prestige of the army in those lands made political interference, even in moments of crisis, more nearly conceivable than was the case in Germany.

The irrationality of rational, professionalized planning could not have been made more patently manifest. Indeed, the uncanny, somnambulent lockstep with which the major powers of Europe marched to war in August 1914 aptly symbolized the central dilemma of our age—the dissonance of the whole introduced, or enormously exacerbated, by a closer harmony and superior organization of its separate parts.

80. On the Schlieffen plan, see Gerhard Ritter, *The Schlieffen Plan: Critique of a Myth* (London, 1958).
81. Gordon A. Craig, *The Politics of the Prussian Army* (New York, 1964), pp. 193–216.

9

World Wars of the Twentieth Century

Men went gladly to war in August 1914 in the more urbanized parts of Europe. Almost everyone assumed that fighting would last only a few weeks. In anticipation of decisive battles, martial enthusiasm bordering on madness surged through German, French, and British public consciousness. Disillusion, when it came, was correspondingly profound, yet for four long, dreary years the will to war continued to prevail even in the face of massive casualty lists and military stalemate on the Western Front.

Reasons for such bizarre behavior can only be surmised. The cult of heroism sustained by an educational system that emphasized patriotism and study of the classics had something to do with what happened. So did the fact that civil strife had seemed imminent within each of the leading countries of Europe in the decade before World War I. To have a foreigner to hate and fear relieved potential combatants from hating and fearing neighbors closer at hand. This was profoundly reassuring to socialists and proletarians as well as to the propertied classes. Perhaps, too, manifold psychological adjustments required by the shift from rural to urban patterns of life found release in an orgy of patriotism and militarism in 1914. The fact that war enthusiasm was far less apparent in eastern Europe supports this view, since urbanization had affected a smaller percentage of the population in that region, where the peasant majority still sought to follow a traditional pattern of life. But despite such efforts at explanation[1] World War I remains more than usually difficult to understand.

1. Marc Ferro, *La Grande Guerre* (Paris, 1969), and Emmanuel Todd, *Le fou et le proletaire* (Paris, 1979) address themselves to this question more imaginatively than most. Todd suggests that the artisan and shopkeeper classes were especially under pressure before 1914 and sublimated sexual as well as economic frustration by transferring hostility to the foreign enemy.

Those who experienced the war were quite unable to fit what happened into any pattern of prior experience. Their initial intoxication with dreams of glory curdled into horror and a sense of helpless entrapment as the slaughter of the trenches persisted month after month. The injection of Wilsonian and Leninist rhetoric in 1917 merely emphasized the unique, exceptional, and unparalleled character of the struggle. Eschatological imagery took hold; and when the war finally ended a swift and strong reaction against everything connected with the bloodletting set in. Most of the survivors acted on the assumption that whatever had happened between 1914 and 1918 was an atavistic aberration from the norms of civilized life.

But even if we take the contemporary judgment at face value and agree that World War I was a kind of Armageddon, bringing a violent, sudden end to an era of European and world history, by now the mere passage of time makes it clear that the Great War also inaugurated a new epoch in world affairs, an epoch in which we, in the 1980s, still find ourselves floundering. It is, therefore, no longer practicable to treat World War I as an unparalled catastrophe interrupting the ordinary course of historical development. If nothing else, World War II proved that the Great War was not unique; and as that conflict in its turn begins to fade from the foreground of contemporary consciousness, it ought to become possible to perceive the two great armed struggles of the twentieth century in a somewhat more enduring perspective.

Balance of Power and Demography in World Wars I and II

Three approaches seem especially promising. First of all the wars may be viewed as another exercise in balance of power politics within a system of rival states. Certainly the way in which German power was countered by the Allies of World Wars I and II conformed in all essentials to two earlier passages of European history: the two bouts of war that constrained Hapsburg power, 1567–1609 and 1618–48; and the more widely separated struggles that checked French preponderance, 1689–1714 and 1793–1815. In each of these cases, as in the years 1914–18 and 1939–45, a coalition of states took the field against the ruler of the day who seemed on the verge of establishing European hegemony; and in each case, too, cross purposes, mutual suspicion, and radical diversity of ideology among the members of the coalition did not prevent the Allies from winning enough of a victory to be able to afford the luxury of quarreling among themselves when the fighting ended.[2]

Soldiers and subjects in past ages were not expected to share in statesmen's calculations of balance of power; but in the two world wars of the twentieth century, citizens and soldiers on both sides and in every belligerent state were invited to believe in war aims which expressly repudiated such calculations as a satisfactory guide to public affairs. To suffer and die maintaining a balance of power that had allowed or even provoked the war was entirely unacceptable to the combatants. Statesmen, too, whether for ideological or other reasons, defied the principles of power politics by their particular actions time and again.[3]

Yet even if statesmen, citizens, and soldiers said and believed that balance-of-power politics was evil and inadequate, the behavior of governments and shifts of public opinion still conformed quite closely to an ineluctable geometry of power. Presumably, as long as sovereign states exist, whenever one of them seems to be growing so powerful as to threaten the continued independence of the others, everything tending to encourage hostility to the potential hegemonial power finds congenial conditions within the states that feel threatened. Rapid changes of mood and popular sympathy can and do occur under such circumstances, forming and dissolving alliances and coalitions in a matter of a few weeks or months. Contrary intentions and conflicting ideals prevailed only when no pressing external threats provoked balance-of-power behavior. This, for example, was the case between the wars when German weakness invited both the Soviet Union and the United States to try deliberately to transcend power politics. Each did so by withdrawing within its boundaries, there to protect a purer and preferred political faith.

Nonetheless, balance of power seems inadequate as a full explana-

2. For a concise statement of this view of the German wars of the twentieth century, see Ludwig Wilhelm Dehio, *The Precarious Balance: The Politics of Power in Europe, 1494–1945* (London, 1963). For a more philosophical study cf. Martin Wight, *Power Politics* (Harmondsworth, 1979).

3. Lenin in Russia, like Woodrow Wilson and Franklin D. Roosevelt in the United States, made a career of repudiating balance-of-power politics as evil and outmoded. Even Hitler sometimes disregarded the rules of the game, most strikingly in 1941 when he relieved Roosevelt of an otherwise intractable dilemma by taking the initiative in declaring war on the United States after the Japanese attack on Pearl Harbor. The Americans reciprocated by declaring war on Germany on 10 December, and were thus able to pursue the "Germany first" strategy already agreed on with Great Britain. Had Hitler not taken the initiative, however, it is hard to see how Roosevelt could have asked Congress to start a war with Germany when the Japanese attack in the Pacific was still to be avenged.

tion of the two wars. The ferocity with which they were fought, and the far-reaching transformations that the war effort precipitated, made society over. War aims and political ideologies may have misled all concerned; but behind the bitter struggles one can surely discern a demographic factor as ineluctable as the geometry of power rivalries.

This perception offers a second approach to an understanding of the two wars. For, as suggested above in chapter 6, if the democratic and industrial revolutions were, among other things, responses to a population squeeze that impinged on western Europe towards the end of the eighteenth century, the military convulsions of the twentieth century can be interpreted in the same way, as responses to collisions between population growth and limits set by traditional modes of rural life in central and eastern Europe in particular, and across wide areas of Asia in rather more diversified and variegated fashion as well. Assuredly, a basic and fundamental disturbance to all existing social relationships set in whenever and wherever broods of peasant children grew to adulthood in villages where, when it came time for them to marry and assume adult roles, they could not get hold of enough land to live as their forefathers had done from time immemorial. In such circumstances, traditional ways of rural life came under unbearable strain. Family duties and moral imperatives of village custom could not be fulfilled. The only question was what form of revolutionary ideal would attract the frustrated young people.

Ever since the mid-eighteenth century, European and world populations have been out of balance. Lowered death rates allowed more children to grow to adulthood than in earlier centuries; but birthrates did not automatically adjust downward. Quite the contrary, they were likely to rise, since with fewer lethal epidemics, couples more often survived throughout their childbearing years.[4]

For a century or more in central and eastern Europe, increasing numbers simply meant increasing wealth. More labor improved cultivation, broke new land to the plow, and intensified agricultural production in many different ways. Nevertheless, such responses had a limit; and by the 1880s it seems clear that diminishing returns had set in drastically in nearly all European villages situated between the Rhine and the Don. This was signalized by two changes. First, between 1880

---

4. On the concept of a "vital revolution" see K. F. Helleiner, "The Vital Revolution Reconsidered," in D. V. Glass and D. E. C. Eversley, *Population in History* (London, 1965), pp. 79–86; Ralph Thomlinson, *Population Dynamics: Causes and Consequences of World Demographic Change* (New York, 1965), pp. 14 ff.

and 1914 emigration assumed extraordinary proportions, carrying millions across the seas to America and projecting other millions eastward into Siberia as well. Second, diverse forms of revolutionary discontent began to affect villagers as well as townspeople in central and eastern Europe during these same decades.

Pressures on village custom and traditional social patterns intensified until 1914, when World War I diverted their expression into new channels and, by killing many millions of people in central and eastern Europe, did something to relieve the problem of rural overpopulation. But it was not until World War II brought much greater slaughter as well as massive flights and wholesale ethnic transfers that central and eastern European populations replicated the French response to the revolutionary upheavals at the beginning of the nineteenth century by regulating births to accord with perceived economic circumstances and expectations. As a result, after 1950 population growth ceased to put serious strain on European society.[5]

Diverse experiences in coping with population growth go far to explain the attitudes and behavior of the European powers on the eve of World War I. As suggested in chapter 6, by mid-century France and Great Britain had each in its own contrasting way gone far to resolve the internal tensions that rapidly rising rural populations had created in those lands between 1780 and 1850.[6] Rising real wages registered this fact during and after the 1850s. Deliberate limitation of births among the French tied population growth to economic experience and expectation. In Great Britain, those who could not find satisfactory work at home went abroad, where careers in lands of European settlement were readily available.[7]

5. For an overview of the population phenomena of the war era see Eugene M. Kulischer, *Europe on the Move: War and Population Changes, 1917–1947* (New York, 1948).

6. Britain's Irish problem was not exactly solved by the catastrophe of the potato blight and resultant famine of 1845–46; but population growth abruptly gave way to population wastage in Ireland, thanks to accelerated emigration and rigorous postponement of the age of marriage until the newlyweds could inherit land. After 1845 the political tensions of Ireland were therefore no longer fed by rising population but took especial venom from the prolonged sexual frustration which became the normal lot of Irish countrymen waiting to inherit land before they dared to marry. On the psychological and sociological consequences of the remarkable demographic regime that prevailed in Ireland after the famine see Conrad Arensburg, *The Irish Countryman* (London, 1937).

7. Chain migration whereby one successful emigrant saved money to finance his relatives' emigration made it possible for even the very poor to get across the ocean in statistically significant numbers. As a result the emptying-out of English villages with the

Russia's position was like that of Great Britain in the sense that migration towards a politically accessible and thinly inhabited frontier was available to rural folk who faced unacceptable constriction of traditional patterns of life in their native villages. Between 1880 and 1914 something over six million Russians migrated to Siberia and about four million established themselves in the Caucasus as well. Simultaneously, from the westernmost provinces of Russia an additional flood of about two and a half million emigrated overseas, though most of these were Poles and Jews, not ethnic Russians.[8] These safety valves were supplemented by expanding urban employment, thanks to railroads and the manifold forms of industrial and commercial expansion provoked by cheapened overland transport. Nevertheless, much of rural Russia simmered with discontent in the first decade of the twentieth century, as demonstrated by the sudden flare-up of revolutionary violence in 1905–6.

The really difficult demographic problem of the late nineteenth and early twentieth centuries came in the regions of Europe between the French and British on the west and the Russians on the east. In Germany, for example, the average annual surplus of births over deaths in the decade 1900–1910 was 866,000, yet Germany's remarkable industrial and commercial expansion provided so many jobs that Polish farm workers had to be imported to cultivate east German estates.[9] Nonetheless, the strains rapid urbanization put upon older patterns of life were very great. Germany's ruling elites were mostly drawn from rural and small-town backgrounds and often felt endangered by the new, thrusting urban elements. Marxist revolutionary rhetoric, popular among industrial workingmen, was particularly frightening. Simultaneously, many Germans felt endangered by impending Slavic inundation from the east. The result was a strong sense of beleaguerment and a more rigid, reckless support of Austria-Hungary in the summer of 1914 than would otherwise have seemed sensible.[10]

---

decay of crop farming after 1873 produced no serious political disturbance in Great Britain. It did raise the tide of emigration from the British Isles to an all-time high in the years 1911–13. Cf. R. C. K. Ensor, *England, 1870–1914* (Oxford, 1936), p. 500.

8. Marcel Reinhard, André Armengaud, and Jacques Dupaquier, *Histoire générale de la population mondiale,* 3d ed. (Paris, 1968), pp. 401, 470; Donald W. Treadgold, *The Great Siberian Migration* (Princeton, 1957), pp. 33–35.

9. Between 1880 and 1914 nearly half a million German farm workers left the east. According to William W. Hagen, *Germans, Poles, and Jews: The Nationality Conflict in the Prussian East, 1772–1914* (Chicago, 1980), the total was 482,062.

10. Analysis of how the "archaic" character of German political leadership on the eve of the war helped to precipitate the catastrophe has become standard among German historians since Fritz Fischer pioneered this approach with his famous books, *Griff nach*

It is ironic to reflect on the difference between German and French developments. Had the German old regime been less successful in coping with the population surge in the nineteenth century, some sort of revolutionary movement might well have come to power in Germany with an attractive, universalist ideology, suited to appeal to other peoples of Europe as the ideals of the French revolutionaries had done in the eighteenth century. But instead, the German bid for European hegemony was fought out in the name of narrowly exclusive, nationalist, and racist principles, designed rather to repel than attract others. Success in industrializing so rapidly, in other words, may have foreclosed Germany's longer-range chances of winning the wars of the twentieth century in the name of some form of revolutionary socialism. Marxist prescriptions for the future thus went astray. Instead, by a twist of fate that would have appalled Karl Marx, after 1917 the Russians made Marxism the ideological instrument of their state power.

Before 1917, however, this remarkable reversal of roles was unimaginable. In the regions of Europe lying east and south of Germany, industrial expansion entirely failed to keep pace with population growth.[11] Consequently, the most acute manifestations of political distress appeared within the borders of the Hapsburg and ex-Ottoman empires. (Russia's Polish provinces belong in this category too.) Overseas emigration, though very great, [12] was insufficient to relieve the problem. Youths who pursued secondary education in hope of qualifying for white-collar employment were strategically situated to communicate revolutionary political ideals to their frustrated contemporaries in the villages. They did so with marked success, beginning as early as the 1870s in Bulgaria and Serbia,[13] and at somewhat

---

der Weltmacht (Düsseldorf, 1961) and *Krieg der Illusionen* (Düsseldorf, 1969) translated as *Germany's War Aims in the First World War* (London, 1967) and *War of Illusions: German Policies from 1911 to 1914* (London, 1975).

11. Paralleling similar failures within the British Isles in such parts as the Scottish Highlands and southern Ireland.

12. About 4 million persons left Hapsburg lands for overseas destinations between 1900 and 1914. Emigration from Russia's western provinces was about 2.5 million, and from Italy was so massive as to depopulate some southern villages. Reinhard et al., *Histoire générale,* pp. 400–401, gives a table of European emigration showing relevant statistics for the pre–World War I decades.

13. In Serbia, the Radical party, founded in 1879, set up a rural party machine and agitational network that changed the basis of politics in that country within a decade or so. Cf. Alex N. Dragnich, *Serbia, Nikola Pašić and Yugoslavia* (New Brunswick, N.J., 1974), pp. 17–22. For Bulgaria, see Cyril Black, *The Establishment of Constitutional Government in Bulgaria* (Princeton, 1943), pp. 39 ff.

later dates in other parts of eastern Europe. The Balkans, accordingly, became the powder keg of Europe. It was appropriate indeed that the spark that triggered World War I was struck by Gavrilo Princip, a youth whose efforts at pursuing a secondary school education had entirely failed to provide him with satisfactory access to adult life but had imbued him with an intense, revolutionary form of nationalism.[14]

World War I did something to relieve rural overcrowding in central and eastern Europe. Millions of peasant sons were mobilized into the rival armies and something like 10.5 million died.[15] In the aftermath, nationalist revolutions in the Hapsburg Empire (1918–19) and socialist revolutions in Russia (1917) did little to relieve peasant overcrowding. Except in Hungary, both forms of revolution did succeed in depriving prewar possessing classes of most of their landed property. But land redistribution among an already impoverished peasantry did little to improve productivity. Indeed it usually worked in an opposite way, since the new owners lacked both capital and know-how with which to farm efficiently. The postwar settlement therefore quite failed to relieve the difficulty of too many people trying to pursue a traditional peasant style of life. The Russians responded between 1928 and 1932 with a state program of industrial investment supported by forcible collectivization of agriculture. In the rest of eastern Europe, when depression came in the 1930s, rural distress commonly found anti-Semitic expression, since Jewish middlemen were numerous enough to be vulnerable to the charge that they prospered by buying cheap and selling dear at the peasantry's expense.

Hence it was not until World War II provoked a far more massive die-off in eastern Europe, totaling perhaps as much as 47 million,[16] that a more brutal but enduring solution to the problem of too many

14. Nationalism appealed more than socialism to east European peasants and former peasants because it could be interpreted as meaning the dispossession of ethnically alien landlords and urban property owners without infringing peasant property in the slightest. The Serbian Radical party, accordingly, shed its founders' socialism as it succeeded in gaining peasant support. On socialist beginnings of the Radicals see Woodford D. McClellan, *Svetozar Marković and the Origins of Balkan Socialism* (Princeton, 1964).

15. This figure is the remainder when French and British war losses are subtracted from the global figure of 13 million for World War I casualties offered by Reinhard et al., *Histoire générale,* p. 488. Estimates are very loose at best, for record keeping broke down in all defeated countries, and epidemics of typhus and influenza killed many civilians as well as soldiers. Such deaths are sometimes classed as war related, sometimes excluded.

16. Ibid., p. 573. Margin for error is even greater in World War II than in World War I calculations, if only because more than half the casualties were civilian.

people trying to live on too little land emerged. For it was during and after World War II that the inhabitants of eastern Europe began to limit births. Birthrates swiftly sank towards a much lower level than before; so low, indeed, that in some countries population replacement ceased to be assured without alien immigration.[17]

As births came into systematic relation with economic expectations all across the face of Europe,[18] the crisis period through which central and eastern Europe had passed between 1880 and 1950 came to an end. Family patterns and sex habits changed; customs and mores of peasant life altered; and the demographic regime that had fomented World Wars I and II ceased to prevail.

Elsewhere in the world, of course, the demographic surge followed different rhythms. In China, for example, collision between mounting rural population and available land became acute as early as 1850 and found expression in the massive and destructive Taiping Rebellion, 1850–64.[19] Asian peasantries did not again respond to revolutionary ideals on a massive scale until after World War I. Suffice it here to refer to the career of Mohandas Gandhi (1869–1948), whose first successful efforts to appeal to the rural classes of India dated from the early 1920s and to that of Mao Tse-tung (1893–1976), whose mobilization of Chinese peasant support for his version of Marxism dated from 1927. The linkages that prevailed in Europe between overcrowding on the land and revolutionary politicization of rural populations were duplicated in much of Asia during ensuing decades,[20] and in some regions of Africa as well. But conditions varied greatly from region to region, and in many tropical climates disease regimes that kept human numbers efficiently in check continued to prevail until after World War II.

17. Cf. Ansley J. Coale et al., eds., *Human Fertility in Russia since the Nineteenth Century* (Princeton, 1979); David M. Heer, "The Demographic Transition in the Russian Empire and the Soviet Union," *Journal of Social History* 1 (1968): 193–240; Reinhard et al., *Histoire générale*, p. 610.

18. With the exception of Albania and Albanian populations inside Yugoslavia, among whom a Moslem heritage and mountainous habitat combined to preserve traditional sexual and family patterns. Cf. John Salt and Hugh Clout, *Migration in Post-war Europe: Geographical Essays* (Oxford, 1976), p. 13. Political manifestations of the resulting population pressure became troublesome in Yugoslavia in 1981.

19. About 40 million died in that rebellion; and an additional 8 million Chinese emigrated to borderlands and overseas in ensuing decades. The country's population of about 430 million in 1850 was cut back to only 400 million in 1870 according to Reinhard et al., *Histoire générale*, p. 476.

20. For China cf. M. P. Redfield, ed., *China's Gentry: Essays in Rural-Urban Relations by Hsiao-tung Fei* (Chicago, 1953).

Japan's twentieth-century imperial aggression coincided with a surge in that nation's population growth that crested only after World War II, although maximal rate of increase came earlier.[21] But World War II brought decisive metamorphosis to Japanese rural life, and, after the war, birthrates started down at almost the same time as in central and eastern Europe. To all appearances, therefore, Japan also passed through its version of the modern demographic crisis during World War II just as most of Europe did.[22]

Obviously, revolutionary expressions of rural frustration when insufficient land is available to allow young people to live as their parents had done have not vanished from the earth. Outbreaks in Latin America, parts of Africa, and in southeast Asia continue to occur. But for World Wars I and II, Japan's population surge, and the chronologically parallel crisis in eastern and central Europe was what mainly mattered. Having changed their demographic pattern, these lands are unlikely to become again the seat of comparable military-political unrest.

But demography and the painful breakup of age-old peasant styles of life, while doing much to explain the bloody character of the two major wars of the twentieth century, do nothing to illuminate the way the more advanced industrial countries reorganized themselves for war along unforeseen and unexpected lines, thereby inaugurating the managed economies that have become a distinctive hallmark of the contemporary world. This, the third approach to an understanding of the two world wars, seems the most promising of them all, inasmuch as the twentieth century may well be witnessing a return to the primacy of command over market as the preferred means for mobilizing

21. Japan's population rose as follows:

	Total	Increment	Percent
1880	36.4 million	—	—
1890	40.5	4.1	11
1900	44.8	4.3	11
1910	50.9	6.1	14
1920	55.9	5.0	10
1930	64.4	8.5	15
1940	73.1	8.7	13.5
1950	83.2	10.1	14

Source: Reinhard et al., *Histoire générale,* pp. 479, 566, 640.

22. For Japanese rural population growth and political protest see Takehiko Yoshihashi, *Conspiracy at Mukden: The Rise of the Japanese Military* (New Haven, 1963); Tadashi Fukutake, *Japanese Rural Society* (Tokyo, 1967); Ronald P. Dore, *Land Reform in Japan* (London, 1959); Cyril E. Black et al., *The Modernization of Japan and Russia* (New York, 1975), pp. 179–85, 281; Carl Mosk, "Demographic Transition in Japan," *Journal of Economic History* 37 (1977): 655–74.

large-scale human effort. I therefore propose to treat the managerial metamorphosis wrought by these two wars at rather greater length, in the belief that this aspect may prove to be their principal and most lasting result for human history.

Managerial Metamorphosis in World War I: First Phase, 1914–16

The unexpected duration of World War I compelled each of the protagonists to organize and reorganize the home front to improve the efficiency and enlarge the scale of the country's war effort. Far-reaching changes in older patterns of management resulted. In particular, innumerable bureaucratic structures that had previously acted more or less independently of one another in a context of market relationships coalesced into what amounted to a single national firm for waging war. Business corporations were the most important of these structures, perhaps, but labor unions, government ministries, and army and navy administrators also played leading roles in defining the new ways of managing national affairs.

Time-tested customs and institutions became soft and malleable in the hands of rival technocratic elites who made millions into soldiers and other millions into war workers. Family life, property rights, access to consumables, locality and class relationships—all altered drastically. Taken together, changes in daily routines and encounters added up to a social metamorphosis as remarkable (and perhaps also as natural) as the metamorphosis of insects.

How did it happen?

At first, everyone assumed that the war would last only a few weeks. On the Continent, the very perfection of rival mobilization plans meant that normal life halted abruptly with the outbreak of hostilities. Only in England did "business as usual" persist.[23] France almost emptied its factories and farms of able-bodied men. The shock was lessened in other countries by the fact that not all eligible males had been trained as soldiers. Political controversy, too, stopped "for the duration" in every belligerent land. Except for a small band of doctrinaires, socialists everywhere betrayed their revolutionary rhetoric and suspended the class struggle in order to repel the national foe.

For thirty-six days it looked as though the expectation of a short war

---

23. The phrase was invented by Winston Churchill, according to Samuel J. Hurwitz, *State Intervention in Great Britain: A Study of Economic Control and Social Response, 1914–1919* (New York, 1949), p. 63.

would turn out to be correct. The Schlieffen plan unrolled almost as the Great General Staff had hoped. German troops turned back the French attack in Lorraine and the Russian advance into East Prussia while their main force, having beaten back the British and Belgians, wheeled across the Low Countries and prepared to encircle the French. But men and horses were stretched to the limit by such marching and fighting; and the French broke off their own offensive in time to launch a major counterattack on the Marne (6–12 September 1914). Accordingly, on 9 September the Germans began to withdraw. Three days later, stalemate set in between exhausted armies, each sheltering in lines of hastily constructed trenches. Ammunition was desperately short at the front, and so were other supplies. Worse still, the tactical stalemate became general in ensuing weeks when repeated efforts to outflank the foe merely prolonged the line of trenches until it became continuous, stretching across France from the Swiss border in the south to a small corner of Belgium in the north. Thereafter the Western Front remained almost stationary for four dreary years, despite enormous efforts on each side to find a way to break through.

This untoward result presented the belligerents with totally unexpected problems. To keep going was difficult; to give up was impossible. As a result, the belligerents were impelled to improvise means to sustain the rival armies, month after month, feeding, equipping, supplying, training, healing, and burying men literally by the millions. Nothing like it had ever been done before. No wonder ancient customs and institutions withered, while new methods and maxims everywhere prevailed.

Of the major belligerents, France was the most drastically affected by the first weeks of war. Initial loss of life was very heavy[24] and the economy came close to foundering. France's crisis was worsened by the fact that when the front stabilized, the part of the country behind German lines was especially important as a source of coal and iron—the sinews of armament manufacture.[25] Even in those arms plants that remained safely behind French lines, manpower was lack-

24. The cult of the offensive had been held very high in the prewar French army with the result that charges across open country in face of magazine rifle and machine gun fire killed about 640,000 men between 1 August and 1 December 1914, according to Joseph Montheilet, *Les institutions militaires de la France, 1814–1924* (Paris, 1932), p. 350. This initial bloodbath amounted to nearly half of French losses during the whole war.

25. No less than 64 percent of French pig iron capacity and 26 percent of French steel capacity was in German hands, together with 85 out of 170 blast furnaces. Cf. Robert Pinot, *Le Comité des Forges en service de la nation* (Paris, 1919), p. 76.

ing, since the able-bodied workers had been drafted like everybody else.[26] Hence when it became clear that the artillery was going to be continually engaged in firing shells across the trench lines in hitherto unimagined numbers,[27] the French minister of war concluded, as early as 20 September 1914, that he would have to release men from the army to manufacture the needed ammunition. At first, confusion prevailed. Employers were authorized to comb railway stations and other likely places in search of suitably skilled men.[28]

From the first, the French authorities saw that improvisation was necessary because so much of the nation's prewar metallurgical plant had fallen into enemy hands. All sorts of firms were therefore called upon to manufacture war materiel by setting up new assembly lines, converting machinery to new uses, and inventing production methods in the light of local conditions and possibilities. Memories of 1793 and the Parisian workshops of that year made massive improvisation easier. So did the readiness of politicians to hand over details to local committees of industrialists, who portioned out contracts and tasks among themselves and coordinated their efforts with the army's overall requirements through frequent conferences with an appropriate cabinet minister.[29]

26. Prewar plans called for production of 10,000–12,000 75mm shells per day in time of war. A work force of 7,600 was therefore kept back at the time of mobilization while the balance of arsenal workers, who totaled 45,000–50,000, were drafted. At Le Creusot, 6,600 out of a work force of 13,000 remained after mobilization in 1914. These figures come from Gerd Hardach, "La mobilization industrielle en 1914–1918: Production, planification et idéologie," in Patrick Fridenson, ed., *1914–1918: L'autre front* (Paris, 1977), p. 83.

27. In all previous wars, field artillery spent nearly all the time trying to get into firing position. Active bombardment of the foe usually lasted only a few hours so that consumption of ammunition had remained correspondingly modest. The trench warfare of 1914–18 reversed matters, for the guns were perpetually in position to fire, and worthwhile enemy targets were always within range. The supply of shells (and of small arms ammunition) therefore became the effective limit on operations as never before. Logistics and, ultimately, industrial capacity to manufacture guns and ammunition became decisive. All the combatants came to recognize this quite unanticipated industrialization of war by the spring of 1915.

28. Not until August 1915 did a public law regulate the status of workers released from the army to work in war production. They remained under military command, but were paid civilian wages, wore a distinctive badge, and could be assigned where most needed without the right to refuse any proffered form of work. Return to the front was the alternative such men faced for any act of indiscipline. See Gilbert Hatry, *Renault: Usine de guerre, 1914–1918* (n.p., n.d.), pp. 79, 92–93.

29. The first such conference took place on 20 September 1914 when a goal of 100,000 75mm shells per day was promulgated by the minister of war. Weekly meetings thereafter changed first to biweekly and then to monthly meetings; and a new Ministry of Munitions took over political responsibility after May 1915. Three perspicacious

In the first furious weeks, cost scarcely mattered. Some 25,000 subcontractors began making munitions of one sort or another and virtually every available machine was put to work somehow. Later, high cost producers were squeezed out, mainly by failing to get allocations of necessary raw materials and fuel. Large new plants constructed from the ground up to produce armaments on an assembly line basis became increasingly important as time passed, though some, among them the largest and most ambitious, had not yet come on stream when the war ended in 1918.[30]

Big business looked after itself very successfully under these circumstances. Businessmen controlled the local councils that allocated scarce commodities—raw materials, fuel, and labor. Large-scale producers were able to reap fat profits from price levels designed to keep marginal firms in business. Mass production methods paid off handsomely for innovative firms with the right political, financial, and industrial connections. Louis Renault, for instance, built up an industrial empire in the war years. By 1918 he had 22,500 workers on his payroll and was turning out shells, trucks, tractors, tanks, airplanes, gun parts, and the like. His role as chairman of the industrial committee of the Paris region gave him an inside track in bidding on new contracts; his reliance on a corps of young engineers to design efficient new production processes made such contracts highly profitable to him and his firm.[31]

Another factor in French success was the character of the labor force. Large-scale industry, still new in France in 1914, was most at home in the regions overrun by the Germans. Hence, customary ways of work scarcely existed for the industrial plants created by the war-

accounts of French war mobilization explain how things were done: Arthur Fontaine, *French Industry during the War* (New Haven, 1926); John F. Godfrey, "Bureaucracy, Industry and Politics in France during the First World War" (D.Phil. thesis, St. Antony's College, Oxford, 1974); and Etienne Clémentel, *La France et la politique économique interaliée* (New Haven, 1931). Gerd Hardach's brief essay, cited above, may also be recommended.

30. The most famous and controversial was a new state arsenal at Roanne, planned in September 1916 and never completed. For details see Godfrey, "Bureaucracy," pp. 314–33. For an upbeat account of a similar venture that barely got under way see Albert G. Stern, *Tanks, 1914–1918: The Logbook of a Pioneer* (London, 1919), pp. 185–201. Stern constructed a factory on French soil using Annamese labor, designed to turn out 300 tanks a month by importing motors from the United States and steel plate from England.

31. Two excellent books illumine the wartime growth of the Renault firm: Hatry, *Renault;* Patrick Fridenson, *Histoire des usines Renault,* vol. 1, *Naissance de la grande entreprise, 1898–1939* (Paris, 1972). For Citroën's and other firms' similar successes see Gerd Hardach, "Französiche Rüstungspolitik 1914–1918" in H. A. Winkler, ed., *Organizierter Kapitalismus* (Göttingen, 1974), pp. 102–4.

time armaments industry. Women, children, foreigners, prisoners of war, and mutilated veterans, together with the soldiers assigned to duty in armaments plants, far outnumbered civilian male workers.[32] Such a work force was more pliable than its German or British counterparts, among whom socialist traditions, shop rules of long standing, and traditional skills all stood in the way of the sort of radical restructuring of work procedures that prevailed in France.

Two other factors also helped. From the political side, the first minister of munitions, Albert Thomas, was a socialist politician and graduate of the Ecole Normale of Paris. He surrounded himself with fellow *normaliens* whose technocratic bent and socialist leanings were like his own. Such managers were more adept at keeping industrialists and workers smoothly in harness than were the haughty army officers who played the parallel role in Germany.[33]

Most important of all was the fact that the French war economy did not depend wholly on its own resources. Large amounts of coal and metal had to be imported from England to replace what had been lost behind German lines. Whenever other critical items ran short, they could be purchased abroad, either in England or in the United States—at least to begin with. But when first the English (in 1915) and then the American (in 1917) markets became overloaded with orders, so that serious delays in delivery multiplied, new means for concerting inter-Allied war production became necessary. Reorganization eventually established an international division of labor, planned at inter-Allied conferences and implemented by international administrative agencies the most important of which was the Allied Maritime Transport Council.

French dependence on Britain and America for fuel, raw materials, and increasingly also for food[34] was registered by mounting war debts that bedeviled postwar international relations. But during the war itself, overseas purchases allowed the French to concentrate their re-

32. Gerd Hardach, *The First World War, 1914–1918* (Berkeley and Los Angeles, 1977), p. 86, gives the following summary of workers in French arms plants in November 1918: 497,000 soldiers; 430,000 women; 425,000 male civilian Frenchmen; 169,000 foreigners and colonials; 137,000 youths below draft age; 40,000 POWs; 13,000 mutilated veterans; making a total of 1,711,000.

33. The biography by B. W. Schaper, *Albert Thomas: Trente ans de réformisme sociale* (Assen, 1959) is apologetic in tone but very informative.

34. In 1917 the French grain harvest dropped from its 1909–13 average of 8.5 million tons to a mere 3.1 million. At one time the food situation became so critical that the army had only a two-day supply of grain in stock; but disaster was forestalled by allocating shipping to bring supplies from overseas. Accordingly, American grain flooded in and food stocks were again adequate early in 1918. See Clémentel, *La France et la politique économique interalliée,* p. 233.

sources on munitions production and front line soldiering to a degree otherwise unattainable. French production of 75 mm shells, for example, became adequate to the demand in 1915 and peaked at over 200,000 per day—twenty times the original scale. Later, a shift to new weapons—big 155 mm artillery pieces, and such novelties as airplanes and tanks—became more important than mere numbers of shells. Here too the French equaled or exceeded what the other great powers were able to accomplish, so much so that when the American Expeditionary Force began to arrive in France, most of its heavy equipment was, by arrangement, supplied from French factories and arsenals.[35] France, more than Britain and far more than America, became the arsenal of democracy in World War I.[36]

The Germans had a different problem. Their industrial resources were far greater than those of France, and in 1914 nearly half the adult male labor force was not immediately affected by mobilization, having been excused from military training.[37] A substantial cushion therefore remained in Germany between absolute limits of production set by available manpower and materials and the escalated demand for shells and more shells that started in October when initial stocks stored in government arsenals began to run out. As a result, officers of the German War Ministry could simply demand more from the civilian economy; and, for many months, more was in fact forthcoming, without the wholesale improvisation and assignment of manpower to which the French resorted from the beginning.

On the other hand, before 1914 Germany had imported a number of key materials for the waging of war. Copper needed to manufacture shell casings and for electrical machinery had come from Chile; so, by coincidence, did nitrate, required for the production of gunpowder and fertilizer. From the moment war broke out, the Royal Navy declared a blockade of Germany's coastline and made access to overseas

35. Practically all the AEF's artillery and tanks were French; so were 4,791 of a total of 6,287 airplanes used by the Americans, not to mention 10 million 75 mm shells. Cf. André Kaspi, *Le temp des Américains: Le concours américain à la France, 1917–1918* (Paris, 1976), pp. 244–45.

36. Cf. figures for production of different types of arms in Hardach, *The First World War,* p. 87. France led the allies in every category except rifles and machine guns according to this compilation. In some lines, e.g., airplanes, France also exceeded German production. See James M. Laux, "Gnôme et Rhône: Une firme de moteurs d'avion durant la Grande Guerre," in Fridenson, *1914–1918: L'autre front,* p. 186.

37. Before the army reforms of 1913 Germany called up only 53.12 percent of the eligible age class, whereas France called up 82.96 percent, i.e., all who were physically fit. These figures come from Hans Herzfeld, *Die deutsche Rüstungspolitik vor dem Weltkrieg* (Bonn-Leipzig, 1923), p. 9.

suppliers increasingly difficult.[38] The British blockade made it obvious that if the German army were not to find its supply of shell casings and gunpowder suddenly cut off, a very careful husbanding of all the copper and nitrate already on hand would be necessary. These matters came to the attention of Walther Rathenau, heir apparent to the German General Electric Company, in the first days of the war. On 8 August 1914 he spoke to the minister of war about the problem and a week later found himself in charge of the allocation of copper and nitrate, together with other scarce raw materials needed for military and industrial production. So was born the Raw Materials Detachment of the War Ministry—the kernel from which an all-embracing system of military management of the German economy was to grow in the next three years.[39]

As befitted a great industrialist, Rathenau set up special corporations to allocate critical materials. In effect a national cartel for each commodity that came into short supply distributed whatever was available among competing users. These cartels, as in France, were managed by business executives, subject to official direction from the War Ministry in matters of general policy. A cat-and-mouse game of economic warfare soon set in between British and German authorities. The Germans sought to purchase needed raw materials wherever they could find them and arrange for import through neutral firms and ports, while the British tried to intercept such deliveries and blacklisted firms known to be trading with the Germans. Little by little the British drew their net closer, so that overseas imports became scarcer and scarcer in the German economy.

Yet the importance of the blockade was much exaggerated at the

38. Prewar planning had not entirely neglected this problem, but German officials assumed that Dutch firms would be able to import everything needed on ships flying the United States flag. Remembering the War of 1812, the Germans assumed that the British would not dare to intercept American ships on the high seas. Cf. Egmont Zechlin, "Deutschland zwischen Kabinettskrieg und Wirtschaftskrieg," *Historische Zeitschrift* 199 (1964): 389–90. In fact, however, Great Britain did persuade the Americans to acquiesce in a long-range blockade of Germany, though friction on details of how to implement the blockade continued to trouble Anglo-American relations until American belligerency turned United States policy around. On the blockade and its complications see the official British account, A. C. Bell, *A History of the Blockade of Germany, Austria-Hungary, Bulgaria and Turkey, 1914–1918* (London, 1961); M. C. Siney, *The Allied Blockade of Germany, 1914–1916* (Ann Arbor, 1957); Hardach, *The First World War*, pp. 11–34.

39. Walther Rathenau, *Tagebuch, 1907–1922* (Düsseldorf, 1967), pp. 186–88. According to L. Burchardt, "Walther Rathenau und die Anfänge der deutschen Rohstoffswirtschaftung im Ersten Weltkrieg," *Tradition* 15 (1970): 169–96, an engineer employed by AEG named Wichard von Moellendorf was the real initiator of the *Kriegsrohstoffsabteilung.*

time and subsequently. Substitutes for many items could in fact be found. Other metals replaced copper in shell casing, for example; and for uses in which copper was irreplaceable, alloying and electroplating made available quantities go much further. Thousands of other adjustments in industrial practice conserved scarce raw materials and avoided serious breakdowns of production. But nothing could replace nitrate in gunpowder. Chemists already understood how to convert nitrogen from the air into nitrate, but because of expense the process had never been tried on an industrial scale. After Germany's initial stocks of powder had been depleted in October 1914, however, continuation of combat depended on the supply of nitrate coming from factories created completely *de novo*. Without such a supply, the war would have come to a speedy close, for smuggling Chilean nitrates past the British blockade was practically impossible.

Accordingly, for the first two years of combat the War Ministry keyed its planning and regulated the scale of national war effort according to the amount of gunpowder available each month. In 1914, 1,000 tons a month was the most that could be produced, whereas the army needed 7,000 tons monthly to keep its guns firing freely. In the fall of 1914 the War Ministry first set a goal of 3,500 tons per month, then raised it to 4,500 tons per month in December 1914, when the prospect of early victory finally faded. In February 1915 the target figure was boosted to 6,000 tons per month. Production of gunpowder lagged behind these goals, but not by much, for in July 1915, 6,000 tons were in fact manufactured. The War Ministry and German industry could feel proud of such a record, even if 6,000 tons of gunpowder each month still fell short of the ever escalating demand.[40]

German industry was also able to supply the army with the thousands of other items it needed in more or less satisfactory amounts. Industrial shortages, when they appeared, were successfully adjusted by assigning priorities among competing users and by seeking substitutes. Manpower was not yet a critical limit, despite substantial drafts from the civilian work force to replace army losses. More ominous were the shortages of food, which became serious enough in May 1916 to provoke the establishment of a special Food Office. Being staffed by civilians, the Food Office did not have jurisdiction over army purchases of food and never managed to create a truly efficient food rationing system.

---

40. Ernst von Wrisberg, *Wehr und Waffen, 1914–1918* (Leipzig, 1922), pp. 86–92. Wrisberg was the officer of the War Ministry in charge of supply and wrote to defend his record against subsequent reproaches of too much "business as usual."

Difficulties at home scarcely mattered as long as German armies remained successful in the field. In spite of powder shortages, the campaigns of 1915 had on the whole gone well for Germany. Victories in the east pushed the Russian front far away from German borders; Serbia was overrun and Turkey successfully repelled an amphibious attack on the Dardanelles. Meanwhile, at home, the rise in powder production slowly restored full striking power to the German artillery.

The Germans' strategic plan for 1916 proposed to take advantage of their superiority in heavy artillery by attacking Verdun. Erich von Falkenhayn, chief of the Great General Staff since the German failure on the Marne in 1914, expected to bleed France white and compel the Republic to sue for peace before Great Britain's new armies could be ready to enter battle. But the attack on Verdun, lasting from February to June 1915, failed to achieve its expected goal, despite heavy loss of life on both sides.

This disappointment was followed by two further shocks to Germany's self-confidence. The British-French attack on the Somme (July–November 1916) showed that Great Britain's resources had indeed been thrown into the war unreservedly. Then in the east a Russian offensive against the Austrians won notable success and persuaded the Rumanians to enter the war on the Allied side. The fact that a shifty Balkan state had opted for Germany's enemy implied that, in Rumanian eyes at least, the war was going to end in an Allied victory.[41] To forestall such a result, a heightened effort on the home front was clearly called for. Germany responded by raising the stakes and intensifying its war effort to match and overmatch British and French mobilization. But before considering the new era inaugurated by Field Marshal Paul von Hindenburg and his quartermaster general, Erich Ludendorff, who took supreme command on 28 August 1916, brief remarks about British, American, and Russian responses to the first years of war are in order.

Unlike the other combatants, the British prepared for a long war from the start. Anything else would have limited their participation to very modest proportions, for only four divisions could be found to take part in the initial battles of 1914. But public opinion rejected a merely marginal role, and when Lord Kitchener, the new secretary for war, called for volunteers he met with massive response. Confusion was enormous, and administrative routines at first took no account of

41. Rumania's king was a Hohenzollern and close relative of the kaiser. His betrayal of kinship added piquancy to the German reaction.

the changed scale of operations. Massive orders were placed with private firms and with Woolwich for everything the new army needed. But such orders had to compete with French and Russian orders, and with demands from the navy as well. The result was instant overload. Deliveries lagged while an inflamed public opinion urged everyone to enlist, regardless of industrial skills or civilian occupation. About 20 percent of the munitions workers actually joined the army in response to these pressures, thereby hampering production of shells and guns that were already in desperately short supply.[42]

Not surprisingly, acute shortages soon began to afflict the British Expeditionary Force in France. In May 1915 the commander, Sir John French, decided to appeal to the public over the head of his military superiors. The resulting scandal provoked a Cabinet crisis and the establishment of a new Ministry of Munitions, headed by Lloyd George. Lloyd George promptly and peremptorily set out to mobilize the entire industrial resources of Great Britain for war. He set production goals that far exceeded anything the War Office asked for or yet conceived to be possible.[43] Voluntarism blended with compulsion in the way the new ministry went about its work. Among its first acts, for example, was to send out questionnaires asking every firm whose address the ministry could discover for an inventory of its machinery and suggestions as to what kind of munitions work it might be able to undertake. In a similar spirit of voluntarism, labor unions were persuaded to suspend traditional work rules and promised not to authorize strikes. This was an important concession, for, as in France, new machinery soon automated a good many production lines, allowing unskilled or semiskilled labor to do what skilled men had done previously. On the other hand, profits were legally limited to not more than 20 percent above the average of the prewar years, and the shrillness of war propaganda against "slackers" put a very real element of compulsion behind the recruiting drives that brought the "Kitchener army" up to a total size of 2,466,000 men by 1916.

Lloyd George gathered a group of "men of push and go" to staff the Ministry of Munitions, drawing them mainly from business and the

42. Cf. Clive Trebilcock, "War and the Failure of Industrial Mobilization, 1899 and 1914," in J. M. Winter, ed., *War and Economic Development* (Cambridge, 1975), pp. 139–64.

43. The spirit of the new regime was reflected by a remark attributed to Lloyd George: "Take Kitchener's maximum, square it, multiply that result by two; and when you are in sight of that, double it again for good luck." R. J. Q. Adams, *Arms and the Wizard; Lloyd George and the Ministry of Munitions, 1915–1916* (College Station, Tex., 1978), p. 174.

professions. Their loosely liberal biases and preconceptions contrasted with the more socialist and technocratic tone of the French
Munitions Ministry and stood in still stronger contrast to the
military-business management of the German war effort. Yet the
practical results were much the same in each country. Shell production
in Britain, for example, multiplied ten times over in the first year, thus
relieving the crisis that had precipitated the establishment of the
Ministry of Munitions in the first place. By July 1916 the volunteer
army was ready for action and brought a weight of artillery to the
Battle of the Somme that dazed and shocked the Germans, whose own
attempt to overwhelm the French at Verdun had to be broken off to
meet the new attack. But that was the only success achieved at the
Battle of the Somme. Enormous casualties,[44] like those the French
had suffered in the first weeks of fighting, took all the bloom off the
war for the British public; and as the trench warfare prolonged itself
endlessly, the Cabinet became increasingly loath to dispatch replacements to France lest still further futile bloodletting ensue.

Across the Atlantic, the United States was in a position to profit
enormously from the upsurge of demand that the war provoked. Export markets formerly supplied by British and German firms beckoned enticingly, especially in Latin America. The result was a boom
of unusual proportions. Early in the war, sales to Germany tapered off
to insignificance. The United States did not insist on defying the
British blockade, even though, when the war started, a blockade conducted at long range had no standing in international law. Yet, as long
as Allied purchases sufficed to keep American farms, factories, and
mines at full stretch, there was little incentive for trying to evade
British trade regulations.

As time passed, therefore, American supply meshed more and more
massively into the Allied war effort. At first the British were able to
pay for their purchases in the ordinary way, even though this involved
selling off capital investments in the United States. Then when ready
cash ran dry, American banks kept business booming by lending
money to the Allies. As American populists later pointed out, this
gave New York bankers an enormous financial stake in an Allied
victory by 1917 and wedded American economic resources more and
more closely to the British and French war effort.

44. Something like 50,000 on the first day; 419,652 in all by official count. John
Keegan, *The Face of Battle* (New York, 1977), pp. 204–80, provides a superb analysis of
the reasons for the British failure at the Somme and, incidentally, explains the realities
of trench warfare for the entire 1915–18 period more concisely and luminously than
anyone else has been able to do.

World markets beyond the borders of the United States were also open to Great Britain and France. Indeed, long-standing imperial roles in Africa, Asia, and Oceania gave the two Allied powers a convenient head start in tapping the globe's resources for their war effort. This meant that planning and control of home production did not have to balance out completely. Shortfalls could be made good by buying abroad in nearly every case. Delays in delivery were awkward but bearable until German submarines in 1917 threatened the Allies' lifeline. Until then, however, a directed economy at home combined very well with old-fashioned market mobilization abroad, financed by American bank loans.

Germany, too, supplemented its own national resources by resort to purchases in adjacent countries like Sweden, the Netherlands, and Switzerland. Occupied Belgium, northern France, and the Polish provinces of Russia were also compelled to provide some of the sinews of war—food, coal, and the like. But the populations of occupied provinces cooperated sluggishly and reluctantly with the German military authorities, and neutrals' sales to Germany were sharply limited by the way the British administered the naval blockade.[45] Hence Germany was mainly dependent on home resources, supplemented by whatever could be gathered within the Hapsburg lands or from Bulgaria, Turkey, and occupied territories. Within that zone, the comparatively high cost of overland transport limited Germany's access to supplies from outside its own borders. Administrative slackness in lands still overwhelmingly peasant in their population had a parallel effect. Moreover, no massive foreign credits assisted Germany in wresting food and other supplies from Allied and conquered peoples. Instead, distrust of an emerging German hegemony intensified as the war years passed, making Germany's Hapsburg, Bulgarian, and Turkish allies less and less enthusiastic in cooperating with anything the Germans proposed or undertook.

The strain on Germany's administrative capacity in the end proved crippling. No one had yet clearly conceived of a way to go about managing an entire national economy without large-scale supplement from outside. Important statistics, e.g., reliable estimates of future food production and consumption, were unavailable or else were disregarded by the military men who had the ultimate say on nearly all disputed points.

45. Beginning in 1915 negotiations between Britain and the Netherlands, Switzerland, and Scandinavian countries restricted imports to the presumed level needed for local consumption.

Russia, too, faced intense internal administrative difficulties as the strain of war set in. It was hard to feed and supply the enormous numbers of men drafted into the tsar's army. But by giving an absolute priority to their military effort the Russians accomplished miracles of production parallel to those the Germans, French, and British were simultaneously bringing to pass. Russia even outstripped the production record of the Hapsburg lands, where internal frictions among the nationalities and administrative *Schlamperei* hampered every departure from routine.[46]

As in France and Germany, the Russians entrusted the allocation of munitions contracts to committees of businessmen. They succeeded in increasing shell production from about 450,000 per month early in 1915 to 4.5 million per month in September 1916; and other forms of munitions manufacture increased more or less in proportion.[47] But profits grew even faster than production, and in 1916 runaway inflation began to register the overload on the Russian economy that the war effort had created. Price levels almost quadrupled between January and December 1916; wages lagged seriously behind prices; and most disastrous of all, peasant food producers found less and less incentive to bring their harvest to market, since consumer goods became so scarce as to be practically unavailable.

Subsistence patterns of village life swiftly reasserted themselves under these circumstances. In 1917 only 15 percent of a reduced harvest was brought to market as compared to 25 percent of the 1913 harvest. The army preempted most of the grain that did become available, so that catastrophic food shortages hit the towns. As a result, by 1917 industrial production plummeted, and army morale soon followed.[48] Munitions shortages at the front played their part, of course; but squandering of materiel through undisciplined fire and poor coop-

---

46. But cf. Robert J. Wegs, *Die österreichische Kriegswirtschaft 1914–1918* (Vienna, 1979) for a record of what was accomplished.

47. Norman Stone, *The Eastern Front* (New York, 1975), pp. 149–52 and passim disproves the notion that Russian armies were starved of munitions in World War I.

48. The following statistics tell the tale.

Grain Harvest (mil. poods)*		Delivered to Towns (mil. poods)		Price Level in Russia		Index of Industrial Production	
1914	4,309	1913–14	390	June 1914	100	1913	100
1915	4,659	1915–16	330	June 1915	115	1914	101.2
1916	3,916	1916–17	295	June 1916	141	1915	113.7
1917	3,809			Dec. 1916	398	1916	121.5
				June 1917	702	1917	77.3
				Dec. 1917	1,172		

*1 pood = 56 pounds. *Source:* Stone, *The Eastern Front*, pp. 209, 287, 295.

eration between Russian artillery and infantry contributed more than was admitted at the time to the disaster that came to Russian arms.[49]

Against Hapsburg troops, Russian armies could still win victories, as the Galician offensive of 1916 showed. But the long series of German victories in the east in 1914 and 1915 demonstrated that mere numbers were an inadequate counter to German technique. Yet as soon as the Germans turned attention to the Western Front in 1916, attacking at Verdun and then parrying the allied assault at the Somme, the Russians regained offensive capability. Clearly, Germany had somehow to become able to mount a massive effort simultaneously on both fronts if such setbacks were to be avoided. In August 1916 Hindenburg took over the Supreme Command, intending to do just that.

Managerial Metamorphosis in World War I:
Second Phase, 1916–18

Before considering the new phase of the conflict inaugurated by the intensification of the German mobilization for war, it is convenient to pause and reflect on some general aspects of the war effort which had begun to alter older patterns of European society profoundly, even before the climactic paroxysms of the final two years of war had had time to make their mark.

In industry, the most important general change was the introduction of mass production methods for manufacturing artillery shells and for nearly every kind of infantry equipment as well. Larger items could not easily be mass produced, yet by the war's end, production lines for cars and trucks and for airplane engines had become standard, especially in France and the United States, where workers' resistance to such radical departures from older industrial practice was much less than in either Germany or Great Britain.[50] As we saw in chapter 7,

49. A striking statistic: Russian rifles fired off 125 rounds per man per month, whereas the French used only 30 rounds and the British 50. Ibid., p. 135. Camouflage and indirect fire, which became normal on the Western Front in 1915, left Russian artillery methods far behind. Using these techniques, German gunners had little difficulty in silencing Russian batteries at long range. Russian infantrymen preferred to attribute the resulting weakness of artillery support to civilian bungling in the rear, whereas in fact deficiencies of Russian military training went far to nullify Russia's real industrial successes in expanding war production.

50. Louis Renault inaugurated his production line for car bodies in 1911 after a visit to the United States. This provoked a strike, but he won it, thus preparing for rapid expansion in the war years when all phases of car, truck, and plane manufacture were organized into assembly lines. Cf. Hatry, *Renault: Usines de guerre,* p. 15; Fridenson, *Histoire des usines Renault,* vol. 1, pp. 73–75.

mass production had been applied to the manufacture of small arms in the United States after the War of 1812, and appropriate machines were subsequently imported into Europe after the Crimean War. In the latter half of the nineteenth century, American businessmen, facing persistent shortages of skilled labor, had applied similar techniques to other kinds of manufacture, most notably in mass producing sewing machines and typewriters. But in Europe little had been done before the sudden emergency of World War I required vast numbers of identical items for military use. Thereupon, jigs and dies, automated machinery and assembly lines, came rapidly into their own.

Radical cheapening of manufactured articles of mass consumption became technically feasible with such methods. As so often before, military demand thus blazed the way for new techniques, and on a very broad front, from shell fuses and telephones to trench mortars and wristwatches. The subsequent industrial and social history of the world turned very largely on the continuing application of the methods of mass production whose scope widened so remarkably during the emergency of World War I. Anyone looking at the equipment installed in a modern house will readily recognize how much we in the late twentieth century are indebted to industrial changes pioneered in near-panic circumstances when more and more shells, gunpowder, and machine guns suddenly became the price of survival as a sovereign state.

Of almost equal importance was the broadened application of deliberate, planned invention to the design of new weapons and machines. As we saw in the preceding chapter, before 1914 deliberate invention was patronized and funded for the most part by the world's leading navies, thanks to the scale of expenditure on warships and the complexity that their armament had attained. World War I brought deliberate invention ashore, and applied it to new and old weapons. The Germans did more to improve the performance of traditional weapons than their rivals, if only because their need to conserve scarce materials dictated careful reconsideration of every aspect of the design and manufacture of artillery and infantry equipment. Newer devices like U-boats and airplanes also underwent very rapid evolution on the Allied as well as on the German side. Experience in battle suggested desirable performance characteristics for all such weapons, which were then translated into reality so far as engineers and designers were able to meet the users' demands. Command invention thus became generalized and applied to every kind of military hardware.

The development of tanks provides the most remarkable example

Command Technology Comes Ashore

During World War I a few visionaries saw that new, gasoline-powered weapons systems could transcend existing muscular limits on land warfare. This sort of thinking achieved only modest success in 1914–18, although tanks and airplanes played a significant part in the final offensives. The photograph upper left shows the most successful World War I tank model, the British Mark V. Below is a photograph of the "Whippet" (Mark A, 1918) whose speed (12.5 km/hour) and range (100 km) were expected to allow tank columns to break clean through the German front so as to

seize headquarters, *disrupt command and supply, and spread panic among front-line troops. The war ended before this bold plan for 1919 could be tested; but twenty years later the German army achieved the intended effect, first in Poland and then in France, using additional refinements such as air-ground cooperation. The photograph on the right shows German troops practicing* Blitzkrieg *tactics on maneuvers late in the 1930s.*

Heinz Guderian, *Die Panzerwaffe* (Stuttgart: Union Deutsche Verlagsgesellschaft, 1943), Abbildungen 7, 12, and 41.

of what could be accomplished along these lines. Early in the war it occurred to several persons that a tracked, armored vehicle might be able to cross enemy trenches with impunity. If equipped with suitable guns, such a vehicle could destroy enemy machine guns and open the path for a general breakthrough. Both British and French authorities acted on this idea. On the British side continuity with naval experience of command technology was assured by the fact that the Bureau of Naval Design took responsibility for the early development of "land cruisers," as tanks initially were called.

When British tanks first went into battle during the closing weeks of the Somme offensive (August 1916) mechanical failures and imperfect coordination with infantry and artillery made the new weapons ineffective. Soon afterwards, the French suffered similar disappointments. Yet a handful of technically minded officers clung to a vision of what yet might be; and by 1917 improved designs (and training) won real if limited successes. When the Allies' final counteroffensives began in June 1918, a new generation of tanks assisted the infantry in battle all along the line. Indeed, the British High Command went so far as tentatively to approve a plan for 1919 which would have inaugurated the tactics of *Blitzkrieg* twenty years before the Germans first actually used tank columns in Poland to penetrate deep in the enemy rear and disrupt command and supply systems.[51]

The remarkable feature of the "Plan 1919" was that its feasibility depended on a weapon that did not exist when the plan was drawn up. New tanks, with improved speed, maneuverability, and range were required for the dash toward the enemy rear which the plan contemplated. Thus, instead of remaining content with the capabilities of existing weapons, as military planners had done before, "Plan 1919" undertook to shape the future by deliberately altering existing technology to make it fit the needs of the plan. The test of action never came of course, and large-scale operations based on improved capabilities of armored vehicles waited until 1939. But by 1918 it was clear that command technology had begun to transform land warfare as pervasively as it had transformed naval warfare in the prewar decades.

Before 1914 the world's leading armies had unanimously resisted rapid, disorganizing technical change. As long as all movement beyond

51. Basil Lidell Hart, *The Tanks: History of the Royal Tank Regiment and its Predecessors,* 2 vols. (London, 1959) is a semiofficial British account. Cf. also J. F. C. Fuller, *Tanks in the Great War, 1914–1918* (London, 1920); and for Plan 1919, R. M. F. Cruttwell, *A History of the Great War, 1914–1918,* 2d ed. (Oxford, 1936), p. 547.

railheads depended on horse-drawn vehicles or human portage, muscular capabilities set a low ceiling on the size and complexity of everything armies could use. But the internal combustion motor lifted that limit in the course of World War I, beginning with the taxicabs that carried French soldiers from Paris for the first Battle of the Marne in 1914. Two years later, trucks traveling along the *voie sacrée* allowed the French to hold Verdun even after rail connections were cut. And by 1918 reconnaisance and pursuit, roles traditionally assigned to cavalry, were being taken over by airplanes and tanks.

Former limits on the industrialization of war were thereby removed. Nevertheless, military exploitation of the possibilities of command invention was really reserved for the future. World War I only opened a door through which armies might march into a mechanical never-never land of the kind that navies had already begun to inhabit. But just as the prospect of what might yet become possible dawned upon a handful of tank enthusiasts and visionaries, the armistice of 1918 called a halt that lasted for about fifteen years.

Technical change was matched by no less deliberate changes in human society and daily routines. Millions of men were drafted into armies and induced to submit to radically new conditions of life—and death. Other millions entered factories, government offices, or undertook some other unaccustomed kind of war work. Efficient allocation of labor soon became a major factor in the war effort of every country; and the welfare of workers, as well as of fighting men, began to matter, since an ill-nourished or discontented work force could not be expected to achieve maximum output. Factory canteens to feed a firm's employees became important as food supplies ran short. Nurseries to provide care for infants freed young mothers for war work too. Special housing was sometimes constructed for war workers or assigned to them. Sports clubs attached to particular plants provided still another kind of fringe benefit and morale booster.[52]

Welfare measures emanating from factory managers went hand in hand with expanding roles for labor unions. In Britain and Germany, where unions had been well entrenched before 1914, government officials found it useful or necessary to rely on cooperation from union leaders in organizing and reorganizing labor for the war effort. When clashes between unions and employers took place, government representatives often favored the unions, even when, as in Germany, traditional antipathy divided the official classes from workers' representa-

---

52. For Renault's efforts along these lines see Hatry, *Renault: Usines de guerre,* pp. 94–102.

tives and spokesmen.[53] The alliance among government bureaucrats, labor bureaucrats, and business bureaucrats to extend their collective jurisdiction and effective control over ordinary human lives was less apparent in France, the United States, and Russia, where unions remained weak or, coming late to the scene, espoused revolutionary or quasi-revolutionary ideologies.[54] Businessmen, whether masquerading as "dollar a year" men in government service or acting privately to capture government contracts, had correspondingly freer scope in directing the French, American, and Russian (to 1917) war economies.

Health, too, became subject to official management. In army ranks, inoculation and other systematic precautions against infectious diseases, which in all earlier wars killed far more soldiers than enemy action, made the long stalemate of the trenches possible. In eastern Europe, public health administration broke down after 1915, so that typhus and other diseases played their usual roles in killing soldiers and civilians alike; but until 1918, when a serious influenza epidemic swept around the entire globe, killing far more persons than died in battle during World War I, army doctors and public health officials managed to keep lethal infections in check on the Western Front, despite miserable conditions in the trenches.[55] On the other hand, little was done to extend preventive medicine to civilians. That had to wait for World War II.

Rationing of food and other consumables had begun to alter accustomed inequalities of consumption within civilian society by 1916, and in the ensuing years increasingly stringent rationing deprived money incomes of much of their peacetime meaning. Taxation and inflation combined in varying proportions in each country to do the same. Ownership of property became less important; ascribed status, deriving from an individual's place in a hierarchy of command— military or civil as the case might be—tended to eclipse inherited rank, although to be sure the two often coincided. Despite carryovers from

53. This is a major theme of Gerald Feldman, *Army, Industry and Labor in Germany, 1914–1918* (Princeton, 1966).

54. Cf. Hatry, *Renault: Usines de guerre*, pp. 119–45, for Renault's difficulties with unions beginning in 1917. For the United States, David M. Kennedy, *Over Here: The First World War and American Society* (New York, 1980), pp. 70–73, 258–64 and passim, has interesting things to say about the wartime roles of rival AF of L and IWW labor leaders. For Russia, Isaac Deutscher, *Soviet Trade Unions* (London, 1950), pp. 1–17.

55. Estimates of deaths from influenza in 1918–19 start at 21 million and rise indefinitely higher. This was more than twice battle deaths in World War I. Cf. Alfred W. Crosby, Jr., *Epidemic and Peace* (Westport, Conn., 1976), p. 207. Venereal disease also attained epidemic proportions in the British army, partly because it was treated as a moral rather than as a medical problem.

the past, what ought to be called national socialism, if Hitler had not preempted the term, emerged from the barracks and purchasing offices of the European armed services and, with the help of a coalition of administrative elites drawn from big business, big labor, academia, and big government, made European society over in an amazingly short time.

Part of the secret of war mobilization was that when it was launched everyone thought it would last for only a few months. Sacrifice of familiar routines and creature comforts mattered less when return to normal as soon as the war had been won was taken for granted by all concerned. This disarmed conservatives time and again. Moreover, the sufferings of soldiers at the front made everything demanded of civilians in the rear seem trivial by comparison and discredited those who sought to hold fast to rights and privileges that the new managers of society found standing in the way of the war effort.

Yet irony and ambiguity lay at the heart of this whole affair. Acceptance of the differentiation between ruler and ruled, shepherd and sheep, staff officer and cannon fodder depended on the strength of a shared conviction that the war had to be fought to a finish, cost what it might. Obedience, sustained by that conviction, paradoxically became an expression of freedom. But if the conviction wavered, still more if it disappeared entirely, then the new ruling elites thrown up by the war were suddenly transmogrified into bloodthirsty and tyrannous usurpers, holding everyone in chains for evil reasons of their own. In other words, freedom and justice changed sides when people ceased to believe that victory at any price was a self-evident good. Whenever and wherever that shift of outlook took hold, the extraordinary enlargement of public power required for efficient mobilization of the home front threatened to break down even more rapidly than it had come into being, though what the alternative might be—civil war, anarchy, defeat, and national humiliation, or, alternatively, the dawn of a new and juster society—remained a matter of faith and fear rather than of foresight.

These dimensions of the war effort became poignantly evident during 1917. The collapse of tsarist autocracy in March of that year seemed to bring Russia into the parliamentary and democratic camp. But the new government never consolidated its legitimacy and failed utterly to solve the food crisis afflicting the cities. The resulting decay of Russia's capacity to wage war reached a climax in November, when Lenin seized power with the professed purpose of giving peace to the people, land to the peasants, and food to the workers of Russian cities.

The war thereupon assumed a new ideological aspect. Lenin's challenge to the legitimacy of all the governments of Europe and the world was explicit and direct. The Marxist-Leninist explanation of how monopoly capitalism had precipitated war and how the resulting disaster could and should be cured by converting international into class war could not be lightly dismissed. Socialists and trade union leaders had to decide whether Lenin was right in summoning them to revolutionary action; and the managerial elites that had come so vigorously to the fore were everywhere alarmed by the prospect of domestic disaffection conjured up by Lenin's words.

Germany's response was to press ahead with an intensified war effort. Hindenberg and Ludendorff, coming to supreme command of the army in August 1916, had already initiated all-out mobilization. They simply cut loose from the War Office's previous habit of keying all planning to calculations of how much powder could be made available each month. Instead, the new planners put military goals first. Having decided on physical requirements for the next season's campaigns, they placed orders for the necessary level of supply, challenging the civilian sector of society to achieve "impossible" goals, if necessary by cutting back drastically on other forms of economic activity. Germany thus became a garrison state, in principle and to a considerable degree also in practice, subordinating everything to the needs of the army as defined by the High Command's strategic plans for the coming year.

The "Hindenburg Plan" of 1916 was originally proclaimed in imitation of Lloyd George's noisy campaign of 1915 to expand munitions production in Britain. Goals were often set arbitrarily and with scant attention to their feasibility. It was partly mere propaganda, as had been true of the British program as well. But in Germany the consequences of exaggeration and overambitious production goals were rather more serious than in Great Britain. Overload swiftly resulted. Coal, steel, and transport all began to run short. Food shortages soon became most critical of all. But Germany could not do much to correct official mistakes by buying abroad, whereas Great Britain and France could compensate for defects of their own planning and overcommitment of their home resources by falling back on the tried and true mechanism of the world market to provide critical items from overseas. The Royal Navy prevented Germany from doing the same. Consequently, all the successes the Germans had in raising their output of munitions after 1916—and they were very great—were counterbalanced by a growingly serious malfunction of the national economy as a whole.

When the Hindenburg Plan was first proclaimed, no one clearly recognized that manpower, food, and fuel were the ultimate regulators of the war effort. In 1916 and 1917, the men in charge assumed that, as in the first years of the war, more could always be wrung out of the civilian economy simply by issuing sterner instructions and demanding more. They were fully determined to do so. Contrary advice seemed defeatist or, when it came from civilians, treasonous. Erich Ludendorff, quartermaster general and the leading spirit at Supreme Headquarters, believed that victory would rest with the nation exhibiting strong enough will and sufficient self-sacrifice. All other variables depended on will power. This being so, the only danger was that weak-kneed civilians—politicians in particular—might betray the German army by stabbing it in the back at the climax of the struggle.

Such principles had deep roots in the Prussian past. Rulers from the Great Elector to Frederick the Great in moments of crisis had commandeered supplies as needed, subordinating private interest ruthlessly to the collective, military effort. That was what had made Prussia great. The fact that a far more complex industrial plant was needed in the twentieth century to supply an army did not change the overriding principle, though the generals in charge often became impatient with the financial claims and controversies that continually embroiled and sometimes obstructed prompt and deferential obedience to their demands. As shortages arose, one after another, the generals relied more and more on big labor and big business to remodel the economy according to military needs. Each party got more or less what it wanted: more munitions for the army, more profits for industrialists,[56] and consolidation of their authority over the work force for union officials.

What was left out was the rural sector where horsepower, manpower, and fertilizer all ran short. Bad weather in 1916 reduced the

56. Rival groupings of industrialists responded to and profited from expansion of munitions production in diverse ways. For an interesting analysis of the splits in German industry see Hartmut Pogge von Strandmann, "Widersprüche in Modernisierungsprozess Deutschlands," in Bernd Jürgen Wendt et al., eds., *Industrielle Gesellschaft und politisches System* (Bonn, 1978), pp. 225–40. Army officers shared with union leaders and socialists a profound distaste for the pecuniary calculations of industrialists. In the closing phases of the war, when worker morale became critical, Ludendorff toyed with the idea of eliminating profits by *étatisation* of munitions firms. Cf. Gerald Feldman, *Army, Industry, and Labor in Germany, 1914–1918* (Princeton, 1966), pp. 494–96. The Marxist view that businessmen called the tune to which the army officers danced, expressed for example in J. Martin Kitchen, *The Silent Dictatorship: The Politics of the German High Command under Hindenburg and Ludendorff, 1916–1918* (London, 1976), seems naively misguided—a clinging to nineteenth-century notions about the sovereignty of market relations in a time when these were being subordinated to the ancient principle of command mobilization.

harvest as well. Efforts to fix agricultural prices misfired, whereupon black marketing proliferated, undermining the legal system of food rationing.[57] By concentrating lopsidedly on producing munitions, the military managers of the German economy thus brought the country to the verge of starvation by the end of 1918.[58]

Subordinating everything to the immediate needs of the army in the hope of winning decisive victory with just one more supreme effort was not necessarily irrational. Victory did come very near in 1918, despite American intervention. Had the Germans won, Hindenburg and Ludendorff and their associates would have seemed paragons and heroes. They did get more munitions. Powder production, the original limit on German warmaking capacity, crested at 14,315 tons in October 1918, and the German army was never seriously hampered in the last years of the war by shortage of materiel.[59] New weapons, e.g., antitank guns, came off production lines as needed. Until November 1918, when manpower, food, and fuel all ran short at once, unforeseen bottlenecks, though they came thick and fast, were always relieved by hasty reallocation of resources.

On the battlefield intensified mobilization brought the expected results. Russia was defeated and dismembered in 1917, and in March 1918 new tactics of infiltration broke the Allied trench lines in France. The victorious Germans lacked the transport to keep advancing, but without the moral and material support of the American Expeditionary Force, some two million strong by November 1918, the weary British and French armies could scarcely have survived the German spring offensives. Thus until the final weeks victory hovered always just beyond the Germans' grasp. As Wellington is reputed to have said of the Battle of Waterloo, World War I was "a near run thing" by anyone's calculation.

The suddenness with which the tide of victory reversed direction after June 1918 gave Germans little time to adjust to defeat. This was especially true within the army, whose leaders had long cultivated a quasi-agonistic attitude towards civilians. Suspicion grew in the last

57. August Skalweit, *Die deutsche Kriegsnährungswirtschaft* (Berlin, 1927) provides much detail of the mismanagement of agriculture.

58. The fact that the Allied blockade was maintained after the armistice through the worst months of food shortage in the winter of 1918–19 made it natural to blame the blockade for the food crisis. But Germany would have been capable of feeding itself, if resources had been reserved for that purpose.

59. Ludwig Wartzbacker, "Die Versorgung des Heeres mit Waffen und Munition," in Max Schwarte, ed., *Der Grosse Krieg* (Leipzig, 1921) 8:129. Von Wrisberg, *Wehr und Waffen, 1914–1918*, pp. 57, 84, although bitterly critical of the Hindenburg program also proudly concludes that manpower and horses, not artillery and munitions, were what limited the German army in its final offensive.

years of the war, especially when strikes and the Reichstag "Peace resolution" of 1917 showed that at least some civilians were not supporting the war effort as the army leaders thought they should. When collapse finally came in November 1918, events reinforced this frame of mind all too aptly. The German army was still on French soil and its leaders could claim with enough plausibility to be convincing to those who wished to believe it, that German soldiers had never been defeated in battle but lost the war because they had been betrayed by treasonous Social Democrats and other revolutionaries in the rear. The Nazi movement founded itself on this myth, and a deep distrust of civilian steadfastness, based on Hitler's memories of 1918, governed Germany's domestic policy during the first phases of World War II.

The manifold success resulting from the intensification of the German war effort after August 1916 created critical problems for the Allies. In particular, unrestricted submarine warfare, launched in February 1917, came close to crippling Great Britain. Antisubmarine weapons, notably depth charges, were invented or improved, but by far the most important means the Allies found for reducing sinkings was to convoy merchant ships with a screen of destroyers and other warships. Yet despite all that the Allied navies could do, for more than a year the stock of shipping diminished faster than new tonnage could be built. This in turn meant that supplies coming from overseas to supplement British, French, and Italian resources dwindled steadily. Careful calculation became necessary; and as available shipping shrank, controls over the uses to which imports were put had to be intensified.

For France this meant that the Ministry of Commerce, headed by Etienne Clémentel, took over the primary role in coordinating war production from the Ministry of Munitions. Clémentel entertained novel ideas about how to institutionalize the wartime economic collaboration of France, Italy, and Britain so as to restrict and restrain German industrial preponderance in peacetime. He soon managed to arouse American suspicions, for such an economic bloc would, indeed, have been directed as much against American as against German industry. As a result, after the United States became an active belligerent, Clémentel's plans and hopes for permanent economic collaboration with Great Britain and Italy had to be shelved, and Wilsonian rhetoric about national self-determination crowded all transnational ideals from the scene.[60]

60. On Clémentel's ideas and the influence of the Ministry of Commerce on the French war effort see Godfrey, "Bureaucracy, Industry and Politics in France during the First World War," pp. 95–215. Clémentel's own book, *La France et la politique économique*

The principal agency coordinating French and British economic planning in the last year of the war was the Allied Maritime Transport Council, set up in December 1917. National calculations of exactly how much tonnage was needed for each vital import were funneled into the council. That body then had to decide on priorities, whenever available shipping fell short of requirements.[61] The fact that after April 1918 new ships were launched faster than the U-boats were able to sink existing vessels enormously facilitated the council's deliberations. Nevertheless, by granting and withholding applications for shipping space, the council was in a position to affect each separate national economy profoundly.

Resort to overseas markets, which had hitherto cushioned the Allied war economies against shortages arising from deficient foresight, was thus also brought within the scope of deliberate management. Something of the sort might have become necessary in any case. For when the United States became an active belligerent, massive orders for the American armed forces swiftly overloaded the country's industrial capacity. Political negotiation then became necessary to protect French and British access to commodities that were in critically short supply in the United States. This situation might have compelled the Europeans to resort to some sort of planning for their overseas purchases anyhow. But shipping shortages made the problem acute and inescapable, and allocation of shipping by the Maritime Transport Council constituted a simple and very efficacious way of compelling each Allied government to control the demand for and uses made of everything imported from overseas.

As far as France was concerned, this meant that the committees of industrialists who had enjoyed a very free hand to manage the country's mobilization in the first years of the war had to conform to requirements and instructions coming from the Ministry of Commerce, even when, as sometimes happened, they found the new rules distasteful or disadvantageous. A far more rigorously *étatist* and technocratic system than anything the socialist minister of munitions, Albert Thomas, had been able or even desired to establish in the first years of the war thus emerged in France under the guidance of the rightist Etienne Clémentel.

---

interalliée, was written for the Carnegie Corporation of New York, and is understandably discrete in describing his unrealized hopes for an anti-German and anti-American European economic community.

61. J. Arthur Salter, *Allied Shipping Control: An Experiment in International Administration* (Oxford, 1921) offers a detailed account of how the chairman of the Council looked back on his accomplishments. For the French side see Jean Monnet, *Mémoires* (Paris, 1976), pp. 59–89.

The British, too, resorted increasingly to compulsory regulation, e.g., in rationing food and other consumer goods. But more of a voluntaristic element survived in Great Britain than on the Continent. Compulsion, introduced for military service in 1916, was never extended to the civilian work force as it was in Germany, though many persons in Britain advocated doing so. Similarly, when shipping shortages threatened the food supply, the government reacted by launching a high-pressure campaign to increase agricultural production and succeeded in bringing some seven and a half million acres of grassland under crops by letting local committees decide whose land should be plowed up by state-owned tractors, grouped into machine tractor stations like those the Russians later used in their collectivization drive of the 1930s. In 1918 this combination of compulsion and voluntarism raised Britain's wheat and potato crop no less than 40 percent above prewar averages and reduced food imports by more than a third.[62]

If one compares the British and French war effort with that of Germany, it is hard to escape the conclusion that the Allies managed somewhat better than their enemy. Britain, in particular, by its policy of limiting profits and through the efficiency of its rationing system,[63] apportioned costs of the war more equably than was true on the Continent or in the United States. A part of this difference rested on political traditions in Britain going back to the eighteenth century, whereby men of property and wealth had become accustomed to paying heavy taxes in wartime. But another factor was the relative ease of controlling an economy in which export and import played so large a role. Goods passing across a dock were hard to conceal from public authorities, whereas in a more nearly self-contained economy, such as that of Germany, no such obvious and easy check point existed. Accurate statistics and equable distribution of scarce goods were much more difficult to achieve in landlocked countries. German shortcomings in the food and agricultural sector were perhaps largely due to this difference between their situation and that confronting British and French administrators.[64]

The war ended before planned integration of the war economies of the great Allied powers went very far. To be sure, two million Ameri-

---

62. Hardach, *The First World War,* pp. 123–31. The high priority accorded to agriculture in Great Britain contrasted sharply with German (and French) policy. No doubt Britain's obvious vulnerability to starvation explained the difference.

63. William Beveridge, *British Food Control* (London, 1928), pp. 217–32.

64. French inattention to agriculture equalled or exceeded German neglect. Cf. Clémentel, *La France et la politique économique interalliée,* p. 233. The United States sent

can soldiers were successfully transported to France, and, to save time and shipping space, their heavy equipment was provided mainly by the French. Other forms of complementarity that had grown up helter skelter during the early years of the war continued to its end, but deliberate management often exacerbated conflicts of interest which a market with freely fluctuating prices would have at least partially disguised. Thus in April 1917, at the height of the shipping crisis, the British withdrew half of the ships they had previously assigned to the task of supplying France and threatened to withdraw the rest in June if the French did not impose stricter controls on imports. The resulting interruption of supplies had the effect of reducing French industrial output, even of munitions, for a few months.[65]

Military command was also integrated among the Allies, but only imperfectly and at the last moment. A decision to unite the Allied armies in France under Field Marshal Ferdinand Foch was taken in March 1918 when the final German offensive had broken through the trench lines; but it never became fully effective. His title as commander in chief did not allow Foch to issue orders to British and American troops without first carefully feeling out the views of his British and American colleagues. Diplomacy and professional consultation, therefore, tempered the military chain of command without preventing the French, British, American, and Belgian armies from coordinating their counteroffensive quite effectively in the last weeks of the war.

Allied responses to the heightened crisis of 1917–18 only adumbrated the possibilities of transnational management. Fuller realization was reserved for World War II. Within national boundaries, however, the mobilization of manpower and resources achieved in Germany, France, and Britain by the end of the war came close to absolute limits set by the manpower and materials available to the planners. The principles of management were clear enough. Experts could calculate what the armed forces needed for conducting planned operations; and administrative skill was sufficient by 1918 to organize the resources of an entire nation as though it were a single firm designed to supply the armed forces with all they required.

Preexisting bureaucracies from private industry, from civil govern-

---

no less than 8.42 million metric tons of food to France between 1914 and 1924 according to William C. Mallendore, *History of the United States Food Administration, 1917–1919* (Stanford, 1941), p. 42.

65. Godfrey, "Bureaucracy, industry and politics in France during the First World War," pp. 84–86; Clémentel, *La France et la politique économique interalliée*, p. 321.

ment, and from the armed services came together to make this possible; but the principles of management—an unobstructed flow-through of appropriately assorted factors of destruction—were the same as those which had been evolved since the 1880s by big business firms for managing the production and distribution of goods for private consumption. Perhaps one may argue that in private businesses costs measured in money mattered so much that planning of material flows was always firmly subordinated to financial calculation, whereas during the war, material factors of production and destruction mattered more than money costs to most of the persons concerned with national planning and management. But financial controls were utilized in each belligerent country too, both at a national, governmental level and within private firms and corporations.

Interplay between financial calculation of costs and quantitative calculation of manpower, food, fuel, transport, and raw materials are always complicated, whether in peace or in war. During World War I only when one of the two got out of control did disaster strike. Russia's inflation and consequent economic dislocation in 1917 and Germany's physical shortages of food and manpower in 1918 brought each to defeat, registering in only slightly divergent ways the limits of deliberate national management within the two countries. Successful maintenance of the war effort required both material and financial plans to work together with reasonable accuracy to the facts. The managers of the major belligerents achieved this during World War I with a degree of success no one had dreamed possible beforehand. In view of the global propagation of managed economies in the second half of the twentieth century, this is likely to seem the major historical significance of World War I in time to come.

Interwar Reaction and Return to Managed Economies during World War II

Among contemporaries and survivors such a judgment would have seemed absurd. As soon as fighting ended, the emergency bureaucracies administering the war effort were disbanded (even in the Soviet Union), and most of the legal constraints that had been imposed on private behavior during the war were canceled. To be sure, revolution and fear of revolution dominated central and eastern Europe until about 1923. Even in the United States, return to normalcy, though an effective political slogan, was never seriously attempted. New possibilities of mass production and urban living, glimpsed during the war, were far too dazzling to abandon with the peace.[66] But private pursuit of the good life, however defined, was taken for granted, and the United States explored the possibilities of mass production of automobiles and other consumables in the 1920s with an enthusiasm unmatched elsewhere.

The Soviet Union stood at the opposite pole, seriously impoverished by civil war and revolution, and ideologically committed to socialism, if necessary in only one country. But there, too, reaction set in. The New Economic Policy of 1921–28 explicitly relied on market incentives to manage agriculture as well as the artisan level of manufacture. In the rest of Europe, residues of the war faded slowly, since boundary changes and land redistribution programs in eastern Europe, reconstruction of war damage in France, catastrophic inflation in Germany, and war debts and reparations everywhere prolonged economic dislocation. New American loans to Germany after 1924 underwrote a brief period of industrial prosperity; but in 1929 the onset of the Great Depression inaugurated a new crisis. Responses varied, but in Russia, Germany, and the United States return to patterns of political management that had been first explored during World War I became unmistakable by the mid-1930s. Japan, too, began to construct a war economy of its own in the Far East after 1932. Then, at the end of the decade, World War II broke out and lasted long enough to make managed economies normal in all of the more industrialized countries of the world.

With the advantages of half a century's perspective, the kinship between wartime mobilization and governmental programs responding to the economic crises of the 1930s seems apparent. But at the time, few recognized or perhaps wished to admit any such thing. Russia's first Five-Year Plan, for example, 1928–32, was trumpeted as a monument to socialism, while its urgent military objectives were systematically disguised.[67] But during the second Five-Year Plan, 1932–37, the rapid growth of arms output made the kinship of

---

66. The United States' GNP approximately doubled during World War I; and for the first time the 1920 census found more than half the population to be urban dwellers. Perhaps the most important result of World War I for the United States was the decisive impetus it gave to the transformation of American agriculture from family farm to agribusiness. High prices, guaranteed by the government, induced a surge in output and encouraged heavy investment in tractors and other farm machinery. On the wartime transformation of United States rural life see David Danbom, *The Resisted Revolution: Urban America and the Industrialization of Agriculture, 1900–1930* (Ames, Iowa, 1979), pp. 97–109.

67. John Ericson, *The Soviet High Command: A Military-Political History* (London, 1962), pp. 303–6.

Soviet-style economic planning with war mobilization more obvious. Certainly the rhetoric of Russian planning was military from the beginning. Heroes of Soviet labor struggled to win victories in production campaigns on both the agricultural and industrial fronts. Propaganda enveloped the whole effort in a haze of ideological enthusiasm, intended to link party and people, rulers and ruled, managers and managed, into a single cooperating whole. War propaganda had aimed at exactly the same result using very similar means.[68]

Despite much wastefulness and years of intense collision with the peasantry, Soviet success in accelerating the pace of industrialization was enormous, as Russia's performance in World War II showed. The Russians had the advantages of a rapidly growing population, abundant natural resources, and an autocratic tradition in politics which made submission to orders more acceptable than would have been the case elsewhere in Europe. At the same time, faith in the future and in the apocalyptic promises of Marxism provided justification for present hardships. The paradoxical combination of quasi-military administration with a revolutionary and libertarian ideology proved potent indeed.

Japan responded to the depression by renewing aggressive expansion on the continent of Asia. In the puppet state of Manchukuo, set up by the Japanese army in 1932, state-owned corporations carried through a very rapid industrial development. Coal and iron production shot upward in much the same way that Russian enterprises were simultaneously developing production from new coal and iron fields in western Siberia.[69] In Japan itself, raw material imports from Manchuria helped to sustain a fivefold increase in heavy industrial output between 1930 and 1942, whereas light industry remained about stable during those years.[70] Armaments were the spark plug and principal growth point of this entire development.

68. John Scott, *Behind the Urals: An American Worker in Russia's City of Steel* (London, 1942), pp. 8–9: "Ever since 1931 or thereabouts, the Soviet Union has been at war. . . . People were wounded and killed, women and children froze to death, millions starved, thousands were court martialed and shot in the campaigns of collectivization and industrialization. I would wager that Russia's battle of metallurgy alone involved more casualties than the battle of the Marne." For the Five-Year Plans as a species of war economy see Moshe Lewin, *Political Undercurrents in Soviet Economic Debates from Bukharin to the Modern Reformers* (Princeton, 1974), pp. 102–12.

69. F. C. Jones, *Manchuria since 1931* (London 1949), pp. 140–60. In 1936 the Japanese inaugurated a five year plan for Manchukuo consciously imitating the Russian model.

70. Jerome B. Cohen, *Japan's Economy in War and Reconstruction* (Minneapolis, 1949), p. 2.

China was quite unable to match Japan's military and economic upthrust. Neither the United States nor the League of Nations was able through remonstrance to prevent the Japanese army from expanding its operations into north China in 1937 and then occupying the entire coastline by 1939. Collisions with Soviet troops along the Manchurian border, however, led to Japanese defeats in 1938 and again on a larger scale in 1939. Vivid recollection of the Russians' formidability in these battles deeply influenced Japan's policy towards the USSR during World War II.[71]

Japan's development towards a war economy between 1930 and 1941 owed less to World War I experience than to the larger pattern of Japan's response to the West since 1853. Management of national effort so as to achieve military power had been central to Japan's entire modernization. World War I represented a phase in that effort when successes at German and Chinese expense had been easily won, only to be compromised after the war when Chinese resistance together with American and European diplomatic pressure persuaded the Japanese to relinquish some of their wartime gains on the Asian mainland, and induced them also to back away from an all-out naval race by subscribing to the Washington Naval Treaties of 1922.[72]

Territorial aggression after 1931 therefore simply reaffirmed a policy that had deep roots in the Japanese past.[73] Peasant land hunger easily translated itself into a public policy of expansion and conquest, especially among junior army officers, who were themselves often of peasant birth. Distrust of greedy capitalists and men of the marketplace also had peasant roots and was abundantly evident among the officers of the Kwangtung army who managed Japan's ventures in Manchuria and China.[74] More generally, command economy, Japanese-style, like command economy Russian-style, had the advantage of building upon patterns of rural life which had never been

71. Ericson, *The Soviet High Command,* pp. 494–99, 517–22, 532–37, offers a clear account of these relatively little known battles.

72. These treaties also headed off an incipient Anglo-American rivalry. They were formally denounced by the Japanese in 1934, with effect in 1936. Competitive naval building therefore escalated sharply as of 1937. Cf. Stephen Roskill, *Naval Policy between the Wars,* vol. 1, *The Period of Anglo-American Antagonism* (London, 1968), and vol. 2, *The Period of Reluctant Rearmament, 1930–1939* (London, 1976).

73. Cf. Edwin O. Reischauer, *Japan Past and Present* (New York, 1964), pp. 158–68. Within the Japanese islands themselves the Japanese people expanded from an initial base in the south through a centuries-long process of conquest and colonization. Hokkaido in the north was settled intensively by Japanese only in the nineteenth and early twentieth centuries.

74. Yoshihashi, *Conspiracy at Mukden,* pp. 116–18.

wholly reconciled to market methods of mobilizing resources or regulating individual rewards for economic activity. High technological skills superimposed upon still powerful residues from a "feudal" past gave both countries a particular advantage in World War II. Hardihood and unquestioning obedience to a command hierarchy when combined with well-designed weapons and a more or less adequate supply system made the Japanese and Russians into very effective soldiers, and allowed the Japanese and Soviet governments noticeably to surpass the military effectiveness attained by either country in World War I.

When it came to coping with the depression of the 1930s in Germany, western Europe, and America, World War I patterns of economic mobilization were much more evident than they were in Japan's case. The Nazi regime in Germany (1933–45) harked back deliberately to wartime propaganda methods for mobilizing sentiment against internal and external foes. As rearmament got seriously underway, after 1935, the role of arms manufacture in the German economy grew in importance, though it did not approach World War I levels until 1942–45. Instead, Hitler reaffirmed the ideal of 1866 and 1870. He aimed to prepare so well that victory would be assured in a short campaign without having to harness current production to a desperate war of attrition as had happened in 1914–18. Officers in charge of armaments supply distrusted this strategy, arguing that preparation for a war of attrition was the only realistic policy. But many German officers shared Hitler's doubts about the willingness of civilians to submit to the sort of prolonged deprivation that such a war was sure to bring; and none of them effectively opposed Hitler's combination of bluff and preparation for *Blitzkrieg*.[75]

In the United States, the elections of 1932 brought Woodrow Wilson's party back to power. The New Deal, proclaimed by President Franklin D. Roosevelt in 1933, like the Nazi regime in Germany, fell back on World War I precedents in trying to do something about the depression which had put some thirteen million persons out of work since 1929.[76] Like Hitler, in his first years of power FDR attempted to

75. General Georg Thomas, chief of the Economic Staff of the Ministry of War, 1934–42 (rechristened Defense Economics and Armaments Office in 1939), was the principal advocate of what he called "armament in depth" as against Hitler's "armament in breadth." Cf. B. A. Carroll, *Design for Total War: Arms and Economics in the Third Reich* (The Hague, 1968), pp. 38–53 and passim. For a penetrating study of the policy of the German army leaders see Michael Geyer, *Rüstung oder Sicherheit: Die Reichswehr in der Krise der Machtpolitik, 1924–1936* (Wiesbaden, 1980), pp. 489–505 and passim.

76. Ellis W. Hawley, "The New Deal and Business," in John Braeman et al., eds., *The New Deal: The National Level* (Columbus, Ohio, 1975), p. 61; William E. Leuchtenburg,

sop up unemployment through programs of public works rather than through military mobilization; and, also like Hitler, it was only when military mobilization got going on a significant scale that the American government really succeeded in eliminating unemployment from the scene.

Among western nations, Germany took the initiative in rearming, starting in 1935. Rearmament, supplemented by large expenditure for public works, allowed Hitler to put the Germans back to work sooner than full employment returned to any other industrial country. He reaped much credit for the feat at home and abroad. In France and Britain, however, heartfelt aversion to any new war checked moves toward rearmament. New weapons were therefore ordered on a smaller scale than in Germany and unemployment remained a problem until after war broke out. Russia, on the other hand, responded to Hitler's threats with a large-scale effort to reequip the Red Army and air force. American rearmament, when it got underway in 1939, was also as much a reaction to German as to Japanese power.

As all the principal industrial countries of the world, one after another, expanded arms manufacture, the pace of improvement in weapons design, having slowed drastically at the end of World War I, suddenly accelerated, especially for airplanes and tanks. Uncontrolled and uncontrollable technical aspects of the arms race, which had become so troublesome in naval design on the eve of World War I, now came to the fore across the whole spectrum of armaments, and in a most confusing way. Superior design of a given year, once put into production, had the effect of saddling the armed forces with obsolete airplanes and tanks two or three years later. The French and Russians, having armed themselves early, suffered from this embarrassment in 1940 and 1941.[77] Conversely, holding back until after a prospective enemy had committed his production lines to a given design could allow a straggler to produce a better machine. The British enjoyed this advantage in 1940 when their new Spitfires proved superior to any German pursuit plane then in existence. On the other hand, the Spit-

---

"The New Deal and the Analogue of War," in John Braeman et al., eds., *Change and Continuity in Twentieth Century America* (Columbus, Ohio, 1964), pp. 82–143; John A. Garraty, "The New Deal, National Socialism, and the Great Depression," *American Historical Review* 78 (1973): 907–44.

77. John F. Milson, *Russian Tanks, 1900–1920* (London, 1970), pp. 59–64. Of some 24,000 Russian tanks operational in June 1941, only 967 were of a new design equivalent or superior to the German tanks of that time. Cf. Andreas Hillgruber, *Hitler's Strategie: Politik and Kriegsführung 1940–1941* (Frankfurt am Main, 1965), p. 509.

fires' scarcity in 1940 constituted a severe limit on the Royal Air Force's ability to repel the German air attack in the Battle of Britain.

No one foresaw or was in possession of enough accurate information to be able to navigate safely between the Scylla of too much too soon and the Charybdis of too little too late. Repeatedly, critical decisions had to be taken in the dark. A nasty mix of faith, hope, and fear activated those who had to decide what kind and how many new weapons to construct. Personal empire building and group rivalries among services, ministries, and firms combined precariously with overall fiscal planning and control. A German four-year plan, proclaimed in 1936, aimed at autarky by developing substitutes for such critical materials as rubber and oil. Memories of the blockade of World War I lay behind that policy. Great Britain hesitated to commit itself to sending an army to France, remembering the futile years in the trenches, and concentrated on naval and air defense. France quailed at the prospect of renewed war against Germany, and was slow to design and even slower to produce new tanks and airplanes. A profound reluctance to prepare for war colored every French and British decision; Hitler had the advantage of being the aggressor, willing to bluff and able to choose the time and place for provoking a crisis.[78]

In Japan and the Soviet Union, a smaller industrial base was compensated for by earlier and more massive commitment to military production. Elsewhere, nothing approaching the all-out mobilization of resources achieved in 1916–18 was even attempted. When war broke out in Europe in 1939, France and Britain still hoped to counter the Nazi *Blitzkrieg* in the east with a *Sitzkrieg* behind carefully prepared defenses in the west while waiting for the naval blockade to damage the German economy and weaken support for Hitler at home. Mobilization plans were based on the expectation of a long war like that of 1914–18. Strategy was dictated by the determination to avoid a repetition of the mass bloodletting which had characterized that war. The French, in particular, underestimated what armored columns,

78. D. C. Watt, *Too Serious a Business: European Armed Forces and the Approach of the Second World War* (London, 1975) is a wise and informative book. See also M. M. Postan, *British War Production* (London, 1952), pp. 9–114; Robert Paul Shaw, Jr., *British Rearmament in the Thirties: Parties and Profits* (Princeton, 1977); Walter Bernhardt, *Die deutsche Aufrüstung 1934–1938: Militärische und politische Konzeptionen und ihre Einschätzung durch die Aliierten* (Frankfurt am Main, 1969); Edward L. Homze, *Arming the Luftwaffe: The Reich Air Ministry and the German Aircraft Industry, 1919–1939* (Lincoln, Neb., 1976). I have been unable to find any comparable survey of French rearmament.

supported by superior air power, could do to disorganize and demoralize the rear of an army that did not want to fight. As a result, Hitler won his greatest victory in May 1940.

The shock of France's fall jarred Great Britain into an all-out effort to safeguard itself from the same fate. Financial limits were withdrawn, and manpower became the principal factor defining what could and could not be done. Management of the war effort benefited from economic theory as developed between the wars as well as from World War I experience. The result was relatively smooth and effective industrial-military effort, sustained by an all but universal popular will to resist the Germans to the end.[79] The United States also stepped up its mobilization at home in reaction to the fall of France, and through the Lend Lease Act (March 1941) made supplies available to the British and to other governments at war with Germany and Japan without requiring or expecting full repayment afterwards. The uncollectible war debts that had blighted international relations between the wars were thereby avoided, despite the fact that the United States began to develop a symbiotic relationship with the British war economy that far surpassed anything attained in World War I. Stalin, on the other hand, in an effort to avoid provoking Hitler, seems to have done little to hurry Russian arms production or reorganize the Red Army after a demoralizing purge of officers in 1937–38. Instead, the Russian dictator sought to assure peace by punctual delivery of large quantities of raw materials and food to Germany as promised in trade agreements supplementary to the Ribbentrop-Molotov agreement of August 1939.[80] This made nonsense of the British blockade and allowed Germany to persist in its prewar policy of refraining from drastic mobilization. Even when, in the fall of 1940, Hitler decided to attack Russia before making peace with Great Britain, the Germans did not depart from this principle. As a result, when German tanks began to roll into Russia in June 1941, the German arms industry was beginning to convert to production for intensified war at sea and in the air against Great Britain.[81]

79. W. K. Hancock and M. M. Gowing, *British War Economy* (London, 1949) is an admirable official history that highlights critical decisions of policy. Postan's *British War Production* is an equally admirable official history of arms manufacture.

80. Ericson, *Soviet High Command,* pp. 575–83.

81. Alan S. Milward, *The German Economy at War* (London, 1965), pp. 43–45; Barry A. Leach, *German Strategy against Russia, 1939–1941* (Oxford, 1973), pp. 133–46 and passim; B. Klein, *Germany's Economic Preparation for War* (Cambridge, Mass., 1959); Andreas Hillgruber, *Hitler's Strategie: Politik und Kriegsführung, 1940–1941* (Frankfurt am Main, 1965), pp. 155–66 and passim.

But the Red Army, unexpectedly, survived the Nazi onslaught. Two days before the Japanese brought the United States into the war as an active belligerent by attacking the United States Navy at Pearl Harbor, Hitler was compelled to announce, on 5 December 1941, that the *Reichswehr's* advance on Moscow had been suspended. This meant that the war of attrition that Hitler had intended to avoid loomed ominously before the Germans once again. But Germany was in a better position to face such a war than had been the case in 1914 inasmuch as a broad expanse of conquered Europe could be organized to supplement Germany's own production. In spite of Nazi doctrine and racial prejudices, therefore, the Germans presided over a transnational war effort from 1942 onwards. As time passed, they also became more ruthless, drawing resources from conquered lands by force and threat of force. Seven and a half million foreign workers supplied about a fifth of the entire German work force by 1944. Some were POWs, some were at least nominally free, but most had been rounded up in manhunts and shipped to Germany as "slave labor."[82] Armaments production peaked in July 1944; thereafter, critical shortages broke out everywhere more or less all at once and brought the German war economy swiftly to collapse by May 1945.[83]

All the other major belligerents also mounted their war effort on a transnational basis. Japan's Co-Prosperity Sphere in the Pacific and Far East was by far the weakest and least well integrated. The vast majority of the population coming under Japanese control were peasants, whose skills, capital, and productive capacities were relatively small and could not readily be enlarged. The most numerous of them, the Chinese, were disinclined to cooperate. Even where Japan's attack on white supremacy met with an initial welcome, relatively few committed themselves wholeheartedly to collaboration with the new Japanese masters. Shipping needed to link the Japanese islands with distant parts soon ran seriously short, owing to sinkings by American submarines and other war losses. By 1943, supplying remote garrisons became impossible; and new designs of airplanes and other weapons

82. Edward L. Homze, *Foreign Labor in Nazi Germany* (Princeton, 1967), pp. 232. Ironically, the experience of work in Germany was a factor in paving the way for postwar European integration. Hitler and his brutal subordinate Fritz Sauckel deserve to rank with Jean Monnet and General George Marshall among the makers of the European Economic Community.

83. Albert Speer, *Inside the Third Reich: Memoirs* (London, 1970); Milward, *German Economy at War;* Alan S. Milward, *The New Order and the French Economy* (London, 1970); Friedrich Forstmeier and Hans-Erich Volkmann, eds., *Kriegswirtschaft und Rüstung, 1939–1945* (Düsseldorf, 1977); and from a Marxist perspective, Dietrich Eicholtz, *Geschichte der deutschen Kriegswirtschaft, 1939–1945* (Berlin, 1969).

fell far behind what was needed to keep pace with improvements elsewhere.[84]

The USSR was transnational in itself, and its war effort was also linked with the Anglo-American economies through Lend Lease and Mutual Aid deliveries. These were never large enough to satisfy Russian requirements and Stalin always suspected that the western powers really wished to see Russia and Germany bleed each other white so as to emerge *tertius gaudens* as he had hoped to do in 1939. Yet by the end of the war, the Red Army owed its mobility in the field very largely to Lend Lease trucks, boots, and food. After 1942, the USSR manufactured weapons and munitions in sufficient quantity to keep the Red Army reasonably well supplied. But this achievement came at extraordinary cost to civilian industrial production, and to agriculture.[85]

Russia's relation to the United States in World War II much resembled the relation of France to Britain and the United States in World War I. In both cases, heavy initial losses of metallurgical plant required radical redeployment of industrial resources in the first months of the war. Yet in both countries, lopsided emphasis on armaments and soldiering paid off in the sense that an industrially weaker country was nonetheless able to meet and repel Germany's attack successfully, but only at a very heavy cost of human life. Moreover, Stalin's Russia continued the tsarist policy of giving absolute priority to armaments and heavy industry against all competing claims on the economy. Russia escaped the food catastrophe of World War I partly because of American food shipments, which fed the army, but mainly because the collectivization of agriculture assured effective administrative methods for delivering grain to urban consumers whether or not the people who did the fieldwork got anything back in the way of consumer goods.[86]

By far the largest and most complex of the transnational war economies was that dominated by the United States, in collaboration with

---

84. Cohen, *Japan's Economy in War and Reconstruction,* pp. 56, 267.
85. The following figures tell the tale (Index: 1940 = 100):

	1941	1942	1943	1944
Gross industrial output	98	77	90	104
of which, Arms	140	186	224	251
Gross agricultural output	62	38	37	54

Source: Alec Nove, *An Economic History of the USSR* (Harmondsworth, 1969), p. 272.

86. In addition to Nove, cited above, see Nikolai Voznesensky, *The Economy of the USSR during World War II* (Washington, D.C., 1948), and Roger A. Clarke, *Soviet Economic Facts, 1917–1970* (London, 1972) for a very convenient summary of officially published statistics.

Great Britain. A plan for all-out mobilization of America's resources achieved definition only a few days before the attack on Pearl Harbor made it politically feasible to implement the Victory Program, as it was called for propaganda purposes. It took two more years before administrative means were fully developed to manage American resources according to plans based on the requirements of future military operations. Along the way, innumerable discrepancies arose between demand and supply, plan and fulfillment. Quarrels over allocation of scarce materials and other factors of production were often very bitter. Nevertheless, the end result was a spectacular increase in American output of war materiel, and of an enormous number of other goods needed to supplement British, Russian, and other Allied war economies as well. The kind of scheduling required to keep a complicated assembly line running smoothly in a great factory was, in effect, applied to the entire national economy of the United States. Increases in productivity and in absolute quantities of physical goods turned out to order were analogous to the increases mass production methods had already made possible when applied within a single firm.[87]

Interlocking with Great Britain became very intimate indeed. British and French experts had a hand in suggesting to Americans how to organize their war effort;[88] and negotiations over allocation of Lend Lease supplies involved continual exchange of information about economic as well as military plans. Britain needed food and raw materials from the United States; in return Britain provided various services to American forces stationed in the British Isles, and lands under British imperial control supplied certain raw materials needed by the United States. But as the war years went on, Great Britain put an increasing proportion of its resources into the armed services and military production and, like Russia, had to rely on imports from the United States to fill widening gaps in home production.

A more or less rational and deliberate division of labor in economic

87. Official figures may be found in U.S., Civilian Production Administration, *Industrial Mobilization for War: History of the War Production Board and Predecessor Agencies, 1940–1945* (Washington, D.C., 1947). Donald M. Nelson, *Arsenal of Democracy* (New York, 1946) is a personal account by the principal administrator of the War Production Board.

88. Jean Monnet, whose public career had started as French representative on the Allied Maritime Transport Council in 1917, was a leading figure in persuading Americans to draw up the Victory Program in 1941. Cf. his *Mémoires*, pp. 179–212. John Maynard Keynes also played an important role in transmitting macroeconomic concepts and expertise to Americans. Cf. Roy F. Harrod, *The Life of John Maynard Keynes* (London, 1951), pp. 505–14, 525–623.

affairs was thus achieved and sustained by the collaboration of British and American officials. The same principle governed Allied military commands. Anglo-American armed forces were controlled in the field by headquarters staffs who established a morale of their own often transcending narrow national identity. At the top of the military chain of command, the Combined Chiefs of Staff, sitting normally in Washington, executed a joint strategy defined from time to time at conferences where President Roosevelt and Prime Minister Churchill (and after November 1943 Marshal Stalin as well) agreed upon future plans of campaign and concerted other aspects of high policy.[89]

By the end of the war, a large number of Allied states and governments in exile, together with such quasi-governmental organizations as the Free French, clustered around the Anglo-American power center, sharing in the bounties of Lend Lease and adding moral and material weight to the Allied cause.

In Africa, India, and Latin America, mobilization for war was less intense. But the resources of these lands were also sucked into the Anglo-American war effort, sometimes through purchases on the open market, and sometimes as a result of administrative action. India, for example, raised a large army for operations against the Japanese in Burma. Manufacture of equipment needed for that army gave special impetus to India's industrialization; and the impress of war work and military service on India's collective consciousness made postwar independence inevitable.[90]

Transnational organization for war thus achieved a fuller and far more effective expression during World War II than ever before. Thanks to the increasing complexity of arms production, a single nation had become too small to conduct an efficient war. This was, perhaps, the main innovation of World War II. Implications for national sovereignty in peacetime were obvious and ran counter to the passionate yearning for local self-government that inspired Asians and Africans to reject colonial status in the first postwar decade.

The results of systematic application of scientific knowledge to

89. Many books have described the Allied strategic management of World War II. Robert E. Sherwood, *Roosevelt and Hopkins: An Intimate History* (New York, 1948) was the earliest inside view and remains one of the most interesting. William H. McNeill, *America, Britain and Russia: Their Cooperation and Conflict, 1941–1946* (London, 1953) represents an early synthesis and interpretation. Opening of archives has not changed the overall picture very much as reference to such a work as John Lewis Gaddis, *The United States and the Origins of the Cold War, 1941–1947* (New York, 1972) will show.

90. Philip Mason, *A Matter of Honour: An Account of the Indian Army, Its Officers and Men* (London, 1974), pp. 495–522; Bisheshwar Prasad, ed., *Expansion of the Armed Forces and Defense Organization, 1939–1945* (n.p., 1956).

weapons design rivaled transnational organization in importance at the time; and since atomic bombs did not dissolve with the peace as international economic structures mostly did, one can argue that this aspect of the war effort was more fateful in the long run.

Scientific advice had been sought in critical questions about arms design long before World War II. Archimedes is reputed to have helped the tyrant of Syracuse in devising new machines of war for use against the Romans in 212 B.C. and Gribeauval was in touch with the top levels of French science in the eighteenth century on questions of ballistics. The renowned physicist Lord Kelvin had advised the British Admiralty about technical questions of ship design as early as 1904; and during World War I the Admiralty established a special board of scientists to help with antisubmarine warfare. Its important result, an echo-ranging device nicknamed ASDIC, did not mature until 1920, too late for use in World War I.[91] On the German side, however, Professor Fritz Haber provided the chemical expertise necessary for the fixation of nitrogen and also invented the first poison gases.[92] Nevertheless, scientific collaboration remained sporadic and marginal during World War I except, perhaps, in the field of airplane design.[93]

World War II was different. The accelerated pace of weapons improvement that set in from the late 1930s, and the proliferating variety of new possibilities that deliberate invention spawned, meant that all the belligerents realized by the time fighting began that some new secret weapon might tip the balance decisively. Accordingly, scientists, technologists, design engineers, and efficiency experts were summoned to the task of improving existing weapons and inventing new ones on a scale far greater than ever before.[94]

91. R. F. Mackay, *Fisher of Kilverstone* (Oxford, 1973), pp. 506–9; Richard Hough, *First Sea Lord* (London, 1969), p. 238.

92. Cf. L. F. Haber, *Gas Warfare, 1916–1945: The Legend and the Facts* (London, 1976), p. 8. Why poison gas was not used in World War II, despite the common expectation beforehand of murderous attack from the air in the first hours of combat, is an interesting and important question. Psychological distaste among military men for a weapon that seemed somehow stealthy and unheroic in use must have played an important part in diverting attention from gas to tanks and airplanes. Barton C. Hacker, "The Military and the Machine: An Analysis of the Controversy over Mechanization in the British Army, 1919–1939" (Ph.D. diss., University of Chicago, 1968) offers a persuasive psychological interpretation of this choice. For German deliberations, see Rolf-Dieter Müller, "Die deutschen Gaskriegsvorbereitungen, 1919–1945: Mit Giftgas zur Weltmacht?" *Militärgeschichtliche Mitteilungen* 1 (1980): 25–54.

93. For the British side see John M. Sanderson, *The Universities and British Industry, 1850–1975* (London, 1972), pp. 228–30; for the United States, Daniel Kevles, *The Physicists* (New York, 1978), pp. 117–38.

94. M. M. Postan et al., *Design and Development of Weapons: Studies in Government and Industrial Organization* (London, 1964) is limited to Great Britain but makes clear the

Battlefield experience was fed back speedily to expert committees charged with correcting faults in existing machines and designing new ones with improved performance. Generations of new tanks, airplanes, and artillery came tumbling off assembly lines as a result, each notably superior to its predecessors and requiring the counter invention of new defensive hardware and tactics. Choices between quantity and quality had always to be made, for if every desirable modification were incorporated into an existing machine, the number of airplanes, tanks, or guns that could be manufactured would have had to be sharply cut back. Interesting national differences manifested themselves. German and British managers tended to prefer quality and made many modifications, whereas the Americans and Russians preferred quantity and refrained from modifications which obstructed full utilization of assembly line techniques. Yet when circumstances seemed to require quantity, the Germans could and did reverse their practice, freezing their designs in the last phases of the war in order to produce maximal numbers of weapons.[95]

The concept of a complete weapons system in which each constituent fitted conveniently with all the rest emerged from World War II design experience. Standard package sizes to fit standardized cargo spaces in railway cars, airplanes, and trucks could save much time and energy in transport, for example. Standardized ammunition for rifles, pistols, and machine guns made supply in the field far simpler. Tanks, infantry carriers, and self-propelled artillery that could travel at the same pace, whether along a road or cross-country, constituted a far more formidable spearhead than when discrepancies of speed or capacity to get across obstacles invited straggling. In these and many other ways the pattern of a smooth flow-through of all the factors of production that allowed modern business corporations to prosper was applied to the assemblage of the factors of destruction with predictable success in reducing costs and increasing output. War, in short,

---

scale and systematic character of scientific involvement in weapons design, especially pp. 433–58, 472–85. For the United States, James Phinney Baxter III, *Scientists against Time* (Boston, 1946) is a well-written official history. P. M. S. Blackett, *Studies of War: Nuclear and Conventional* (Edinburgh, 1962), pp. 101–19 and 205–34 offers a more personal view; Reginald Victor Jones, *Most Secret War* (London, 1978) is even more personal in describing counterintelligence coups. I have not found any serious account of German, Japanese, or Russian scientific mobilization.

95. Alan S. Milward, *War, Economy and Society, 1939–1945* (Berkeley, 1977), pp. 184–93; Postan, *British War Production.* The British Spitfire underwent more than 1,000 technical modifications between 1938 and 1945, adding 100 miles per hour to its top speed in the process.

became well and truly industrialized as industry became no less well and truly militarized.

More spectacular and perhaps more important were new devices that came into being before and during World War II. At the beginning, radar was the most notable such innovation. British scientists and engineers discovered how to use reflections of short radio waves to locate airplanes at sufficient distances to allow their interception by fighter pilots during the Battle of Britain. Radar continued to develop very rapidly during the war and found new uses in navigation and gun laying; but other technologies—jet airplanes, proximity fuses, amphibious vehicles, guided missiles, rockets, and, most complicated of all, atomic warheads—soon rivaled radar's early importance.

Decisions about how to exploit these new technologies, as well as less bizarre choices between new designs for tanks, guns, and airplanes, played a very important role in determining the course and outcome of military operations. If Hitler had not refused to put his full support behind the V-2 rocket until July 1943, for example, it is hard to believe that the Allied landings in Normandy could have taken place,[96] since the harbors of southern England where the cross-channel flotillas assembled presented excellent targets for V-2 rockets. On the other hand, if European refugee scientists had not persuaded the British and American governments to mount the enormous effort of research and development required to produce the first atomic bomb,[97] not only would the final stages of the Japanese war have taken a different turn, but postwar international relations would have been profoundly different, since it is hard to believe that any government would have undertaken the enormous expenses of such a risky project in time of peace. (When the Manhattan Project was at its peak, 120,000 persons worked at it, including an extraordinary proportion of the world's leading physicists. The cost was over two billion dollars; and until the final tests, no one could be absolutely sure that atomic theory could be embodied in the engineering of an explodable warhead.)

In these and innumerable other cases, some famous and others presumably buried in some forgotten file among the might-have-beens

96. Cf. Walter Dornberger, *V2* (London, 1954), pp. 93, 100; Dwight D. Eisenhower, *Crusade in Europe* (New York, 1948), p. 260.
97. Martin J. Sherwin, *A World Destroyed: The Atomic Bomb and the Grand Alliance* (New York, 1975) is a recent and readable as well as judicious account. Margaret Gowing, *Britain and Atomic Energy, 1939–1945* (London, 1964) is a fine official history.

of history, the irrationality of scientific and managerial rationality applied to warfare was repeatedly demonstrated in ways more dramatic than ever before. For with the discovery of atomic explosives, human destructive power reached a new, suicidal level, surpassing previous limits to all but unimaginable degree.

Welfare and warfare were also more closely linked than during World War I. Advances in knowledge about human dietary requirements made between the wars allowed food rationing to become scientific in the sense that vitamin, calorie, and protein requirements for different categories of the population could be accurately calculated and, within limits of supply, provided. In Great Britain, health actually improved during the war, thanks largely to the rationing of food. Skilled medical teams swiftly suppressed epidemics among civilian populations, which on several occasions briefly threatened to interfere with operational plans;[98] and military medicine made World War II far safer for uniformed personnel outside the battle zone than had ever been the case before. New drugs like sulfanilamide and penicillin, and insecticides like DDT, reduced the risks of infection and changed whole environments—abruptly.

German slave labor camps and the extermination centers where millions of Jews and other enemies of the Nazi regime were starved and slaughtered constituted a macabre counterpart to the sort of welfare by administrative fiat that kept the labor forces of each of the combatant nations in more or less optimal working condition. Extremes of inhumanity, bureaucratized and rendered efficient by the same methods used for managing other aspects of the war effort, illustrate more poignantly than any other event of modern history the moral ambivalence implicit in every increase in human power to manage and control our natural and social environment. POW camps in other countries, and wholesale displacements of distrusted ethnic groups, such as occurred in both the United States and the Soviet Union during the war, also exhibited the demonic side of the administrative virtuosity that flourished so luxuriantly during the two wars of the twentieth century.

Planning for peace, on the other hand, though confidently undertaken long before the fighting ended, met with only limited success. An international relief agency, UNRRA, did forestall starvation in the

---

98. A typhus epidemic in Naples in 1943 was nipped in the bud by wholesale delousing with DDT; and two outbreaks of bubonic plague in North Africa were no less expeditiously snuffed out by Allied medical teams. Cf. Harry Wain, *A History of Preventive Medicine* (Springfield, Ill., 1970), p. 306.

immediate postwar months. But American hopes for really effective peace-keeping machinery and for a liberal economic order in international trade were destined to disappointment. Instead, within no more than two years of the end of hostilities, both the United States and the Soviet Union reverted to transnational economic and military organization of the sort that had proved its effectiveness so tellingly during World War II. An arms race revived in 1950, after the Russians exploded an atomic bomb in 1949. The Korean War, 1950–53, gave further impetus. The world has lived ever since in the shadow of the mushroom cloud. The resulting dilemmas of our age require a final chapter.

10

The Arms Race and Command Economies since 1945

When World War II ended in 1945, return to prewar conditions was not a viable ideal. In many parts of the earth, old political regimes were discredited and unpopular. This was true in the defeated countries and in most European colonies, even in places where there had been little or no active fighting. Both in liberated and in occupied Europe wartime destruction and dislocations assured continuing misery long after fighting had stopped. Even among the victors, war mobilization had attained such an extreme that spontaneous return to normal, however normal might be defined, was no longer possible. Cancellation of wartime regulations was not enough; planned mobilization demanded planned demobilization and conscious redeployment of resources. Thus national and transnational management and command economies were as necessary after the war as during it. American efforts to institute a liberalized international trading system were rendered futile by these facts.

What happened in the postwar years was, in its way, as surprising as the achievements of wartime production and destruction. Methods that had summoned enormous numbers of tanks, airplanes, and other weapons into existence during the war when applied to the tasks of reconstruction lost little of their magic—at least in the first years when what to do was easy to define and agree upon. The recovery of western Europe with the help of credits from the United States, 1948–53, was spectacularly swift. The USSR and eastern Europe did not lag very far behind, thanks to a still abundant pool of manpower and natural resources hitherto but slenderly exploited for industrial purposes. Japan also began to exhibit an industrial and commercial dynamism after 1950 that eventually left even Germany and the United States behind, thanks to its unique adaptation of traditional forms of social solidarity to industrial and urban conditions of life.

With the defeat of Germany and Japan, the four transnational war economies dissolved into two rival blocs. Germany was divided into zones of occupation. Its wartime dependencies in Europe split into an eastern zone dominated by the USSR and a western zone where the United States soon took the leading role. Japan's Co-Prosperity Sphere also split up. Mainland China went Communist in 1949; Korea and Indochina divided; most of the rest, including Japan itself, came within the American sphere of influence. The "iron curtain" in Europe provoked noisy controversy, but no actual fighting. Partitioning the Co-Prosperity Sphere, on the contrary, triggered long-drawn-out wars in China (1944–49), Korea (1950–53), and Indochina (1946–54, 1955–75), as well as lesser armed conflicts in Indonesia, Malaya, and Burma.

Many former colonial lands tried hard to protect newly won political sovereignty by resisting more than marginal association with either the Soviet or the American power blocs. In practice however, new governments needed economic help and found themselves dependent on credits from abroad, provided either by their former imperial masters or by the American or Russian aspirants to vacated imperial roles. The "Third World" of new nations and uncommitted peoples was, nonetheless, a reality in the postwar decades, modifying the simple polarity of the cold war.

Despite intense initial difficulties, the USSR reverted to autarky after 1945, casting off the reliance on Lend Lease supplies from the United States that had developed in the last stages of the war. To be sure, reparations in kind from conquered Germany and trade deals with east European countries that were markedly advantageous to the USSR helped the Russians to survive the first desperate months when war damages were only beginning to be repaired. Frictions first with Britain, then with the United States, kept alive a sense of beleaguerment among the Communist elites. Stalin declared and probably believed that there was only a "temporary political" difference between Nazi Germany and other capitalist states.[1] Stalin's Marxism thus took it for granted that the imperatives compelling Hitler to attack the Motherland of Socialism in 1941 were just as ineluctably at work

---

1. In an interview with the American politician Harold Stassen on 9 April 1947, published in *New York Times,* 4 May 1947. For a collection of Stalin's most striking references to the inevitable final conflict between capitalism and socialism see Historicus, "Stalin on Revolution," *Foreign Affairs* 27 (1949): 175 ff.

within British and American society in the postwar years. Consequently Soviet reconstruction had to compete from the beginning
with continuing military expenditures. In particular, Russia's efforts to
develop atomic bombs like those the Americans had used against
Japan in 1945 must have had the highest priority at a time when
civilian levels of consumption within the USSR were still at a very low
ebb indeed. Stalin also maintained such large forces in eastern Europe
that American and other observers believed the Red Army was able
and might be tempted to overrun the entire European continent.

Between 1946 and 1949 American countermoves consolidated a
rival transnational economic and military power structure, somewhat
disingenuously dubbed the "Free World." In many senses it was freer
than the lands dominated by the USSR. Public expression of dissent
was not systematically repressed; and labor, food, fuel, and raw materials were not allocated by governmental fiat on anything like the scale
that prevailed within Communist-ruled lands. Individual choices
about work, consumption, and leisure activities remained correspondingly broader than anything available within the Communist
camp. Yet individual and small group choices operated in a society
dominated by a new symbiosis of public and private administrators.
Managed economies became normal in all industrially advanced
countries; and as long as public consensus about the general goals of
such management could be maintained, no one objected very vigorously. In other words, among the great majority of Americans, west
Europeans, and Japanese, freedom collapsed into obedience and conformity to bureaucratically channeled behavior. The springs of obedience and conformity within the Communist lands were similar
inasmuch as most Russians and east Europeans, together with the
enormous Chinese population, also willingly accepted goals defined by
their bureaucratic superiors and behaved accordingly. Their rewards
were smaller than in the West and Japan, where living standards rose
rapidly and soon surpassed prewar levels. But standards of consumption rose in Communist lands too, so the difference was only one of
degree.

Diminished allocation of resources through direct governmental
action and the enhanced scope for fluctuating prices as regulators of
economic behavior presumably improved the general efficiency of
Free World as compared to Communist society. American corporate
managers, though able to allocate resources by simple command
within their corporations, were constantly brought up against the
necessity of buying and selling goods and services to others who were

not directly under their control. Insofar as their partners in such transactions were large corporations and governments, oligopolistic and monopolistic market confrontations ensued. In these instances, prices were set by diplomatic negotiation rather than by competition from some mythical "outside." But in transactions with private citizens and other weakly organized market partners, corporate and governmental buyers and sellers were usually able to set prices at levels favorable to themselves. They did so simply by regulating supply to keep the price of whatever they offered for sale at the level they preferred.

As long as large-scale buyers and sellers could operate in a setting of weakly organized trading partners, a remarkable exactitude of large-scale management became possible. Financial planning and material planning matched up. Prosperity set in as war damages were repaired. New investment proliferated and full employment, or close to it, became a reality. The dysfunction of the prewar depression years vanished thanks to a happy collaboration between skilled large-scale corporate management on the one hand and governmental fiscal policy on the other, enlightened by the new science of macroeconomics and backed by enlarged expenditures for arms and welfare. A veritable managerial revolution in the leading capitalist countries seemed to have made industrial nations masters of their collective destinies as never before. Moreover, since the principal governments concerned remained elective, the interests and needs of ordinary folk at home were safeguarded by a democratic franchise.

On the other hand, when operating in poorly organized foreign countries, large American and European corporations escaped many of the political constraints familiar to them at home. Agricultural producers, together with lands supplying minerals and other raw materials, were seldom capable of organizing themselves in such a way as to meet foreign corporations on anything like even terms. When in 1973 governments of oil exporting countries succeeded in doing so, the Free World's postwar pattern of command and corporate economy faced its first severe shock in more than two decades.[2]

In the immediate aftermath of World War II, the United States took the lead in renewing a transnational military command to safeguard the sphere of influence that fell to the Americans with the decay of British power. The North Atlantic Treaty Organization, established in

2. Cf. the astringent exploration of the interface of politics and economics to be found in Robert Gilpin, *United States Power and the Multinational Corporation* (New York, 1975); Charles E. Lindblom, *Politics and Markets: The World's Political-Economic Systems* (New York,1977); Gavin Kennedy, *The Economics of Defense* (London, 1975).

1949, entrusted the task of marshaling west European defenses against the Red Army to an American commander in chief. At first, Russian soldiers stationed in east European lands seemed a better guardian of Soviet interests than locally recruited forces. But when West Germany joined NATO in 1955 the Russians responded by establishing a military alliance and command system—the so-called Warsaw Pact—that was a mirror image of NATO. Elsewhere, in southeast Asia and the Middle East, American efforts to set up comparable regional defense organizations met no significant success. Only in Europe did the two super powers confront one another across a well-defined boundary, on either side of which carefully matched polyethnic garrisons developed war plans, carried out training exercises, and indulged in various kinds of war gaming of a sort which in prewar years had existed only within national frontiers. The World War II experience of transnational organizations for war was thus institutionalized in time of peace. National sovereignty, as once conceived, disappeared, more through fear than from any positive conviction of the merits of newfangled transnational military organization.

Economic and psychological factors played their part in eroding national sovereignty in Europe; but an even more important factor was the drastic new threat that nuclear weaponry presented. NATO came into being, initially, in response to the presence of large Red Army forces in eastern Europe. Their mere numbers seemed capable of overrunning the entire continent at will, unless American military force, backed by the ultimate atomic sanction, were permanently committed to defending the European bridgehead projecting so precariously from Russia's vast Eurasian sphere of management and control.

The Russians, on the other hand, were quite unwilling to remain indefinitely at the mercy of American bombers. Stalin spared no effort to achieve atomic capability. In 1949, five months after NATO was established, the USSR exploded its first nuclear device. This provoked surprise and dismay in the United States, for nearly all Americans had been sure that the Russians would not be able to master the complexities of atomic technology for many years. Russian prowess in science, engineering, and weapons design was further demonstrated by the next round of the postwar arms race. For in 1950 the American government reacted to the loss of its atomic monopoly by deciding, reluctantly, to press ahead with the development of a far more terrible weapon, the fusion or H-bomb. The Russians kept pace, exploding their first hydrogen bomb only nine months after the United States in November 1952 had used Eniwetok atoll in the Pacific for its first experimental test of the fusion reaction.

Even though complex in construction, hydrogen warheads could readily be made far lighter than the first clumsy uranium and plutonium bombs. This made rockets an obvious and preferred instrument for their delivery. No means of intercepting a speeding rocket existed, and Germany's bombardment of England by V-2s in 1944 had shown how effective such weapons could be. The Americans accordingly put new urgency into rocket research and development, beginning in the early 1950s; but the Russians started a good deal sooner than the United States at a time when heavier atomic warheads required larger and more powerful rockets to get off the ground.[3] As a result, in October 1957 the Russians launched a rocket powerful enough to put a small satellite—*Sputnik*—into orbit around the earth, and in ensuing months sent larger and larger payloads after it into space.[4]

The Russian achievement left no doubt of their technical capacity to drop atomic warheads anywhere on the face of the earth. American rockets lagged behind in size and power until 1965. This did not mean that American ability to deliver atomic warheads really fell short of Russian capabilities, for United States bombers, stationed within easy striking distance of the Soviet Union, together with newer submarine-based missiles, capable of being launched from beneath the seas, kept Russian cities under the same threat of annihilation that hung over the people of the United States after 1958.

Americans were not comforted by knowing that their new vulnerability merely brought them to the level of their rivals. For generations before *Sputnik,* the territory of the United States had been immune to any real danger of foreign attack. As a result, the shock of discovering that this was no longer the case and that Russians had outdistanced America's own vaunted technical skill in at least one important field

3. At the conclusion of World War II the United States organized a strategic airforce and soon developed bases from which airplanes could carry atomic bombs to any part of the USSR. For a decade thereafter, a strong vested interest in piloted planes as the supreme deterrent inhibited American research and development of long-range rockets. Cf. Edmund Beard, *Developing the ICBM: A Study in Bureaucratic Politics* (New York, 1976).

4. The first Sputnik weighed 84 kilograms; a second, launched a month later, weighed 508 kilograms; and in 1965 the Russians put a payload of no less than 12,200 kilograms into orbit. Cf. Charles S. Sheldon, *Review of the Soviet Space Program with Comparative United States Data* (New York, 1968), pp. 47–49.

proved unusually intense.[5] Not surprisingly, the so-called "missile gap" became a point of controversy in the presidential election of 1960. The new Democratic administration that took office in 1961 was committed to surpassing the Soviets in rocket technology, whether on the moon or on the earth.

The Russians, on the other hand, tried to exploit their technical lead by asserting full equality with the United States the world around. However, in October 1962 Premier Nikita Khrushchev's scheme for installing intermediate-range missiles in Cuba, where they would have been capable of attacking most American cities, failed when the United States Navy prevented delivery of some of the necessary equipment. After a tense confrontation, the Soviets backed down and agreed to withdraw their missiles from Cuba. But this humiliation triggered a vast expansion of the Soviet fleet in the following years, aimed, clearly, at equaling or surpassing American power on and especially underneath the sea.[6]

Arms competition between the USA and the USSR therefore attained a new and enlarged scale in the 1960s. Emphasis was on new technologies and new weapons. Research and development mattered more than current capabilities. A breakthrough in the future, whether defensively or offensively, might alter or even upset the balance of terror that arose in the decade after 1957 as the two countries installed hundreds of long-range missiles and so became capable of destroying each other's cities in a matter of minutes.

The United States government responded to the new sense of danger by pouring money into research and development with a prodigal hand. Not all was military, for the men directing national policy—especially those deriving from Harvard University and MIT—believed that the ultimate test of American society in its competition with the Soviets boiled down to finding out which contestant could develop superior skills in every field of human endeavor. Entering upon such a competition, a wise and resolute government could expect to commission task forces, composed of suitably trained and supremely ingenious technicians, to develop an unending succession of new devices for peace and war. This would guarantee prosperity at home and security abroad. But success would come only if skill were

5. Robert A. Divine, *Blowing in the Wind: The Nuclear Test Ban Debate, 1954–1963* (New York, 1978) explores these political and psychological strains persuasively.

6. Donald W. Mitchell, *A History of Russian and Soviet Sea Power* (New York, 1974), pp. 518–19. For a convenient summary of divergent interpretations of the Cuban missile crisis see Robert A. Divine, ed., *The Cuban Missile Crisis* (Chicago, 1971).

cultivated wherever it could be found, and if it were encouraged by the removal of long-standing fiscal limitations on education, research, and development.

The ensuing academic boom, led by natural science, was matched only by the boom in aerospace and electronics. In effect the managerial elites that had come so powerfully to the fore during World War II now found a new, more technocratic outlet for their ambitions and skills. For their cold war had to be fought on a wide front. Social engineering to achieve a better society mattered as much as the improvement of military hardware.

The prevailing confidence in the nation's ability to solve all problems and overcome all obstacles took dramatic form in 1961 when President John F. Kennedy announced that the United States would put a man on the moon within the decade. The task was entrusted to a civilian agency, NASA (National Aeronautics and Space Administration). But new technologies allowing men and machines to move about in space always had military implications and applications. This made the separation of military from civilian research and development of space technology almost meaningless. [7]

The Soviet Union strained to keep up, announcing a new party program in 1961 that promised to overtake the United States level of per capita production within the decade so as to be able to inaugurate communism (from each according to his ability, to each according to his need) in the 1980s. Premier Khrushchev's technocratic faith was, indeed, very similar to that which inspired President Kennedy's circle of policy makers. Both drew upon their memories of what had been done during and immediately after World War II to achieve impossible production goals by resort to deliberate social and technical engineering.

Most other countries despaired of the race. France, however, rebelling against what General Charles de Gaulle felt to be undue American partiality for Britain and Germany, withdrew from NATO and embarked on a national program of research and development *à l'Américaine.* Only so, de Gaulle felt, could France escape from becoming a quasi-colonial dependency of American (or, alternatively, of Russian) technocracy. [8] In the Far East, China and Japan both made

7. John M. Logsdon, *The Decision to Go to the Moon: Project Apollo and the National Interest* (Cambridge, Mass., 1970); Alfred Charles Bernard Lovell, *The Origins and International Economics of Space Exploration* (Edinburgh, 1973).
8. Robert Gilpin, *France in the Age of the Scientific State* (Princeton, 1968) offers a sympathetic analysis of French reaction to American example in the 1960s. I also owe much to two unpublished papers by Walter A. McDougall, "Technology and Hubris in

belated efforts to enter the technological space race, but only the USSR had the means and motivation to match the American effort step by step. The following tally of launches into space, 1957–72, provides an indication of the domination achieved by the two super powers in space technology during the first fifteen years: USSR, 612; USA, 537; France, 6; Japan, 4; China, 2; and Great Britain, 1.[9]

The USSR invested heavily in a new navy during the 1960s as well as in rocketry and space vehicles. In all probability, military research and development in the Soviet Union more or less matched the sums allocated to the same purpose in the United States. But comparisons are very inexact, because of budgetary obfuscation on both sides as well as the arbitrary values each country assigned to recondite new devices. When there was only one manufacturer and only one buyer for some new kind of technology, as was universally the case in the space race, what costs and overheads to count in or exclude from the pricing of a given piece of machinery became a more or less metaphysical exercise in accountancy. There was no doubt, however, that expenditures on both sides dwarfed peak World War II outlays on technological innovation.[10]

Vast expenditure brought extraordinary results. Undoubtedly the greatest spectacle was the landing on the moon by American astronauts in 1969. Probes of other planets sent back data of great interest to astronomers, and scanning satellites harvested enormous amounts of new information about the surface of the earth itself. In the weapons field, science fiction and technological fact interpenetrated one another in a fashion outsiders can only dimly understand. Control devices to alter missile trajectories in flight attained great sophistication in the 1970s for example. This complicated the task of interception enormously. Indeed, no reliable way of attacking approaching missiles could be found. For at least a quarter of a century

---

the Early Space Age" and "Politics and Technology in the Space Age—Towards the History of a Saltation."

9. A. C. B. Lovell, *The Origins and International Economics of Space Exploration* (Edinburgh, 1973), p. 28.

10. For what little it is worth, a Swedish estimate of research and development expenditures came up with a figure of between 4.1 and 6.1 billion dollars for Soviet military spending in 1972 compared to 7.2 billion for the United States. Stockholm International Peace Research Institute, *Resources Devoted to Military Research and Development* (Stockholm, 1972), p. 58. These figures exclude NASA's disbursements, despite the military relevancy of many NASA programs. Military items masquerading in civilian dress in the Soviet budget were probably equally massive, and perhaps greater. The additional difficulty in equating American with Russian prices makes comparison well-nigh impossible, as the authors of this study admit.

after the missile race went into high gear, lasers and other "death rays" capable of destroying enemy warheads with the speed of light remained fictional. The balance of terror therefore continued more or less intact, despite all the efforts Americans and Russians put into finding a way to shield themselves from the specter of sudden annihilation.

In one respect, the balance of terror became more stable. The development of spy satellites from 1960 onwards gave each side sure and complete access to information about the other's missile installations on land. This greatly advantaged the Americans, who found it far harder to keep secrets than the Russians did. Presumably, mutual acceptance of satellite surveillance from outer space arose as an accidental by-product of the fact that when Russia launched the first satellite, its path, inevitably, transgressed national frontiers. The Soviet government was therefore unable to object when the United States followed suit. The further fact that neither power was able to shoot down enemy satellites when first they began to traverse space above their respective home territories made it necessary to acquiesce in what could not be prevented. Soon afterwards, the United States developed satellites carrying high-resolution cameras that could relay fine details of the Russian landscape back to earth. The Russians did object to this, but only half-heartedly.

Satellite surveillance at once dispelled many uncertainties about Soviet missiles. Indeed, in 1960 when the "spies in the skies" first started to work their magic, American officials discovered that the missile gap was mythical. The Soviets had not in fact yet invested in expensive rocket arrays poised to attack American cities, even though their technical capacity to do so had been proved. Each side subsequently did install hundreds of missiles at carefully prepared launch sites. But throughout the process, satellite surveillance detected every new installation. Each government could feel confident of the facts so miraculously made manifest since, even if perfect camouflage were possible for a completed launch site, during construction telltale signs were sure to show.

During the 1960s, therefore, each watched while the other installed intercontinental ballistic missiles (ICBMs) to match those they were themselves emplacing. Simultaneously, each power built and deployed submarines capable of lying silent beneath the sea for weeks at a time before launching atomic warheads from below the surface.[11]

11. The accelerating pace of technical advance resulting from massive and systematic research and development programs is illustrated by the fact that it took forty years for

This buildup produced a balance of nuclear forces approximately as shown in table 2.

Table 2. Nuclear Weapons

	1970	1980
Long-range bombers		
USA	512	348
USSR	156	156
Submarine-launched missiles		
USA	656	576
USSR	248	950
ICBMs		
USA	1,054	1,052
USSR	1,487	1,398
Total nuclear warheads		
USA	4,000	9,200
USSR	1,800	6,000

Source: Stockholm International Peace Research Institute, *Yearbook 1981*, table 2:1, p. 21.

Clearly, by the beginning of the 1970s, substantial equality had been achieved in the sense that each power was in a position to wreak such damage on the other that building additional missiles seemed wasteful. A five-year Strategic Arms Limitation Treaty (SALT), signed in 1972, accordingly set a ceiling on such weaponry. This did not, however, halt the arms race. Research and development teams merely shifted attention to other kinds of weapons not mentioned in the treaty for the good reason that they did not yet exist. By the end of the 1970s therefore, several new weapons systems were ready to make the transition from experimental laboratories to production lines. But which weapons to build and how much of the nation's resources to commit to the escalation of the arms race remained, in 1981, a disputed matter in the United States. No doubt similar disputes were in progress within the Soviet Union, even though public airing of alternatives, such as was necessary in the United States to persuade Congress to vote funds, did not take place.

---

self-propelled torpedoes to increase their range from 220 yards when first invented in 1866 to 2,190 yards in 1905, but only six to rise to 18,590 in 1913, whereas the range of the Polaris missiles, installed in U.S. submarines for the first time in 1959, increased from 1,200 to 2,500 miles in a mere five years. For torpedo ranges see Edwin A. Gray, *The Devil's Device* (London, 1975), Appendix; for Polaris ranges see SIPRI *Yearbook, 1968–69* (London, 1969), p. 98.

New models of old weapons with improved performance capabilities were disturbing enough to the world's power balances. The further possibility that some device of a quite different kind might suddenly open a new avenue for paralyzing violence also prevented the world's great powers from settling down to any stable, trusting accommodation with one another. Breakthroughs in chemical or biological warfare might at any time create an end run around the atomic balance of terror. But what seemed particularly promising for the 1980s were various kinds of "death rays" traveling with the speed of light. Such beams, launched from space vehicles, might be expected to intercept incoming missiles, or perhaps even destroy them in their launch sites. The merest glimmer of such a possibility introduced a profound instability in the balance of terror that had prevailed since the 1960s.

Clearly, competition for strategic advantage by dint of some new breakthrough in the design of a secret weapon was impossible to exorcise in a world where rival states feared one another. Mounting costs, as successive generations of weapons became more and more elaborate, constituted a brake of sorts. But interested parties, seeking new contracts in the USA or assignment of new resources of manpower and materiel in the USSR, could always point with alarm to research and development efforts undertaken by the other side. Political managers had somehow to balance demands from the civilian economy against the ravenous appetite for new resources that military research and development teams regularly exhibited. Decisions for and against particular weapons systems and development programs in the United States often induced a mirror image response in the USSR. But much remained secret, especially in Russia. The fiscal and moral uncertainties as well as the technological and engineering uncertainties that had manifested themselves so fatefully before World War I in connection with the Anglo-German naval race[12] haunted policy makers in both countries. The difference was that the cost of error had multiplied many times over in the intervening decades.

Space spectaculars tended, perhaps, to disguise the fact that the arms race was not limited to the USA and USSR, nor were the two superpowers solely concerned with rockets and atomic warheads. Table 3 summarizes the extraordinary growth of military expenditure that took place in the post–World War II decades. These figures are liable to enormous errors because of budgetary subterfuges and the arbitrary exchange rates that must be assigned in reducing money

12. See above, chap. 8.

Table 3. Military Expenditures at Constant Prices
(In billions, 1978 dollars)

	1950	1955	1960	1965	1970	1975	1980
USA	39.5	98.2	100.0	107.2	130.9	101.2	111.2
NATO total	67.3	142.6	150.3	168.1	194.0	184.9	193.9
USSR	37.7	51.2	48.0	65.9	92.5	99.8	107.3
Warsaw Pact	40.7	54.2	51.3	71.3	100.8	110.3	119.5
Uncommitted states	25.7	29.6	34.6	57.9	85.7	123.7	141.9
World total	133.7	226.4	236.2	297.3	380.5	418.9	455.3

Source: Stockholm International Peace Research Institute, *Yearbook 1981*, Appendix 6A, p. 156.

costs to a common dollar denominator. Nevertheless, whatever distortions survive these more or less neutral Swedish efforts to get at the truth, it remains indubitable that superpower military spending had its counterpart among other governments. Indeed, the rate of increase in military spending by Third World countries in the 1970s exceeded the growth rate of great power expenditures.

The arms race thus proved contagious, affecting all parts of the earth. An especial peak (or depth?) may be discerned in the Middle East, where oil revenues and unstable regimes overlapped the Arab-Israeli and other apparently irreconcilable local conflicts. As a recipe for disaster, developments since 1947 in the Middle East were hard to equal, though bloodshed in southeast Asia was greater, while race and tribal wars in Africa were restrained more by poverty and a resulting shortage of highly lethal weapons than by any sort of prudence.

The two superpowers were in a poor position to control the situation. In the 1960s, if not before, the American and Russian governments realized that even after a successful surprise atomic attack, awesome retaliation would follow. Their new power to destroy therefore ceased to be a practicable instrument of policy. Other governments soon saw the same thing and felt freer than before to defy the USA and the USSR. The French withdrawal from NATO in 1966 and a growing restiveness in eastern Europe registered this fact. As the capacity for mutual destruction became more and more assured, the two superpowers were in danger of becoming a pair of Goliaths, hampered by the very formidability of their weaponry. Paradoxically helpless, they were as unable to use atomic warheads as to do without them.

Such a situation, transmuting unimaginable power into its opposite at the wave of a wand, was without historical precedent. Yet it occurred in a world where nuclear proliferation remained both a possibility and a reality, although exactly how many governments possessed atomic warheads or the means to deliver them remained secret. Only six states have exploded warheads in public,[13] but several others have been widely suspected of possessing warheads manufactured from plutonium produced in nuclear power plants.[14]

In the postwar decades, neither the nuclear umbrella nor the efforts of international peace-keeping bodies sufficed to prevent local wars and guerrilla actions from breaking out and running their course repeatedly. Armed conflicts numbered in the hundreds; and the combatants, dependent on outside sources of arms in nearly every case, almost invariably sought help from one or the other of the superpowers, directly or indirectly.[15] Staying aloof from such affairs was difficult. Substantial numbers of American troops engaged in the Korean War, 1950–53, for example, and even larger numbers later fought vainly in Vietnam, 1964–73. The Russians, for their part, invaded unruly eastern European countries in 1956 and again in 1968, and tried the same thing in Afghanistan in 1979. The United States met qualified success in Korea and humiliating defeat in Vietnam. It remains to be seen whether the Russians' qualified successes in Hungary and Czechoslovakia will be followed by a different result in Afghanistan.

The quite extraordinary power of a technically proficient society to exert overwhelming force on its enemies depends, after all, on prior agreement about the ends to which collective skill and effort ought to be directed. Maintaining such agreement is not automatic or assured. This became clear in the United States during the Vietnam War, when the cause for which Americans were fighting became so dubious as to make withdrawal politically necessary. American technological superiority did not defeat the Viet Cong. Acts of destruction merely hardened Vietnamese opinion against the foreigners. Escalation of-

13. Between 16 July 1945 and 31 December 1979 known atomic explosions were as follows: USA, 667; USSR, 447; France, 97; UK, 33; China, 26; and India, 1. SIPRI *Yearbook 1981,* App. 11B, p. 382.

14. In 1979 no fewer than thirty-six countries had nuclear power plants within their borders capable of producing fissionable material. Efforts to monitor and control the use of such material by the United States and other suppliers were fragile to say the least. Some countries (Israel for example) had probably breached such regulations. But, if so, the matter remained secret and rumor often may have outrun reality.

15. International arms sales remained under governmental control after World War II, as much in the free world as in the Communist. Evasions of official regulations, though real, were marginal. For a perspicacious account see John Stanley and Maurice Pearton, *The International Trade in Arms* (London, 1972).

fered no solution, short of all-out attack on the north, or a level of destruction in the south that would have destroyed most of the human beings whose liberties the United States claimed to defend.

Moreover, as Vietnamese feeling solidified against the invaders, American opinion at home divided more and more sharply as to the justice and wisdom of armed intervention in Vietnam. Distrust of the military, of high technology, and of the administrative-academic-military-industrial elites that had guided the American response to *Sputnik* became widespread. The high hopes and brash self-confidence with which the American government had launched its adventure into space in the 1960s evaporated, leaving a sour taste behind. Large numbers of young people espoused some form of counterculture, deliberately repudiating the patterns of social management that had attained such heights during and after World War II.

In extreme forms, their rebellion was suicidal, as many drug-takers' shortened lives showed. It was also ineffective in inventing viable alternatives to bureaucratic, corporate management. Cheap, mass-produced goods required flow-through technology which only large-scale bureaucratically managed corporations could sustain; and a world safe for such behemoths must presumably regulate their interactions bureaucratically as well. Spontaneity, personal independence, and small group solidarity against outsiders have very limited scope in such a society. But the material impoverishment that thoroughgoing return to any of these older values and patterns of behavior entailed was a far higher price than most of the rebels were prepared to pay.

Nevertheless, flow-through technologies remained extremely vulnerable to disruption. The factory efficiency that cheapened costs of production required precise coordination of many subsidiary flows. Interruptions anywhere along the line turned efficiency into its opposite very quickly. Discontented and disaffected groups, if appropriately organized, could therefore obstruct the industrial process easily enough, as successful strikes since the 1880s had demonstrated more than once.

On the other hand, the price of survival for even the most incandescently revolutionary group was the generation of its own power-wielding internal bureaucracy. And bureaucratically organized revolutionaries, if genuinely powerful, found themselves swiftly coopted into the labyrinthine tasks of state management. The public life of Germany and Great Britain since World War I exhibited these compulsions quite clearly; but the Soviet Union carried the bureaucratic transmutation of protest into governance to a kind of logical completion, making a once revolutionary party and radically disruptive unions into undisguised instruments of state control over the industrial working force and society at large.

The hard fact remained that only by organizing bureaucratically could groups assert themselves effectively in a bureaucratic world. This deprived the counterculture of the 1960s of enduring importance. Yet American technocrats and politicians were compelled to recognize hitherto unsuspected limits to their new powers of social management. The great administrative machines created by and constituting the skeleton of the national state could not decide at will what ends to pursue, nor who should manage whom. Reason and calculation came a poor second in settling such questions to ideals and feelings. Manipulative propaganda could only establish the emotional climate for mass obedience by staying within limits set by inherited, widely prevalent beliefs. Fissiparousness, inherent in a highly skilled and sharply differentiated society, put enormous strains on political leadership. These strains were not significantly relieved by the fact that politicians and statesmen could call on the most expert systems analysis, cost-benefit calculations, and other instruments of modern industrial, corporate management.[16]

Perhaps the most fundamental shift of the postwar decades was a widespread withdrawal of loyalty from constituted public authorities. Ethnic, regional, and religious groupings gained importance at the expense of the national state while at the same time various transnational collective identities and administrative structures also waxed stronger than ever before. Within what units and to what ends the technical virtuosity of modern management would be exercised was a question that therefore attained a new vibrancy in the 1960s and 1970s. This was especially apparent in the more advanced industrialized countries, where old-fashioned patriotism seemed clearly on the wane. How it will be answered in years to come may well turn out to be the capital question of humanity's future.

Soviet society was not immune. Khrushchev's confident promises of the early 1960s soured when it became apparent that enhanced productivity, upon which everything depended, was not forthcoming merely on the strength of exhortation from the Communist party to work harder in order to enjoy a better life sometime in the future.

16. Two books aptly illustrate aspects of this impasse: the cocky assurance of Alain C. Enthoven and K. Wayne-Smith, *How Much Is Enough? Shaping the Defense Program, 1961–1969* (New York, 1971) and the quizzical skepticism of Don K. Price, *The Scientific Estate* (Cambridge, Mass., 1965).

Khrushchev's notorious secret denunciation of Stalin in 1956 unleashed previously pent-up criticism among members of the managerial elites. Methods of Soviet planning came under scrutiny, for example, and debates as to how to assure a more efficient use of resources attained quite unaccustomed candor. Experiments in administrative reform were tried in the mid-1960s; but when the debates became too revelatory of internal difficulties and differences of opinion, public discussion was shut down again.[17] Thereafter, as previously in Soviet (as also in prerevolutionary Russian) history, police pressure inhibited free expression of dissent.

Yet the personal courage needed to defy official repression gave unusual weight to the voices of those who continued to dare. Throughout the postwar era, dissidence within the Communist world proliferated, beginning as early as 1946, when Yugoslavia split away from the rest of the Communist world. Other nations subsequently did the same, most notably the Chinese in 1961. Such splits reflected national feeling and diversity. So did some expressions of dissent from within the Soviet Union, especially among Jews and Moslems. But in addition, a few distinguished scientists and men of letters attacked repression of truth and personal freedom within the USSR. Such individuals were able to circulate their views through secret channels, within and also outside of the Soviet Union.

This proved, if proof were needed, that the few individuals who dared to defy party authorities were supported by many others who sympathized with the dissidents sufficiently to pass their writings from hand to hand and through secret channels to persons living beyond the reach of the Soviet police. A second sign of disillusionment with official ideology was the vogue for pop music and other imports from the youth culture of the West. A real if tenuous counterculture thus emerged in the Soviet Union which offended the pieties and proprieties of the Russian establishment even more radically than the parallel youthful rebelliousness grated upon capitalist-corporate values in the United States.

Strains on consensus within state boundaries, however, merely tended to make the police and armed forces more important. Except for France and Britain, none of the major industrialized countries had to call on its armed forces to put down domestic disorder during the postwar decades. In poorer countries, however, intenser dissension brought the military to the fore, time and again. In any modern state,

17. Moshe Lewin, *Political Undercurrents in Soviet Economic Debates from Bukharin to the Modern Reformers* (Princeton, 1974), pp. 127 ff. offers an intriguing overview.

weaponry in the hands of police and soldiers exercises an ultimate veto on internal political processes, unless the discipline and cohesion of the armed forces breaks down. Preservation of discipline in difficult times calls for isolation and withdrawal from civil society, particularly when that society becomes permeated with serious dissent. Maintenance of suitable skills, on the other hand, calls for interpenetration with some at least of the technically proficient elites of civil society. Yet such elites are especially likely to become impatient with an inefficient or corrupt government, believing that they can do better themselves. Who manages whom and for what ends becomes problematic indeed when technical elites and elites from the armed forces collide in this fashion with other groups in society.

When such collisions led to coups d'état, bringing military personnel to power, it was difficult for the new rulers to retain the cohesion and morale that allowed them to seize power in the first place. Programs for reform, however heartfelt at the moment of taking office, were always difficult to put into practice; and when opportunities for personal enrichment and sensuous enjoyment multiplied, as always happened to men in possession of political power, ideals nurtured in the barracks and military schools were likely to go by the board. Often as not, such betrayal deprived the military regime of legitimacy in its own eyes and in the eyes of others. Most modern military dictatorships have therefore been short-lived.

Alliance of throne and altar constituted the traditional time-tested solution to the problem of sustaining legitimacy for long periods of time. The difficulty in the twentieth century was to find a faith and priesthood capable of supporting governments that had to rule in the absence of any well-defined popular consensus. The secular faiths of the eighteenth and nineteenth centuries showed signs of losing their power in industrially advanced countries. Indeed, the weakening of public consensus was a register of this decay. To be sure, Marxist and nationalist ideals had proved effective for mobilizing predominantly peasant populations against European administrators and foreign capitalists in the immediate postwar decades. But when revolutionary parties took power and confronted the practical tasks of daily administration, nationalist principles and Marxist faith constituted sadly inadequate guides to action. Disappointment and disillusion therefore regularly set in.

In some parts of the world, traditional religions, sometimes in sectarian form, offered an alternative. This was especially true in Islamic lands. An age-old antagonism to Christianity and Judaism dating back

to the very foundation of Islam, made it easy to attack foreign influence and corruption and rally mass followings for the defense of the
true faith. But a regime seeking to be true to the Koran had difficulty
in coping with twentieth-century technology since those who mastered the technology of the West were unlikely to remain fanatically
faithful to Mohammed's revelation.

An enemy at the gates has always been the best substitute for spontaneous consensus at home. Fear of what a foe would do if allowed to
cross the frontier will often breed obedience, if only on the ancient
principle "better the scoundrels one knows that the scourge one
fears." Wars and rumors of war against near neighbors can therefore
be expected to flourish luxuriantly in those parts of Africa, Asia, and
Latin America where public consensus is weak and precarious. Peasant
ways of life face enormous strain wherever population has become too
great to allow the rising generation to find enough land to live on and
raise a family in traditional fashion. The restless and impassioned
search for new faiths, new land, new ways of life provoked by such
circumstances is sure to disturb any and every form of constituted
governmental authority until such time as the demographic crisis
somehow diminishes. To judge from Europe's history between 1750
and 1950, this will take a long time and may cost many lives.

Wars and preparations for wars are therefore likely to remain very
prominent in most of the Third World. The enormous arms buildup
occurring in those lands since the 1960s testifies to this fact. As in
earlier ages, such expenditures are not always purely wasteful from an
economic point of view. New skills, needed to maintain such complicated pieces of machinery as modern combat airplanes, have wider
application. Given suitable conditions, they can, as in nineteenth-
century Japan, promote industrial growth. On the other hand, heavy
investment in armaments may choke off other kinds of development.
Overall, there seems to be no coherent relationship between Third
World rates of economic growth since 1945 and rates of military
expenditure.[18]

Inability to maintain domestic peace, however, is a sure path to
economic regression. Insofar as maintenance of public order becomes
problematic so that governments fear their own people as much or
more than any external foe, police equipment takes precedence. Recent statistics show that since the mid 1960s new nations have invested
more heavily in police forces than in armament aimed at foreign

18. Cf. Gavin Kennedy, *The Military in the Third World* (London, 1974), pp.
174–89.

enemies.[19] Whether better-organized repression will suffice to prop up existing regimes in the absence of real consent remains to be seen. Military forms of discipline and policies intended to insulate armed personnel from the rest of the population surely offer some prospect of success. European sovereigns of the Old Regime, after all, exercised this sleight of hand triumphantly in times past. Moreover, as armaments become more expensive as well as more lethal, small professional armies are likely to supplant the mass armies of conscripts that dominated European warfare in the nineteenth and early twentieth centuries. If so, governments and their armed forces can perhaps afford to dispense with popular support, and rely on force and the threat of force, exercised by specialized professionals kept systematically separate from the subjected population at large. Such a pattern of governance would conform to the norms of the past, however much at odds they may be with modern political rhetoric and democratic theory.

On the other hand, contemporary forms of mass communication probably act in an opposite sense and make such old-fashioned polarity between armed rulers and a subject population persistently unstable. To be sure, selective recruitment into the armed services from some special segment of the population can be counted on to induce a social distance between the armed forces and ordinary civilians and subjects. But whether such an armed force can monopolize organized violence within state boundaries depends largely on whether discontented revolutionary groups have access to arms; and this in turn depends on the policies of other governments as well as on the fanaticism of the revolutionaries. As long as the globe is divided among rival states, revolutionaries have a good chance of finding some foreign patron and supplier of arms. Under these circumstances, strengthening the police and army does not seem likely to assure political stability in those parts of the world where a rural population surge generates widespread and radical discontent with the way things are.

In Europe, the United States, and the Soviet Union population pressures are of a different kind. How to come to terms with immigrants and aliens, whether Latino in the United States or Moslem in

---

19. Morris Janowitz, *Military Institutions and Coercion in the Developing Nations* (Chicago, 1977), p. 35, says that expenditures for police forces in Africa, 1966–75, rose by 144 percent while costs of armies rose by only 40 percent in the same decade. His figures show that almost every government in the world has increased expenditures for the means of internal coercion more rapidly than other defense costs. There is some indication, too, that police consolidation made coups d'état harder to pull off and therefore fewer in the 1970s than had been true in the 1960s. Ibid., pp. 42, 70.

Europe and the USSR is sufficiently delicate to require very careful management. But the problem does not threaten the existing political order. Neither does the divergence between the interests of the military-technical elite and the rest of society, however real the competition for resources may be. For half a century, military-industrial elites have nearly always prevailed over domestic rivals without much difficulty. Time and again fear of the foreign foe persuaded the political managers and the population at large to acquiesce in new efforts to match and overtake the other side's armament. The escalating arms race, in turn, helped to maintain conformity and obedience at home, since an evident outside threat was, as always, the most powerful social cement known to humankind.

Yet how far such shadow boxing can go is problematical. Atomic warheads changed the rules; and the absurdity of devoting enormous resources to the creation of weapons no one dares to use is obvious to all concerned. This means that the vast armed establishments currently protecting the NATO and Warsaw Pact powers against one another are liable to catastrophe not merely from the external attack they are designed to survive but also from internal decay. Such decay is facilitated by the way in which long-standing notions of heroism and the military calling meet with frustration in technically up-to-date armies and navies. Push-button war is the antithesis of muscular prowess; and the niggling routine of bureaucratic record-keeping is no less at odds with naive but heartfelt feelings about what fighting men should be and do. Such tensions are as old as the bureaucratization and industrialization of war; but the dawn of the rocket age, with its overwhelming preponderance of action at a distance, from which the muscular and merely human input has almost drained away, constitutes a mutation of the art of war with which soldiers' psychology does not easily keep up.[20]

All the same, short of defeat in war, drastic demoralization of military personnel is perhaps unlikely. Traditional methods for inculcating and sustaining military discipline remain very effective. Close order drill has lost none of its capacity to arouse elemental sociality among those who participate in it hour after hour. Its utter irrelevance in modern combat may not matter. Other rituals and routines, too, may arise and exert self-perpetuating power to channel and stabilize behavior both within the armed services and in civil society at large.

20. For remarks about the conflict between heroic and technocratic roles see Jacques van Doorn, ed., *Military Profession and Military Regimes: Commitments and Conflicts* (The Hague, 1969).

Routine and ritual constitute the standard substitute for faith of the incandescent, personal, and revolutionary kind. As such faiths—Marxist or liberal-democratic, as the case may be—fade towards mere shibboleth, ritual and routine alone remain.

In times past, routine and ritual prevailed in European and all other armed forces. Technical upheavals were few and far between, however important for the ebb and flow of peoples and the tides of victory and defeat. Perhaps the extraordinary disturbance arising across the past century and a half, ever since the industrialization of war got seriously under way, will eventually be contained so that the world's armed forces can again sink back into the sustaining and restraining regime of unchanging routine.

On the other hand, as long as rivalry between mutually suspicious states continues, deliberate organized invention seems certain to persist, cost what it may. Absolute economic limits are scarcely in sight. Every productive resource not needed for bodily life is, in principle, available for defense; and the enhanced productivity of automated machinery is so great that the practical limits on military expenditure are limits on the efficiency of human organization for war rather than anything else. Once again one comes up against the question of consensus and obedience. Material limits are comparatively trivial.

One might, perhaps, suppose that absolute physical limits to weaponry were close at hand. After all, escape velocities for ballistic missiles were attained as long ago as 1957. The next generation of weaponry may act from space with the speed of light, as do control and guidance systems already in use. But attainment of the physical world's absolute speed limit would not hinder rival research and development teams from seeking to improve control and precision of aim, while developing methods of protection against interference from without. Stabilization of weapons systems, if it ever comes, seems unlikely to arise from exhaustion of the frontiers of scientific research and engineering.

To halt the arms race, political change appears to be necessary. A global sovereign power willing and able to enforce a monopoly of atomic weaponry could afford to disband research teams and dismantle all but a token number of warheads. Nothing less radical than this seems in the least likely to suffice. Even in such a world, the clash of arms would not cease as long as human beings hate, love, and fear one another and form into groups whose cohesion and survival is expressed in and supported by mutual rivalry. But an empire of the earth could be expected to limit violence by preventing other groups from arming themselves so elaborately as to endanger the sovereign's easy superiority. War in such a world would therefore sink back to proportions familiar in the preindustrial past. Outbreaks of terrorism, guerrilla action and banditry would continue to give expression to human frustration and anger. But organized war as the twentieth century has known it would disappear.

The alternative appears to be sudden and total annihilation of the human species. When and whether a transition will be made from a system of states to an empire of the earth is the gravest question humanity confronts. The answer can only come with time.

Conclusion

Understanding current affairs requires a bold imaginative effort. Amidst a plethora of data, one must somehow decide what to pay attention to and treat as important even though it means disregarding all the rest. The possibility of error inheres in such a situation, but that is no different from the other uncertainties surrounding human life always and inevitably. It was by learning to concentrate attention on a tiny segment of the total sensory input available to their central nervous systems that our remote ancestors became skilled and successful hunters, and then proceeded to transform the earth's natural ecology by a long series of inventions, implemented through collective social effort. Words and symbols, allowing the mind to focus attention arbitrarily on some aspects of a situation while neglecting all the rest, were the supreme instruments through which these extraordinary changes were wrought. In using words to understand contemporary circumstances, we are therefore doing no more—and no less—than our predecessors have done for many thousands of years.

Emboldened by this reflection, one may in imagination try to think ahead to an age when our contemporary dilemmas of political rivalry and competitive armament have been resolved without entirely destroying human society and civilization. From the perspective of a few hundred years, it seems to me, our successors are likely to perceive the millennium with which this book has been concerned as an extraordinary period of upheaval. For a thousand years modes of political control and public management of human effort lagged behind transport and communication nets so seriously as to allow private and small group initiatives and self-interest to play a quite exceptional, transitional role in governing day-to-day behavior. The unseen hand of the market came into its own, regulating the working lives of millions and hundreds of millions of human beings through fluctuating prices. New techniques and complementarities of resources found unexpected scope, allowing larger populations to survive. Presently, invention itself became conscious and deliberate; production became systematically organized within larger and larger units; and in the twentieth century techniques of bureaucratic management and data retrieval at last began to catch up with communications and transport until global government became feasible.

Once the feasible became actual, planning that took full account of collateral costs quickly brought a halt to breakneck technical change. Deliberate adjustment of population numbers to available resources presently achieved sufficient accuracy to cushion human hurts arising from systematic discrepancies between economic expectation and actual experience. Peace and order improved. Life settled down towards routine. The era of upheaval had come to a close. Political management, having monopolized the overt organization of armed force, resumed its primacy over human behavior. Self-interest and the pursuit of private profit through buying and selling sank towards the margins of daily life, operating within limits and according to rules laid down by the holders of political-military power. Human society, in short, returned to normal. Social change reverted to the leisurely pace of preindustrial, precommercial times. Adaptation between means and ends, between human activity and the natural environment and among interacting human groups achieved such precision that further changes became both unnecessary and undesirable. Besides, they were not allowed.

Competitive and aggressive propensities found satisfactory outlet in sport. Intellectual and literary creativity flagged as administrative and customary routines became well defined. But historians and society at large sometimes looked back on the perils of the past in wonder—tinged with awe—at the reckless rivalries and restless creativity of the millennium of upheaval, A.D. 1000–2000.

We who have not escaped from that millennium may well do the same. Awesome power and awful dilemmas have never been so closely juxtaposed. What we believe and how we act therefore matter more than in ordinary ages. Clear thinking and bold action, based as always on inadequate evidence, are all we have to see us through to whatever the future holds. It will differ from anyone's intentions as radically as the actual past differed from our forefathers' plans and wishes. But study of that past may reduce the discrepancy between expectation and reality, if only by encouraging us to expect surprises —among them, a breakdown of the pattern of the future suggested in this conclusion. For however horrendous it is to live in the face of uncertainty, the future, like the past, depends upon humanity's demonstrated ability to make and remake natural and social environments within limits set mainly by our capacity to agree on goals of collective action.

Index

389